WEBSTER'S
NEW BOOK OF
FACTS

WEBSTER'S
NEW BOOK OF
FACTS

COMPACT EDITION

World Book Marketing, Inc.
22 Fifth Street
Taunton MA 02780
(058) 880 - 5555

© Geddes & Grosset Ltd., New Lanark, Scotland 1990

Published by Russell, Geddes & Grosset, Windsor Court,
New York, N.Y. U.S.A.

Printed in the U.S.A.

This book is not published by the original publishers of
Webster's Dictionary or by their successors.

FACTS ABOUT WORDS

Abbreviations

A

a at; to, in algebra, known quantity, constant

A1 first class

A ace, acre, America, American, April, argon

A angstrom unit

AA Alcoholics Anonymous, Associate of Arts, anti-aircraft

AAA Agricultural Adjustment Administration, Amateur Athletic Association, American Automobile Association

AAAL American Academy of Arts and Letters

AAAS American Association for the Advancement of Science

AAG Assistant Adjutant General

A and M agricultural and mechanical, ancient and modern

AAR against all risks

AAU Amateur Athletic Union

AAUP American Association of University Professors

AAUW American Association of University Women

AB able-bodied seaman, airman basic. Alberta. [*artium baccalaureus*] bachelor of arts

ABA American Bankers Association, American Bar Association, American Basketball Association, American Booksellers Association

abbr abbreviation

ABC American Bowling Congress, American Broadcasting Company, Australian Broadcasting Company

ABCD accelerated business collection and delivery

abd or **abdom** abdomen, abdominal

abl ablative

abn airborne

abp archbishop

abr abridged, abridgment

abs absolute, abstract

ABS American Bible Society

abstr abstract

abt about

ac account, acre

Ac actinium

AC air-conditioning, alternating current, (*ante Christum*) before Christ

acad academic, academy

AC and U Association of Colleges and Universities

acc accusative

accel accelerando

acct account, accountant

accus accusative

ACE American Council on Education

ack acknowledge, acknowledgment

ACLU American Civil Liberties Union

ACP American College of Physicians

acpt acceptance

ACS American Chemical Society, American College of Surgeons

act active, actor, actual

ACT American College Test, Association of Classroom Teachers, Australian Capital Territory

actg acting

ACW alternating continuous waves

AD active duty, after date, [*anno domini*] in the year of our Lord

ad advertisement

ADA American Dental Association, average daily attendance

ADC aide-de-camp. Air Defense Command

ADD American Dialect Dictionary

addn addition

addnl additional

ADF automatic direction finder

ADH antidiuretic hormone

ad inf to infinity [*ad infinitum*]

ad int ad interim

ADIZ air defense identification zone

adj adjective, adjunct, adjustment, adjutant

ad loc [*ad locum*] to or at the place

adm administration, administrative

admin administration

admrx administratrix

ADP automatic data processing

adv advert. (*adversus*) against

ad val ad valorem

advt advertisement

AEC Atomic Energy Commission

AEF American Expeditionary Force

aeq (*aequalis*) equal

aero aeronautical, aeronautics

aet *or* **aetat** (*aetatis*) of age, aged

af affix

AF air force, audio frequency

Af Africa, African

AFB air force base

AFBS American and Foreign Bible Society

AFC American Football Conference, automatic frequency control

aff affirmative

afft affidavit

AFL American Football League, American Federation of Labor

AFL—CIO American Federation of Labor and Congress of Industrial Organizations

aft afternoon

AFT American Federation of Teachers, automatic fine tuning

AFTRA American Federation of Television and Radio Artists

Ag (L. *argentum*) silver

AG adjutant general, attorney general

agcy agency

AGR advanced gas-cooled reactor

agr *or* **agric** agricultural, agriculture

agt agent

AH ampere-hour, (*anno hegirae*) in the year of the Hegira (the flight of Mohammed from Mecca to Medina, 622 A.D.)

AHC Army Hospital Corps

AHL American Hockey League

AI ad interim, artificial insemination, artificial intelligence

AIA Associate of the Institute of Actuaries

AID Agency for International Development

AIDS acquired immune (or immuno-) deficiency syndrome

AIM American Indian Movement

AIME American Institute of Mining Engineers, Associate of the Institute of Mechanical Engineers

AK Alaska

aka also known as

AKC American Kennel Club

Al aluminium

AL Alabama, American League, American Legion

Ala Alabama

ALA American Library Association

alc alcohol

alk alkaline

allo allegro

alt alternate, altitude

Alta Alberta

alw allowance

Am America, American, americium

AM (*ante meridiem*) before midday, (*artium magister*) master of arts

AMA American Medical Association

AMD Army Medical Department

Amer America, American

Amer Ind American Indian

Amn airman

amp ampere

amp hr ampere-hour

AMS Agricultural Marketing Service, Army Medical Staff

amnt amount

AMU atomic mass unit

AMVETS American Veteran (of World War I)

AN airman (Navy)

ANA American Newspaper Association, American Nurses Association

anat anatomical, anatomy

ANC Army Nurse Corps

Angl Anglican

anhyd anhydrous

ann annals, annual

anon anonymous

ANOVA analysis of variance

AO account of

AP additional premium, antipersonnel, Associated Press, author's proof

APB all points bulletin

APC armored personnel carrier, Army Pay Corps

API air position indicator

APO army post office

appl applied

approx approximate, approximately

appt appoint, appointed, appointment

apptd appointed

Apr April

APR annual percentage rate

apt apartment, aptitude

aq aqua, aqueous

Ar argon

AR accounts receivable, acknowledgment of receipt, all risks, Arkansas

ARC American Red Cross

arch archaic, architect, architecture

Arch Archbishop

arg argent, argument

arith arithmetic, arithmetical

Ariz Arizona

Ark Arkansas

ARP air-raid precautions

arr arranged, arrival, arrive

art article, artificial

As arsenic

AS after sight, American Samoa, Anglo-Saxon

ASA American Standards Association

ASAP as soon as possible

asb asbestos

ASCAP American Society of Composers, Authors and Publishers

ASCU Association of State Colleges and Universities

ASF American Stock Exchange

ASEAN Association of Southeast Asian Nations

ASI airspeed indicator

ASL American Sign Language

ASR airport surveillance radar, air-sea rescue

assn association

assoc associate, associated, association

ASSR Autonomous Soviet Socialist Republic

asst assitant

Assyr Assyrian

ATS American Tract Society, American Temperance Society

astrol astrologer, astrology

astron astronomer, astronomy

ASV American Standard Version

Atl Atlantic

atm atmosphere, atmospheric

attn attention

atrib attributive, attributively

AUA American Unitarian Association

Au (*aurum*) gold

aud audit, auditor

Aug August

Aus Austria, Austrian, Australia, Australian

AUS Army of the United States

Austral Australia

auth authentic, authorized

auto automatic

av avenue, average, avoidupois

AV ad valorem, audiovisual, Authorized Version

AVC automatic volume control

avdp avoirdupois

ave avenue

avg average

AWACS airborne warning and control system

AYC American Youth Congress

AYD American Youth for Democracy

AZ Arizona

B

B boron

Ba barium

BA Bachelor of Arts

BAEd Bachelor of Arts in Education

BAg Bachelor of Agriculture

bal balance

B and B bed-and-breakfast

b and w black and white

Bapt Baptist

bar barometer, barometric

BAr Bachelor of Architecture

BAS Bachelor of Agricultural Science, Bachelor of Applied Science

Bart baronet

BBC British Broadcasting Corporation

bbl barrel, barrels

BC before Christ, British Columbia

BCD binary-coded decimal

BCh Bachelor of Chemistry

bcn beacon

BCSE Board of Civil Service Examiners

bd ft board foot

bdl *or* **bdle** bundle

bdrm bedroom

Be beryllium

BE Bachelor of Education, Bachelor of Engineering, bill of exchange

BEC Bureau of Employees' Compensation

BEd Bachelor of Education

BEF British Expeditionary Force

beg begin, beginning

Belg Belgian, Belgium

BEM British Empire Medal

BEngr Bachelor of Engineering

BFA Bachelor of Fine Arts

BG *or* **B Gen** brigadier general

BH bill of health

bhd bulkhead

BHE Bureau of Higher Education

bhp bishop

BIA Bachelor of Industrial Arts, Braille Institute of America, Bureau of Indian Affairs

bib Bible, biblical

biog biographer, biographical, biography

biol biologic, biological, biologist, biology

bk bank, book

Bk berkelium

bkg banking, bookkeeping, breakage

bkgd background

bks barracks

bkt basket, bracket

bl bale, barrel, block

BL Bachelor of Law, Bachelor of Letters, bill of lading, breadth/length

bldg building

bldr builder

Blitt *or* **BLit** (*baccalaureus litterarum*) Bachelor of Letters, Bachelor of Literature

blk black, block, bulk

blvd boulevard

BMR basal metabolic rate

BNDD Bureau of Narcotics and Dangerous Drugs

BO back order, body odor, branch office, buyer's option

BOD biochemical oxygen demand, biological oxygen demand

bor borough

bot botanical, botanist, botany, bottle, bottom, bought

BP bills payable, blood pressure, blueprint, boiling point

BPD barrels per day

bpi bits per inch, bytes per inch

Br Britain, British, bromine

BR bills receivable

brig brigade, brigadier

Brig Gen brigadier general

Brit Britain, British

brl barrel

bro brother, brothers

bros brothers

BS Bachelor of Science, balance sheet, bill of sale, British Standard

BSA Boy Scouts of America

BSI British Standards Institution

bskt basket

Bt baronet

btry battery

Btu British thermal unit

bu bureau, bushel

bur bureau

bus business

BV Blessed Virgin

BW bacteriological warfare, biological warfare, black and white

BWI British West Indies

BYO bring your own

C

C carbon

ca circa

Ca calcium

CA California, chartered accountant, chief accountant

CAB Civil Aeronautics Board

CAD computer-aided design

CAF cost and freight

CAGS Certificate Advanced Graduate Study

CAI computer-aided instruction, computer-associated instruction

cal calendar, caliber, calorie, small calorie

Cal California, large calorie

calc calculate, calculated

Calif California

CAM computer-aided manufacturing

can canceled, cancellation

Can *or* **Canad** Canada, Canadian

canc canceled

C and F cost and freight

C and W country and western

cap capacity, capital, capitalize

CAP Civil Air Patrol

caps capitals, capsule

Capt captain

card cardinal

CAS certificate of advanced study

cat catalog, catalyst

cath cathedral, cathode

CATV community antenna television

caus causative

cav cavalry, cavity

Cb columbium

CBC Canadian Broadcasting Corporation

CBD cash before delivery

CBI computer-based instruction, Cumulative Book Index

CBS Columbia Broadcasting System

CBW chemical and biological warfare

cc cubic centimeter

CC carbon copy, chief clerk

CCF Cooperative Commonwealth Federation (of Canada)

cckw counterclockwise

CCTV closed-circuit television

CCU cardiac care unit, coronary care unit, critical care unit

ccw counterclockwise

cd candela

Cd cadmium

CD carried down, certificate of deposit, civil defense, (*corps diplomatique*) diplomatic corps

CDD certificate of disability for discharge

cdg commanding

CDR commander

CDT central daylight time

Ce cerium

ce chemical engineer, civil engineer

CEA College English Association, Council of Economic Advisors

CED Committee for Economic Development

cem cement

cent centigrade, central, centium, century

Cent Central

CENTO Central Treaty Organization

CEO chief executive officer

CER conditioned emotional response

cert certificate, certified

CETA Comprehensive Employment and Training Act

cf (*confer*) compare

Cf californium

CF carried forward, cost and freight, cystic fibrosis

CFI cost, freight, and insurance

cfm cubic feet per minute

cfs cubic feet per second

CG center of gravity, coast guard, commanding general

cg *or* **cgm** centigram

CGT (*Confederation Generale du Travail*) General Confederation of Labor

ch chain, chapter, church

CH clearinghouse, courthouse, customhouse

chan channel

chap chapter

chem chemical, chemist, chemistry

chg change, charge

chm chairman, checkmate

Chmn chairman

chron chronicle, chronological, chronology

Ci curie

CI certificate of insurance, cost and insurance

CIA Central Intelligence Agency

CIC Commander in Chief

CID Criminal Investigation Department

cie (*compagnie*) company

CIF cost, insurance and freight

C in C commander in chief

CIP Cataloging in Publication

cir circle, circuit, circumference

circ circular

cit citation, cited, citizen

civ civil, civilian

CJ chief justice

ck cask, check

cl centiliter, class

Cl chlorine

CL center line, civil law, common law

cld called, cleared

Clev Cleveland

clin clinical

clk clerk

clr clear, clearance

CLU chartered life underwriter

cm centimeter, cumulative

Cm curium

CMA certified medical assistant

cmd command

cmdg commanding

cmdr commander

CMG Companion of the Order of St Michael and St George

cml commercial

CMSgt chief master sergeant

CN credit note

CNO chief of naval operations

CNS central nervous system

co company, county

Co cobalt

CO cash order, Colorado, commanding officer, conscientious objector

c/o care of

cod codex

COD cash on delivery

C of S chief of staff

col color, colored, column

col *or* **coll** collateral, college

Col colonel, Colorado

COL colonel, cost of living

collat collateral

colloq colloquial

Colo Colorado

comb combination, combined

comd command

comdg commanding

comdr commander

comdt commandant

COMECON Council for Mutual Economic Assistance

coml commercial

comm command, commerce, commission, committee, communication

commo commodore

comp compare, complex

compd compound

comr commissioner

conc concentrate, concentrated

conf conference, confidential

Confed Confederate

cong congress, congressional

Conn Connecticut

consol consolidated

cont containing, contents, continent, continued

contd continued

contg containing

contrib contribution, contributor

CORE Congress of Racial Equality

corp corporal, corporation

corr correct, corrected, corresponding

cos cosine

COS cash on shipment, chief of staff

cp compare, coupon

CP candlepower, charter party, communist party

CPA certified public accountant

CPB Corporation for Public Broadcasting

CPCU chartered property and casualty underwriter

cpd compound

CPFF cost plus fixed fee

CPI consumer price index

Cpl corporal

CPO chief petty officer

CPOM master chief petty officer

CPOS senior chief petty officer

CPS characters per second, cycle per second

CPT captain

cpu central processing unit

Cr chromeum

CR carrier's risk, cathode ray

CRC Civil Rights Commission

cresc crescendo

crim criminal

crit critical, criticism, criticized

CRT cathode-ray tube

cryst crystalline, crystallized

Cs cesium

CS capital stock, chief of staff, Christian Science, civil service

C/S cycles per second

CSA Confederate States of America

CSC Civil Service Commission

CSM command sergeant major

CSO chief signal officer, chief staff officer

CST central standard time

ct carat, cent, count, county, court

CT central time, certificated teacher, Connecticut

CTC centralized traffic control

ctf certificate

ctg *or* **ctge** cartage

ctn carton

cto concerto

c to c center to center

ctr center, counter

cu cubic, cumulative

Cu (*cuprum*) copper

CU close-up

cum cumulative

cur currency, current

CV cardiovascular, curriculum vitae

cvt convertible

cw clockwise

CW chemical warfare, chief warrant officer

CWO cash with order, chief warrant officer

cwt hundred weight

CY calendar year

cyl cylinder

CYO Catholic Youth Organization

CZ Canal Zone

D

d deceased, penny

D Democrat, deuterium

da deka-

DA days after acceptance, deposit account, district attorney

DAB Dictionary of American Biography

dag dekagram

dal dekaliter

dam dekameter

DAR Daughters of the American Revolution

dat dative

DAV Disabled American Veterans

db debenture

db *or* **dB** decibel

DB daybook

DBE Dame Commander of the Order of the British Empire

dbl double

DBMS data base management system

DC direct current, District of Columbia

dd dated, delivered

DD days after date, demand draft, dishonorable discharge, due date

DDC Dewey Decimal Classification

DDD direct distance dialing

DDS Doctor of Dental Science, Doctor of Dental Surgery

DE Delaware

deb debenture

dec deceased, declaration, declared, decorative, decrease

Dec December

def defendant, defense, deferred, defined, definite

deg degree

del delegate, delegation, delete

Del Delaware

dely delivery

dem demonstrative, demurrage

Dem Democrat, Democratic

Den Denmark

dent dental, dentist, dentistry

dep depart, department, departure, deposit, depot, deputy

dept department

der or **deriv** derivation, derivative

DEW distant early warning

DF damage free, direction finder

DFC Distinguished Flying Cross

DFM Distinguished Flying Medal

dft defendant, draft

dg decigram

DG director general, (*Dei gratia*) by the grace of God

dia diameter

diag diagonal, diagram

dial dialect

diam diameter

dict dictionary

dim diminutive

dip diploma

dir director

disc discount

dist distance, district

distr distribute, distribution

div dividend, division

DJ disc jockey, district judge, Doctor of Jurisprudence

DJIA Dow-Jones Industrial Average

dkg dekagram

dkl dekaliter

dkm dekameter

dl deciliter

DLitt or **DLit** (*doctor litterarum*) Doctor of Letters, Doctor of Literature

DLO dead letter office, dispatch loading only

dm decimeter

DM deutsche Mark

DMZ demilitarized zone

dn down

DNB Dictionary of National Biography

do ditto

DOA dead on arrival

DOB date of birth

doc document

DOD Department of Defense

DOE Department of Energy

dol dollar

DOM (*Deo optimo maximo*) to God, the best and greatest

DOS disk operating system

DOT Department of Transportation

doz dozen

DP data processing, dew point

DPH department of public health

dr dram

Dr doctor

DR dead reckoning

DSM Distinguished Service Medal

DSO Distinguished Service Order

DSP (*decessit sine prole*) died without issue

DST daylight time, double time

dup duplex, duplicate

DV (*Deo volente*) God willing

DVM Doctor of Veterinary Medicine

DW deadweight

dwt deadweight ton, pennyweight

DX distance

dy delivery, deputy, duty

Dy dysprosium

dynam dynamics

dz dozen

E

ea each

E Earl, Easter, English

E and OE errors and omissions excepted

EB eastbound

eccl ecclesiastic, ecclesiastical

ECG electrocardiogram

ECM European Common Market

ecol ecological, ecology

econ economics, economist, economy

ed edited, edition, editor, education

EDP electronic data processing

EDT eastern daylight time

educ education, educational

EEC European Economic Community

EEG electroencephalogram, electroencephalograph

EENT eye, ear, nose, and throat

EEO equal employment opportunity

eff efficiency

EFT *or* **EFTS** electronic funds transfer (system)

eg (*exempli gratia*) for example

EHF extremely high frequency

EHP effective horsepower, electric horsepower

EHV extra high voltage

elec electric, electrical, electricity

elem elementary

elev elevation

ELF extremely low frequency

ELSS extravehicular life support system

EM electromagnetic, electron microscope

emer emeritus

emf electromotive force

emp emperor, empress

enc *or* **encl** enclosure

ENE east-northeast

eng engine, engineer, engineering

Eng England, English

ENS ensign

env envelope

EO executive order

EOM end of month

EP extended play

EPA Environmental Protection Agency

eq equal, equation

equip equipment

equiv equivalency, equivalent

Er erbium

Es einsteinium

ESE east-southeast

ESL English as a second language

esp especially

Esq esquire

est established, estimate, estimated

EST eastern standard time

esu electrostatic unit

ESV earth satellite vehicle

ET eastern time, extra-terrestrial

ETA estimated time of arrival

et al *et alii* (masc.), *et aliae* (fem.) or *et alia* (neut.) and others

etc et cetera, and the rest

ETD estimated time of departure

ETO European theater of operations

et seq (*et sequens*) and the following one

et ux (*et uxor*) and wife

Eu europium

Eur Europe, European

EVA extravehicular activity

ex example, exchange, excluding, executive, express, extra

exch exchange, exchanged

exec executive

exhbn exhibition

exor executor

expy expressway

ext extension, exterior, external

F

f Fahrenheit, farad, faraday, and the following one

F fluorine

FA field artillery, fielding average, football association

FAA Federal Aviation Administration, free of all average

fac facsimile, faculty

FADM fleet admiral

fam familiar, family

F and A fore and aft

FAO Food and Agriculture Organization of the United Nations

FAQ fair average quality

far farthing

FAS free alongside ship

fath fathom

FBI Federal Bureau of Investigation

FCA Farm Credit Administration

FCC Federal Communications Commission

fcp foolscap

FDA Food and Drug Administration

FCIC Federal Deposit Insurance Corporation

Fe (*ferrum*) iron

Feb February

fec (*fecit*) he made it

fed fedcral, fcderation

fem female, feminine

FERA Federal Emergency Relief Administration

ff folios, and the following ones, fortissimo

FHA Federal Housing Administration

fict fiction, fictitious

FIFO first in, first out

fig figurative, figuratively, figure

fin finance, financial, finish

FIO free in and out

fir firkin

fl florin (*floruit*) flourished

FL Florida

Fla Florida

fl oz fluid ounce

FLSA Fair Labor Standards Act

fm fathom

Fm fermium

FM field manual

FMB Federal Marine Board

FMCS Federal Mediation and Conciliation Service

fn footnote

fo *or* **fol** folio

FO foreign office

FOB free on board

FOC free of charge

fp freezing point

FPA Foreign Press Association, free of particular average

FPC Federal Power Commission

fps feet per second, foot-pound-second, frames per second

fr father, franc, from

Fr francium

freq frequency

Fri Friday

FRS Federal Reserve System

frt freight

frwy freeway

FS Foreign Service

FSLIC Federal Savings and Loan Insurance Corporation

FSP Food Stamp Program

ft feet, foot

FTC Federal Trade Commission

fth fathom

ft lb foot-pound

fur furlong

fut future

fwd foreword, forward

FWD front-wheel drive

FX foreign exchange

FY fiscal year

FYI for your information

fz (*forzando, forzato*) accented

G

g gauge, gold, grain, acceleration of gravity, gram, gravity

Ga gallium, Georgia

GA general assembly, general average, Georgia

gal gallery, gallon

galv galvanized

GAO General Accounting Office

gar garage

GATT General Agreement on Tariffs and Trade

GAW guaranteed annual wage

gaz gazette

GB Great Britain

GCA ground-controlled approach

GCB Knight Grand Cross of the Bath

Gd gadolinium

GDR German Democratic Republic

Ge germanium

GE gilt edges

gen general, genitive, genus

Gen AF general of the air force

Gent gentleman, gentlemen

genl general

geog geographic, geographical, geography

geol geologic, geological, geology

geom geometric, geometrical, geometry

ger gerund

GGPA graduate grade-point average

GHQ general headquarters

hi gill

GI gastrointestinal, general issue, government issue

GM general manager, grand master, guided missile

GMT Greenwich mean time

GMW gram-molecular weight

gn guinea

GNI Gross national income

GNP gross national product

GO general order

GOP Grand Old Party (Republican)

gov government, governor

govt government

gp group

GP general practice

GPD gallons per day

GPH gallons per hour

GPM gallons per minute

GPO general post office, Government Printing Office

GPS gallons per second

gr grade, grain, gram, gravity, gross

grad graduate, graduated

gram grammar, grammatical

gro gross

gr wt gross weight

GSA General Services Administration, Girl Scouts of America

GSC general staff corps

GSO general staff officer

GSV guided space vehicle

GT gross ton

Gt Brit Great Britain

gtd guaranteed

gyn gynecology

H

ha hectare

hab corp habeas corpus

Hb hemoglobin

hc (*honoris causa*) for the sake of honor

HC Holy Communion, House of Commons

HCF highest common factor

hd head

HD heavy duty

hdbk handbook

He helium

HE Her Excellency, His Excellency

HEW Department of Health, Education and Welfare

hf half

Hf hafnium

HF high frequency

hg hectogram

Hg (*hydrargyrum*) mercury

HH Her Highness, His Highness, His Holiness

HI Hawaii

Hind Hindustani

hist historian, historical, history

hl hectoliter

HL House of Lords

hld hold

HLS (*hoc loco situs*) laid in this place, holograph letter signed

hlt halt

hm hectometer

HM Her Majesty, Her Majesty's, His Majesty, His Majesty's

HMC Her Majesty's Customs, His Majesty's Customs

HMS Her Majesty's ship, His Majesty's ship

HN head nurse

Ho holmium

hon honor, honorable, honorary

hor horizontal

hort horticultural, horticulture

hosp hospital

HP high pressure, hire purchase, horsepower

HQ headquarters

hr hour

HR House of Representatives

HRH Her Royal Highness, His Royal Highness

HRIP here rests in peace

hrzn horizon

HS high school

HSGT high-speed ground transport

HST Hawaiian standard time

ht height

HUD Department of Housing and Urban Development

HV high velocity, high-voltage

hvy heavy

HWM high-water mark

hwy highway

Hz hertz

I

Ia *or* **IA** Iowa

IAAF International Amateur Athletic Federation

IABA International Amateur Boxing Association

IAEA International Atomic Energy Agency

IALC instrument approach and landing chart

IATA International Air Transport Association

ib *or* **ibid** ibidem

IBM intercontinental ballistic missile

IBRD International Bank for Reconstruction and Development

ICA International Cooperation Administration, International Cooperative Alliance

ICAO International Civil Aviation Organization

ICBM intercontinental ballistic missile

ICC Indian Claims Commission, International Chamber of Commerce, Interstate Commerce Commission

ICFTU International Confederation of Free Trade Unions

ICJ International Court of Justice

ICRC International Committee of the Red Cross

ICU intensive care unit

id idem

ID Idaho, identification

i e (*id est*) that is

IFC International Finance Corporation

IG inspector general

Il Illinois

ill illustrated, illustration, illustrator

IL Illinois

illust *or* **illus** illustrated, illustration

ILO International Labor Organization

ILS instrument landing system

IMF International Monetary Fund

imit imitative

immun immunity, immunization

imp imperative, imperfect, import

in inch

In indium

IN Indiana

inc including, incorporated, increase

incl including, inclusive

incog incognito

ind independent, industrial, industry

Ind Indian, Indiana

inf infantry, infinitive

infl influenced

inq inquire

INRI (*Jesus Nazarenus Rex Iudaeorum*) Jesus of Nazareth, King of the Jews

ins inches, insurance

INS Immigration and Naturalization Service

intl *or* **intnl** international

intrans intransitive

in trans (*in transitu*) in transit

intsv intensive

IOC International Olympic Committee

IPA International Phonetic Alphabet, International Phonetic Association

ipm inches per minute

IPPF International Planned Parenthood Federation

ips inches per second

iq (*idem quod*) the same as

Ir iridium

IR infrared, inland revenue, intelligence ratios, internal revenue

IRA Irish Republican Army

IRBM intermediate range ballistic missile

irreg irregular

IRS Internal Revenue Service

ISBN International Standard Book Number

ISC interstate commerce

ISSN International Standard Serial Number

ital italic, italicized

ITO International Trade Organization

IU international unit

IV intravenous, intravenously

IWW Industrial Workers of the World

J

j joule

JA joint account, judge advocate

JAG judge advocate general

Jan January

Jap Japan, Japanese

Jav Javanese

JBS John Birch Society

JCS joint chiefs of staff

jct junction

JD justice department, juvenile delinquent, (*juris doctor*) doctor of jurisprudence, doctor of law

JP justice of the peace

Jr junior

jt *or* **jnt** joint

jun junior

Jun June

junc junction

juris jurisprudence

juv juvenile

K

k karat, kilogram, king, knight, kopeck, krona, kronor

K (*kalium*) potassium, Kelvin

Kan *or* **Kans** Kansas

kb *or* **kbar** kilobar

KB kilobyte

KC Kansas City, King's Counsel, Knights of Columbus

kcal kilocalorie, kilogram calorie

KCB Knight Commander of the Order of the Bath

kc/s kilocycles per second

KD knocked down

Ken Kentucky

kg kilogram

KG Knight of the Order of the Garter

KGB (*Komitet Gosudarstvennoi Bezopasnosti*) (Soviet) State Security Committee

kHz kilohertz

KIA killed in action

KJV King James Version

KKK Ku Klux Klan

kl kiloliter

km kilometer

KMPS kilometers per second

kn knot

K of C Knights of Columbus

kph kilometers per hour

Kr Krypton

KS Kansas

kt karat, knight

kv kilovolt

kw kilowatt

kwhr *or* **kwh** kilowatt-hour

Ky *or* **KY** Kentucky

L

L lady, lake, land, latitude, law, leaf, league, left, length, liberal, lira, liter, lodge, lord

La lanthanum, Louisiana

LA law agent, Los Angeles, Louisiana

Lab Labrador

lam laminated

lang language

lat latitude

Lat Latin, Latvia

LAT local apparent time

lb (*libra*) pound

LB Labrador

lc lowercase

LC landing craft, letter of credit, Library of Congress

LCD lowest common denominator

LCF lowest common factor

LCJ Lord Chief Justice
LCM lowest common multiple
LD lethal dose
LDC less developed country
ldg landing, loading
LDS Latter-day Saints
lect lecture, lecturer
leg legal, legislative, legislation
legis legislation, legislative, legislature
lex lexicon
lexicog lexicography
LF low frequency
lg large, long
LH left hand
Li lithium
LI Long Island
lib liberal, librarian, theory
lieut lieutenant
LIFO last in, first out
lin lineal, linear
ling linguistics
liq liquid, liquor
lit liter, literal, literally, literary, literature
lith lithographic, lithography
ll lines
LL limited liability
LM Legion of Merit, lunar module
LMT local mean time
lndg landing
LNG liquefied natural gas
loc cit (*loco citato*) in the place cited
LP low pressure
LPG liquified petroleum gas
LPGA Ladies Professional Golf Association
Lr lawrencium
LS (*locus sigilli*) place of the seal

LSS lifesaving station, life-support system
Lt lieutenant
LT long ton
LTC *or* **Lt Col** lieutenant colonel
Lt Comdr lieutenant commander
ltd limited
LTG *or* **Lt Gen** lieutenant general
lt gov lieutenant governor
LTJG lieutenant, junior grade
Lu lutetium
lub lubricant, lubricating
LVT landing vehicle, tracked
LWM low-water mark
LWV League of Women Voters
LZ landing zone

M

m much, meter (*mille*) thousand
M monsieur
ma *or* **mA** miliampere
MA Massachusetts, (*magister artium*) master of arts
MAD mutual assured destruction
MAE *or* **MA Ed** master of arts in education
mag magnesium, magnetism, magnitude
Maj major
Maj Gen major general
man manual
Man Manitoba
manuf manufacture, manufacturing
MAP modified American plan
mar maritime
Mar March
masc masculine

MASH mobile army surgical hospital

Mass Massachusetts

math mathematical, mathematician

matric matriculated, matriculation

max maximum

mb millibar

MB bachelor of medicine, Manitoba, megabyte

MBA master of business administration

mbd million barrels per day

MBE Member of the Order of the British Empire

MBS Mutual Broadcasting System

mc megacycle, millicurie

MC Member of Congress

mcf thousand cubic feet

mig microgram

MCPO master chief petty officer

Md Maryland

MD Maryland, (*medicinae doctor*) doctor of medicine

mdse merchandise

MDT mountain daylight time

Me Maine, methyl

ME Maine

meas measure

mech mechanical, mechanics

med medicine, medieval medium

Med Mediterranean

MEd master of education

met meteorological, meteorology, metropolitan

METO Middle East Treaty Organization

Mex Mexican, Mexico

MF medium frequency, mezzo forte, microfiche

mfd manufactured

mfg manufacturing

MFN most favored nation

mfr manufacture, manufacturer

mg milligram

Mg magnesium

mgd million gallons per day

mgr manager, monseigneur, monsignor

mgt management

MH medal of honor, mobile home

MHz megahertz

mi mile, mileage, mill

MI Michigan, military intelligence

MIA missing in action

Mich Michigan

mid middle

midn midshipman

mil military, million

min minimum, minute

Minn Minnesota

misc miscellaneous

Miss Mississippi, mistress, (unmarried woman)

Mk Mark

mks meter-kilogram-second

mktg marketing

ml milliliter

MLA Member of the Legislative Assembly

MLD median lethal dose, minimum lethal dose

MLF multilateral force

Mlle mademoiselle

Mlles mesdemoiselles

mm millimeter

MM messieurs, mutatis mutandis

Mme madame

Mm manganese

MN Minnesota

mo month

Mo Missouri, molybdenum

MO mail order, medical officer, Missouri, modus operandi, money order

mod moderate, modern, modification, modified, modulo, modulus

modif modification

mol molecular, molecule

MOl manned orbiting laboratory

Mont Montana

MP melting point, member of parliament, metropolitan police, military police, military policeman

mpg miles per gallon

mph miles per hour

MR map reference, mentally retarded

Mr mister

mRNA messenger RNA

Mrs mistress (married woman)

ms millisecond

MS manuscript, master of science, military science, Mississippi, motorship, multiple sclerosis

Ms mistress (woman, marital status unmarked)

MSc master of science

msec millisecond

msg message

MSG master sergeant, monosodium glutamate

msgr monseigneur, monsignor

MSgt master sergeant

MSS manuscripts

MST mountain standard time

mt mount, mountain

MT Montana, mountain time

mtg meeting, mortgage

mtge mortgage

mun *or* **munic** municipal

mus museum, music, musical, musician

mv *or* **mV** millivolt

MV motor vessel

MVA Missouri Valley Authority

MW megawatt

MWe megawatts electric

mxd mixed

N

n neuter, neutron, north, northern, noun, number

N newton, nitrogen

Na (*natrium*) sodium

NA no account, North America, not applicable

NAACP National Association for the Advancement of Colored People

NAB New American Bible

NACU National Association of Colleges and Universities

NAM National Association of Manufacturers

NAMH National Association for Mental Health

NAS National Academy of Sciences, naval air station

NASA National Aeronautics and Space Administration

nat national native, natural

NATO North Atlantic Treaty Organization

naut nautical

Nb niobium

NB New Brunswick, northbound, nota bene

NBA National Basketball Association, National Boxing Association

NBC National Broadcasting Company

NBS National Bureau of Standards

NC no charge, no credit, North Carolina

NCAA National Collegiate Athletic Association

ncv no commercial value

Nd neodymium

ND North Dakota

N Dak North Dakota

Ne neon

NE Nebraska, New England, northeast

NEA National Education Association

Neb *or* **Nebr** Nebraska

NEB New English Bible

neg negative

nem con (*nemine contradicente*) no one contradicting

nem diss (*nemine dissentiente*) no one dissenting

neut neuter

Nev Nevada

New Eng New England

NF Newfoundland, no funds

NFC National Football Conference

NFL National Football League

Nfld Newfoundland

NFS not for sale

ng nanogram

NG national guard, no good

NH New Hampshire

NHL National Hockey League

NHP nominal horsepower

Ni nickel

NIH National Institutes of Health

NJ New Jersey

NL National League, new line, (*non licet*) it is not permitted

NLF National Liberation Front

NLRB National Labor Relations Board

NLT night letter

NM nautical mile, New Mexico, no mark

N Mex New Mexico

NMI no middle initial

NMR nuclear magnetic resonance

NNE north-northeast

NNW north-northwest

no north, northern, (*numero*) number

No nobelium

nom nominative

non seq (*non sequitur*) it does not follow

NOP not otherwise provided for

Nor Norway, Norwegian

NORAD North American Air Defense Command

norm normal

nos numbers

NOS not otherwise specified

Nov November

Np neptunium

NP Notary Public

NPR National Public Radio

nr near

NRA National Recovery Administration, National Rifle Association

NRC National Research Council, Nuclear Regulatory Commission

NS new style, not specified, not sufficient, Nova Scotia

NSA National Security Agency

NSC National Security Council

NSW New South Wales

NT New Testament, Northern Territory, Northwest Territories

NTP normal temperature and pressure

nt wt *or* **n wt** net weight

NV Nevada, nonvoting

NW northwest

NWT Northwest Territories

NY New York

NYA National Youth Administration

NYC New York City

NYSE New York Stock Exchange

NZ New Zealand

O

o ohm

O Ohio, oxygen

o/a on or about

OAS Organization of American States

OAU Organization of African Unity

ob (*obit*) he died, she died

OBE Officer of the Order of the British Empire

obj object, objective

OCR optical character reader, optical character recognition

oct octavo

Oct October

OD on demand, overdose, overdrawn

OE Old English

OECD Organization for Economic Cooperation and Development

OED Oxford English Dictionary

OF outfield

off office, officer, official

offic official

OH Ohio

OHMS on Her Majesty's service, on His Majesty's service

OIT Office of International Trade

OK Oklahoma

Okla Oklahoma

OM order of merit

On *or* **ONT** Ontario

OP out of print

op cit (*opere citato*) in the work cited

OPEC Organization of Petroleum Exporting Countries

opp opposite

opt optical, optician

OR Oregon, owner's risk

orch orchestra

ord order, ordinance

Oreg *or* **Ore** Oregon

org organic, organization, organized

orig original, originally, originator

Os osmium

OS old style, ordinary seaman, out of stock

OT occupational therapy, Old Testament, overtime

OTC over-the-counter

OTS officers' training school

OW one-way

Oxon (*Oxonia*) Oxford

oz (*onza*) ounce, ounces

P

p page, penny, peseta, peso

P phosphorus

Pa Pennsylvania, protactinium

PA particular average, Pennsylvania, per annum, personal appearance, power of attorney, press agent, private account

p and h postage and handling

P and L profit and loss

par paragraph, parallel

part participle, particular

pass passenger, passive

pat patent

path *or* **pathol** pathological, pathology

PAU Pan American Union

PAYE pay as you earn, pay as you enter

payt payment

Pb (*plumbum*) lead

PB power brakes

PBS Public Broadcasting Service

PBX private branch exchange

PC Peace Corps, percent, percentage, personal computer, postcard

pct percent, percentage

pd paid

Pd palladium

PD per diem, police department

PDD past due date

PDT Pacific daylight time

PE physical education, printer's error, probable error

P/E price/earnings

pen peninsula

PEN International Association of Poets, Playwrights, Editors, Essayists and Novelists

Penn Pennsylvania

per period, person

perf perfect, perforated, performance

perh perhaps

perm permanent

perp perpendicular

pers person, personal, personnel

pert pertaining

pfd preferred

PGA Professional Golfers' Association

ph phase

PH public health, Purple Heart

phar pharmacy

pharm pharmaceutical, pharmacist, pharmacy

PhB (*philosophiae doctor*) Bachelor of Philosophy

PhD (*philosophiae doctor*) Doctor of Philosophy

phon phonetics

photog photographic, photography

phr phrase

phys physics

pinx (*pinxit*) he painted it, she painted it

pk park, peak, peck, pike

PK psychokinesis

pkg package

pkng packaging

pkt packet, pocket

pkwy parkway

pl place, plate, plural

PL partial loss, private line

plat plateau, platoon

plf plaintiff

PLO Palestine Liberation Organization

PLSS portable life-support system

pm phase modulation, premium

Pm promethium

PM paymaster, permanent magnet, police magistrate, postmaster, (*post meridiem*) after midday, postmortem, prime minister, provost marshal

pmk postmark

pmt payment

PN promissory note

Po polonium

PO petty officer, postal order, post office, purchase order

POC port of call

POD pay on delivery, post office department

POE port of embarkation, port of entry

poly polytechnic

POO post office order

pop popular, population

por portrait

POR pay on return

Port Portugal, Portuguese

pos position, positive

poss possessive

pp pages, (*per procurationem*) by proxy

PP parcel post, past participle, postpaid, prepaid

ppd post paid, prepaid

ppm parts per million

PPS (*post postscriptum*) an additional postscript

ppt parts per thousand, parts per trillion

pptn precipitation

PQ previous question, Province of Quebec

pr pair, price, printed

Pr praseodymium

PR payroll, proportional representation, public relations

PRC People's Republic of China

prec preceding

pred predicate

pref preface, preferred, prefix

prem premium

prep preparatory, preposition

pres present, president

Presb Presbyterian

prev previous, previously

prf proof

prim primary, primitive

prin principal, principle

priv private, privately, privative

PRN (*pro re nata*) for the emergency, as needed

PRO public relations officer

prob probable, probably, probate, problem

proc proceedings

prod product, production

prof professional, professor

prom promontory

pron pronoun, pronounced, pronunciation

prop property, proposition, proprietor

pros prosody

Prot Protestant

prov province, provincial, provisional

PS (*postscriptum*) postscript

pseud pseudonym, pseudonymous

psi pounds per square inch

PST Pacific standard time

psych psychology

psychol psychologist, psychology

pt part, payment, pint, point, port

Pt platinum

PT Pacific time, part-time, physical therapy, physical training

pta peseta

PTA Parent-Teacher Association

ptg printing

PTO Parent-Teacher Organization, please turn over

Pu plutonium

pub public, publication, published, publisher, publishing

publ publication, published, publisher

PUD pickup and delivery

PVA polyvinyl acetate

PVC polyvinyl chloride

pvt private

PVT pressure, volume, temperature

PW prisoner of war

pwr power
pwt pennyweight
PX please exchange, post exchange

Q

q quart, quartile, quarto, query, question
QB queen's bench
QC quality control, queen's counsel
QED (*quod erat demonstrandum*) which was to be demonstrated
QEF (*quod erat faciendum*) which was to be done
QEI (*quod erat inveniendum*) which was to be found out
QMG quartermaster general
qp *or* **q pl** (*quantum placet*) as much as you please
qq questions
qr quarter, quire
qs (*quantum sufficit*) as much as suffices
qt quantity, quart
qtd quartered
qto quarto
qty quantity
qu *or* **ques** question
quad quadrant
qual qualitative, quality
quant quantitative
quar quarterly
Que Quebec
quot quotation
qv (*quod vide*) which see

R

r radius, repeat, Republican, ruble, rupee
R radical, registered trademark
Ra radium

RA regular army, Royal Academician, Royal Academy
RAAF Royal Australian Air Force
rad radical, radian, radiator, radio, radius, radix
RAF Royal Air Force
RAM random access memory
R & B rhythm and blues
R & D research and development
R & R rest and recreation, rest and recuperation
Rb rubidium
RBC red blood cells, red blood count
RBE relative biological effectiveness
RC Red Cross, Roman Catholic
RCAF Royal Canadian Air Force
RCMP Royal Canadian Mounted Police
RCN Royal Canadian Navy
rct recruit
rd road, rod, round
RD refer to drawer
RDA recommended daily allowance, recommended dietary allowance
RDF radio direction finder, radio direction finding
Re rhenium
rec receipt, record, recording, recreation
recd received
recip reciprocal, reciprocity
rec sec recording secretary
rect receipt, rectangle, rectangular, rectified
red reduce, reduction
ref reference, referred, refining, reformed, refunding
refl reflex, reflexive
refrig refrigerating, refrigeration
reg region, register, registered, registration, regular
regd registered

regt regiment

rel relating, relative, released, religion, religious

relig religion

rep report, representative, republic

Rep Republican

repl replace, replacement

req request, require, required, requisition

reqd required

res research, reservation, reserve, residence, resolution

resp respective, respectively

retd retained, retired, returned

rev revenue, reverse, review, reviewed, revised, revision, revolution

Rev reverend

rf refunding

RF radio frequency

rh relative humidity

Rh rhodium

rhet rhetoric

RI refractive index, Rhode Island

RIP (*requiescat in pace*) may he rest in peace, may she rest in peace

rit ritardando

riv river

rm ream, room

RMS Royal Mail Service, Royal Mail Steamship

Rn radon

RN registered nurse, Royal Navy

rnd round

ROG receipt of goods

ROI return of investment

Rom Roman, Romance, Romania, Romanian

ROM read-only memory

ROP record of production

rot rotating, rotation

ROTC Reserve Officers' Training Corps

RP Received Pronunciation, reply paid, reprint, reprinting

RPM revolutions per minute

RPO railways post office

RPS revolutions per second

rpt repeat, report

RR railroad

RS Royal Society

RSV Revised Standard Version

RSVP (*réspondez s'il vous plaît*) please reply

RSWC right side up with care

rt right

RT radiotelephone, room temperature

rte route

rtw ready-to-wear

Ru ruthenium

RV recreational vehicle

rwy *or* **ry** railway

S

s saint, schilling, senate, shilling, sine, singular, small, south, southern

S sulfur

SA Salvation Army, seaman apprentice, (*sine anno*) without year, without dates, South Africa, South America, South Australia

SAC Strategic Air Command

SAE self-addressed envelope, stamped addressed envelope

SALT Strategic Arms Limitation Talks

SAM surface-to-air missile

S & M sadism and masochism

sanit sanitary, sanitation

SASE self-addressed stamped envelope

Sask Saskatchewan

sat saturate, saturated, saturation

Sat Saturday

satd saturated

S Aust South Australia

sb substantive

Sb (*stibium*) antimony

SBA Small Business Administration

SBN Standard Book Number

sc scale, scene, science, (*sculpsit*) he carved it, she carved it, he engraved it, she engraved it

Sc scandium, Scots

SC small capitals, South Carolina, supreme court

sch school

sci science, scientific

SCP single-cell protein

SCPO senior chief petty officer

sct scout

SD South Dakota, special delivery, stage direction

SDA specific dynamic action

S Dak South Dakota

SDI Strategic Defense Initiative

SDR special drawing rights

Se selenium

SE southeast, Standard English, stock exchange

SEATO Southeast Asia Treaty Organization

sec second, secretary, (*secundum*) according to

sect section, sectional

secy secretary

sed sediment, sedimentation

sel selected, selection

sen senate, senator, senior

sep separate, separated

Sep September

sepd separated

Sept September

seq (*sequens*) the following

serg *or* **sergt** sergeant

serv service

sf *or* **sfz** sforzando

SF science fiction, sinking fund

SFC sergeant first class

SG sergeant, solicitor general, specific gravity

sgd signed

Sgt sergeant

Sgt Maj sergeant major

sh share

shipt shipment

shpt shipment

sht sheet

shtg shortage

Si silicon

SI (*Système International d'Unitéds*) International System of Units

SIDS sudden infant death syndrome

sig signal, signature, signor

SIG special interest group

sigill (*sigillum*) seal

sin sine

sing singular

SJ Society of Jesus

SK Saskatchewan

sl slightly, slow

SL salvage loss, sea level, south latitude

SLBM submarine-launched ballistic missile

sld sailed, sealed, sold

SLR single lens reflex

Sm samarium

SMaj sergeant major

SMSgt senior master sergeant

SMV slow-moving vehicle

Sn [*stannum*] tin

SNG substitute natural gas, synthetic natural gas

so south, southern

SO seller's option, strikeout

soc social, society

sociol sociologist, sociology

soln solution

SOP standard operating procedure

soph sophomore

sp species, specific, specimen, spelling

SP self-propelled, shore patrol

SPCA Society for the Prevention of Cruelty to Animals

SPCC Society for the Prevention of Cruelty to Children

spec special, specifically

specif specific, specifically

sp gr specific gravity

SPOT satellite positioning and tracking

SPQR (*senatus populusque Romanus*) the senate and the people of Rome

sq squadron, square

Sr senior, senor, señor, sister, strontium

Sra senora, señora

SRO standing room only

Srta senorita, señorita

SS saints, same size, Social Security, steamship

SSA Social Security Administration

SSE south-southeast

SSG *or* **SSgt** staff sergeant

SSM staff sergeant major

SSW south-southwest

st stanza, state, street

St saint, stratus

ST short ton, single throw, standard time

sta station, stationary

stat (*statim*) immediately

stbd starboard

std standard

Ste (*sainte*) saint (*fem.*)

ster *or* **stg** sterling

stge storage

stk stock

STOL short takeoff and landing

stor storage

STP standard temperature and pressure

STV subscription television

sub subaltern, subtract, suburb

subj subject, subjunctive

suff sufficient, suffix

Sun Sunday

supp *or* **suppl** supplement, supplementary

supr supreme

supt superintendent

sur surface

surg surgeon, surgery, surgical

surv survey, surveying, surveyor

sv sailing vessel, saves, (*sub verbo* or *sub voce*) under the word

svgs savings

sw switch

SW shortwave, southwest

sym symbol, symmetrical

syn synonym, synonymous

syst system

T

T tritium

Ta tantalum

TA teaching assistant

TAC Tactical Air Command

tan tangent

tb tablespoon, tablespoonful

Tb terbium

TB trial balance, tubercle bacillus

tbs *or* **tbsp** tablespoon, tablespoonful

Tc technetium

tchr teacher

TD touchdown, Treasury Department

TDN total digestible nutrients

TE tellurium

tech technical, technically, technician, technological, technology

TEFL teaching English as a foreign language

tel telegram, telegraph, telephone

teleg telegraphy

temp temperance, temperature, template, temporal, temporary

Tenn Tennessee

TESL teaching English as a second language

TESOL Teachers of English to speakers of Other Languages

Test Testament

Tex Texas

TG transformational grammar, type genus

Th thorium, Thursday

Thurs *or* **Thu** Thursday

Ti titanium

tk tank, truck

tkt ticket

TL total loss, truckload

TLC tender loving care

TLO total loss only

tlr tailor, trailer

Tm thulium

TM trademark, transcendental meditation

TMO telegraph money order

tn ton, town, train

TN Tennessee, true north

tng training

tnpk turnpike

topog topography

tot total

tpk *or* **tpke** turnpike

tps townships, troops

tr translated, translation, translator, transpose

trans transaction, transitive, translated, translation, translator

transl translated, translation

transp transportation

trib tributary

trop tropic, tropical

ts tensile strength

tsp teaspoon, teaspoonful

TT telegraphic transfer, Trust Territories

Tu Tuesday

TU trade union, transmission unit

TUC Trades Union Congress

Tues *or* **Tue** Tuesday

TV television, terminal velocity, transvestite

TX Texas

U

U university, uranium

UAE United Arab Emirates

UAR United Arab Republic

UC undercharge, uppercase

ugt urgent

UHF ultrahigh frequency

UK United Kingdom

ult ultimate, ultimo

UN United Nations

unan unanimous

UNESCO United Nations Educational, Scientific, and Cultural Organization

UNICEF United Nations International Children's Emergency Fund

univ universal, university

UNRWA United Nations Relief and Works Agency

uns unsymmetrical

UPC Universal Product Code

UPI United Press International

US United States Army, United States of America

USAF United States Air Force

USCG United States Coast Guard

USDA United States Department of Agriculture

USIA United States Information Agency

USM United States Mail

USMC United States Maritime Corps

USN United States Navy

USO United Service Organizations

USPS United States Postal Service

USS United States ship

USSR Union of Soviet Socialist Republics

usu usual, usually

UT Universal time, Utah

util utility

UV ultraviolet

UW underwriter

ux wife

UXB unexploded bomb

V

v vector, verb, versus, very, volt, voltage, vowel

V vanadium

Va Virginia

VA Veterans Administration, vice admiral, Virginia, visual aid, volt-ampere

vac vacuum

VADM vice admiral

val value, valued

var variant, variety, various

VAT value-added tax

vb verb, verbal

VC veterinary corps, vice-chancellor, vice-consul, Victoria Cross, Vietcong

VD vapor density, venereal disease

VDT video display terminal

VDU visual display unit

veg vegetable

vel vellum, velocity

vert vertebrate, vertical

VFD volunteer fire department

VG very good, vicar-general

VHF very high frequency

vi verb intransitive

VI Virgin Islands, viscosity index, volume indicator

vic vicinity

Vic Victoria

vil village

vis visibility, visual

VISTA Volunteers in Service to America

viz vicelicet

VLF very low frequency

VOA Voice of America

voc vocational, vocative

vocab vocabulary

vol volcano, volume, volunteer

VOLAR volunteer army

VOM volt ohm meter

VP variable pitch, various places, verb phrase, vice president

VRM variable rate mortgage

vs verse, versus

VS veterinary surgeon

vss verses, versions

V/STOL vertical short takeoff and landing

Vt Vermont

VT vacuum tube, variable time, Vermont

VTOL vertical takeoff and landing

VTR video tape recorder, video tape recording

VU volume unit

Vulg Vulgate

vv verses, vice versa

W

W (*Wolfram*) tungsten

WA Washington, Western Australia

war warrant

W Aust Western Australia

WC water closet, without charge

Wed Wednesday

WFTU World Federation of Trade Unions

WH watt-hour

WHA World Hockey Association

whf wharf

WHO World Health Organization

whr watt-hour

whs *or* **whse** warehouse

whsle wholesale

wi when issued

WI West Indies, Wisconsin

WIA wounded in action

wid widow, widower

wk week, work

wkly weekly

WL waterline, wavelength

WNW west-northwest

WO warrant officer

w/o without

W/O water-in-oil

WOC without compensation

WP without prejudice

WPM words per minute

wpn weapon

WR warehouse receipt

WRAC Women's Royal Army Corps

WRAF Women's Royal Air Force

WRNS Women's Royal Naval Service

wrnt warrant

WSW west-southwest

wt weight

WT watertight, wireless telegraphy

WV *or* **W Va** West Virginia

WVS Women's Voluntary Services

WW warehouse warrant, with warrants, world war

w/w wall-to-wall

Wy *or* **Wyo** Wyoming

X

x cross, ex, experimental, extra

XC ex coupon

XD *or* **x div** ex dividend

Xe xenon

XI *or* **x in** *or* **x int** ex interest

XL extra large, extra long

Y

y yard, year, yen

Y ytrium

Yb ytterbium

YB yearbook

yd yard

YO year old

YOB year of birth
yr year, younger, your
yrbk yearbook
Yug Yugoslavia

Z

z zero, zone
Zn zinc
ZPG zero population growth
Zr zirconium

Computer Acronyms and Abbreviations

A

A/D *abbrev for* analog to digital.

ADP *abbrev for* automatic data processing

ALGOL *acronym* Algorithmic-Oriented Language, a high-level programing language

ALU *abbrev for* arithmetic and logic unit

ANSI *abbrev for* American National Standards Institute

APL *abbrev for* A Programing Language

ARQ *abbrev for* automatic request for data correction

ASCII *acronym* American Standard Code for Information Interchange

ASR *abbrev for* automatic send and receive

ATLAS *acronym* Automatic Tabulating, Listing and Sorting System; Automated Telephone Line Address System

ATM *abbrev for* automated teller machine

B

BASIC *acronym* Beginner's All-purpose Symbolic Instruction Code

BCD *abbrev for* binary-coded decimal

BIM *acronym* Beginning of Information Mark

BIT *acronym* Binary digit

BOF *acronym* Beginning Of File

BPI *abbrev for* bits per inch

BPS *abbrev for* bits per second

C

CAD *acronym* Computer-Aided Design

CAD/CAM *acronym* Computer-Aided Design and Manufacture

CAL *acronym* Computer-Assisted Learning

CAM *acronym* Computer-Aided Manufacture

CAT *abbrev for* catalogue

CBL *abbrev for* computer-based learning

CBT *abbrev for* computer-based training

CCD *abbrev for* charge-coupled device

CD-ROM *abbrev for* compact disc read-only memory

CGA *abbrev for* color graphics adapter

CMI *abbrev for* computer-managed instruction

CML *abbrev for* computer-managed learning

CMOS *abbrev for* complementary metal oxide semiconductor

COBOL *acronym* Common Business-Oriented Language

COM *acronym* Computer Output on Microfilm

COMMS *abbrev for* communications

CP/M *abbrev for* control, program, monitor

CPS *abbrev for* characters per second

CPU *abbrev for* central processing unit

CRC *abbrev for* cyclic redundancy check

CR *abbrev for* carriage return

CRT *abbrev for* cathode-ray tube

CTRL *abbrev for* control key

CUG *abbrev for* closed user group

D

D/A *abbrev for* digital to analog

DATEL *trademark, acronym* Data Telecommunications

DDA *abbrev for* direct data entry

DFS *abbrev for* disk filing system

DIN *abbrev for* Deutsche Industrie Norm, the German industry standard

DMS *abbrev for* direct memory access

DOS *acronym* Disk-Operating System

DP *abbrev for* data processing

DTL *abbrev for* diode transistor logic

E

EARCOM *acronym* Electrically Alterable Read-Only Memory

EBDIC *acronym* Extended Binary Decimal Code for information exchange

ECMA *abbrev for* European Computer Manufacturers' Association

EDI *abbrev for* electronic data interchange

EDP *abbrev for* electronic data processing

EEPROM *acronym* Electrically Erasable Programmable Read-Only Memory

EFIT *acronym* Electronic Facial Identification Technique

EFTPOS *acronym* Electronic Funds Transfer at Point Of Sale

EGA *abbrev for* enhanced graphics adapter

ELSI *abbrev for* extra large-scale integration

EMAIL *acronym* Electronic Mail

ENIAC *acronym* Electronic Numeral Integrator And Calculator

EOF *abbrev for* end-of-file marker

EPROM *acronym* Erasable Programmable Read-Only Memory

EROPS *acronym* Extended Range Operations

ESC *abbrev for* escape key

ESPRIT *acronym* European Community Research and Development Programme in Advanced Information Technology

EXP *abbrev for* exponential function

EXPUT *acronym* Extraction of input data

F

FET *abbrev for* field-effect transistor

FF *abbrev for* form feed

FIFO *acronym* First In First Out

FORTRAN *acronym* Formula Translation, a high-level language

FM *abbrev for* frequency modulation

G

GEM *acronym* Graphics Environmental Manager

GIGO *acronym* Garbage In Garbage Out

GUI *acronym* Graphical User Interface

H

HEX *abbrev for* hexadecimal

HRG *abbrev for* high resolution graphics

Hz *abbrev for* Hertz, unit of frequency

I

IAL *abbrev for* International Algebraic Language

IAR *abbrev for* instruction address register

IAS *abbrev for* immediate access store

IBM *abbrev for* International Business Machines

IC *abbrev for* integrated circuit

ICL *abbrev for* International Computers Limited

ID *abbrev for* identification code

IDP *abbrev for* integrated data processing

IEEE *abbrev for* American Institute of Electrical and Electronic Engineers

IFIP *abbrev for* International Federation for Information Processing

IKBS *abbrev for* intelligent knowledge-based system

INTELSAT *acronym* International Telecommunications Satellite consortium

I/O *abbrev for* input and output

IP *abbrev for* information provider

ISBN *abbrev for* International Standard Book Number

ISDN *abbrev for* Integrated Services Digital Network

ISO *abbrev for* International Organization for Standardization

IT *abbrev for* Information Technology

J

JCL *abbrev for* job control language

K

KEPROM *acronym* Keyed-access Erasable Programmable Read-Only Memory

K *abbrev for* Kilo (1024 in computer storage)

kHx *abbrev for* kilohertz

L

LAN *acronym* Local Area Network

LCD *abbrev for* liquid crystal display

LED *acronym* Light Emitting Diode

LIFO *acronym* Last In First Out

LISP *acronym* List Processor, a high-level programing language

LPM *abbrev for* lines per minute

LSE *abbrev for* Language Symbolique d'Enseignement

LSI *abbrev for* large-scale integration

M

MACRO *abbrev for* macro code

MAP *acronym* Microprocessor Application Project

Mb *abbrev for* megabyte

MHz *abbrev for* megahertz

MICR *abbrev for* magnetic ink character recognition

MICRO *abbrev for* microcomputer

MIPS *acronym* Millions of Instructions Per Second

MIS *acronym* Management Information System

MISP *acronym* Microelectronics Industry Support Program

MMI *abbrev for* man-machine interface

MODEM *acronym* Modulator-Demodulator

MOS *acronym* Metal-Oxide Semiconductor

MOSFET *acronym* Metal-Oxide Semiconductor Field-Effect Transistor

MP/M *abbrev for* multi-user CP/M

MPU *abbrev for* microprocessor unit

MSDOS *trademark, abbrev for* Microsoft Disk-Operating System

MSI *abbrev for* medium-scale integration

N

NAK *acronym* Negative Acknowledgment

NCR *abbrev for* National Cash Register; 'no carbon required' copying paper

NLQ *abbrev for* near letter quality

NMOS *abbrev for* n-type metal-oxide semiconductor

NRZI *abbrev for* non-return to zero indicator

O

OCR *abbrev for* optical character recognition

OEM *abbrev for* original equipment manufacturer

OMR *abbrev for* optical mark recognition

OPAMP *acronym* Operational Amplifier

OP-CODE *acronym* Operation Code

P

PCB *abbrev for* printed circuit board

PC-DOS *trademark, abbrev for* Personal Computer Disk Operating System

PIXEL *abbrev for* picture elements

PIO *abbrev for* programmable input/output

PMOS *abbrev for* p-type metal-oxide semiconductor

POS *acronym* Point Of Sale terminal

PROM *acronym* Programmable Read-Only Memory

PSS *abbrev for* packet switching service

PSTN *abbrev for* public switched telephone network

PSU *abbrev for* power supply unit

Q

QWERTY the standard typewriter keyboard

R

RAM *acronym* Random Access Memory

RGB *abbrev for* red, green, blue (color video signal system)

RJE *abbrev for* remote job entry

RO *abbrev for* receive-only terminal

ROM *acronym* Read-Only Memory

RPN *abbrev for* reverse polish notation

RTL *abbrev for* resistor transistor logic

R/W *abbrev for* read/write

S

SAM *acronym* Serial Access Memory

SSI *abbrev for* small-scale integration

SYSOP *acronym* System Operator

T

TELECOMMS *abbrev for* telecommunications

TRL *abbrev for* transistor-resister logic

TTL *abbrev for* transistor-transistor logic

U

UART *acronym* Universal Asynchronous Receiver Transmitter

UCSD *abbrev for* University College of San Diego

UHF *abbrev for* ultrahigh frequency

ULA *acronym* Uncommitted Logic Array

UNIVAC *acronym* Universal Automatic Computer

USART *acronym* Universal Synchronous/Asynchronous Receiver Transmitter

USRT *acronym* Universal Synchronous Receiver Transmitter

V

VAD *acronym* Value-Added and Data

VDU *abbrev for* visual display unit

VHF *abbrev for* very high frequency

VLF *abbrev for* very low frequency

VLSI *abbrev for* very large-scale integration

VLT *abbrev for* variable list table

W

WAN *acronym* Wide Area Network

WIMP *acronym* Window, Ikon, Mouse Program

WP *abbrev for* word processor; word processing

WYSIWYG *acronym* What You See Is What You Get

Phrases and quotations from Latin, Greek and modern foreign languages

A

abiit, excessit, evasit, erupit (L.) he is gone, he is off, he has escaped, he has broken away. — Cicero, *In Catilinam,* II. i. 1.

ab imo pectore (L.) from the bottom of the heart.

à bon chat, bon rat (Fr.) to a good cat, a good rat — well matched: set a thief to catch a thief.

ab ovo usque ad mala (L.) from the egg to the apples — of a Roman banquet: from the beginning to the end.

absens haeres non erit (L.) the absent one will not be the heir — out of sight, out of mind.

ab uno disce omnes (L.) from one (offense) learn all (the race). — Virgil, *Aen.,* I. 65-66: hence, from one example you may know the rest.

abusus non tollit usum (L.) abuse does not do away with use — i.e. an abuse is not a reason for giving up the legitimate use of a thing.

a capite ad calcem (L.) from head to heel.

à chacun son goût (Fr.) to everyone his own taste. See also **chacun (à) son goût.**

à chaque saint sa chandelle (Fr.) every saint his candle: to every patron his meed of service.

Acherontis pabulum (L.) food for Acheron — of a bad person. — Plautus, *Casina,* II. i. 12.

actum est de republica (L.) it is all up with the state.

actum ne agas (L.) do not do what is already done — quoted as a proverb by Terence, *Phormio.,* II. iii. 72 (or 1. 419).

ad Calendas Graecas (L.) at the Greek Calends — i.e. never, as the Greeks had no Calends.

adhuc sub judice lis est (L.) the dispute is still before the court. — Horace, *A.P.,* 78.

ad majorem Dei gloriam (L.) for the greater glory of God — the Jesuit motto.

adscriptus glebae (L.) bound to the soil — of serfs.

ad utrumque paratus (L.) prepared for either case.

ad vitam aut culpam (L.) for life or till fault: of appointments, for life unless misconduct necessitates dismissal.

advocatus diaboli (L.) devil's advocate. See Dict.

aequam memento rebus in arduis servare mentem (L.) remember to keep a calm mind in difficulties. — Horace, *Od.,* II. iii. 1.

aequitas sequitur legem (L.) equity follows law.

age quod agis (L.) do what you are doing — i.e. with all your powers.

aide-toi, le ciel t'aidera (Fr.) help yourself and Heaven will help you.

aliquando bonus dormitat Homerus (L.) See **indignor.**

aliquid haeret (L.) something sticks.

Allah il Allah, a corr. of Ar. *lā ilāha illā 'llāh* = there is no God but the God.

Allahu akbar (Ar.) God is great.

alter ipse amicus (L.) a friend is another self.

amabilis insania (L.) a pleasing madness or rapture. — Horace, *Od.,* III. 4. 5-6.

amantium irae amoris integratio est (L.) lovers' quarrels are a renewal of love. — Terence, *Andr.,* III. iii. 23.

amare et sapere vix deo conceditur (L.) to be in love and to be wise is scarce granted even to a god. — Laberius.

amari aliquid (L.) some touch of bitterness. — Lucretius, *De Rer. Nat.,* iv. 1130.

a mensa et toro (L.) from bed and board.

amicus Plato, amicus Socrates, sed magis amica veritas (L.) Plato is dear to me (or is my friend), Socrates is dear, but truth is dearer still. — L. version of saying attributed to Aristotle.

amicus usque ad aras (L.) a friend as far as the altars — i.e. as far as may be without offense to the gods.

amor sceleratus habendi (L.) the accursed love of possessing. — Ovid, *Met.,* I. 131.

amor vincit omnia (L.). See **omnia.**

anathema sit (L.) let him be accursed. — 1 Cor. xvi. 22.

anch' io son pittore (It.) I, too, am a painter (said by Correggio on looking at Raphael's 'St Cecilia').

anērithmon gelasma. See **kymatōn anērithmon gelasma.**

anguis in herba (L.) a snake in the grass. — Virgil, *Ecl.,* III. 93.

anima naturaliter Christiana (L.) a soul naturally Christian, i.e. one who behaves like a Christian without the benefit of Christian revelation. — Tertullian, *Apologia,* xvii.

animula vagula (L.) little soul flitting away — beginning of a poem ascribed to the dying Hadrian, translated or paraphrased by Prior, Pope, Byron, and Dean Merivale.

à nos moutons. See **revenons.**

ante Agamemnona. See **vixere fortes.**

a parte ante (L.) on the side before, from past eternity — opp. to **a parte post,** in future eternity.

a posse ad esse (L.) from the possible to the actual.

après moi (nous) le déluge (Fr.) after me (us) the deluge: then the deluge may come when it likes — attributed to Mme. de Pompadour and to Louis XV. Cf. **emou thanontos.**

aquila non capit muscas (L.) an eagle does not catch flies.

arbiter elegantiae (L.) judge of good taste — said by Tacitus, *Annals*, XVI. 18, of Gaius Petronius, an exquisite at the court of Nero (prob. same as Petronius Arbiter). — Also quoted as **arbiter elegantiarum.**

Arcades ambo (L.) Arcadians both: two of the same stamp. — Virgil, *Ecl.*, VII. 4. — Rendered by Byron blackguards both, *Don Juan*, IV. xciii.

ariston men hydōr(Gr.) water is best. — Pindar, *Olympian Odes,* i. 1.

ars est celare artem (L.) true art is to conceal art.

ars longa, vita brevis (L.) art is long, life is short. — Seneca, *De Brevitate Vitae*, 1. Cf. **ho bios brachys.**

asbestos gelōs (Gr.) inextinguishable laughter. — Homer, *Iliad*, I. 599, etc.

asinus ad lyram (L.) an ass at the lyre, one ignorant of music or art: one unsuited to an occupation. — From a Greek proverbial expression *onos pros lyran.*

astra castra, numen lumen (L.) the stars my camp, God my lamp.

Athanasius contra mundum (L.) Athanasius against the world: one resolute man facing universal opposition.

atra cura (L.) black care. See **post equitem.**

at spes non fracta (L.) but hope is not yet crushed.

au bout de son latin (Fr.) at the end of his Latin, at the end of his knowledge, at his wits' end.

auctor quae pretiosa facit (L.) gifts that the giver adds value to. — Ovid, *Her.*, XVII. 71-2.

audentes fortuna juvat (L.) fortune favors the daring. — Virgil, *Aen.*, X. 284.

audi alteram partem (L.) hear the other side. — St Augustine, *De Duabus Animabus*, XIV. 2.

auditque vocatus Apollo (L.) and Apollo hears when invoked. — Virgil, *Georg.*, IV. 7.

aufgeschoben ist nicht aufgehoben (Ger.) put off is not given up.

aujourd'hui roi, demain rien (Fr.) king today, nothing tomorrow.

au plaisir de vous revoir (Fr.) till I have the pleasure of seeing you again.

auribus teneo lupum (L.) I am holding a wolf by the ears. — Terence, *Phormio*, III. ii. 21.

auri sacra fames (L.) accursed hunger for gold. — Virgil, *Aen.*, III. 57.

au royaume des aveugles les borgnes sont rois (Fr.) in the kingdom of the blind the one-eyed are kings. — As a Latin proverb, *beati monoculi in regione caecorum.*

aurum omnes, victa jam pietate, colunt (L.) all worship gold, piety being overthrown. — Propertius, III. xiii. 48.

auspicium melioris aevi (L.) augury of a better age.

aussitôt dit, aussitôt fait (Fr.) no sooner said than done.

Austriae est imperare orbi universo (L.) it is Austria's part to command the whole world — often **A.E.I.O.U.**

aut amat aut odit mulier, nihil est tertium (L.) a woman either loves or hates, there is no third course. — Syrus, 42.

autant d'hommes (or **de têtes**), **autant d'avis** (Fr.) so many men, so many minds. Cf. **quot homines.**

aut Caesar aut nullus, or **nihil** (L.) either Caesar or nobody (nothing): all or nothing.

aut insanit homo aut versus facit (L.) either the man is mad or he is making verses. — Horace, *Sat.*, II. vii. 117.

aut inveniam viam aut faciam (L.) I shall either find a way or make one.

aut non tentaris aut perfice (L.) either do not attempt or else achieve. — Ovid, *A.A.*, I. 389.

aut prodesse volunt aut delectare poetae (L.) poets seek either to profit or to please. — Horace, *A.P.*, 333.

aut regem aut fatuum nasci oportet (L.) one should be born either king or fool. — Proverb; quoted by Seneca.

autres temps, autres mœurs (Fr.) other times, other manners.

aut vincere aut mori (L.) to conquer or die.

aut vitam aut culpam. An incorrect variant of **ad vitam aut culpam** (q.v.).

aux absents les os (Fr.) the bones to the absent.

aux grands maux les grands remèdes (Fr.) to desperate evils, desperate remedies.

auxilium ab alto (L.) help from on high.

ave, Caesar (or **imperator), morituri te salutant** (L.) hail, Caesar, men doomed to die salute thee (said by gladiators).

a verbis ad verbera (L.) from words to blows.

à vieux comptes nouvelles disputes (Fr.) old accounts breed new disputes.

a vinculo matrimonii (L.) from the bond of matrimony.

avi numerantur avorum (L.) ancestors of ancestors are counted [to me].

avis au lecteur (Fr.) notice to the reader.

avise la fin (Fr.) weigh well the end.

avito viret honore (L.) he is green with ancestral honours.

avoir la langue déliée (Fr.) to have the tongue unbound, to be glib of speech.

B

barba tenus sapientes (L.) sages as far as the beard — i.e. with an appearance of wisdom only.

battre la campagne (Fr.) to scour the country, to beat the bush.

bayer aux corneilles (Fr.) to gape at the crows, to stare vacantly.

beatus ille qui procul negotiis . . . paterna rura bobus exercet suis (L.) happy he who, far removed from business . . . tills with his own oxen the fields that were his father's.— Horace, *Epod.*, ii. 1.

bella gerant alii, tu, felix Austria, nube (L.) let others wage wars; do thou, lucky Austria, make marriages. — Matthias Corvinus of Hungary.

bella, horrida bella (L.) wars, horrid wars. — Virgil, *Aen.*, VI. 86.

bellaque matribus detestata (L.) and wars abhorred by mothers. — Horace, *Od.*, I. i. 24-5.

bellum nec timendum nec provacandum (L.) war is neither to be feared nor provoked (Pliny the Younger, *Panegyricus*, 16, **nec times bellum, nec provocas).**

belua multorum capitum (L.) monster with many heads— the irrational mob. — Horace, *Epistolae*, I. i. 76.

beneficium accipere libertatem est vendere (L.) to accept a favor is to sell one's liberty. — Syrus, 49.

bene orasse est bene studuisse (L.) to have prayed well is to have endeavored well.

bene qui latuit bene vixit (L.) he has lived well who has lived obscure. — Ovid, *Trist.*, III. iv. 25.

benigno numine (l.) with favoring godhead.— Horace, *Od.*, III. iv. 74.

bibere venenum in auro (L.) to drink poison from a cup of gold.

biblia abiblia (Gr.) books that are no books.

bis dat qui cito dat (L.) he gives twice who gives promptly. — Proverb; by Bacon.

bis peccare in bello non licet (L.) in war one may not blunder twice.

bis pueri senes (L.) old men are twice boys.

blandae mendacia linguae (L.) falsehoods of a smooth tongue.

bon avocat, mauvais voisin (Fr.) a good lawyer is a bad neighbor.

bon jour, bonne œuvre (Fr.) better day, better deed.

bonnes nouvelles adoucissent le sang (Fr.) good news sweetens the blood.

borgen macht sorgen (Ger.) borrowing makes sorrowing.

boutez en avant (Fr.) push forward.

brevis esse laboro, obscurus fio (L.) I labor to be brief, and I become obscure. — Horace, *A.P.*, 25-26.

briller par son absence (Fr.) to be conspicuous by its absence.

brûler la chandelle par les deux bouts (Fr.) to burn the candle at both ends.

buen principio, la mitad es hecha (Sp.) well begun is half-done.

C

cadit quaestio (L.) the question drops.

caeca invidia est (L.) envy is blind. — Livy, xxxviii. 49.

caelebs quid agam (L.) (you wonder) what I, a bachelor, am about. — Horace, *Od.*, III.viii. 1.

caelum non animum mutant qui trans mare currunt (L.) they change their sky, not their mind, who scour across the sea. — Horace, *Epist.*, I. xi. 27.

Caesar non supra grammaticos (L.) Caesar has no authority over the grammarians.

ça ira (Fr.) it will go — refrain of a famous song of the French Revolution.

callida junctura (L.) a skilful connection. — Horace, *A.P.*, 47-48.

candida Pax (L.) white-robed Peace. — Tibullus, I. x. 45.

cantabit vacuus coram latrone viator (L.) the empty-handed traveler will sing in presence of the robber. — Juvenal, X. 22.

carent quia vate sacro (L.) because they lack a sacred bard. — Horace, *Od.*, IV. ix. 28.

carpe diem, quam minimum credula postero (L.) enjoy the present day, trust the least possible to the future. — Horace, *Od.*, I. xi. 8.

causa sine qua non (L.) an indispensable cause.

cave quid dicis, quando, et cui (L.) beware what you say, when, and to whom.

cedant arma togae (L.) let arms yield to the gown: let military authority yield to civil. — Cicero, *De Officiis*, I. xxii. 77, *in Pisonem*, xxx. 73.

cela va sans dire (Fr.) that goes without saying: of course.

cela viendra (Fr.) that will come.

celui qui veut, peut (Fr.) who will, can.

ce monde est plein de fous (Fr.) this world is full of madmen.

c'en est fait de lui (Fr.) it is all up with him.

ce n'est que le premier pas qui coûte (Fr.). See **il n'ya.**

certum est quia impossibile est (L.) it is certain because it is impossible. — Tertullian.

c'est-à-dire (Fr.) that is to say.

c'est égal (Fr.) it's all one (to me): it makes no odds.

c'est le commencement de la fin (Fr.) it is the beginning of the end.— Attrib. to Talleyrand..

c'est magnifique, mais ce n'est pas la guerre (Fr.) it is magnificent, but it is not war (said at Balaklava by a French general watching the charge of the Light Brigade).

c'est pire (or **plus**) **qu'un crime, c'est une faute** (Fr.) it is worse than a crime, it is a blunder (on the execution of the Duc d'Enghien; attributed to various persons, incl. Boulay de la Meurthe).

c'est selon (Fr.) that is according to the circumstances.

c'est (une) autre chose (Fr.) that is quite another thing.

ceterum censeo (L.) but I think (said of persistent obstruction like that of Cato).

chacun (à) son goût (Fr.) everyone to his taste. Also **à chacun son goût.**

chapeaux bas (Fr.) hats off.

cherchez la femme (Fr.) look for the woman: there's a woman at the bottom of it. — Dumas *père*.

che sarà sarà (It.) what will be will be.

chiesa libera in libero stato (It.) a free church in a free state (Cavour's ideal for Italy).

chi tace confessa (It.) who keeps silence, confesses.

circulus in probando (L.) arguing in a circle, using the conclusion as one of the arguments.

civis Romanus sum (L.) I am a Roman citizen. — Cicero, *In Verrem,* VI. 57.

clarior e tenebris (L.) the brighter from the darkness.

clarum et venerabile nomen (L.) an illustrious and venerable name. — Lucan, IX. 202.

cogito, ergo sum (L.) I think, therefore I am. (Descartes's fundamental basis of philosophy.)

comitas inter gentes, or **comitas gentium** (L.) See **comity** in Dict.

conditio sine qua non (L.) an indispensable condition.

conjunctis viribus (L.) with united powers.

conquiescat in pace (L.) may he [or she] rest in peace.

conscia mens recti (L.) a mind conscious of rectitude. — Ovid, *Fast.,* IV. 311. Cf. **mens sibi.**

consensus facit legem (L.) consent makes law or rule.

consuetudo pro lege servatur (L.) custom is held as a law.

consule Planco (L.) when Plancus was consul, when I was a young man. — Horace, *Od.,* III. xiv. 28.

contraria contrariis curantur (L.) opposites are cured by opposites.

corruptio optimi pessima (L.) the corruption of the best is the worst of all.

cosi fan tutte (It.) so do they all (of women): they are all like that.

coûte que coûte (Fr.) cost what it may.

crambe repetita (L.) cauld kale het again — cold cabbage warmed up. — Juvenal, VII. 154.

credat Judaeus Apella, non ego (L.) let the Jew Apella believe that, for I don't. — Horace, *Sat.,* I. v. 100.

credo quia absurdum (L.) I believe it because it is absurd; — **quia impossibile** because it is impossible (based on Tertullian; see **certum est quia impossibile est).**

crescit eundo (L.) it grows as it goes. — Lucretius VI. 341.

cucullus non facit monachum (L.) the cowl does not make the monk.

cuilibet (or cuicunque) in arte sua (perito) credendum est (L.) every (skilled) person is to be trusted in his own art. — Coke.

cujus regio, ejus religio (L.) whose the region, his the religion — the principle that the established religion should be that of the prince in each state.

curiosa felicitas (L.) studied felicity of expression — said by Petronius Arbiter, *Saturae (Satyricon),* 118, 5 of Horace's style: (*loosely*) curious felicity.

D

da dextram misero (L.) give the right hand to the unhappy.

da locum melioribus (L.) give place to your betters. — Terence, *Phormio*, III. ii. 37.

damnosa haereditas (L.) an inheritance of debts (*Roman law*): any hurtful inheritance.— Gaius, *Institutes*, ii. 163.

damnum absque injuria (L.) loss without legal injury.

das Ding an sich (Ger.) the thing in itself.

das Ewig-Weibliche zieht uns hinan (Ger.) the eternal feminine draws us upward. — Goethe, *Faust*, at end.

data et accepta (L.) expenditures and receipts.

date obolum Belisario (L.) give a penny to Belisarius (ascribed to the great general when reduced to beggary).

Davus sum, non Oedipus (L.) I am Davus, not Oedipus — no good at riddles. — Terence, *Andria*., I. ii. 23.

de die in diem (L.) from day to day.

de gustibus non est disputandum (L.) there is no disputing about tastes.

de l'audace, encore de l'audace, et toujours de l'audace (Fr.) to dare, still to dare, and ever to dare (Danton's famous phrase).

delenda est Carthago (L.) Carthage must be wiped out (a saying constantly repeated by Cato).

de mal en pis (Fr.) from bad to worse.

de minimis non curat lex (L.) the law does not concern itself about very small matters. — Bacon, Letter cclxxxii.

de mortuis nil nisi bonum (L.) say nothing but good of the dead.

de nihilo nihilum. See **gigni.**

de omni re scibili et quibusdam aliis (L.) about all things knowable, and some others.

de pis en pis (Fr.) worse and worse.

der grosse Heide (Ger.) the great pagan (Heine's name for Goethe).

desipire in loco. See **dulce.**

desunt cetera (L.) the rest is wanting.

de te fabula narratur (L.) the story is about you. — Horace, *Sat.*, I. i. 69-70.

detur digniori (L.) let it be given to the more worthy; **detur pulchriori** let it be given to the fairer.

deus nobis haec otia fecit (L.) it is a god that hath given us this ease. — Virgil, *Ecl.*, I. 6.

dicamus bona verba (L.) let us speak words of good omen. — Tibullus, II, ii. 1.

Dichtung und Wahrheit (Ger.) poetry and truth.

dictum de dicto (L.) hearsay report.

dictum sapienti sat est (L.) a word to the wise is enough (usu. quoted as **verbum**). — Plautus, *Persa*, IV. vii. 19.

diem perdidi (L.) I have lost a day (said by the Emperor Titus).

Dieu défend le droit (Fr.) God defends the right; **Dieu vous garde** God keep you.

Die Wacht am Rhein (Ger.) the Watch on the Rhine (a famous German patriotic song).

digito monstrari (L.) to be pointed out with the finger: to be famous. — Persius, I. 28.

dignus vindice nodus (L.). See **nec deus intersit.**

di grado in grado (It.) by degrees.

dis aliter visum (L.) the gods have adjudged otherwise. — Virgil, *Aen.*, II. 428.

disjecta membra (L.) scattered limbs (after Ovid, *Met.*, III. 724); **disjecti membra poetae** limbs of the dismembered poet. — Horace, *Sat.*, I. iv. 62.

distinguo (L.) I distinguish.

divide et impera (L.) divide and rule.

docendo discimus (L.) we learn by teaching.

doctor utriusque legis (L.) doctor of both laws (civil and canon).

doli capax (L.) capable of committing a wrong — opp. to *doli incapax.*

Domine. dirige nos (L.) Lord, direct us (the motto of London).

Dominus illuminatio mea (L.) the Lord is my light.

domus et placens uxor (L.) a home and a pleasing wife. — Horace, *Od.*, II. xiv. 21-22.

dorer la pilule (Fr.) to gild the pill.

dormitat Homerus (L.). See **indignor.**

dos moi pou stō kai tēn gēn kinēsō (Gr.) give me where to stand, and I will move the earth (attributed to Archimedes).

do ut des (L.) I give that you may give.

dulce, 'Domum' (L.) sweet strain, 'Homeward' — from a Winchester school song sung before the holidays; **dulce est desipere in loco** it is pleasant to play the fool on occasion. — Horace, *Od.*, IV. xii. 28; **dulce et decorum est pro patria mori** it is sweet and glorious to die for one's country. — Horace, *Od.*, III. ii. 13.

dum casta (L.) while (she is) chaste.

dum spiro, spero (L.) while I breathe, I hope.

dum vivimus, vivamus (L.) let us live while we live.

dux femina facti (L.) a woman was leader in the deed. — Virgil, *Aen.*, I. 364.

E

écrasez l'infâme (Fr.) crush the vile thing. Voltaire against the Roman Catholic Church of his time.

edax rerum. See **tempus.**

ego et rex meus (L.) I and my kng. — Cardinal Wolsey.

ebeu fugaces . . . labuntur anni (L.) alas! the fleeting years slip away. — Horace, *Od.*, II. xiv. 1-2.

eile mit Weile (Ger.) make speed with leisure. Cf. **festina lente.**

ein Mal, kein Mal (Ger.) just once counts nothing.

ek parergou (Gr.) as a by-work.

Ēli, Ēli, lama sabachthani (Matt. xxvii. 46), **Eloi, Eloi, lamma sabachthani** (Mark xv. 34) (Gr. transliterations of Aramaic) my God, my God, why hast thou forsaken me?

emou thanontos gaia michthētō pyri (Gr.) when I am dead let earth be mingled with fire. Cf. **après moi le déluge.**

entbehren sollst du, sollst entbehren (Ger.) thou must abstain, abstain thou must. — Goethe, *Faust*, Part I. (Studierzimmer, ii).

en toutōi nika (Gr.) conquer in this (sign). See **in hoc (signo) vinces.**

epea pteroenta (Gr.) winged words. — Homer (*Iliad*, I, 201, etc.).

ephphatha (Aramaic) be opened (Mark vii. 34).

e pluribus unum (L.) one out of many — before 1956 regarded as motto of the United States.

eppur si muove (It.) it does move all the same (attrib. to Galileo after he had recanted his doctrine that the earth moves round the sun).

erectos ad sidera tollere vultus (L.). See **os homini.**

ergo bibamus (L.) therefore let us drink.

Erin go bragh (Ir.) Erin forever.

errare est humanum (L.) to err is human.

es korakas (Gr.) to the ravens: go and be hanged.

esse quam videri (L.) to be, rather than to seem.

est modus in rebus (L.) there is a mean in (all) things. — Horace, *Sat.*, I. i. 106.

esto perpetua (L.) be lasting.

est quaedam flere voluptas (L.) there is in weeping a certain pleasure. — Ovid, *Trist.*, IV. iii. 37.

et hoc (or id) genus omne (L.) and all that sort of thing.

et in Arcadia ego (L.) I, too, lived in Arcadia. (Inscription from tomb, used in Poussin's picture 'The Arcadian Shepherds').

et tu, Brute (L.) you too, Brutus. (Caesar's alleged exclamation when he saw Brutus amongst his assassins.)

eventus stultorum magister (L.) the outcome is the schoolmaster of fools. — Livy, XXII, 39.

ex abusu non arguitur ad usum (L.) from the abuse no argument is drawn against the use. Cf. **abusus non.**

exceptio confirmat (or probat) regulam (L.) the exception proves the rule. (See **except** in Dict.)

exegi monumentum aere perennius (L.) I have reared a monument more lasting than brass. — Horace, *Od.*, III. xxx. 1.

exempla sunt odiosa (L.) examples are hateful.

exitus acta probat (L.) the outcome justifies the deed. — Ovid, *Her.*, II. 85.

ex nihilo (or **nilo**) **nihil** (or **nil**) **fit** (L.) out of nothing nothing comes. See **gigni.**

ex pede Herculem (L.) (we recognise) Hercules from his foot.

experientia docet stultos (L.) experience teaches fools.

experto crede, or (Virgil, *Aen.*, XI. 283) **credite** (L.) trust one who has tried, or had experience.

expertus metuet, or **metuit** (L.) he who has experienced it will fear (or fears). — Horace, *Epist.*, I. xviii, 87.

exstinctus amabitur idem (L.) the same man (maligned living) when dead will be loved. — Horace, *Epist.*, II. i. 14.

ex ungue leonem (L.) (judge, or infer) the lion from his claws.

F

faber est quisque fortunae suae (L.) every man is the fashioner of his own fortunes.— Proverb quoted by Sallust, *De Republica.* I.

fable convenue (Fr.) fable agreed upon — Voltaire's name for history.

facile est inventis addere (L.) it is easy to add to things invented already.

facilis descensus Averno, or **Averni** (L.) descent to Avernus is easy. — Virgil, *Aen.*, VI. 126.

facinus majoris abollae (L.) the crime of a larger cloak, i.e. of a philosopher. — Juvenal, III. 115.

facit indignatio versum (L.) indignation makes verse. — Juvenal. I. 79.

facta non verba (L.) deeds, not words.

factum est (L.) it is done.

facundi. See **fecundi.**

faire bonne mine (Fr.) to put a good face on the matter.

falsus in uno, falsus in omnibus (L.) false in one thing, false in all.

fama nihil est celerius (L.) nothing is swifter than rumour. — Livy.

fama semper vivat (L.) may his (or her) fame live for ever.

far niente (It.) doing nothing.

farrago libelli. See **quicquid.**

fas est et ab hoste doceri (L.) it is right to learn even from an enemy. — Ovid, *Met.*, IV. 428.

Fata obstant (L.) the Fates oppose. — Virgil, *Aen.*, IV. 440.

Fata viam invenient (L.) the Fates will find out a way. — Virgil, *Aen.*, X. 113.

favete linguis (L.) favor me with your tongues — keep silent to avoid ill omen. — Horace, *Od.*, III. i. 2.

fecundi (or **facundi**) **calices quem non fecere disertum?** (L.) whom have not full cups made eloquent? — Horace, *Epist.*, I. v. 19.

felicitas multos habet amicos (L.) prosperity has many friends.

felix qui potuit rerum congnoscere causas (L.) happy is he who has been able to understand the causes of things. — Virgil, *Georg.*, II. 490.

fendre un cheveu en quatre (Fr.) to split a hair in four.

fenum (or **foenum**) **habet in cornu** (L.) he has hay on his horn (sign of a dangerous bull). — Horace, *Sat.*, I. iv. 34.

festina lente (L.) hasten gently.

fiat experimentum in corpore vili (L.) let experiment be made on a worthless body.

fiat justitia, ruat caelum (L.) let justice be done, though the heavens should fall.

fiat lux (L.) let there be light.

fide, sed cui vide (L.) trust, but take care in whom.

fidus Achates (L.) faithful Achates (friend of Aeneas): hence, a close friend. — Virgil.

finem respice (L.). See **respice finem.**

finis coronat opus (L.) the end crowns the work.

fin mot de l'affaire (Fr.) the bottom of the matter, the explanation.

flectere si nequeo superos, Acheronta movebo (L.) if I can't move the gods, I'll stir up hell. — Virgil, *Aen.*, VII. 312.

foenum. See **fenum.**

forsan et haec olim meminisse juvabit (L.) perhaps some day we shall like to remember even these things. — Virgil, *Aen.*, I. 203.

Fors Clavigera (L.) Fortune the club-bearer (used as a title by Ruskin).

fortes Fortuna adjuvat (L.) Fortune helps the brave (Terence, *Phorm.*, I. iv. 26): **forti et fideli nihil difficile** to the brave and faithful nothing is difficult; **fortis cadere, cedere non potest** the brave man may fall, he cannot yield.

fortiter in re, suaviter in modo (L.). See **suaviter.**

Fortuna favet fatuis (L.) Fortune favors fools; **Fortuna favet fortibus** Fortune favors the bold.

frangas, non flectes (L.) you may break, you shall not bend.

fraus est celare fraudem (L.) it is a fraud to conceal a fraud.

frontis nulla fides (L.) no reliance on the face, no trusting appearances.— Juvenal, II. 8.

fruges consumere nati (L.) born to consume the fruits of the soil. — Horace, *Epist.*, I. ii. 27.

fugit hora (L.) the hour flies. — Persius, V. 153.

fuimus Troes; fuit Ilium (L.) we were Trojans; Troy was. — Virgil, *Aen.*, II. 325.

fulmen brutum (L.) a harmless thunderbolt.

furor arma ministrat (L.) rage supplies arms. — Virgil, *Aen.*, I. 150.

G

gaudet tentamine virtus (L.) virtue rejoices in trial.

geflügelte Worte (Ger.) winged words. See **epea.**

genus irritabile vatum (L.) the irritable tribe of poets. — Horace, *Epist.*, II. ii. 102.

gibier de potence (Fr.) gallows-bird.

gigni de nihilo nihilum, in nihilum nil posse reverti (L.) from nothing nothing can come, into nothing nothing can return. — Persius, III. 84.

giovine santo, diavolo vecchio (It.) young saint, old devil.

gli assenti hanno torto (It.) the absent are in the wrong.

gloria virtutis umbra (L.) glory (is) the shadow of virtue.

glückliche Reise (Ger.) prosperous journey to you.

gnōthi seauton (Gr.) know thyself.— Inscribed on the temple of Apollo at Delphi. See also **nosce teipsum.**

Gott mit uns (Ger.) God with us — Hohenzollern motto.

gradu diverso, via una (L.) with different step on the one way.

gradus ad Parnassum (L.) a step, or stairs, to Parnassus, a Latin or Greek poetical dictionary.

Graeculus esuriens (L.) the hungry Greekling. — Juvenal III. 78.

Graecum est: non legitur (L.) this is Greek; it is not read (placed against a Greek word in mediaeval MSS, a permission to skip the hard words).

grande chère et beau feu (Fr.) ample cheer and a fine fire; **grande fortune, grande servitude** great wealth, great slavery.

gratia placendi (L.) the delight of pleasing.

graviora manent (L.) greater dangers remain (Virgil, *Aen.*, VI. 84); **graviora quaedam sunt remedia periculis** some remedies are more grievous than the perils (Syrus).

gravis ira regum est semper (L.) the anger of kings is always serious.

grosse Seelen dulden still (Ger.) great souls suffer in silence. — Schiller, *Don Carlos,* I. iv., end of scene.

grosse tête et peu de sens (Fr.) big head and little wit.

gutta cavat lapidem (L.) the drop wears away the stone. — Ovid, *Pont.*, IV. x. 5.

H

habendum et tenendum (L.) to have and to hold.

habent sua fata libelli (L.) books have their destinies. — Maurus, *De Litteris, Syllabis et Metris.*

hanc veniam petimusque damusque vicissim (L.) this liberty we ask and grant in turn. — Horace, *A.P.,* 11.

Hannibal ad portas (L.) Hannibal at the gates. — Cicero, *Philippica,* I. v. 11.

haud longis intervallis (L.) at no long intervals.

helluo librorum (L.) a glutton of books.

heu pietas! heu prisca fides! (L.) alas for piety! alas for the ancient faith! — Virgil, *Aen.*, VI. 879.

hiatus valde deflendus (L.) a gap deeply to be deplored.

hic finis fandi (L.) here (was, or let there be) an end of the speaking.

hinc illae lacrumae (L.) hence [came] those tears. — Terence, *Andria*, I. i. 99; also Horace, *Epist.*, I. xix. 41.

hinc lucem et pocula sacra (L.) from this source [we draw] light and draughts of sacred learning.

ho bios brachys, hē de technē makrē (Gr.) life is short and art is long. — Attributed to Hippocrates.

hoc age (L.) this do.

hoc erat in votis (L.) this was the very thing I prayed for. — Horace, *Sat.*, II. vi. 1.

hoc opus, hic labor est (L.) this is the toil, this the labor. — Virgil, *Aen.*, VI. 129.

hoc saxum posuit (L.) placed this stone.

hoc (or sic) volo, sic jubeo, sit pro ratione voluntas (L.) this (thus) I will, thus I command, be my will sufficient reason. — Juvenal, VI. 223.

hodie mihi, cras tibi (L.) me today, you tomorrow.

hominibus plenum, amicis vacuum (L.) full of men, empty of friends.

hominis est errare (L.) it belongs to man to err.

homo alieni juris (L.) one under control of another; **homo antiqua virtute ac fide** a man of the antique virtue and loyalty (Terence, *Adelphi*, III. iii. 88 or 1. 442); **homo homini lupus** man is a wolf to man; **homo multarum literarum** a man of many literary accomplishments; **homo mullius coloris** a man of no color, one who does not commit himself; **homo sui juris** one who is his own master; **homo sum: humani nihil a me alienum puto** I am a man: I count nothing human indifferent to me (Terence, *Heaut.*, I. i. 25); **homo trium litterarum** man of three letters — i.e. *fur* = thief; **homo unius libri** a man of one book.

hon hoi theoi philousi apothnēskei neos (Gr.) whom the gods love dies young. — Menander. Cf. **quem di diligunt . . .**

honi soit qui mal y pense (O.Fr.) the shame be his who thinks ill of it — the motto of the Order of the Garter.

honneur et patrie (Fr.) honor and native land.

honores mutant mores (L.) honors change manners.

honor virtutis praemium (L.) honor is the reward of virtue.

honos alit artes (L.) honor nourishes the arts (Cicero, *Tusculanae Disputationes*, I. ii. 4); **honos habet onus** honor has its burden.

hora fugit (L.) the hour flies.

horas non numero nisi serenas (L.) I number none but shining hours. [Common on sundials.]

horresco referens (L.) I shudder in relating. — Virgil, *Aen.*, II, 204.

horribile dictu (L.) horrible to relate.

hostis honori invidia (L.) envy is an enemy to honor; **hostis humani generis** enemy of the human race.

humanum est errare (L.) to err is human.

hurtar para dar por Dios (Sp.) to steal in order to give to God.

hypage Satana (Gr.) away Satan. — Matt. iv. 10.

hypotheses non fingo (L.) I do not frame hypotheses (i.e. unverifiable speculations). — Newton.

I

ich dien (Ger.) I serve.

ici on parle français (Fr.) here French is spoken.

idem velle atque idem nolle ea demum firma amicitia est (L.) to like and dislike the same things is indeed true friendship. — Sallust, *Catalina*, 20.

Iesus Hominum Salvator (L.) Jesus, Saviour of men.

ignorantia legis neminem excusat (L.) ignorance of the law excuses nobody.

ignoti nulla cupido (L.) for a thing unknown there is no desire. — Ovid, *A.A.*, III. 397.

ignotum per ignotius (L.) the unknown by the still more unknown.

i gran dolori sono muti (It.) great griefs are mute.

il a inventé l'histoire (Fr.) he has invented history.

il a le diable au corps (Fr.) the devil is in him: he is full of devilment, or of vivacity, wit, enthusiasm, etc.: he can't sit still.

il a les défauts de ses qualités (Fr.) he has the defects that answer to his good qualities.

il faut de l'argent (Fr.) money is necessary.

il faut laver son linge sale en famille (Fr.) one should wash one's dirty linen in private.

il gran rifiuto (It.) the great refusal (the abdication of Pope Celestine V). — Dante, *Inferno*, III. 60.

Ilias malorum (L.) an Iliad of woes.

ille crucem sceleris pretium tulit, hic diadema (L.) that man got a cross, this man a crown, as the price of his crime. — Juvenal, XIII. 105.

ille terrarum mihi praeter omnes angulus ridet (L.) that corner of the earth to me smiles sweetest of all. — Horace, *Od.*, II. vi. 13-14.

il meglio è l'inimico del bene (It.) the better is the enemy of the good.

il n'y a pas à dire (Fr.) there is nothing to be said.

il n'y a que le premier pas qui coûte (Fr.) it is only the first step that counts. (Mme du Deffand on St Denis walking after decapitation.)

ils n'ont rien appris ni rien oublié (Fr.) they have learned nothing and forgotten nothing [said of the French *Émigrés*, often of the Bourbons].

impar congressus Achilli (L.) unequally matched against Achilles. — Virgil, *Aen.*, I. 475.

incedis per ignis suppositos cineri doloso (L.) you walk on fires covered with treacherous ash. — Horace, *Od.*, II. i. 7-8.

incidis in Scyllam cupiens vitare Charybdim (L.) you fall into Scylla trying to avoid Charybdis. — Philip Gaultier de Lille.

incredulus odi (L.) I hate and disbelieve. — Horace, *A.P.*, 188.

indignor quandoque bonus dormitat Homerus (L.) I am annoyed whenever good Homer slumbers. — Horace, *A.P.*, 359. Usually cited as **aliquando** (=sometimes) **bonus**, etc.

infandum, regina, jubes renovare dolorem (L.) thou bidst me, queen, renew unspeakable woes. — Virgil, *Aen.*, II. 3.

in hoc (signo) vinces (L.) in this sign thou wilt conquer — i.e. in the Cross [the motto of Constantine the Great]. See **en toutōi nika.**

in magnis et voluisse sat est (L.) in great things even to have wished is enough. — Propertius, II. x. 6.

in meditatione fugae (L.) in contemplation of flight.

inopen me copia fecit (L.) plenty has made me poor. — Ovid, *M.*, III. 466.

integer vitae scelerisque purus (L.) blameless in life and clear of offense. — Horace, *Od.*, I. xxii. 1.

inter arma silent leges (L.) amid wars laws are silent (Cicero).

interdum stultus bene loquitur (L.) sometimes a fool speaks a right.

invita Minerva (L.) against the will of Minerva: uninspired. — Horace, *A.P.*, 385.

ira furor brevis est (L.) rage is a brief madness. — Horace, *Epist.*, I. ii. 62.

Italia irredenta (It.) unredeemed Italy — the parts of Italy still under foreign domination after the war of 1866 — South Tirol, etc.

J

jacta est alea (L.) the die is cast (quoted as said by Caesar at the crossing of the Rubicon).

je n'en vois pas la nécessité (Fr.) I don't see the necessity for that [said by the Comte d'Argental in reply to a man who pleaded, 'But one must live somehow'].

joci causa (L.) for the joke.

judex damnatur cum nocens absolvitur (L.) the judge is condemned when the guilty is acquitted. — Syrus, 247.

Jup(p)iter optimus maximus (L.) Jupiter best and greatest; **Jup(p)iter Pluvius** rain-bringing Jupiter; **Jup(p)iter Tonans** Jupiter the thunderer.

justum et tenacem propositi virum (L.) a man upright and tenacious of purpose. — Horace, *Od.*, III. iii. 1.

j'y suis, j'y reste (Fr.) here I am, here I stay [said by Macmahon at the Malakoff].

K

kai ta leipomena, kai ta loipa (Gr.) and the rest: and so on.

kalos kagathos, kalokagathos (Gr.) good and honorable: a perfect gentleman.

kat' exochēn (Gr.) pre-eminently: *par excellence*.

keine Antwort is auch eine Antwort (Ger.) no answer is still an answer: silence gives consent.

Kirche, Küche, Kinder (Ger). church, kitchen, children — said, e.g. during the Nazi period, to be the proper interests of a German woman.

ktēma es aei (Gr.) a possession for ever.

kymatōn anērithmon gelasma (Gr.) innumerable smiles of the waves. — Aeschylus, *Prom.*, 89-90.

L

laborare est orare (L.) work is prayer.

labore et honore (L.) by labor and honor.

labuntur et imputantur (L.) [the moments] slip away and are laid to our account (inscription on sundials). Also **pereunt et imputantor** (q.v.).

la donna è mobile (It.) woman is changeable.

la garde meurt et ne se rend pas (Fr.) the guard dies, it does not surrender.

la grande nation (Fr.) the great nation — i.e. France.

lā ilāha illā 'llāh (Ar.) there is no god but God.

langage des halles (Fr.) language of the market-place.

l'appétit vient en mangeant (Fr.) appetite comes as you eat.

la propriété c'est le vol (Fr.) property is theft [from Proudhon].

la reyne le veult (s'avisera) (Norm. Fr.). See **le roy**.

lasciate ogni speranza, voi che'ntrate (It.) abandon all hope ye who enter. — Dante, *Inferno*, III. 9. From the inscription over the gate of hell.

latet anguis in herba (L.) there is a snake hidden in the grass. — Virgil, *Ecl.*, III. 93.

laudator temporis acti (L.) one who praises past times. — Horace, *A.P.*, 173.

le génie n'est qu'une grande aptitude à la patience (Fr.) genius is merely a great aptitude for patience (attributed to Buffon).

le grand monarque (Fr.) the great king — i.e. Louis XIV.

le jeu ne vaut pas la chandelle (Fr.) the game is not worth the candle.

l'empire c'est la paix (Fr.) the empire means peace [said by Louis Napoleon in 1852].

le roy (or la reyne) le veult (Norm. Fr.) the king (or queen) wills it — form of royal assent.

le roy (la reyne) s'avisera (Norm. Fr.) the king (or queen) will deliberate — form of refusal.

le style est l'homme (même) (Fr.) the style is the man himself (from Buffon).

l'état, c'est moi (Fr.) I am the state [alleged to have been said by Louis XIV].

liberté, égalité, fraternité (Fr.) liberty, equality, fraternity — a slogan of the French Revolution.

limae labor (L.) the labor of the file, of polishing. — Horace, *A.P.*, 291.

littera scripta manet (L.) what is written down is permanent. See **vox audita.**

lucri causa (L.) for the sake of gain.

lucus a non lucendo (L.) the grove (*lucus*) (is so named) from its *not* shining (*lucendo*).

ludere cum sacris (L.) to trifle with sacred things.

l'union fait la force (Fr.) union makes strength.

lupus in fabula (L.) the wolf in the fable: talk of the devil. — Terence, *Adelphi.*, IV. i. 21.

M

macte virtute (L.) be honored in your valor, virtue — used by Cicero, Virgil, Livy (**macte virtute esto** — Cato to one coming out of a resort of vice, acc. to Horace, *Sat.*, I. ii. 31-32).

magna est veritas et praevalebit (L.) truth is great and will prevail (Vulgate, **et prevalet).**

magni nominis umbra (L.) the mere shadow of a mighty name. — Lucan, I. 135.

man spricht Deutsch (Ger.) German spoken here.

matre pulchra filia pulchrior (L.) a daughter fairer than her fair mother. — Horace, *Od.*, I. xvi. 1.

maxima debetur puero reverentia (L.) the greatest reverence is due to the boy — i.e. to the innocence of his age. — Juvenal, XIV, 47.

mea virtute me involvo (L.) I wrap myself in my virtue. — Horace, *Od.*, III. xxix. 54-55.

mēden agan (Gr.) [let there be] nothing in excess.

medio tutissimus ibis (L.) thou wilt go safest in the middle. — Ovid, *Met.*, II. 137.

mega biblion, mega kakon (Gr.) big book, great evil.

mē kinei Kamarinan (Gr.) do not stir up Kamarina (a pestilent marsh in Sicily): let well alone.

mens sana in corpore sano (L.) a sound mind in a sound body.— Juvenal, X. 356.

mens sibi conscia recti (L.) a mind conscious of rectitude. — Virgil, *Aen.*, I. 604. Cf. **conscia mens recti.**

mirabile dictu (L.) wonderful to tell; **mirabile visu,** wonderful to see.

mole ruit sua (L.) falls by its own weight. — Horace, *Od.*, III. iv. 65.

monstrum horrendum, informe, ingens (L.) a frightful monster, ill-shapen, huge. — Virgil, *Aen.*, III. 658.

morituri te salutant. See **ave.**

muet comme un poisson (Fr.) dumb as a fish.

N

natura abhorret vacuum (L.) nature abhors a vacuum.

naturam expellas furca, tamen usque recurret (L.) though you drive out nature with a pitchfork, yet will she always return. — Horace, *Epist.*, I. x. 24.

natura non facit saltus (or saltum) (L.) nature does not make leaps (or a leap).

naviget Anticyram (L.) let him sail to Anticyra [where hellebore could be had, to cure madness]. — Horace, *Sat.*, II. iii. 166.

nec cupias, nec metuas (L.) neither desire nor fear.

nec deus intersit nisi dignus vindice nodus inciderit (L.) let not a god intervene unless a knot occur worthy of the untier. — Horace, *A.P.*, 191-2.

ne cede malis (L.) yield not to misfortune. — Virgil, *Aen.*, VI. 95.

necessitas non habet legem (L.) necessity has no law.

nec pluribus impar (L.) no unequal match for several (suns). — Louis XIV's motto.

nec scire fas est omnia (L.) it is not permitted to know all things. — Horace, *Od.*, IV. iv. 22.

ne exeat (L.) let him not depart.

negatur (L.) it is denied.

nemo me impune lacessit (L.) no one provokes me with impunity — the motto of the kings of Scotland and of the Order of the Thistle; **nemo repente fuit turpissimus** no one ever became utterly bad all at once. — Juvenal, II 83.

ne obliviscaris (L.) do not forget.

neque semper arcum tendit Apollo (L.) Apollo does not always bend his bow. — Horace, *Od.*, II. x. 19-20.

ne quid nimis (L.) [let there be] nothing in excess.

nescis, mi fili, quantilla prudentia mundus regatur (L.) you know not, my son, with what a small stock of wisdom the world is governed. — Attributed to Oxenstierna and others.

nescit vox missa reverti (L.) a word published cannot be recalled. — Horace, *A.P.*, 390.

n'est-ce-pas? (Fr.) is it not so?

ne sutor ultra crepidam (L.). See **sutor.**

ne temere (L.) not rashly — a papal decree of 1907 denying recognition to the marriage of a Catholic unless contracted before a priest.

nicht wahr? (Ger.) is it not true? isn't that so?

nihil tetigit quod non ornavit. See **nullum.**

nil actum credens dum quid superesset agendum (L.) thinking nothing done while anything was yet to do. — Lucan, II. 657; **nil admirari** to wonder at nothing. — Horace, *Epist.*, I. vi. 1; **nil desperandum** nothing is to be despaired of. — Horace, *Od.*, I. vii. 27.

n'importe (Fr.) no matter.

nisi Dominus frustra (L.) except the Lord (keep the city, the watchman waketh but) in vain. — Ps. cxxvii — the motto of Edinburgh.

nitor in adversum (L.) I strive in opposition. — Ovid, *Met.*, II. 72.

non amo te, Sabidi, nec possum dicere quare (L.) I do no love thee, Sabidius, nor can I tell you why. — Martial, I. xxxiii.

non compos mentis (L.) not of sound mind.

non est inventus (L.) he has not been found (he has absconded).

non licet (L.) it is not allowed.

non liquet (L.) it is not clear.

non mi ricordo (It.) I don't remember.

non multa, sed multum (L.) not many, but much.

non nobis, Domine (L.) not unto us, O Lord. — Psalm cxv.

non olet pecunia (L.) the money does not stink. — Attributed to Vespasian, of revenue from an unsavoury source.

non omnia possumus omnes (L.) we cannot all do everything. — Virgil, *Ecl.*, viii. 63.

non omnis moriar (L.) I shall not wholly die. — Horace, *Od.*, III. xxx. 6.

non placet (L.) it does not please — a negative vote.

non possumus (L.) we cannot — a form of refusal.

non tali auxilio nec defensoribus istis tempus eget (L.) not for such aid nor for these defenders does the time call. — Virgil, *Aen.*, II. 521.

nonumque prematur in annum (L.) and let it be kept unpublished till the ninth year. — Horace, *A.P.*, 388.

non ut edam vivo sed ut vivam edo (L.) I do not live to eat, but eat to live. — Quintilian.

nosce teipsum (L.) know thyself — a translation of **gnōthi seauton** (q.v.).

nous avons changé tout cela (Fr.) we have changed all that. — Molière, *Le Médecin malgré lui*, II. iv.

nous verrons (ce que nous verrons) (Fr.) we shall see (what we shall see).

nulla dies sine linea (L.) no day without a line, without painting (or writing) a little.

nulla nuova, buona nuova (It.) no news is good news.

nullius addictus (or **adductus**) **jurare in verba magistri** (L.) bound to swear to the words of no master, to follow no one blindly or slavishly. — Horace, *Epist.*, I. i. 14.

nullum (scil. **scribendi genus**) **quod tetigit non ornavit** (L.) he touched no form of literature without adorning it. From Johnson's epitaph on Goldsmith.

nunc est bibendum (L.) now is the time to drink. — Horace, *Od.*, I. xxxvii. 1.

O

obscurum per obscurius (L.) (explaining) the obscure by means of the more obscure.

oderint dum metuant (L.) let them hate so long as they fear. — Accius, *Atreus*, Fragment IV; quoted in Cicero, *Philippica*, I. xiv.

odi profanum vulgus et arceo (L.) I loathe and shun the profane rabble. — Horace, *Od.*, iii. i. 1.

O fortunatos nimium, sua si bona norint, agricolas (L.) Oh too happy farmers, if they but knew their luck. — Virgil, *Georg.*, II. 458.

ohe! jam satis (L.) hold! enough now (a common phrase).

ohne Hast, ohne Rast (Ger.) without haste, without rest. — Goethe's motto.

olim meminisse juvabit. See **forsan.**

omne ignotum pro magnifico (L.) everything unknown (is taken to be) magnificent. — Tacitus, *Agric.*, 30.

omnem crede diem tibi diluxisse supremum (L.) believe each day to have dawned as your last. — Horace, *Epist.*, I. iv. 13.

omne tulit punctum qui miscuit utile dulci (L.) he has carried every vote who has combined the useful with the pleasing. — Horace, *A.P.*, 343.

omne vivum ex ovo (L.) every living thing comes from an egg. — Attributed to Harvey.

omnia mea mecum porto (L.) all I have I carry with me.

omnia mutantur. See **tempora mutantur.**

omnia vincit amor, et nos cedamus amori (L.) love overcomes all things, let us too yield to love. — Virgil, *Ecl.*, X. 69.

ore rotunda (L.) with round, full voice (mouth). — Horace, *A.P.*, 323.

O sancta simplicitas! (L.) O holy simplicity!

os homini sublime dedit caelumque tueri jussit et erectos ad sidera tollere vultus (L.) he gave man an up-turned face and bade contemplate the heavens and raise looks to the stars. — Ovid, *Met.*, I. 85.

O si sic omnia! (L.) Oh that he had done all things thus, or Oh that all things were thus!

O tempora! O mores! (L.) O the times! O the manners! Occurs in Cicero's first speech against Catiline.

otia dant vitia (L.) idleness begets vice.

otium cum dignitate (L.) dignified leisure.

ouk esti? (Gr.) is it not so?

ovem lupo committere (L.) to entrust the sheep to the wolf.

P

pace tua (L.) by your leave.

pallida Mors aequo pulsat pede pauperum tabernas regumque turres (L.) pale Death knocks with impartial foot at poor men's huts and kings' castles. — Horace, *Od.*, I. iv. 13-14.

palmam qui meruit ferat (L.) let him who has won the palm wear it. — Dr Jortin, *Lusus Poetici*, viii. 20.

panem et circenses (L.) bread and (Roman) circus-games — food and amusements at public expense. — Juvenal, X. 81.

panta men kathara tois katharois (Gr.) all things are pure to the pure. — Titus, I. 15.

panta rhei (Gr.) all things are in a flux (a saying of Heraclitus).

parcere subjectis et debellare superbos (L.) to spare the vanquished and put down the proud. — Virgil, *Aen.*, VI. 854.

par nobile fratrum (L.) a noble pair of brothers. — Horace, *Sat.*, II. iii. 243.

parturiunt montes, nascetur ridiculus mus (L.) the mountains are in travail, an absurd mouse will be born. — Horace, *A.P.*, 139.

parva componere magnis. See **si parva.**

pas op (Afrik.) look out.

pathēmata mathēmata (Gr.) sufferings [are] lessons.

paulo majora canamus (L.) let us sing of rather greater things. — Virgil, *Ecl.*, IV. 1.

pax vobiscum (L.) peace be with you.

peccavi (L.) I have sinned.

pecunia non olet. See **non olet pecunia.**

pereant qui ante nos nostra dixerunt (L.) perish those who have said our good things before us. — Attributed to Donatus and to Augustine.

pereunt et imputantur (L.) [the moments, hours] pass away and are reckoned to our account.

perfervida. See **praefervida.**

per varios casus, per tot discrimina rerum (L.) through various chances, through so many crises of fortune. — Virgil, *Aen.*, I. 204.

pleon hēmisy pantos (Gr.) the half is more than the whole. — Hesiod, *Erga*, 40.

plus ça change, plus c'est la même chose (Fr.) the more that changes the more it is the same thing (no superficial or apparent change alters its essential nature).

poeta nascitur, non fit (L.) the poet is born, not made.

pollōn onomatōn mia morphē (Gr.) one shape of many names. — Aeschylus, *Prometheus*, 210.

polyphloisboio thalassēs (Gr.) of the much-sounding sea. — Homer, *Il.*, I. 34; also Hesiod, *Erga*, 648.

populus vult decipi, ergo decipiatur (L.) the public wishes to be fooled, therefore let it be fooled. — Ascribed to Cardinal Caraffa.

poscimur (L.) we are called on [to sing, etc.].

post equitem sedet atra cura (L.) behind the horseman sits black care. — Horace, *Odes*, III. i. 40.

post hoc, ergo propter hoc (L.) after this, therefore because of this (a fallacious reasoning).

pour encourager les autres (Fr.) to encourage the others (Voltaire, *Candide,* on the shooting of Admiral Byng); **pour faire rire,** to raise a laugh; **pour mieux sauter** see **reculer** below; **pour passer le temps** to pass away the time; **pour prendre congé,** or **PPC,** to take leave.

praefervida (misquoted as **perfervida**). See **Scotorum.**

principiis obsta (L.) resist the first beginnings. — Ovid, *R.A.*, 91. Cf. **venienti,** etc.

probatum est (L.) it has been proved.

probitas laudatur et alget (L.) honesty is commended and left out in the cold. — Juvenal, I. 74.

procul este, profani (L.) keep your distance, uninitiated ones. — Virgil, *Aen.*, VI. 258.

proh pudor! (L.) oh, for shame!

proxime accessit (*pl.* **accesserunt**) (L.) came next [to the prizeman].

pulvis et umbra sumus (L.) we are dust and a shadow. — Horace, *Od.*, IV. vii. 16.

purpureus pannus (L.) a purple patch. — From Horace, *A.P.*, 15-16.

Q

quamdiu se bene gesserit (L.) during good behavior.

quantum mutatus ab illo (L.) how changed from that (Hector who came back clad in Achilles's spoils). — Virgil, *Aen.*, II. 274.

que diable allait-il faire dans cette galère? (Fr.) what the devil was he doing in that galley? — Molière, *Les Fourberies de Scapin,* II. vii.

quem di diligunt adolescens moritur (L.) whom the gods love dies young. — Plautus's translation of **hon hoi theoi . . .**

quem Iupiter vult perdere dementat prius, or **quem deus perdere vult, prius dementat** (L.) whom Jupiter (a god) wishes to destroy, he first makes mad.

que sais-je (sçai-je)? (Fr.) what do I know? — Montaigne's motto.

que voulez-vous? (Fr.) what would you?

quicquid agunt homines . . . nostri est farrago libelli (L.) whatever men do is the medley of our little book. — Juvenal, I. 85-86.

quicquid delirant reges plectuntur Achivi (L.) whatever madness possesses the chiefs, it is (the common soldiers or people of) the Achaeans who suffer. — Horace, *Epist.*, I. ii. 14.

quicunque vult salvus esse (L.) whosoever will be saved (the beginning of the Athanasian creed).

quid hoc sibi vult? (L.) what does this mean?

quid rides? mutato nomine de te fabula narratur (L.) why do you laugh? with change of name the story is about you. — Horace, *Sat.*, I. i. 69-70.

quién sabe? (Sp.) who knows?

quieta non movere (L.) not to move things that are at rest — to let sleeping dogs lie.

qui facit per alium facit per se (L.) he who acts through another is himself responsible.

quis custodiet ipsos custodes? (L.) who will guard the guards themselves? — Juvenal, VI. 347-8.

quis desiderio sit pudor aut modus tam cari capitis? (L.) what shame or stint should there be in mourning for one so dear? — Horace, *Od.,* I. xxiv. 1.

qui s'excuse s'accuse (Fr.) he who excuses himself accuses himself.

quis separabit? (L.) who shall separate [us]?

qui tacet consentit (L.) who keeps silence consents.

qui va là? (Fr.) who goes there?

quod avertat Deus (L.) which may God avert.

quod bonum, felix, faustumque sit (L.) may it be right, happy, and of good omen.

quod erat demonstrandum (L.), or **Q.E.D.,** which was to be proved or demonstrated; **quod erat faciendum,** or **Q.E.F.,** which was to be done.

quod ubique, quod semper, quod ab omnibus (L.) what everywhere, what always, what by all (has been believed). — St Vincent of Lérin's definition of orthodoxy.

quorum pars magna fui (L.) in which I bore a great share. — Virgil, *Aen.,* II. 6.

quot homines, tot sententiae (L.) as many men, so many minds or opinions. — Terence, *Phormio,* II. iv. 14 (or 1. 454).

quousque tandem abutere, Catilina, patientia nostra? (L.) how far, O Catiline, will you abuse our patience?— Cicero, *In Catilinam.*

quo vadis? (L.) whither goest thou?

R

rara avis (L.) a rare bird, rare person or thing. — Juvenal, VI. 165.

rari nantes in gurgite vasto (L.) here and there some swimming in a vast whirlpool. — Virgil, *Aen.,* I. 118.

reculer pour mieux sauter (Fr.) to draw back to take a better leap.

redolet lucerna (L.) it smells of the lamp.

re galantuomo (It.) the honest king — king and gentleman [said of Victor Emmanuel II].

religio loci(L.) the religious spirit of the place. — Virgil, *Aen.,* VIII. 349.

rem acu tetigisti (L.) you have touched the thing with a needle, hit it exactly. — Proverbial expression used by Plautus.

remis velisque (L.) with oars and sails; also **remis ventisque** with oars and winds (Virgil, etc.): with all vigor.

res angusta domi (L.) straitened circumstances at home. — Juvenal, III. 165.

res ipsa loquitur (L.) the thing speaks for itself: the accident is in itself evidence of negligence.

respice finem (L.) look to the end. — Playfully perverted into **respice funem,** beware of the (hangman's) rope.

resurgam ((L.) I shall rise again.

retro me, satana (L.) in Vulgate, **vade retro me, satana,** get thee behind me, Satan (Matt. xvi. 23, Mark viii. 33, Luke iv. 8): stop trying to tempt me.

revenons à nos moutons (Fr.) let us return to our sheep, i.e. our subject. — From the mediaeval farce, *L'Avocat Pathelin.*

rhododaktylos Eōs (Gr.) rosy-fingered Dawn.— Homer, *Odyssey,* II. 1.

rien ne va plus (Fr.) lit. nothing goes any more — used by croupiers to indicate that no more bets may be made.

risum teneatis, amici? (L.) could you keep from laughing, friends? — Horace, *A.P.,* 5.

Roma locuta, causa finita (L.) Rome has spoken, the cause is ended.

ruat caelum. See **fiat justitia.**

rudis indigestaque moles (L.) a rude and shapeless mass. — Ovid, *Met.,* I. 7.

ruit. See **mole.**

rus in urbe (L.) the country in town. — Martial, XII. 57, 21.

rusticus expectat dum defluat amnis (L.) waits like the yokel for the river to run by. — Horace, *Epist.,* I. ii. 42.

S

salaam aleikum (Ar.) peace be upon you.

salus populi suprema lex esto (L.) let the welfare of the people be the final law (Cicero, *De Legibus,* III. iiii:
    suprema est lex).

sans peur et sans reproche (Fr.) without fear and without reproach.

sapere aude (L.) dare to be wise. — Horace, *Epist.,* I. ii. 40.

sartor resartus (L.) the tailor retailored.

sauter à pieds joints (Fr.) to take a standing jump.

sauve qui peut (Fr.) save himself who can: every man for himself.

Scotorum praefervida ingenia (L.) the ardent tempers of the Scots. — Buchanan, *Hist. Scot.,* XVI. li.

selon les règles (Fr.) according to the rules.

semel insanivimus omnes (L.) we have all played the fool once. — J. B. Mantuanus, *Ecl.,* i. 217.

se non è vero, è ben trovato (It.) if it is not true, it is cleverly invented.

sero venientibus ossa (L.) the bones to the late-comers.

sic itur ad astra (L.) such is the way to the stars. — Virgil, *Aen.,* IX. 641.

si componere magnis parva, etc. See **si parva, etc.**

sic transit gloria mundi (L.) so passes away earthly glory.

sic volo. See **hoc volo.**

sic vos non vobis (L.) thus do you, not for yourselves. — Ascribed to Virgil.

Sieg heil (Ger.) victory hail!

si jeunesse savait, si vieillesse pouvait (Fr.) if youth but knew, if age but could.

s'il vous plait (Fr.) if you please.

similia similibus curantur (L.) likes are cured by likes — a hair of the dog that bit one.

si monumentum requiris, circumspice (L.) if you seek (his) monument, look round you (inscription for the architect Christopher Wren's tomb in St Paul's).

simplex munditiis (L.) elegant in simplicity. — Horace, *Od.*, I. v. 5.

sine Cerere et Libero friget Venus (L.) without Ceres and Bacchus (food and drink) Venus (love) is cold. — Terence, *Eun.*, IV. v. 6.

sine ira et studio (L.) without ill-will and without favor.

sint ut sunt aut non sint (L.) let them be as they are or not at all.

si parla Italiano (It.) Italian spoken.

si parva licet componere magnis (L.; Virgil, *Georg.*, IV. 176); **si componere magnis parva mihi fas est** (Ovid, *Met.*, V. 416-7) if it is permissible to compare small things to great.

siste, viator (L.) stop, traveler.

si vis pacem, para bellum (L.) if you would have peace, be ready for war.

skias onar anthrōpos (Gr.) man is a dream of a shadow. — Pindar., *Pyth.*, VIII. 95.

solitudinem faciunt, pacem appellant (L.) they make a desert and call it peace. — Tacitus, *Agric.*, 30.

solventur risu tabulae: tu missus abibis (L.) the bills will be dismissed with laughter — you will be laughed out of court. — Horace, *Sat.*, II. i. 86.

solvitur ambulando (L.) (the problem of reality of motion) is solved by walking — by practical experiment, by actual performance.

spero meliora (L.) I hope for better things.

splendide mendax (L.) splendidly false, nobly lying. — Horace, *Od.*, III. xi. 35.

spretaeque injuria formae (L.) (and) the insult of beauty slighted. — Virgil, *Aen.*, I. 27.

stans pede in uno (L.) standing on one foot. — Horace, *Sat.*, I. iv. 10.

stat pro ratione voluntas (L.) See **hoc volo.**

stet fortuna domus (L.) may the fortune of the house last long.

Sturm und Drang (Ger.) storm and stress.

sua si bona. See **O fortunatos,** etc.

suaviter in modo, fortiter in re (L.) gentle in manner, resolute in deed.

suggestio falsi. See **suppressio veri,** etc.

sunt lacrimae rerum (L.) there are tears for things (unhappy). — Virgil, *Aen.*, I. 462.

suo motu on one's own initiative.

suppressio veri suggestio falsi (L.) suppression of truth is suggestion of the false. (In law, **suppressio veri** is passive, **suggestio falsi** active, misrepresentation.)

sursum corda (L.) lift up your hearts.

surtout, pas de zèle (Fr.) above all, no zeal.

sutor ne supra crepidam judicaret (L.) let not the cobbler criticise (a work of art) above the sandal. See **ultracrepidate** in Dict.

T

tacent, satis laudant (L.) their silence is praise enough. — Terence, *Eun.*, III. ii. 23.

tantae molis erat Romanam condere gentem (L.) a task of such difficulty was it to found the Roman race. — Virgil, *Aen.*, I. 33.

tantaene animis caelestibus irae? (L.) are there such violent passions in celestial minds? — Virgil, *Aen.*, I. 11.

tempora (orig. **omnia) mutantur, nos et mutamur in illis** (L.) the times (all things) change, and we with them.

tempus edax rerum (L.) time, consumer of things. — Ovid, *Met.*, XV. 234.

tempus fugit (L.) time flies.

thalassa, thalassa! or **thalatta thalatta!** (Gr.) the sea, the sea! (the exulting cry of Xenophon's men on beholding the sea). — Xenophon, *Anabasis,* IV. 7.

timeo Danaos et dona ferentes (L.) I fear the Greeks, even when bringing gifts. — Virgil, *Aen.*, II. 49.

tiré à quatre épingles (Fr.) as neat as can be.

ton d'apameibomenos prosephē (Gr.) addressed him in reply. — Homer (*passim*).

totus, teres, atque rotundus (L.) complete, smooth, and round. — Horace, *Satires,* II. vii. 86.

toujours perdrix (Fr.) partridge every day — too much of a good thing.

tout comprendre c'est tout pardonner (Fr.) to understand all is to pardon all; **tout est perdu fors l'honneur** all is lost but honor [attrib. to Francis I after Pavia]; **tout vient (à point) à qui sait attendre** all things come to him who can wait.

traduttore traditore (It.) a translator is a traitor or betrayer: *pl.* **traduttori traditori.**

tria juncta in uno (L.) three things in one.

U

ubi bene, ibi patria (L.) where it goes well with me, there is my fatherland.

ubi saeva indignatio ulterius cor lacerare nequit (L.) where fierce indignation can tear his heart no longer. — Part of Swift's epitaph.

und so weiter (Ger.), or **u.s.w.,** and so forth.

urbi et orbi (L.) to the city (Rome) and to the world, to everyone.

uti possidetis (L.) lit. as you possess — the principle of letting e.g. belligerents keep what they have acquired.

V

vade in pace (L.) go in peace.

vade retro me, satana. See **retro.**

varium et mutabile semper femina (L.) woman is ever a fickle and changeable thing.— Virgil, *Aen.*, IV. 569.

vedi Napoli, e poi muori (It.) see Naples, and die.

veni Creator Spiritus (L.) come, Creator Spirit — the beginning of an early Latin hymn.

venienti occurrite morbo (L.) run to meet disease as it comes. — Persius, III. 63.

veni, vidi, vici (L.) I came, I saw, I conquered. — Ascribed to Caesar on his victory over Pharnaces.

vera incessu patuit dea (L.) the true goddess was revealed by her gait. — Virgil, *Aen.*, I. 405.

verbum sapienti sat est (L.) a word to the wise is enough — often abbrev. *verb. sap.* and *verb. sat.* See **dictum.**

veritas odium parit (L.) truth begets hatred. — Terence, *Andria,* I. i. 41.

vestigia . . . nulla retrorsum (L.) no footprints backwards (at the lion's den): sometimes used to mean no going back. — Horace, *Epist.*, I. i. 74-75.

victrix causa deis placuit, sed victa Catoni (L.) the gods preferred the winning cause, but Cato the losing. — Lucan, I. 128.

video meliora proboque, deteriora sequor (L.) I see the better course and approve it, I follow the worse. — Ovid, *Met.*, VII. 20.

vigilate et orate (L.) watch and pray.

viresque acquirit eundo (L.) (Fama, hearsay personified) gains strenght as she goes. — Virgil, *Aen.*, IV. 175.

Virgilium vidi tantum (L.) I just saw Virgil [and no more]. — Ovid, *Trist.*, IV. x. 51.

virginibus puerisque canto (L.) I sing for maidens and boys — for the young person. — Horace, *Od.*, III. i. 4.

virtus post nummos (L.) virtue after money — i.e. money first. — Horace, *Epist.*, I. i. 54.

vita brevis, ars longa (L.) life is short, art is long (see **ho bios,** etc.); **vita sine litteris mors est** life without literature is death.

vive la bagatelle (quasi-Fr.) long live folly.

vive ut vivas (L.) live that you may live; **vive, valeque** life and health to you.

vivit post funera virtus (L.) virtue lives beyond the grave.

vixere fortes ante Agamemnona multi (L.) many brave men lived before Agamemnon. — Horace, *Od.*, IV. ix. 25-26.

vogue la galère! (Fr.) row the boat: row on: come what may!

volenti non fit injuria (L.) no wrong is done to one who consents.

volo, non valeo (L.) I am willing, but unable.

volto sciolto e pensieri stretti (It.) open face, close thoughts.

vous l'avez voulu, George Dandin (Fr.) you would have it so. — Molière, *George Dandin,* Act 1.

vox audita perit, littera scripta manet (L.) the heard word is lost, the written letter abides; **vox et praeterea nihil** a voice and nothing more (of a nightingale).

W

Wahrheit und Dichtung (Ger.) truth and poetry.

Wein, Weib, und Gesang (Ger.) wine, women and song.

wer da? (Ger.) who is there?

wie geht's? (Ger.) how are you?

Z

zonam perdidit (L.) he has lost his money-belt: he is in needy circumstances; **zonam solvere** to loose the virgin zone, i.e. marry.

Personal names

Masculine names are marked *m.*, feminine names *f.*

A

Aaron, *m.* (Heb.) lofty, mountaineer. — Ar. *Harun, Haroun.*

Abel, *m.* (Heb.) breath, vanity.

Abigail, *f.* (Heb.) father rejoiced, or father of exaltation. — Dims. **Abby, Nabby, Gail.**

Abner, *m.* (Heb.) the (divine) father (is) light.

Abraham, Abram, *m.* (Heb.) perhaps father of a multitude, high father. — Dims. **Abe, Aby, Bram.**

Absalom, *m.* (Heb.) father of peace.

Ada, *f.* prob. for **Adelaide** or other Gmc. name in Adel-, Adal- (noble).

Adalbert. See **Albert.**

Adam, *m.* (Heb.) man, earth, red earth. — Scottish dims. **Edie, Yiddie.**

Adela, *f.* (Gmc.) noble. — Fr. *Adèle.*

Adelaide, *f.* Fr. *Adélaïde* from Ger. *Adelheid* (from *Adelheidis*), noble kind (i.e. sort).

Adeline, Adelina *f.* (Gmc.) noble. — Dim. **Addy.**

Adolphus, *m.* (Gmc.) noble wolf. — Fr. *Adolphe,* It. and Sp. *Adolfo,* Ger. *Adolf,* O.E. *Æthelwulf.*

Adrian, Hadrian, *m.* (L.) of Adria (in Italy).

Aeneas, Eneas, *m.* (Gr.) commended. — Fr. *Enée.* — Used for **Angus.**

Afra, *f.* (Heb.) dust. (Now rare.)

Agatha, *f.* (Gr.) good.

Agnes, *f.* (Gr.) chaste.— Dims. **Aggie, Aggy, Annis, Annot, Nance, Nancy, Nessa, Nessie, Nesta.** — L. *Agneta.* It. *Agnese,* Fr. *Agnès,* Sp. *Inés.* — Confused with **Ann.**

Aileen, *f.* Anglo-Irish form of **Helen.**

Ailie, *f.* Scottish dim. of **Alison, Alice,** and **Helen.**

Alan, Allan, Allen, *m.* (prob. Celt.) harmony. — Fr. *Alain,* W. *Alun.*

Alaric, *m.* (Gmc.) noble ruler.

Alasdair, Alastair, Alister, *m.* See **Alexander.**

Alban, *m.* (L.) of Alba (near Rome).

Albert, *m.* (Gmc.) nobly bright. — Dims. **Al, Bert, Bertie.** — Obs. Scot. **Halbert** (dims. **Hab, Habbie, Hob, Hobbie**). — L. *Albertus,* Fr. *Albert,* It. and Sp. *Alberto,* Ger. *Adalbert, Albert, Albrecht,* O.E. *Æthelbeorht.*

Aldis, Aldous, Aldus, *m.* (Gmc.) old.

Aldred, *m.* See **Eldred.**

Alethea, *f.* (Gr.) truth.

Alexander, *m.* (Gr.) defender of men. — Also (from Gael.) **Alasdair, Alastair, Alister.** — Scot. **Elshender.** — Dims. **Alec(k), Alex, Alick, Eck, Ecky, Sanders, Sandy,** or (as an Englishman's nickname for a Scotsman) **Sawnie.** — Fr. *Alexandre,* It. *Alessandro,* Sp. *Alejandro.* — Fem. **Alexandra, Alexandrina.** — Dim. **Alexa, Sandra.**

Alexis, *m.* (Gr.) help. — Fem. **Alexia.**

Alfonso. See **Alphonsus.**

Alfred, *m.* (Gmc.) elf counsel (good counsellor). — Dims. **Alf, Alfie.** — L. *Alfredus, Aluredus,* O.E. *Ælfred.*

Algernon, *m.* (O.Fr.) moustached. — Dim. **Algy.**

Alice, Alicia, *f.* (Gmc.) from O.Fr. *Aliz* for Gmc. *Adalheidis* (see **Adelaide**). — Dims. **Ailie, Allie, Ally, Ellie, Elsie.** See also **Alison.**

Aline, *f.* for **Adeline.**

Alison, *f.* a form of **Alice,** mainly Scots, now considered a separate name. — Dims. **Ailie, Elsie.**

Allan, Allen. Forms of **Alan.**

Alma, *f.* (L.) fostering. nourishing, loving.

Almeric, *m.* See **Emery.**

Aloys, Aloysius. See **Lewis.**

Alphonsus, *m.* (Gmc.) noble ready.— Ger. *Alfons,* Sp. *Alfonso, Alonso,* Port. *Afonso,* Fr. *Alphonse,* It. *Alfonso.*

Althea, *f.* (Gr.) a healer, or wholesome.

Amabel, *f.* (L.) lovable. — Derivative **Mabel.**

Amadeus, *m.* (L.) love God. — Fr. *Amédée.*

Amalia. See **Amelia.**

Amanda, *f.* (L.) lovable.

Ambrose, *m.* (Gr.) of the immortals, divine. — L. *Ambrosius,* It. *Ambrogio,* W. *Emrys.*

Amelia, *f.* (Gmc.) struggling, labor. — Gr. *Amalia,* Fr. *Amélie,* It. *Amelia, Amalia.* — Dim. **Millie.**

Amos, *m.* (Heb.) strong, bearing a burden.

Amy, *f.* (Fr.) beloved. — L., It., Sp. *Amata,* Fr. *Aimée.*

Amyas, *m.* prob. for **Amadeus.**

Anastasia, *f.* (Gr.) resurrection.

Andrew, *m.* (Gr.) manly. — Dims. **Andie, Andy, Dandy, Drew.** — Gr., L., Ger. *Andreas,* Fr. *André,* It. *Andrea,* Sp. *Andrés.* — Fem. **Andrea, Andrina.**

Aneurin, Aneirin, *m.* (W.) meaning doubtful, perh. for L. *Honorius.*

Angela, *f.* (Gr.) angel, messenger. — Deriv. **Angelica.** — Dim. **Angelina.**

Angus, *m.* (Celt.) perh. one choice. — Gael. *Aonghas.* — **Aeneas** is used as a substitute.

Ann, Anne, Anna, Hannah, *f.* (Heb.) grace. — Dims. **Anita** (Sp.), **Annette** (Fr.), **Annie, Nan, Nana, Nance, Nancy, Nanna, Nannie, Nanny, Nina, Ninette** (Fr.), **Ninon** (Fr.)

Annabel, Annabelle, Annabella, Annaple, *f.* prob. for **Amabel.**

Annis, Annot. Dims. of **Agnes.**

Anselm, *m.* (Gmc.) god-helmet.

Anthea, *f.* (Gr.) flowery.

Anthony, Antony, *m.* (L.) from a Roman family name, meaning unknown. — Dims. **Tony, Nanty.** — L. *Antonius,* Fr. *Antoine,* It. and Sp. *Antonio,* Ger. *Antonius, Anton.* — Fem. **Antonia.** — Dims. **Antoinette** (Fr.), **Net, Nettie, Netty.**

April, *f.* (L.) from the name of the month.

Arabella, *f.* origin and meaning doubtful; perh. for **Amabel,** or perh. (L. *orabilis*) easily entreated. — Dims. **Bel, Bell, Bella, Belle.**

Archibald, *m.* (Gmc.) genuine and bold. — Dims. **Arch, Archie, Archy, Baldie.** — L. *Archibaldus,* Fr. *Archembault,* It. *Arcibaldo,* O.E. *Eorconbeald.*

Arnold, *m.* (Gmc.) eagle strength. — Fr. *Arnaud, Arnaut.*

Arthur, *m.* (Celt.) perh. bear, or (Ir.) stone; or from a Roman family name *Artorius.* — L. *Arturus,* It. *Arturo.*

Asa, *m.* (Heb.) healer.

Athanasius, *m.* (Gr.) undying.

Athelstan, Athelstane, *m.* (Gmc.) noble stone.— O.E. *Æthelstän.*

Aubrey, *m.* (Gmc.) elf rule. — Ger. *Alberich,* O.E. *Ælfric.*

Audrey, *f.* (Gmc.) noble power. — O.E. *Æthelthryth,* whence the form **Etheldreda.**

Augustine, Austin, *m.* (L.) belonging to Augustus. — L. *Augustinus,* Ger. and Fr. *Augustin,* It. *Agostino,* Sp. *Agustin.*

Augustus, *m.* (L.) venerable, exalted. — Dims. **Gus, Gussie, Gustus.** — Ger. *August,* Fr. *Auguste.* — Fem. **Augusta.**

Aurelius, *m.* (L.) golden (Roman family name). — Fem. **Aurelia.** — Dim. **Aurelian,** *m.*

Aurora, *f.* (L.) dawn.

Austin. See **Augustine.**

Ava, *f.* origin and meaning uncertain. — perh. Latin.

Averil, *m.* and *f.* (Gmc.) perh. boar-favor. Associated in people's minds with Avril.

Avice, Avis *f.* origin obscure.

Avril *m.* and *f.* (Fr.) April.

Aylmer, Elmer, *m.* (Gmc.) noble, famous. — O.E. *Æthelmær.* Or from the surname.

Aylwin, *m.* (Gmc.) noble friend. — O.E. *Æthelwine.*

B

Baldwin, *m.* (Gmc.) bold friend. — L. *Balduinus,* Fr. *Baudouin,* It. and Sp. *Baldovino,* Ger. *Balduin.*

Balthazar, Balthasar, *m.* (Babylonian *Bal-sarra-uzur,* whence *Belshazzar*) Bel defend the king. — Ger. *Balthasar,* Fr. *Balthazar,* It. *Baldassare,* Sp. *Baltasar.*

Baptist, *m.* (Gr.) baptiser. — Ger. *Baptist,* Fr. *Baptiste, Batiste,* It. *Battista,* Sp. *Bautista* Fem. **Baptista.**

Barbara, *f.* (Gr.) foreign, stranger. — Dims. **Bab, Babs, Babbie,** (Scot. **Baubie), Barbie.**

Bardolph, *m.* (Gmc.) bright wolf.— Fr. *Bardolphie,* It. *Bardolfo.*

Barnabas, Barnaby, *m.* (Heb.) son of exhortation. — Dim. **Barney.**

Barney, *m.* See **Bernard, Barnabas.**

Barry, *m.* (Ir.) spear.

Bartholomew, Bartlemy, *m.* (Heb.) son of Talmi. — Dims. **Bart, Bat.** — L. *Bartholomaeus,* Fr. *Barthélemy, Bartholomé,* It. *Bartolomeo,* Sp. *Bártolo, Bártolomé, Bartolomeo,* Ger. *Bartholomäus, Barthel.*

Basil, *m.* (Gr.) kingly. — L. *Basilius,* Fr. *Basile,* It. and Sp. *Basilio.*

Beatrice, Beatrix, *f.* (L.) making happy. — Obs. form **Bettrice.** — Dims. **Bee, Beatty, Trix, Trixie.**

Beck, Becky, *f.* See **Rebecca.**

Belinda, *f.* (Gmc.) the second part meaning snake, the first unexplained. — O.H.G. *Betlindis.*

Bell, Belle, Bella, *f.* See **Isabella,** also **Annabel, Arabella.**

Benedict, Benedick, Bennet, *m.* (L.) blessed. — L. *Benedictus,* Ger. *Benedikt,* Fr. *Benoît,* It. *Benedetto,* Sp. *Benedicto, Benito.* — Fem. **Benedicta.**

Benjamin, *m.* (Heb.) son of the right hand (i.e. of good fortune). — Dims. **Ben, Benjie, Bennie.** — It. *Beniamino,* Sp. *Benjamin.*

Berenice, *f.* (Gr.) a Macedonian form of *Pherenikē,* victory-bringer. See also **Veronica.**

Bernard, *m.* (Gmc.) bear-hard. — Dims. **Bernie, Barney.** — L. *Bernardus,* Fr. *Bernard, Bernardin,* It. *Bernardo, Bernardino,* Sp. *Bernardo, Bernal,* Ger. *Bernhard, Barend, Berend.* — Fem. **Bernadette.**

Bert, Bertie, *m.* for **Albert, Bertram** or **Herbert.** — Both are used for any name ending in -bert, and (*f.*) for **Bertha.**

Bertha, *f.* (Gmc.) bright. — Dims. **Bert, Bertie.** — Ger. *Berta, Bertha,* Fr. *Berthe,* It. and Sp. *Berta,* O.E. *Bercta.*

Bertram, *m.* (Gmc.) bright raven. — Dims. **Bertie, Bert.** — Fr. *Bertrand,* It. *Bertrando,* Sp. *Beltrán.*

Beryl, *f.* (Gr.) from the precious stone.

Bess, Bessie, Beth, Betsy, Bettina, Betty. See **Elizabeth.**

Bevis, *m.* from a French form of the Germanic name *Bobo* (Frankish), *Bobba* (O.E.).

Biddy, *f.* See **Bridget.**

Bill, *m.* See **William.**

Blanche, Blanch, *f.* (Fr.—Gmc.) white. — It. *Bianca,* Sp. *Blanca,* Ger. *Blanka,* Fr. *Blanche.*

Blodwen, *f.* (W.) white flower.

Bob. See **Robert.**

Boris, *m.* (Russ.) fight.

Bram. See **Abraham.**

Brenda, *f.* perh. a fem. form of the Norse name *Brand,* brand, or sword, or a fem. form of **Brendan;** a Shetland name popularised by Scott's *Pirate.*

Brendan, *m.* (Ir.) meaning uncertain — stinking hair has been suggested.

Brian, *m.* (Celt.) meaning doubtful.

Bridget, Brigid, *f.* (Celt.) strength; name of a Celtic fire-goddess, an Irish saint; partly from the Swedish saint *Brigitto* (prob. a different name). — Dim. **Biddy.** — Fr. *Brigide, Brigitte,* Sp. *Brigida,* It. *Brigida, Brigita.*

Bronwen, *f.* (W.) white breast.

Bruce, *m.* from the surname.

Bruno, *m.* (Gmc.) brown.

C

Caleb, *m.* (Heb.) dog, or bold.

Camilla, *f.* (L.) a free-born attendant at a sacrifice; in Virgil, name of a queen of the Volsci. — Fr. *Camille.*

Candida, *f.* (L.) white.

Carlotta, *f.* See **Charles.**

Carmen, *f.* Sp. form of Heb. *Carmel,* the garden.

Carol, Carola, Carole, Caroline, Carolyn, *f.* See under **Charles.**

Casimir, Kasimir, *m.* (Pol.) proclamation of peace.

Caspar, Kaspar, *m.* See **Jasper.**

Cassandra. See Dict.

Catherine, Catharine, Katherine, Katharine, Kathryn, Catherina, Katrine, Katerina, Katrina, Kathleen, *f.* from Gr. *Aikaterinē,* of unknown origin, later assimilated to *katharos,* pure. — Fr. *Catherine,* It. *Caterina,* Sp. *Catalina,* Ger. *Katharina,* Dan., etc. *Karin, Karen,Gael. Catriona.* — **Casey, Cathie, Cathy, Kate, Katie, Katy, Kathie, Kathy, Kay, Kit, Kittie, Kitty.**

Catriona. See **Catherine.**

Cecil, *m.* (L.) the Roman family name *Caecilius* (lit. blind). — Fem. **Cecilia, Cecily, Cicely, Sisley.** — Fr. *Cécile,* Ger. *Cācilia,* Ir. *Sile* (see **Celia**). — Dims. **Sis, Cis, Sissy, Sissie, Cissy, Cissie.**

Cedric, *m.* prob. a mistake of Scott's for *Cerdic* (name of the first king of the West Saxons, but apparently not really English — perh. a British name).

Celeste, Celestine, *f.* (L.) heavenly.

Celia, Caelia, *f.* fem. of the Roman family name *Caelius* (poss. heavenly). — Fr. *Célie*; Ir. *Sile* (anglicised *Sheila, Shelagh,* etc.) — Sometimes used for **Cecilia.**

Charis, *f.* (Gr.) grace.

Charity, *f.* (Eng.) charity. — Deriv. **Cherry.**

Charles, *m.* (Gmc.) manly. — Also **Carol.** — L. *Carolus,* Fr. *Charles,* Ger. *Carl, Karl.,* It. *Carlo,* Sp. *Carlos,* Czech *Karol,* Gael. *Tearlach.* — Dims. **Charlie, Charley.** — Fem. **Carol, Carole, Carola, Caroline, Carolyn, Carlotta, Charlotte.** — Dims. **Caddie, Carrie, Lina, Lottie, Chat, Chatty, Sharley.**

Cherry, *f.* from the fruit, or see **Charity.**

Chloe, *f.* (Gr.) a green shoot, verdure.

Chloris, *f.* (Gr.) name of a flower-goddess, also greenfinch or a kind of grape.

Christabel, *f.* (L.—Gr.) anointed, or Christ, and (L.) fair.

Christian, *m.,* also *f.* belonging to Christ. — L. *Christianus,* Fr. *Chrétien,* It. and Sp. *Cristiano.* — Dims. **Chris, Christie, Christy.** — Fem. **Christiana, Christina, Christine, Kirsteen.** — Dims. **Chris, Chrissie, Kirsty, Teenie, Tina.**

Christopher, *m.* (Gr.) carrying Christ. — L. *Christophorus,* Fr. *Christophe,* It. *Cristoforo,* Sp. *Cristóbal,* Ger. *Christoph.* — Dims. **Chris, Kester, Kit** (Scot. fem. **Crystal, Chrystal).**

Cicely. See **Cecilia.**

Clara, Clare, Claire, Clarinda, *f.* (L.) bright. — Fr. *Claire,* Ger. *Klara,* It. *Chiara.* —Derivatives **Clarice, Clarissa.**

Clarence, *m.* from the dukedom.

Claribel, *f.* (L.) brightly fair.

Claud, Claude, Claudius, *m.* (L.) lame. — Fem. **Claudia** (Fr. *Claude).*

Clement, *m.* (L.) mild, merciful. — Dim. **Clem.** — Fem. **Clemency, Clementina, Clementine.**

Clive, *m.* from the surname.

Clotilda, Clothilda, *f.* (Gmc.) famous fighting woman. — Fr. *Clot(h)ilde.*

Clovis, *m.* See **Lewis.**

Colette, *f.* See **Nicholas.**

Colin, *m.* orig. a dim. of **Nicholas;** used also for **Columba;** now regarded as a separate name.

Colley, orig. dim. of **Nicholas.**

Connor, *m.* (Ir.) high desire. — Ir. *Conchob(h)ar,* or *Conchub(h)ar.* — Dims. **Corney, Corny.** — **Cornelius** is used as a substitute.

Conrad, Conrade, Konrad, *m.* (Ger.) bold in counsel. — Ger. *Konrad,* It. *Corrado.*

Constance, *f.* (L.) constancy. — L. *Constantia,* Fr. *Constance,* It. *Costanza,* Ger. *Konstanze.* — Dims. **Con, Connie.** — **Constant,** *m.* firm, faithful. — L. *Constans, Constantius.* It. *Costante, Costanzo,* Ger. *Konstanz.* — Deriv. **Constantine,** *m.*

Cora, *f.* a modern name, prob. from Gr. *koré,* girl.

Coralie, *f.* (Fr.) perh. coral, a modern French invention.

Cordelia, *f.* perh, (L.) warm-hearted.

Corinne, Corinna, *f.* (L.—Gr.) maiden.

Cornelius, *m.* (L.) a Roman family name, prob. related to L. *cornu,* horn. — Used for **Connor.** — Dims. **Corney, Corny.** — Fem. **Cornelia.**

Cosmo, *m.* (Gr.) order. — It. *Cosimo, Cosmo,* Fr. *Cosme, Côme,* Sp. *Cosme.*

Craig, *m.* from the surname.

Cressida, *f.* (Gr.) English form of *Chryseis,* accus. *Chryseida,* daughter of *Chryses.*

Crispin, Crispian, Crispinian, Crispus, *m.* (L.) curly.

Crystal. See **Christopher.**

Cuthbert, *m.* (O.E.) well-known, bright. — Dim. **Cuddie.**

Cynthia, *f.* (Gr.) of Mount Cynthus, an epithet of Artemis.

Cyprian, *m.* (Gr.) of Cyprus.

Cyril, *m.* (Gr.) lordly.

Cyrus, *m.* (Pers.) throne. — Dim. **Cy.**

D

Daisy, *f.* (Eng.) a translation of Fr. *Marguerite.* See **Margaret.**

Damian, *m.* (Gr.) perh. connected with *damaein,* to tame.

Daniel, *m.* (Heb.) the Lord is judge. — Dims. **Dan, Danny.**

Daphne, *f.* (Gr.) laurel.

Daryl, *m.* (O.E.) darling.

David, *m.* (Heb.) beloved. — Dims. **Dave, Davie, Davy** (obs. **Daw, Dawkin**). — Fem. **Vida** (Scot. **Davina**).

Dawn, *f.* (Eng.) dawn.

Deborah, *f.* (Heb.) bee. — Dims. **Deb, Debbie, Debby.**

Deirdre, *f.* (Ir.) meaning doubtful.

Delia, *f.* (Gr.) of the island of Delos.

Demetrius, *m.* belonging to Demeter.

Denis, Dennis, *m.,* **Denise,** *f.* See **Dionysius.**

Derek, Derrick, *m.* See **Theodoric.**

Desideratus, Desiderius, *m.* (L.), **Désiré,** *m.* (Fr.) longed for. — Fem. **Desiderata, Désirée.**

Desmond, *m.* (Ir.) from the surname or the district.

Diana, *f.* (L.) goddess: the Roman goddess identified with Artemis. — Dims. **Di, Die, Diane.**

Dick, Dickie, Dickon. See **Richard.**

Diggory, *m.* (Fr.) from *Degarre,* a hero of romance, an exposed child (prob. Fr. *égaré, astray*).

Dilys, *f.* (W.) sure, constant, genuine.

Dinah, *f.* (Heb.) judged, or dedicated.

Dionysius, *m.* (Gr.), **Denis, Dennis** (Fr.—Gr.) belonging to Dionysus or Bacchus. — Fr. *Denis, Denys,* It. *Dionigi,* Sp. *Dionisio.* — Fem. **Dionysia, Denise.**

Dod, Doddy. See **George.**

Dolores, *f.* (Sp.) sorrows. — Dim. **Lola.**

Dolly, Doll, Dol. See **Dorothy.**

Dominic(k), *m.* (L.) Sunday. — L. *Dominicus,* It. *Domenico,* Sp. *Domingo,* Fr. *Dominique.*

Donald, *m.* (Celt.) world chief. — Gael. *Domhnall.* — Dims. **Don, Donnie.**

Donna, *f.* (It.) mistress, lady.

Dora, *f.* prob. a dim. of **Dorothy;** used also for **Theodora** and names of like ending.

Dorcas, *f.* (Gr.) gazelle.

Doreen, *f.* (Ir.) sullen; or for **Dorothy.**

Doris, *f.* (Gr.) the name of a sea-nymph; meaning doubtful.

Dorothy, Dorothea, *f.* (Gr.) gift of God. — Fr. *Dorothée, Dorette,* Ger. *Dorothea.* — Dims. **Dol, Doll, Dolly, Dora Do, Dot.**

Dougal, Dugald, *m.* (Celt.) dark stranger. — Gael. *Dùghall.*

Douglas, *m.* (and *f.*) from the surname, or the river.

Drew. See **Andrew.**

Dudley, *m.* from the surname.

Duke. See **Marmaduke.**

Dulcie, *f.* (L.) sweet — a modern invention.

Duncan, *m.* (Celt.) brown, brown warrior. — Gael. *Donnchadh.*

Dwight, *m.* from the surname.

E

Eamon, *m.* Irish form of **Edmund.**

Earl, Earle, *m.* (U.S.) from the title.

Ebenezer, *m.* (Heb.) stone of help. — Dim. **Eben.**

Ed, Eddie, dims. of **Edgar, Edmund, Edward, Edwin.**

Edgar, *m.* (O.E.) happy spear. — O.E. *Ēadgar.* — Dims. **Ed, Eddie, Eddy, Ned, Neddie, Neddy.**

Edie. See **Adam, Edith.**

Edith, *f.* (O.E.) happy or rich war. — O.E. *Ēadgyth.* — Dims. **Edie, Edy.**

Edmund, *m.* (O.E.) happy protection.— Fr. *Edmond,* Ir. *Eamon.* — Dims. **Ed, Eddie, Eddy, Ned, Neddie, Neddy.**

Edna, *f.* (Heb.) meaning uncertain.

Edward, *m.* (O.E.) rich guard. — Ger. *Eduard,* Fr. *Édouard,* It. *Eduardo, Edoardo, Odoardo.* — Dims. **Ed, Eddie, Eddy, Ned, Neddie, Neddy, Ted, Teddie, Teddy.**

Edwin, *m.* (O.E.) prosperity or riches, friend. — Dims. **Ed, Eddie, Eddy, Ned, Neddie, Neddy.**

Effie, *f.* dim. of **Euphemia.**

Egbert, *m.* (O.E.) sword-bright.

Eileen, *f.* (Ir.) an old Irish name perh. meaning pleasant; used as a substitute for **Helen.**

Eirene. See **Irene.**

Elaine, *f.* an O.Fr. form of **Helen.**

Eldred, Aldred, *m.* (O.E.) old counsel. — O.E. *Ealdred.*

Eleanor, Eleanore, Elinor, Leonora, *f.* Same as **Helen.** — It. *Eleonora,* Ger. *Eleonore, Lenore,* Fr. *Éléonore, Aliénor.*—Dims. **Ella, Ellen, Nell, Nellie, Nelly, Nora.**

Eleazer, *m.* (Heb.) God is help.

Elfleda, *f.* (O.E. *Æthelflaed*) noble-clean, and (O.E. *Ælflæd*) elf-clean.

Elfreda, *f.* (O.E.) elf-strength. — O.E. *Ælfthryth.*

Elgiva, *f.* (O.E.) elf-gift. — O.E. *Ælfgyfu,* or noble gift (O.E. *Æthelgyfu*).

Eli, *m.* (Heb.) height.

Elias, Elijah, *m.* (Heb.) the Lord is Yah.

Elizabeth, Elisabeth, Eliza, *f.* (Heb.) God an oath. — Fr. *Élizabeth, Élise,* It. *Elisabetta, Elisa,* Ger. *Elisabeth, Elise,* Sp. *Isabel* (q.v.). — Dims. **Bess, Bessie, Bessy, Bet, Beth, Betsy, Bettina, Betty, Elsie, Libby, Lisa, Liza, Lisbeth, Lizbeth, Liz, Lizzie.**

Ella, *f.* (Gmc.) all. — Also a dim. of **Eleanor** or of **Isabella** or other name in -ella.

Ellen, *f.* a form of **Helen,** also used for **Eleanor.**

Elma, *f.* for **Wilhelmina,** or a combination of **Elizabeth Mary.**

Elmer. See **Aylmer.**

Eloisa. See **Heloise.**

Elsa, Elsie. See **Elizabeth, Alison, Alice.**

Elshender. Scots form of **Alexander.**

Elspeth, Elspet. Scots forms of **Elizabeth.**

Elvira, *f.* (Sp.) prob. of Gmc. origin, elf-counsel.

Emery, Emory, Almeric, *m.* (Gmc.) work-rule, energetic rule. — L. *Amalricus,* Ger. *Emerich,* It. *Amerigo.*

Emily, Emilia, fem. of the Roman family name *Aemilius.* — L. *Aemilia,* Ger. *Emilie,* Fr. *Émilie,* It. *Emilia.* — Sometimes confused with **Amelia.**

Emlyn, *m.* (W.) meaning uncertain. — L. *Aemilianus,* pertaining to the family *Aemilius,* has been suggested.

Emma, *f.* (Gmc.) whole, universal. — Also a shortened form of various names beginning Ermin-, Irmin-. — Dims. **Emm, Emmie.**

Emmanuel, Immanuel, *m.* (Heb.) God with us. — Sp. *Manuel,* Port. *Manoel.*

Emmeline, Emeline, *f.* prob. for **Amelia.**

Emrys, *m.* Welsh form of **Ambrose.**

Ena, *f.* (Ir.) fire; or a shortened form of **Eugenia** or other name of similar sound.

Enid, *f.* (W.) possibly wood-lark.

Enoch, *m.* (Heb.) poss. consecrated, or teaching.

Ephraim, *m.* (Heb.) fruitful.

Erasmus, *m.* (Gr.) lovely, deserving love. — Dim. **Rasmus.**

Erastus, *m.* (Gr.) lovely. — Dim. **Rastus.**

Eric, *m.* (Gmc.; O.N. *Eirikr*) perh. sole ruler. — Ger. *Erich,* O.E. *Yric.* — Fem. **Erica** (associated with Gr. *ereikē,* heath).

Ermentrude, Irmentrude, *f.* (Gmc.) prob. Ermin (the god) and strength.

Ernest, *m.* (Gmc.) earnest. — Ger. *Ernst,* It. and Sp. *Ernesto.* — Dim. **Ernie.** — Fem. **Ernestine.**

Esau, *m.* (Heb.) hairy.

Esme, *m., f.* (Fr.) beloved (a Scottish name).

Esmeralda, *f.* (Sp.) emerald.

Estella, Estelle, *f.* See **Stella.** Perh. sometimes for **Esther.**

Esther, Hester, *f.* poss. Pers., star; or Babylonian, *Ishtar,* the goddess Astarte. — Dims. **Essie, Hetty.**

Ethel, *f.* (O.E.) noble (not used uncompounded in O.E.).

Ethelbert, *m.* (O.E.) noble-bright.

Etheldred, -a. See **Audrey.**

Ethelind, Ethelinda, *f.* (Gmc.) noble snake.

Etta, *f.* See **Henrietta.**

Eugene, *m.* (Gr.) well-born. — L. *Eugenius,* Fr. *Eugiène,* Ger. *Eugen.* — Dim. **Gene.** — Fem. **Eugenia.** — Fr. *Eugénie.* — Dims. **Ena, Gene.**

Eulalia, *f.* (Gr.) fair speech.

Eunice, *f.* (Gr.) happy victory.

Euphemia, *f.* (Gr.) of good report. — Dims. **Effie, Euphan, Euphie, Phemie, Phamie.**

Eusebius, *m.* (Gr.)) pious.

Eustace, Eustachius, *m.* (Gr.) rich in corn (Gr. *eustachys,* confounded with *eustathēs,* stable). — Ger. *Eustachius,* Fr. *Eustache,* It. *Eustachio,* Sp. *Eustaquio.* — Fem. **Eustacia.**

Eva, Eve, *f.* (Heb.) life. — Fr. *Ève,* Ger., It., Sp. *Eva.* — Dims. **Evie, Evelina** (q.v.), **Eveleen** (Ir.).

Evan, *m.* Anglicised Welsh form of **John.** — W. *Ifan.*

Evangeline, *f.* (Gr.) bringer of good news.

Evelina, *f.,* **Eveline,** *f.,* **Evelyn,** *m.* and *f.,* partly dims. of **Eve,** partly from the surname Evelyn, partly from Gmc. *Avilina* from the same *Avi.*

Everard, *m.* (Gmc.) boar-hard. — Ger. *Eberhard, Ebert,* Fr. *Évraud.*

Ewan, Ewen, *m.* See **Owen.**

Ezekiel, *m.* (Heb.) God will strengthen.— Ger. *Ezechiel, Hesechiel,* Fr. *Ézéchiel.* — Dim. **Zeke.**

Ezra, *m.* (Heb.) help. — L. *Ezra, Esdras,* Fr. *Esdras,* Ger. *Esra.*

F

Fabian, *m.* — L. *Fabianus,* a derivative of the family name *Fabius,* perh. connected with *faba,* bean.

Faith, *f.* (Eng. or Fr.) faith.

Fanny, *f.* See **Francis.**

Farquhar, *m.* (Gael.) manly. — Gael. *Fearachar.*

Faustina, Faustine, *f.* (L.) fortunate.

Fay, *f.* (Fr.) perh. faith, perh. fairy.

Felix, *m.* (L.) happy. — Fem. **Felicia, Felice** (confused with **Phyllis**) happy, **Felicity,** happiness.

Fenella, *f.* anglicisation of Gael. *Fionnghuala,* white shoulder.— Ir. *Finola.*

Ferdinand, *m.* (Gmc.) journey-risk. — Ger. *Ferdinand,* Fr. *Ferdinand, Ferrand,* Sp. *Fernando, Hernando,* It. *Ferdinando, Ferrando.*

Fergus, *m.* (Gael.) supremely choice.— Gael. *Fearghas.*

Fidelia, *f.* (L.) faithful.

Finlay, Findlay, Finley, *m.* (Gael.) a sunbeam.

Fiona, *f.* (Gael.) fair.

Flavia, *f.* (L.) yellow, fair.

Fleur, *f.* (Fr.) flower.

Flora, *f.* (L.) name of the Roman flower-goddess. — Dims. **Flo, Florrie.**

Florence, *f.* (L.) blooming; also born in Florence.— L. *Florentia* (masc. *Florentius*). — Dims. **Flo, Florrie, Flossie, Floy.**

Francis, *m.* (Fr.) Frankish, French. — L. *Franciscus,* Fr. *François,* It. *Francesco,* Sp. *Francisco,* Ger. *Franz, Franziskus.* — Dims. **Frank, Francie, Frankie.** — Fem. **Frances.** — L. *Francisca,* Fr. *Françoise,* It. *Francesca* (dim. *Franceschina*), Sp. *Francisca,* Ger. *Franziska.* — Dims. **Fanny, Frank, Francie, Francine.**

Freda, *f.* dim. of **Winifred,** or for **Frieda.**

Frederick, Frederic, *m.* (Gmc.) peace-rule. — L. *Fredericus, Fridericus,* Ger. *Friedrich, Fritz,* Fr. *Frédéric,* It. *Federico, Federigo,* Sp. *Federico.* — Dims. (both genders) **Fred, Freddie, Freddy.** — Fem. **Frederica.** — Ger. *Friederike,* Fr. *Frédérique.*

Frieda, *f.* (Gmc.) peace. — Used as a dim. for any feminine name with the element *fred* or *frid.*

Fulk, Fulke, *m.* (Gmc.) people.

G

Gabriel, *m.* (Heb.) God is mighty, or man of God. — Dims. **Gabe, Gabby.** — Fem. **Gabrielle.**

Gail, *f.* dim. of **Abigail** — now regarded as a name in its own right.

Gareth, *m.* O.Fr. *Gahariet,* prob. from some W. name.

Gary, Garry, *m.* perh. a dim. of **Gareth;** perh. for **Garvey** (Gmc.) spear-bearer.

Gaspar, *m.* See **Jasper.**

Gavin, Gawain, *m.* (W.) perh. white hawk.

Gay, *m. and f.* (Eng.) gay.

Gemma, *f.* (It.) a gem.

Gene, for **Eugene, Eugenia.**

Genevieve, *f.* (Fr. — Celt.) meaning obscure. — Fr. *Geneviève.*

Geoffrey, Jeffrey, *m.* (Gmc.). Two names have run together — district-peace (O.H.G. *Gaufrid*) and traveller-peace (O.H.G. *Walahfrid*). — L. *Gaufridus, Galfridus,* Sp. *Geofredo,* Fr. *Goffroi.* — Dims. **Geoff, Jeff.** — Confounded with **Godfrey.**

George, *m.* (Gr.) husbandman. — L. *Georgius,* Fr. *Georges, George,* Ger. *Georg,* It. *Giorgio,* Sp. *Jorge,* Gael. *Seóras.* — Dims. **Geordie, Georgie, Georgy, Dod, Doddy.** — Fem. **Georgia, Georgiana, Georgette, Georgina.** — Dim. **Georgie.**

Gerald, *m.* (Gmc.) spear-wielding. — L. *Geraldus, Giraldus,* Fr. *Géraud, Giraud, Girauld,* It. *Giraldo,* Ger. *Gerold, Gerald.* — Fem. **Geraldine.**

Gerard, *m.* (Gmc.) spear-hard. — L. *Gerardus,* Fr. *Gérard,* It. *Gerardo,* Ger. *Gerhard.*

Gerda, *f.* (O.N.) in Norse mythology, the name of the wife of the god Frey.

German, *m.* (L.) German. — Fem. **Germaine.**

Gerrie, Gerry, *m.* Dims. of **Gerald, Gerard.**

Gertrude, *f.* (Gmc.) spear-might. — Dims. **Gert, Gertie, Trudy.**

Gervase, *m.* (Gmc.) spear-servant. — Also **Gervas, Jervis.**

Gideon, *m.* (Heb.) hewer.

Gil. See **Gilbert, Giles.**

Gilbert, *m.* (Gmc.) bright hostage. — L. *Gilbertus,* Fr. *Guilbert, Gilbert,* It. and Sp. *Gilberto,* Ger. *Gilbert, Giselbert.* — Dims. **Gib, Gibbie, Gil.**

Giles, *m.* (Fr. — Gr.) kid. — L. *Aegidius,* Fr. *Gilles,* Ger. *Agidius,* It. *Egidio,* Sp. *Egidio, Gil.*

Gill, Gillian, *f.* See **Julian.** — Also **Jill, Jillian.**

Gladys, *f.* W. *Gwladys* for **Claudia.**

Glenda, *f.* poss. valley (see **glen** in Dict.).

Gloria, *f.* (L.) glory.

Glyn, *m.* (W.) valley. — Fem. **Glynis.**

Godfrey, *m.* (Gmc.) God's peace. — L. *Godofridus,* Fr. *Godefroi,* Ger. *Gottfried,* It. *Goffredo, Godofredo,* Sp. *Godofredo, Gofredo.* — Confused with **Geoffrey.**

Godwin, *m.* (O.E.) God-friend.

Gordon, *m.* from the surname.

Grace, *f.* (Fr.) grace.

Graham, *m.* from the surname — also sometimes **Graeme.**

Gregory, *m.* (Gr.) watcher. — L. *Gregorius,* Ger. *Gregor, Gregorius,* Fr. *Grégoire,* It. and Sp. *Gregorio.* — Dim. **Greg.**

Greta. See **Margaret.**

Griffith, *m.* (W.) ruddy, rufous. — W. *Gruffydd.*

Grizel, Grizzel, Grissel, Grisell, Griselda, Grizelda, *f.* (Gmc.) perh. grey war, perh. Christ war. — Ger. *Griseldis,* It. *Griselda.*

Gustavus, *m.* (Gmc.) meditation (?) staff. — L. *Gustavus,* Swed. *Gustaf.* Ger. *Gustav,* Fr. *Gustave.*

Guy, *m.* (Gmc.) perh, wood, perh. wide. — O.H.G. *Wido, Wito,* L., Ger., It., and Sp. *Guido,* Fr. *Guy, Guyon.*

Gwendolen, *f.* (W.) white (second element obscure). — Dims. **Gwen, Gwenda, Gwennie.**

Gwillym, Gwilym. See **William.**

Gwyneth, *f.* (W.) blessed.

H

Hab, Habbie. See **Albert.**

Hadrian. See **Adrian.**

Hal. See **Henry.**

Halbert, *m.* an old Scots form of **Albert.**

Hamish, *m.* See **James.**

Hannah, *f.* See **Ann.**

Harold, *m.* (Gmc.) army rule.

Harriet, Harriot, fem. forms of **Henry.** — Dim. **Hatty.**

Hartley, *m.* from the surname.

Hatty. See **Henry.**

Hazel, Heather, *f.* from the plants.

Hector, *m.* (Gr.) holding fast. — Dim. **Heck.** — Ger. *Hektor,* It. *Ettore,* Sp. *Héctor.*

Hedwig, *f.* (Ger.) contention-fight.

Helen, Helena, Ellen, *f.* (Gr.) bright. — L. *Helena,* Fr. *Hélène,* Ger. *Helene,* It. and Sp. *Elena.* — Dims. **Nell, Nellie, Nelly.**

Helga, *f.* (Gmc., Norse) holy.

Heloise, Eloise, Eloisa, *f.* (Gmc.) sound or whole, and wide. — Fr. *Héloïse.*

Henry, Harry, *m.* (Gmc.) house ruler. — L. *Henricus, Enricus,* Fr. *Henri,* It. *Enrico,* Sp. *Enrique,* Ger. *Heinrich* (dims. *Heinz, Heinze, Hinz, Hinze*), Du. *Hendrik.* — Fem. **Henrietta, Harriet, Harriot.** — Fr. *Henriette,* It. *Enrichetta,* Sp. *Enriqueta.* — Dims. **Hatty, Hetty.**

Herbert, *m.* (Gmc.) army-bright. — Ger. *Herbert,* It. *Erberto,* Sp. *Heriberto.* — Dims. **Bert, Bertie.**

Hercules, *m.* L. name of the Greek hero Herakles, glory of Hera (Greek goddess). — It. *Ercole.*

Herman, Hermann, *m.* (Gmc.) army man, warrior. — Ger. *Hermann.*

Hermione, *f.* (Gr.) a derivative of *Hermes* (Greek god).

Hester. See **Esther.**

Hetty, dim. of **Hester** and **Henrietta.**

Hew, another spelling of **Hugh,** preferred by certain families.

Hezekiah, *m.* (Heb.) Yah is strength, or has strength. — Fr. *Ézéchias,* Ger. *Hiskia.*

Hilary, *m.* and *f.* (L.) cheerful. — L. and Ger. *Hilarius,* Fr. *Hilaire,* It. *Ilario,* Sp. *Hilario.* — Also fem. **Hilaria.**

Hilda, *f.* (Gmc.) battle.

Hildebrand, *m.* (Gmc.) battle sword.

Hildegard, *f.* (Gmc.) know battle.

Hiram, Hyram, *m.* (Heb.) noble.

Hob, Hobbie, *m.* for **Halbert, Robert.**

Hodge, *m.* for **Roger.**

Homer, *m.* (U.S.) from the name of the poet.

Honor, Honora, Honoria, *f.* (L.) honor, honorable. — Dims. **Nora, Norah** (Ir. **Noreen**). — Masc. **Honorius.**

Hope, *m.* and *f.* (Eng.) hope.

Horace, Horatio, *m.* (L.) the Roman family name *Horatius.* — Fem. **Horatia.**

Hortensia, *f.* (L.) fem. of a Roman family name — gardener.

Hubert, *m.* (Gmc.) mind-bright.

Hugh, Hew, Hugo, *m.* (Gmc.) mind. — L., Ger., Sp. *Hugo,* Fr. *Hugues,* It. *Ugo, Ugone.* — Dims. **Huggin, Hughie** (obs. **Huchon**).

Hulda, *f.* (Gmc.) name of a Germanic goddess — gracious. Also (Norse) covered.

Huldah, *f.* (Heb.) weasel.

Humbert, *m.* (Gmc.) prob. giant-bright. — It. *Umberto.*

Humphrey, Humphry, *m.* (Gmc.) prob. giant-peace. — Ger. *Humfried,* Fr. *Onfroi,* It. *Onofrio,* Sp. *Hunfredo.* — Dims. **Humph, Numps, Dump, Dumphy.**

Hyacinth, *m.* and *f.* (Gr.) the flower hyacinth (masc. in Greek).

Hyram. See **Hiram.**

I

Iain, Ian, *m.* Gaelic for **John.**

Ianthe, *f.* (Gr.) violet flower (name of a sea-nymph).

Ida, *f.* (Gmc.) labor.

Ifan, *m.* Welsh form of **John.**

Ifor, *m.* Welsh form of **Ivo, Ivor.**

Ignatius, *m.* Latinised from a late Greek form of the Roman (perh. orig. Samnite) family name *Egnatius* (meaning unknown), assimilated to L. *ignis,* fire.. — Fr. *Ignace,* Ger. *Ignaz,* It. *Ignazio,* Sp. *Ignacio.* See **Inigo.**

Igor, *m.* Russian form of the Scandinavian name *Ingvarr,* watchfulness of Ing (the god Frey).

Ike. See **Isaac.**

Immanuel. See **Emmanuel.**

Imogen, *f.* prob. a misprint for *Innogen* in Shakespeare's *Cymbeline,* poss. O. Ir., a daughter, girl.

Ines, Inez, *f.* Sp. See **Agnes.**

Ingeborg, *f.* (Scand.) stronghold of Ing (the god Frey).

Ingram, *m.* raven of Ing (Frey).

Ingrid, *f.* (Scand.) ride of Ing (Frey), or maiden of the Ingvaeones.

Inigo, *m.* (Sp.) either a form of **Ignatius** or another name confused with it. — L. *Enecus, Ennecus,* Sp. *Íñigo.*

Iona, *f.* from the place-name.

Ira, *m.* (Heb.) watchful.

Irene, Eirene, *f.* (Gr.) peace.

Iris, *f.* (Gr.) rainbow, iris (plant) — name of the Greek goddess Hera's messenger.

Irmentrude. See **Ermentrue.**

Isaac, Izaak, *m.* (Heb.) laugh. — Dims. **Ik, Ike, Iky.**

Isabella, Isabel, Isobel, or (Scots) **Iseabail, Ishbel, Isbel,** *f.* (Sp. — Heb.) forms of **Elizabeth,** now regarded as an independent name. — Sp. *Isabel,* Fr. *Isabelle (Isabeau),* It. *Isabella.* — Dims. **Bel, Bell, Belle, Bella, Ella, Ib, Ibby, Isa, Tib, Tibbie, Tibby.**

Isaiah, *m.* (Heb.) Yahwe helps. — L. *Isaias,* Ger. *Jesaias,* Fr. *Isaïe, Esaïe,* Sp. *Isaias,* It. *Isaia.*

Isodor, Isidore, Isadore, *m.* (Gr.) perh. gift of Isis. — Sp. *Isidro, Isidoro.* — Fem. **Isidora, Isadora.**

Isla, *f.* from the place-name.

Isold, Isolde, Isolda, Isolt, *f.* perh. (Gmc.) ice-rule; or a Welsh name.

Israel, *m.* (Heb.) ruling with the Lord.

Ivan, *m.* (Russ.) See **John.**

Ivo, Ivor, *m.* prob. Celtic, but perh. from a Gmc. root meaning yew. — W. *Ifor,* Fr. *Ives, Yves, Ivon, Yvon;* fem. *Ivette, Yvette, Ivonne, Yvonne.*

Ivy, *m.* and *f.* (Eng.) from the plant.

J

Jabez, *m.* (Heb.) perh. sorrow, perh. height.

Jack, *m.* See **John.**

Jacob, *m.* (Heb.) follower, supplanter, or deceiver. — It. *Giacobbe,* Sp. *Jacob.* — Dim. **Jake.** See also **James.**

James, *m.* Same as **Jacob.** — L. *Jacobus* (later Jacŏbus (-o-), Jacŏmus, whence the forms with *m*), Fr. *Jacques,* It. *Jacopo, Giacomo, Iachimo,* Sp. *Jacobo, Diego, Jaime, Jago,* Ger. *Jakob,* Gael. *Seamas, Seamus, Seumas* (Anglicised vocative **Hamish**). — Dims. **Jim, Jimmie, Jimmy, Jem, Jemmie, Jamie, Jeames.** — Fems. **Jacoba, Jacobina, Jacqueline, Jaqueline, Jacquetta, Jamesina, Jemima** has nothing to do with **James.**

Jan. See **John.**

Jane, Jean, Joan, Jo(h)an(n)a, Joann(e), fems. of **John.** — L. *Johanna,* Fr. *Jeanne* (dim. *Jeannette*), It. *Giovanna,* Sp. *Juana* (dim. *Juanita*), Ger. *Johanna,* Gael. *Seonad* (Anglicised *Shona*), *Sine* (Anglicised *Sheena*), W. *Sian.* — Dims. **Janet, Janetta, Janey, Janie, Janice, Jeanette, Jeannie, Jen, Jenny, Jennie, Jess, Jessie, Jessy, Netta, Nettie, Nita** — some of them regarded as separate names.

Janet, *f.* a dim. of **Jane,** regarded as an independent name.

Janice, *f.* orig. a dim. of **Jane,** now regarded as a separate name.

Jared, *m.* (Heb.) descent.

Jasmine, *f.* from the flower. — Deriv. **Jessamine.**

Jason, *m.* poss. Gr. rendering of Heb. Joshua or Jesus, or simply (Gr.) a healer.

Jasper, Gaspar, *m.* prob. Pers. treasure-bringer. — Fr. *Gaspard,* Ger. *Kaspar.*

Jean, *f.* See **Jane,** etc. For Fr. *m.* see **John.**

Jedidiah, Jedediah, *m.* (Heb.) Yah is friend.

Jeffrey, *m.* See **Geoffrey.**

Jem, Jemmie. Dims. of **James.**

Jemima, *f.* (Heb.) meaning unknown (day, dove, pure, fortunate have been suggested). — Not connected with **James.** — Dim. **Mima.**

Jennifer, Jenifer, *f.* the orig. Cornish form of W. *Guinevere,* perh. white wave, or white phantom. — Dims. **Jen, Jennie, Jenny.**

Jenny, Jennie, *f.* See **Jane, Jennifer.**

Jeremiah, Jeremias, Jeremy, *m.* (Heb.) Yah is high, or heals, or founds. — Dim. **Jerry.**

Jerome, *m.* (Gr.) holy name. — L. and Ger. *Hieronymus,* Fr. *Jérôme,* It. *Geronimo, Gerolamo, Girolamo,* Sp. *Jerónimo.*

Jerry, *m.* dim. of **Jeremy,** also of **Gerald, Gerard, Jerome.**

Jervis, *m.* See **Gervase.**

Jess, Jessie, *f.* forms of **Janet,** chiefly Scots. See **Jane.**

Jessamine. See **Jasmine.**

Jesse, *m.* (Heb.) Yah is.

Jessica, *f.* (app. Heb.) perh. Yah is looking.

Jethro, *m.* (Heb.) superiority.

Jill, Jillian, *f.* See **Julian.**

Jim, Jimmie. See **James.**

Jo, for **Joanna, Joseph, Josepha, Josephine.**

Joachim, *m.* (Heb.) Yah has set up. — Sp. *Joaquin,* It. *Gioacchino.*

Joan, Jo(h)an(n)a, Joann, Joanne. See **Jane.**

Joannes. See **John.**

Job, *m.* (Heb.) perh. pious, or persecuted, afflicted. — Ger. *Hiob,* It. *Giobbe.*

Jocelyn, Jocelin, *m.* and *f.* perh. (Gmc.) one of the Geats (a people of southern Sweden), or (L.) connected with **Justin, Justus.** Also fem. **Joceline.**

Jock, *m.* See **John.**

Joe, Joey, for **Joseph, Josepha, Josephine.**

Joel, *m.* (Heb.) Yah is the Lord.

John, *m.* (Heb.) poss. Yah is gracious. — L. *Jo(h)annes,* Fr. *Jean,* It. *Giovanni (Gian, Gianni),* Sp. *Juan,* Port. *João,* Ger. *Johann, Johannes* (dim. *Hans.*), Du. *Jan,* Russ. *Ivan,* Ir. *Seán,* (Anglicised *Shane, Shawn*), *Eoin,* Gael. *Iain (Ian),* W. *Ifan.* — Dims. **Johnnie, Jack** (from **Jankin), Jackie,** (Scot. **Jock, Jockie), Jan,** obs. **Jankin.** — Fem. see under **Jane.**

Jonas, Jonah, *m.* (Heb.) dove.

Jonathan, *m.* (Heb.) Yah has given.

Joseph, *m.* (Heb.) Yah increases. — L. *Josephus,* Fr. *Joseph,* It. *Giuseppe* (dim. *Beppo*), Sp. *José* (dims. *Pepe, Pepillo, Pepito*), Ger. *Joseph, Josef.* — Dims. **Jo, Joe, Joey, Jos.** — Fem. **Josepha, Josephine.** — Dims. **Jo, Joe, Josie, Jozy.**

Joshua, *m.* (Heb.) Yah delivers. — L. and Ger. *Josua,* Fr. and Sp. *Josué,* It. *Giosuè.* — Dim. **Josh.**

Josiah, Josias, *m.* (Heb.) Yah supports.

Joy, *f.* (Eng.) joy.

Joyce, *f.* (Gmc.) a Geat (see **Jocelyn**).

Judith, *f.* (Heb.) Jewess. — Dims. **Judy, Judie.**

Julian, *m., f.* (L.) derived from, belonging to Julius. — Dim. **Jule.** — Fem. **Juliana, Jillian, Gillian.** — Dim. **Jill.**

Julius, *m.* (L.) a Roman family name, perh. downy-bearded. — Dim. **Jule.** — Fr. *Jules,* It. *Giulio.* — Fem. **Julia.** —Dims. **Julie, Juliet.**

June, *f.* (L.) from the month.

Justus, *m.* (L.) just. — Derivs. **Justin** (fem. **Justina, Justine), Justinian.**

K

Karen, Karin, Kate, Katherine, Katharine, Kathryn, Kathleen, Katrine, Katerina, Katrina, Kay. See **Catherine.**

Keith, *m.* from the surname or place-name.

Kenelm, *m.* (O.E. *Cenhelm*) keen helmet.

Kenneth, *m.* (Gael.) handsome. — Gael. *Caioneach.* — Dims. **Ken, Kennie, Kenny.**

Kester, *m.* See **Christopher.**

Kevin, *m.* (Ir.) comely birth.

Keziah, *f.* (Heb.) cassia.

King, *m.* (U.S.) from the title.

Kirsty, Kirsteen, *f.* See **Christian.**

Kit. See **Christopher, Catherine.** — **Kitty.** See **Catherine.**

L

Lachlan, *m.* (Gael.) warlike. — Dims. **Lachie, Lachy.**

Lalage, *f.* (L. — Gr.) talkative, prattling. — Dim. **Lallie.**

Lambert, *m.* (Gmc.) land-bright.

Lance, *m.* (Gmc.) land. — Dims. **Lancelot, Launcelot.**

Laura, *f.* (L.) Laurel. — Also **Laurinda, Lorinda.** — Dims. **Lauretta, Lolly.**

Laurence, Lawrence, *m.* (L.) laurel. — L. *Laurentius,* It. *Lorenzo,* Ger. *Lorenz.* — Dims. **Larry, Laurie, Lawrie.**

Lavinia, *f.* (L.) origin unknown (second wife of Aeneas).

Lazarus, *m.* (Gr. *Lazaros* from Heb.) a form of **Eleazar.**

Lea, Leah, *f.* (Heb.) a cow.

Leander, *m.* (Gr.) lion man.

Lee, Leigh, *m.* and *f.* from the surname.

Leila, *f.* (Pers.) night.

Lemuel, *m.* (Heb.) consecrated to God.

Lena, *f.* See **Helena, Magdalen.**

Leo, *m.* (L.) lion. — Fem. **Leonie.**

Leonard, *m.* (Gmc.) lion-hard.

Leonora, *f.* See **Eleanor.**

Leopold, *m.* (Gmc.) people-bold. — Ger. *Luitpold, Leopold.*

Leslie, *m.,* **Lesley,** *f.,* from the surname or place-name.

Lettice, Letitia, Laetitia, *f.* (L.) gladness. — Dim. **Lettie, Letty.**

Lewis, Louis, Ludovic(k), Lodowick — also **Aloys, Aloysius,** *m.* (Gmc.) famous warrior. — L. *Ludovicus, Aloysius,* Fr. *Louis* (from *Chlodowig, Clovis*), Prov. *Aloys,* It. *Ludovico, Luigi, Aloysio,* Sp. *Luis, Aloisio,* Ger. *Ludwig.* — Dims. **Lewie, Louie, Lew.** — Fem. **Louisa, Louise.** — Dims. **Lou, Louie.** — Fr. *Louise (Lisette),* It. *Luisa,* Ger. *Luise.*

Liam, *m.* Irish form of **William.**

Libby. See **Elizabeth.**

Lily, Lil(l)ian, Lil(l)ias, *f.* prob. partly from the flower, partly for **Elizabeth.**

Linda, Lynda, *f.* (Gmc.) short for any feminine name ending in -lind (snake). — Now regarded as a name in it own right. — Dim. **Lindy.**

Lindsay, Lindsey, *m.* and *f.* from the surname.

Lionel, *m.* (L.) young lion.

Liz, Lizzie, Lisa, Liza, Lisbeth, Lizbeth. See **Elizabeth.**

Llewelyn, *m.* (W.) meaning doubtful.

Lloyd, *m.* (W.) grey.

Lodowick. See **Lewis.**

Lois, *f.* prob. (Gr.) good.

Lola, *f.* for **Dolores,** or **Carlotta.**

Lord, *m.* (U.S.) from the title.

Lorenzo, *m.* See **Laurence.**

Lorinda, *f.* See **Laura.**

Lorna, *f.* invented by R. D. Blackmore for the heroine of his novel *Lorna Doone.*

Lorraine, *f.* (Fr.) from the region of France.

Lottie, *f.* See under **Charles.**

Louis, *m.,* **Louisa, Louise,** *f.* See **Lewis.**

Lucas, *m.* See **Luke.**

Lucius, *m.* (L.) a Roman name probably connected with L. *lux,* light. — Fem. **Luce, Lucy, Lucinda, Lucilla, Lucil(l)e.**

Lucretius, *m.* (L.) a Roman name perh. meaning gain. — Fem. **Lucretia, Lucrece.**

Ludovic(k). See **Lewis.**

Luke, Lucas, *m.* (L.) of Lucania (in Italy).

Luther, *m.* (Gmc.) famous warrior. — L. *Lutherus,* Fr. *Lothaire,* It. *Lotario.*

Lydia, *f.* (Gr.) Lydian woman.

M

Mabel, *f.* See **Amabel.**

Madel(e)ine. See **Magdalen(e).**

Madge, *f.* See **Margaret.**

Madoc, *m.* (W.) fortunate.

Maeve. See **Meave.**

Magdalen(e), Madel(e)ine, *f.* of Magdala on the Sea of Galilee. — Dims. **Maud, Maude, Maudlin.**

Maggie, Mag. Dims. of **Margaret.**

Magnus, *m.* (L.) great.

Maida, *f.* origin obscure.

Màiri *f.* See **Mary.**

Maisie, *f.* dim. of **Margaret,** now also sometimes regarded as a name in its own right.

Malachi, *m.* (Heb.) messenger of Yah.

Malcolm, *m.* (Gael.) Columba's servant.

Malise, *m.* (Gael.) servant of Jesus.

Mamie, *f.* a chiefly American dim. of **Mary,** used also for **Margaret.**

Manuel, Manoel. See **Emmanuel.**

Marcia, Marcius. See **Mark.**

Marcus. See **Mark.**

Margaret, *f.* (Gr.) pearl. — Fr. *Marguerite* (dim. *Margot*), It. *Margherita,* Sp. *Margarita,* Ger. *Margarete* (dims. *Grete, Gretchen*). — Dims. **Madge, May, Maggie, Margie, Margery, Marjory, Meg, Meggie, Meta, Maisie, Mysie, Peg, Peggie, Peggy, Greta, Rita.**

Maria, Marie. See **Mary.**

Marian, Marion, Marianne, *f.* (Fr.) orig. dims. of **Mary;** used also for the combination **Mary Ann.** — Dims. **Maynie, Mysie.**

Marigold, *f.* from the flower.

Marilyn. See **Mary.**

Marina, *f.* (L.) of the sea.

Marjory, Margery, *f.* orig. a dim. of **Margaret,** now regarded as a name in its own right.

Mark, Marcus, *m.* (L.) a Roman name prob. derived from Mars (the god). — L. *Marcus,* Sp. *Marcos,* Ger. *Markus.* — Derivatives **Marcius** (fem. **Marcia**), strictly a Roman family name perh. of like origin, **Marcellus** (fem. **Marcella**).

Marlene, *f.* (Gmc.) perh. a compound of **Mary** and **Helena.**

Marmaduke, *m.* prob. (Celt.) servant of Madoc.— Dim. **Duke.**

Martha, *f.* (Aramaic) lady, mistress. — Dims. **Mat, Mattie, Matty, Pat, Pattie, Patty.**

Martin, Martyn, *m.* (L.) prob. warlike, of Mars.

Mary, Maria, Marie, Miriam, *f.* (Heb.) prob. wished-for child; less probably rebellion. — Gr. *Mariam,* L., It., Ger. *Maria,* Sp. *Maria,* Fr. *Marie* (dim. *Marion*), Gael. *Màiri.* — Dims. **May, Moll, Molly, Mally, Mamie, Marietta, Marilyn, Maureen, Minnie, Poll, Polly.**

Mat, Matty. See **Martha, Matilda, Matthew.**

Mat(h)ilda, *f.* (Gmc.) battle-might. — Dims. **Mat, Matty, Maud, Maude, Patty, Tilly, Tilda.**

Matthew, Matthias, *m.* (Heb.)gift of Yah. — Gr. *Matthaios,* L. *Matthaeus,* Fr. *Matthieu,* It. *Matteo,* Sp. *Mateo,* Ger. *Matthäus.* — Dims. **Mat, Matty.**

Maud, Maude, *f.* See **Matilda, Magdalen.**

Maudlin. See **Magdalen(e).**

Maurice, Morris (L.) Moorish, dark-colored. — L. *Mauritius,* Fr. *Maurice,* It. *Maurizio,* Sp. *Mauricio,* Ger. *Moritz.*

Mavis, *f.* (Eng.) thrush.

Maximilian, *m.* (L.) a combination of *Maximus,* greatest, and *Aemilianus.* — Dim. **Max.**

Maxwell, *m.* from the surname. — Dim. **Max.**

May, *f.* partly for **Mary,** partly from the month. — Dim. **Minnie.**

Meave, Maeve, *f.* (Ir.) the goddess, or legendary queen of Connaught, Medb, or Meadhbh.

Meg. See **Margaret.**

Melanie, *f.* (Gr.) black.

Melicent, *f.* See **Millicent.**

Melissa, *f.* (Gr.) bee.

Mercy, *f.* (Eng.) mercy. — Sp. *Mercedes* (mercies).

Meredith, *m.* and *f.* from the surname.

Meta. See **Margaret.**

Mhairi, *f.* (Gael.) vocative case of **Màiri,** used erroneously as its equivalent. See **Mary.**

Micah, *m.* (Heb.) contraction of *Micaiah* — who is like Jehovah?

Michael, *m.* (Heb.) who is like the Lord? — Fr. *Michel,* It. *Michele,* Sp. and Port. *Miguel,* Ger. *Michael* (dim. *Michel*). — Dims. **Mick, Micky, Mike.** — Fem. **Michaela, Michelle.**

Mildred, *f.* (Gmc.; O.E. *Mildthryth*) mild power. — Dim. **Millie.**

Miles, *m.* (Gmc.) meaning doubtful, perh. merciful.

Millicent, Melicent, *f.* (Gmc.) work-strong. — Fr. *Mélisande.* — Dim. **Millie.**

Millie, *f.* See **Mildred, Millicent, Emilia, Amelia.**

Mima, *f.* See **Jemima.**

Mina, Minella, *f.* See **Wilhelmina.**

Minna, *f.* (Gmc.) memory, or love.

Minnie, for **Minna, Mary, May,** or **Wilhelmina.**

Mirabel, *f.* (L.) wonderful.

Miranda, *f.* (L.) to be admired or wondered at.

Miriam. See **Mary.**

Moira, Moyra, *f.* (Ir.) perh. great; (Gr.) a fate.

Moll, Molly, *f.* See **Mary.**

Mona, *f.* (Ir.) noble.

Monica, *f.* the name, possibly African, of St Augustine's mother; sometimes understood as (Gr.) alone, solitary.

Montagu(e), *m.* from the surname. — Dim. **Monty.**

Morag, *f.* (Gael.) great.

Morgan, *m.* (W.) sea, sea-shore. — Fem. **Morgan, Morgana.**

Morna, *f.* (Gael.) beloved.

Morris. See **Maurice.**

Mortimer, *m.* from the surname.

Morven, Morwen(n)a, *f.* (Celt.) perh. a wave of the sea.

Moses, *m.* meaning obscure. — Gr. *Mōysēs,* Ger. *Moses,* Fr. *Moïse,* It. *Moisè, Mosé,* Sp. *Moisés.*

Moyna, *f.* perh. the same as **Mona.**

Mungo, *m.* (Gael.) amiable.

Murdo, Murdoch, *m.* (Gael.) seaman.

Muriel, *f.* (Celt.) perh. sea-bright.

Murray, *m.* from the surname.

Myfanwy, *f.* (W.) perh. *mabanwy,* child of water, or *my-manwy,* my fine one.

Myra, *f.* app. an arbitrary invention; sometimes used as an anagram of **Mary.**

Myrtle, Myrtilla, *f.* from the shrub.

Mysie, *f.* for **Margaret, Marian.**

N

Nadine, *f.* Fr. form of Russ. *Nadezhda,* hope.

Nahum, *m.* (Heb.) consoling.

Nan, Nana, Nanna, Nannie, Nanny, *f.* See **Ann.**

Nance, Nancy, *f.* See **Ann, Agnes.**

Nanty, *m.* dim. of **Anthony.**

Naomi, *f.* (Heb.) pleasant.

Nat, for **Nathaniel, Nathan, Natalia.**

Natalia, Natalie, (L.). See **Noel.**

Nathan, *m.* (Heb.) gift. — Dim. **Nat.**

Nathaniel, *m.* (Heb.) gift of God. — Also **Nathanael.** — Dim. **Nat.**

Ned, Neddie, Neddy, dims. of **Edward;** also of **Edgar, Edmund, Edwin.**

Nehemia, *m.* (Heb.) consolation of Yah.

Neil. See **Nigel.**

Nell, Nellie, Nelly, *f.* dims. of **Helen, Ellen, Eleanor.**

Nessa, Nessie, Nesta, dims. of **Agnes.**

Netta, Nettie, dims. of **Janet(ta), Henrietta, Antoinette.**

Neville, *m.* from the surname.

Niall. See **Nigel.**

Nicholas, Nicolas, *m.* (Gr.) victory of the people. — Dims. **Nick, Colin** (q.v.), **Colley, Nicol, Nichol.** — Fem. **Nicola, Nicole.** — Dims. **Nicolette, Colette.**

Nicodemus, *m.* (Gr.) victory of the people. — Dims. **Nick, Noddy.**

Nigel, Neil, Niall, *m.* perh. (Ir.) champion, but understood as dim. of L. *niger,* black.

Nina, Ninette, Ninon. See **Ann.**

Ninian, *m.* (Celt.) meaning unknown. — Also (Scot.) **Ringan.**

Nita, *f.* for **Juanita.** See **Jane.**

Noah, *m.* (Heb.) rest.

Noel, *m.* and *f.* (Fr. — L.) birthday, i.e. Christmas. — Fr. *Noël,* It. *Natale.* — Fem. also **Noele, Noelle, Natalia, Natalie.**

Noll, Nolly, *m.* See **Olive.**

Nora, Norah, *f.* orig. for **Honora, Leonora, Eleanor.** — Dim. (Ir.) **Noreen.**

Norma, *f.* (L.) a rule, precept.

Norman, *m.* (Gmc.) Northman.

Norna, *f.* (Gmc.) a Norn or Fate.

O

Obadiah, *m.* (Heb.) servant, or worshipper, of the Lord.

Octavius, Octavus, *m.* (L.) eighth. — Dims. **Tavy, Tave.** — Fem. **Octavia.**

Odette, *f.* See **Ottilia.**

Odo, *m.* See **Otto.**

Olaf, *m.* (Scand.) ancestor-relics.

Olga, *f.* (Russ. — Gmc.) holy.

Olive, Olivia, *f.* (L.) olive. — Dim. **Livy.** — **Oliver,** *m.* (Fr.) olive-tree (but poss. orig. another name assimilated). — Dims. **Noll, Nolly.**

Olwen, *f.* (W.) white track.

Olympia, *f.* (Gr.) Olympian.

Oona(gh). See **Una.**

Ophelia, *f.* prob. (Gr.) help.

Orlando. See **Roland.**

Osbert, *m.* (Gmc.) god-bright.

Oscar, *m.* (Gmc.) god-spear.

Osmund, Osmond, *m.* (Gmc.) god-protection.

Osric, *m.* (Gmc.) god-rule.

Oswald, *m.* (Gmc.) god-power.

Oswin, *m.* (Gmc.) god-friend.

Ottilia, Otilie, *f.* (Gmc.) heritage. — Dim. **Odette.**

Otto, Odo, Otho, *m.* (Gmc.) rich. — It. *Ottone.*

Oughtred. See **Ughtred.**

Owen, *m.* (W.) said to mean youth. — Ir. and Gael. *Ewan, Ewen* (Eoghan.) — Used as a substitue for **Eugene.**

P

Paddy, dim. of **Patrick, Patricia.**

Pamela, *f.* prob. an invention of Sir Philip Sidney's.

Pansy, *f.* (Fr.) thought; or from the name of the flower.

Parnel, *f.* See **Petronella.**

Pat, dim. of **Patrick, Patricia, Martha.**

Patience, *f.* patience.

Patrick, *m.* (L.) nobleman, patrician. — Dims. **Pat, Paddy.** — Fem. **Patricia.** — Dims. **Pat, Paddy.**

Patty, f. dim. of **Martha, Patience.**

Paul, Paullus, Paulus, *m.* (L.) little. — It. *Paolo,* Sp. *Pablo.* — Deriv. **Paulinus.** — Fem. **Paula, Paulina, Pauline.**

Pearl, *f.* pearl.

Peg, Peggy, *f.* dims. of **Margaret.**

Penelope, *f.* (Gr.) perh. weaver. — Dims. **Pen, Penny.**

Pepe, Pepito. See **Joseph.**

Percival, Perceval, *m.* (Fr.) penetrate the valley.

Percy, *m.* from the surname.

Perdita, *f.* (L.) lost.

Peregrine, *m.* (L.) wanderer, traveler, pilgrim. — Dim. **Perry.**

Perkin. See **Peter.**

Pernel. See **Petronella.**

Persis, *f.* (Gr.) Persian.

Peter, *m.* (Gr.) rock. — Also **Piers.** — L. *Petrus,* Fr. *Pierre,* It. *Pietro,* Sp. and Port. *Pedro,* Ger. *Peter, Petrus,* Norw. *Peer.* — Dims. **Pete, Peterkin, Perkin.**

Petronella, Petronilla, *f.* (L.) from the Roman family name *Petrōnius..* — Contracted **Parnel, Pernel.**

Phelim, *m.* (Ir.) ever good.

Philemon, *m.* (Gr.) affectionate.

Philip, *m.* (Gr.) lover of horses. — L. *Philippus,* Fr. *Philippe,* It. *Filippo,* Sp. *Felipe,* Ger. *Philipp.*— Dims. **Phil, Pip.** — Fem. **Philippa.** — Dim. **Pippa.**

Phillis, Phylis, Phillida, Phyllida, *f.* (Gr.) a leafy shoot.

Philomena, *f.* (Gr.) I am loved, or strong in friendship.

Phineas, Phinehas, *m.* (Heb.) meaning obscure — explained as Negro, oracle, serpent's mouth, etc.

Phoebe, *f.* (Gr.) shining, a name of Artemis as moon-goddess.

Phyllis, Phyllida. See **Phillis.**

Piers, *m.* See **Peter.**

Pip, *m.,* **Pippa,** *f.* See **Philip.**

Polly, *f.* See **Mary.**

Poppy, *f.* from the flower.

Primrose, *f.* from the flower.

Priscilla, *f.* (L.) dim. of the Roman name *Priscus* (former).

Prudence, *f.* prudence. — Dim. **Prue.**

Q

Queenie, *f.* from *queen.*

Quintin, Quentin, *m.* (L.) fifth. — L. *Quintianus.*

R

Rab, Rabbie. See **Robert.**

Rachel, Rachael, *f.* (Heb.) ewe. — Ger. *Rahel,* Fr. *Rachel,* It. *Rachele,* Sp. *Raquel.* — Dim. **Ray, Rae.**

Rae. Same as **Ray.**

Ralph, *m.* (Gmc.) counsel-wolf. — O.E. *Rædwulf,* Fr. *Raoul.*

Ranald, *m.* See **Reginald.**

Randal, Randolph, *m.* (Gmc.) shield-wolf.

Raoul, *m.* See **Ralph.**

Raphael, *m.* (Heb.) God heals. — It. *Raffaele, Raffaello.*

Rasmus, Rastus. See **Erasmus, Erastus.**

Ray. See **Rachel, Raymond.** — Also an independent name, *f.* and *m.*

Raymond, Raymund, *m.* (Gmc.) counsel (or might) protector. — Ger. *Raimund,* Sp. *Ramón, Raimundo,* It. *Raimondo.* — Dim. **Ray, Rae.**

Rayner, *m.* (Gmc.) counsel (or might), army (or folk).

Rebecca, Rebekah, *f.* (Heb.) noose. — Dims. **Beck, Becky.**

Reginald, Reynold, Ronald, Ranald, *m.* (Gmc.) counsel (or power) rule. — Ger. *Reinwald, Reinhold, Reinalt,* Fr. *Regnault, Regnauld, Renaud,* It. *Rinaldo, Reinaldo.* — Dims. **Reg, Reggie, Rex, Ron, Ronnie.**

René, *m.* (Fr.), **Renatus,** *m.* (L.) born again. — Fem. **Renée, Renata.**

Reuben, *m.* (Heb.) behold a son, or renewer.

Rex, *m.* (L.) king. — Also for **Reginald.**

Reynold, *m.* See **Reginald.**

Rhoda, *f.* (Gr.) rose.

Rhona, *f.* origin and meaning obscure, poss. conn. with **Rowena.**

Rhys, *m.* (W.) perh. impetuous man.

Richard, *m.* (Gmc.) rule-hard. — It. *Riccardo,* Sp. *Ricardo.* — Dims. **Dick, Dickie, Dicky, Dicken, Dickon, Rick, Richie** (obs. **Diccon, Hick**). — Fem. **Ricarda.**

Ringan, *m.* See **Ninian.**

Rita, *f.* See **Margaret.**

Robert, Rupert, *m.* (Gmc.) fame-bright. — L. *Robertus,* Fr. *Robert,* It. and Sp. *Roberto,* Ger. *Robert, Ruprecht, Rupprecht.* — Dims. **Bert, Bertie, Bob, Bobbie, Bobby, Dob, Dobbin Rob, Robbie, Robin,** Scots. **Rab, Rabbie.** — Fem. **Roberta, Robina.**

Roderick, *m.* fame-rule. — Ger. *Roderich,* Fr. *Rodrigue,* It. *Rodrigo, Roderico,* Sp. *Rodrigo, Ruy.* — Dims. **Rod, Roddy.**

Rodney, *m.* and *f.* from the surname or place-name. — Dim. **Rod.**

Rodolph. See **Rudolf.**

Roger, *m.* (Gmc.) fame-spear. — O.E. *Hrōthgār,* Ger. *Rüdiger,* Fr. *Roger,* It. *Ruggero, Ruggiero,* Sp. *Rogerio.* — Dims. **Hodge, Hodgkin.**

Roland, Rowland, *m.* (Gmc.) fame of the land. — Ger., Fr. *Roland,* It. *Orlando,* Sp. *Roldán, Rolando.*

Rolf, *m.* See **Rudolf.**

Roma, *f.* from the name of the city.

Rona, *f.* (Gael.) seal. — Not conn. with **Rhona.**

Ronald, *m.* See **Reginald.**

Rory, *m.* (Ir.) red.

Rosalind, Rosaline, *f.* (Gmc.) horse-snake, but associated with **Rose** (fair rose).

Rosamund, Rosamond, *f.* (Gmc.) horse protection. — Associated with **Rose** (L. *rosa munda,* fine or pure rose, *rosa mundi,* rose of the world).

Rose, Rosa, *f.* (L.) rose. It may also be sometimes Gmc., horse. — Derivatives **Rosabel, Rosabella, Rosalia, Rosalie** (L. *rosalia,* the hanging of rose garlands on tombs). — Dims. **Rosetta, Rosie.**

Roseanna, Rosana, Roseanne, Rosemarie, *f.* compounds of **Rose** with **Anna, Anne, Marie.**

Rosemary, *f.* from the plant; also for **Rose Mary.**

Rowena, *f.* perh. Geoffrey of Monmouth's mistake for W. *Rhonwen,* white skirt.

Roy, *m.* (Gael.) red.

Ruby, *f.* from the stone. — Also **Rubina.**

Rudolf, Rudolph, Rodolph, Rolf, *m.* (Gmc.) fame-wolf.

Rufus, *m.* (L.) red.

Rupert, Rupprecht. See **Robert.**

Ruth, *f.* (Heb.) meaning obscure; used sometimes with associations with English *ruth.*

S

Sadie, Sal, Sally. See **Sarah.**

Salome, *f.* (Heb.) perfect, or peace.

Samantha, *f.* (Heb.) meaning obscure.

Samson, Sampson, *m.* (Heb.) of the sun. — Gr. *Sampsōn.* Fr. *Samson,* Ger. *Simson,* It. *Sansone,* Sp. *Sansón.*

Samuel, *m.* (Heb.) heard by God, or name of God. — Dims. **Sam, Sammy.**

Sancho, *m.* (Sp.) holy.

Sandra, *f.* It. dim. of **Alessandra;** sometimes used as a diminutive of **Alexandra** but now regarded as a separate name.

Sandy, *m.* See **Alexander.**

Sarah, Sara, *f.* (Heb.) princess, queen. — Dims. **Sadie, Sal, Sally.**

Saul, *m.* (Heb.) asked for.

Seamas, Seamus, *m.* See **James.**

Seán, *m.* See **John.**

Sebastian, *m.* (Gr.) man of Sebasteia (in Pontus). — Gr. *sebastos,* august, venerable.

Secundus, *m.* (L.) second.

Selina, *f.* poss. connected with **Celia,** but associated with Gr. *selēnē,* moon.

Senga, *f.* backward spelling of Agnes.

Seonad, *f.* See **Jane.**

Septimus, *m.* (L.) seventh.

Serena, *f.* (L.) calm, serene.

Seth, *m.* (Heb.) substitute, or compensation.

Seumas. See **James.**

Sextus, *m.* (L.) sixth.

Shamus, for **Seamus** (see **James**).

Shane, Shawn, *m.* See **John.**

Sharon, *f.* (Heb.) a Biblical place-name.

Sheena, *f.* See **Jane.**

Sheila, Sheelagh, *f.* See **Celia** and **Cecilia.**

Shirley, *f.* from the surname or place-name.

Sholto, *m.* perh. (Gael). sower, propagator.

Shona, Sian, *f.* See **Jane.**

Sibyl, now **Sybil, Sibylla,** *f.* (L.) a Sibyl. — Dim. **Sib.**

Sidney, Sydney, *m.* and *f.* from the surname.

Siegfried, Sigurd, *m.* (Gmc.), victory-peace.

Sigismund, Siegmund, *m.* (Gmc.) victory-protection.

Sigrid *f.* (O.N.) prob. victorious (second element obscure).

Silas, Silvanus, Silvester, Sylvester, Silvius, Sylvius, *m.* (L.) living in the woods. — Fem. **Silvia, Sylvia.**

Simon, Simeon, *m.* (Heb.) perh. hearing; perh. also (Gr.) snub-nosed. — Dims. **Sim, Simmy, Simkin.**

Solomon, *m.* (Heb.) peaceable. — Ger. *Salomo,* Fr. *Salomon,* It. *Salomone,* Sp. *Salomón,* Port. *Salamão.* — Dims. **Sol, Solly.**

Sophia, Sophie, Sophy, *f.* (Gr.) wisdom. — Russ. (dim.) **Sonia, Sonya.**

Sophronia, *f.* (Gr.) prudent, temperate, of sound mind.

Stanislas, Stanislaus, *m.* (Pol.) camp-glory.

Stanley, *m.* from the surname or place-name.

Stella, *f.* (L.) star. — Also **Estella, Estelle.**

Stephen, *m.* (Gr.) crown. — L. *Stephanus,* Fr. *Etienne,* It. *Stefano,* Sp. *Esteban,* Ger. *Stephan.* — Dims. **Steenie, Steve, Stevie.** — Fem. **Stephana, Stephanie.**

Stewart, Steuart, Stuart, *m.* from the surname.

Susan, Susanna, Susannah, *f.* (Heb.) lily. — Fr. *Suzanne.* — Dims. **Sue, Suke, Suky, Susie, Susy.**

Sybil. See **Sibyl.**

Sydney. See **Sidney.**

Sylvius, Sylvester, Sylvia. See **Silas.**

T

Tabitha, *f.* (Aramaic) gazelle.

Taffy, Welsh form of **David.**

Talbot, *m.* from the surname.

Tam, Tammie. See **Thomas.**

Tamsin, *f.* a dim. of **Thomasina,** orig. Cornish. Now regarded as a separate name.

Tania, Tanya, *f.* a dim. of Russ. *Tatiana.*

Ted, Teddie, Teddy. Dims. of **Edward.**

Terence, *m.* (L.) the Roman family name *Terentius;* used with its dim. **Terry** as a substitute for Ir. *Turlough,* like Thor.

Teresa, Theresa, Theresia, *f.* (Gr.) origin unknown — more probably connected with the island of Therasia than with reaping (Gr. *therizein,* to reap). — It. and Sp. *Teresa,* Fr. *Thérèse,* Ger. *Theresia, Therese.* — Dims. **Terry, Tessa, Tracy.**

Terry. See **Terence, Teresa.**

Tessa. See **Teresa.**

Thaddaeus, Thaddeus, *m.* (Heb.) meaning obscure. — Used with its dims. **Thaddy, Thady** as a substitute for the Irish name **Tadhgh,** poet, which formerly in the form **Teague** served as a general nickname for an Irishman, as Pat, Paddy, now.

Thea, *f.* (Gr.) goddess.

Thecla, *f.* (Gr.) god-famed.

Thelma, *f.* poss. (Gr.) will, popularized by Marie Corelli.

Theobald, Tybalt, *m.* (Gmc.) people-bold. — Fr. *Thibaut, Thibault,* It. *Tebaldo,* Sp. *Teobaldo.*

Theodore, *m.* (Gr.) gift of God. — Fem. **Theodora.**

Theodoric, Theoderic, *m.* (Gmc.) people-rule — Ger. *Dietrich* (dim. *Dirk.*). — Dim. **Derrick, Derek.**

Theodosius, *m,* (Gr.) gift of God. — Fem. **Theodosia.**

Theophilus, *m.* (Gr.) beloved of God (or the Gods). — Fem. **Theophila.**

Theresa, Theresia. See **Teresa.**

Thomas, *m.* (Heb.) twin. — Fr., Ger. *Thomas,* It. *Tommaso,* Sp. *Tomás.* — Dims. **Tom, Tommy** (Scot. **Tam, Tammie**). — Fem. **Thomasa, T(h)omasina, Tomina.**

Thorold, *m.* (Gmc.) Thor-strength.

Tib, Tibbie, *f.* dims. of **Isabella,** mainly Scottish.

Tilly, *f.* See **Matilda.**

Timothy, *m.* (Gr.) honored of God. — Dims. **Tim, Timmie.**

Titus, *m.* (L.) a Roman praenomen — meaning unknown.

Toby, Tobias, *m.* (Heb.) Yah is good.

Tom, Tommy, Tomina. See **Thomas.**

Tony, *m.* Dim. of **Anthony.**

Tracy, *m.* and *f.* deriv. of **Teresa;** the masc. form perh. from the surname.

Trevor, *m.* from the surname.

Tristram, Tristrem, Tristan, *m.* (Celt.) perh. tumult.

Trix, Trixy. See **Beatrice.**

Trudy. See **Gertrude.**

Turlough, *m.* (Ir. *Toirdhealbhac*) like Thor. — Represented by **Terence, Terry, Charles.**

Tybalt, *m.* See **Theobald.**

U

Uchtred, Ughtred, Oughtred, *m.* perh. (O.E.) thought-counsel.

Ulick, *m.* an Irish form of **Ulysses,** but perh. really for a native name.

Ulric, *m.* (Gmc.) wolf-rule. — Ger. *Ulrich.* — Fem. **Ulrica.** — Ger. *Ulrike.*

Ulysses, *m.* (L. form of Gr.) angry, or hater. — Gr. *Odysseus,* L. *Ulysses, Ulixes.* See **Ulick.**

Una, *f.* (L.) one, from Spenser's heroine, personification of truth, but perh. suggested by Ir. **Oona(gh)** meaning obscure.

Urban, *m.* (L.) of the town, urbane.

Uriah, *m.* (Heb.) perh. Yah is light.

Ursula, *f.* (L.) little she-bear.

V

Valentine, *m.* and *f.* (L.) healthy.

Valeria, *f.* (L.) fem. of a Roman family name. — Also **Valerie, Valery.** — Derivative **Valerian** *m.*

Vanessa, *f.* a name invented by Swift from *Esther Van*homrigh.

Venetia, *f.* (L.) Venetian; perh. also a Latinisation of **Gwyneth.**

Vera, *f.* (L.) true; also (Russ.) faith.

Vere, *m.* and *f.* from the surname.

Verena, *f.* the name of a Swiss martyr (*c.* 300 A.D.).

Verity, *f.* (L.) truth.

Veronica, *f.* (L.) true image; or (Gr.) a form of **Berenice.**

Vesta, *f.* (L.) the Roman hearth-goddess.

Victor, *m.* (L.) conqueror. — Dim. **Vic.** — **Victoria,** *f.* victory. — Dim. **Vicky.**

Vida, a fem. dim. of **David.**

Vincent, *m.* (L.) conquering.

Viola, Violet, *f.* (L.) violet (flower).

Virgil, *m.* (L.) from the Roman family name; perh. specif. for the poet Publius *Vergilius* Maro.

Virginia, (L.) fem. of a Roman family name.

Vivian, *m.* and (chiefly in the form **Vivien**) *f.* (L.) lively. — Also **Vyvyen, Vyvian.**

W

Walter, *m.* (Gmc.) rule-people (or army). — L. *Gualterus,* Ger. *Walter, Walther,* Fr. *Gautier, Gauthier,* Sp. *Gualterio,* It. *Gualtieri.* — Dims. **Wat, Watty, Wally, Walt.**

Wanda, *f.* (Gmc.) stock or stem.

Warren, *m.* (Gmc.) a folk-name — meaning. uncertain.

Wendy, *f.* an invention of J. M. Barrie's.

Wilfrid, Wilfred, *m.* (Gmc.) will-peace.

Wilhelmina (Ger. *Wilhelmine*), a fem. formed from *Wilhelm* (see **William**). — Dims. **Elma, Wilma, Wilmett, Wilmot, Mina, Minnie, Minella.**

William, *m.* (Gmc.) will-helmet. — L. *Gulielmus, Guilielmus,* Ger. *Wilhelm,* Fr. *Guillaume,* It. *Guglielmo,* Sp. *Guillermo, Guillelmo,* Ir. *Liam,* W. *Gwillym, Gwilym.* — For fem. see **Wilhelmina.**

Winifred, *f.* prob. orig. W, the same as *Guinevere* (white-mane), but assimilated to the English masculine name *Winfred, Winfrith* (friend of peace). — Dims. **Win, Winnie, Freda.**

Winston, *m.* (Eng.) from the place-name.

X

Xavier, *m.* (Sp. — Ar.) splendid.

Y

Yoland, f. app. a mediaeval form of *Violante,* a derivative of **Viola.**

Yve, Yves, Yvon, Fr. derivative of **Ivo.** — Fem. **Yvonne, Yvette.**

Z

Zachariah, Zechariah, Zachary, *m.* (Heb.) Yah is renowned. — Dims. **Zach, Zack.**

Zara, *f.* (Heb.) poss. bright as the dawn.

Zedekiah, *m.* (Heb.) Yah is might.

Zeke, *m.*, dim. of **Ezekiel.**

Zena, *f.* perh. Pers., a woman.

Zenobia, *f.* (Gr.) life from Zeus (but perh. a Semitic name in Greek guise).

Zillah, *f.* (Heb.) shade.

Zoe, *f.* (Gr.) life.

Classified word-lists

air and space vehicles aerobus, airdrome, aerodyne, aerohydroplane, airplane, aerostat, air-ambulance, air-bus, airship, all-wing airplane, amphibian, autogiro, balloon, biplane, blimp, bomber, cable-car, camel, canard, chopper, comsat, convertiplane, crate, delta-wing, dirigible, dive bomber, fan-jet, fighter, fire-balloon, flying boat, flying saucer, flying wing, glider, gondola, gyrocopter, gyroplane, helibus, helicopter, hoverbus, hovercar, hovercraft, hovertrain, hydro-airplane, hydrofoil, hydroplane, intercepter, jet, jetliner, jetplane, lem, mictolight, module, monoplane, multiplane, plane, rocket, rocket-plane, runabout, sailplane, satellite, seaplane, space platform, space probe, space shuttle, spacecraft, spaceship, spitfire, sputnik, step-rocket, stol, strato-cruiser, stratotanker, swingtail cargo aircraft, swing-wing, tanker, taube, téléférique, tow-plane, tractor, triplane, troop-carrier, tube, tug, turbojet, twoseater, UFO, warplane, zeppelin.

alphabets and writing systems Chalcidian alphabet, cuneiform, Cyrillic, devanagari, estrang(h)elo, finger-alphabet, futhark, Glagol, Glossic, Greek, Gurmukhi, hieroglyphs, hiragana, ideograph, kana, katakana, Kuffic, linear A, linear B, logograph, nagari, naskhi, og(h)am, pictograph, Roman, runic, syllabary.

anatomical abductor, acromion, adductor, alvine, ancon, astragalus, atlas, aural, auricular, axilla, biceps, blade-bone, bone, brachial, bregma, buccal, calcaneum, calcaneus, capitate, cardiac, carpal, carpus, cartilage, cephalic, cerebral, cholecyst, clavicle, coccyx, celiac, collar-bone, concha, coracoid, crural, cuboid, cuneiform, deltoid, dental, derm, derma, dermal, dermic, diaphragm, diencephalon, digital, diploe, diverticulum, dorsal, dorsolumbar, dorsum, duodenal, duodenum, dura mater, earlap, elbow, enarthrosis, encephalic, encephalon, endocardiac, endocardial, endocardium, endocrinal, endocrine, epencephalic, epencephalon, epidermal, epidermic, epidermis, epididymis epigastric, epigastrium, epiglottic, epiglottis, epithelium, eponychium, erythrocyte, esophagus, ethmoid, extensor, Fallopian tubes, false rib, femur, fenestra ovalis, fenestra rotunda, fibula, flexor,

anatomical *continued*

floating rib, fontanel(le), fonticulus, foramen magnum, forearm, forebrain, forefinger, foreskin, fourchette, frenum, frontal, funiculus, funny bone, gastric, gastrocnemius, gena, genal, genial, genitalia, genu, gingival, glabella, glabellar, gladiolus, glossa, glossal, glottal, glottic, glottis, gluteus, gnathal, gnathic, gonion, gracilis, gremial, gristle, groin, gula, gular, gullet, guttural, hallux, ham, hamate, hamstring, helix, hemal, hematic, hepatic, hind-brain, hindhead, hip-bone, hip-girdle, hock, huckle-bone, humeral, humerus, hyoid, hypogastrium, hypothalamus, iliac, ilium, incus, inguinal, innominate, innominate bone, intercostal, ischium, jugular, labial, lachrymal, lacrimal, leucocyte, ligament, lumbar, lumbrical, lunate, luz, malar, malleolus, malleus, mamillar(y), mammary, mandible, mandibular, manubrium, marriage-bone, mastoid, maxilla, maxillary, membral, mental, merrythought, metacarpal, metatarsal, mons veneris, mount of Venus, muscle, nasal, nates, navicular, neural, obturators, occipital, occiput, occlusal, occlusion, occlusor, ocular, odontic, omentum, omohyoid, omoplate, optical, orbicularis, orbit(a), origin, os innominatum, oscheal, oscular, ossicle, otic, otolith, palatal, palatine, palpebral, parasphenoid, parietal, paroccipital, parotid, patela, patellar, pecten, pectoral, pedal, pelvic girdle, pelvis, periotic, perone, phalanges, pisiform, plantar, popliteal, poplitic, prefrontal, premaxilla, premaxillary, pronator, prootic, prosencephalon, psoas, pubis, pudenda, pulmonary, quadriceps, radius, renal, rhomboid, rib, rictal, sacrocostal, sacrum, sartorius, scaphoid, scapula, sesamoid, shoulder-blade, shoulder-bone, skull, soleus, spade-bone, sphenoid, spine, splinter-bone, stapes, sternum, stirrup-bone, supinator, sural, talus, tarsal, temporal, tendon, thigh-bone, tibia, trapezium, trapezius, trapezoid, triceps, triquetral, turbinal, tympanic, ulna, umbilicus, unguis, urachus, uterus, uvula, vagus, vas deferens, velum, vermis, vertebra, vertebrae, vertex, vesica, voice-box, vomer, vulva, windpipe, wisdom tooth, womb, wrist, xiphisternum, xiphoid, zygapophysis, zygoma, zygomatic.

architecture and building abacus, abutment, acrolith, acroter, acroterial, acroterion, acroterium, alcove, annulet, anta, antefix, areostyle, architrave, ashlar, ashler, astragal, baguette, bandelet, banderol(e), barge-board, barge-couple, barge-stones, battlement, bellcote, bema, bratticing, canephor, canton, cartouche, caryatid, Catherine-wheel, cavetto, centering, cinque-foil, concha, corbeil, corbel, corner-stone, corona, cradling, crenel, crocket, crossette, cruck, cul-de-four, dado, decorated, demi-bastion, demi-lune, dentil, diaconicon, diaper, diastyle, diglyph, dimension work, dinette, dipteros, distyle, ditriglyph, dodecastyle, dog-leg(ged), dogtooth, dome, domed, domical, donjon, Doric, dormer, double-glazing, doucine, drawbridge, drawing-room, dreamhole, dressing, drip, dripstone, dromic, dromos, drum, dry-stone, duplex, Early English, eaves, echinus, egg-and-anchor, egg-and-

architecture and building *continued*

dart, egg-and-tongue, egg-box, el, elevation, Elizabethan, embattlement, embrasure, emplection, encarpus, engage, engaged, engrail, enneastyle, entresol, epaule, epaulement, epistyle, eustyle, exedra, extrados, eye-catcher, façade, fan tracery, fan vaulting, fanlight, fascia, fastigium, feathering, fenestella, fenestra, fenestral, fenestration, festoon, fillet, finial, flamboyant, flèche, Flemish bond, fletton, fleuron, foliation, fornicate, fortalice, French sash/window, frieze, fronton, furring, fusarol(e), fust, gable, gablet, galilee, gambrel roof, gargoyle, gatehouse, glacis, glyph, gopura(m), gorgerin, Gothic, gradin(e), griff(e), groin, groundplan, groundsel, guilloche, gutta, hagioscope, half-timbered, hammer-beam, hammer-brace, hance, hanging buttress, harling, haunch, haute époque, headstone, heart, helix, herringbone, hexastyle, hip, hip-knob, holderbat, hood-mold(ing), hypostyle, imbrex, imbricate, imbrication, imperial, impost, impostume, intercolumniation, intrados, jamb, javelin, jerkinhead, knosp, lierne, linen-fold, linen-scroll, lintel, mansard(-roof), mascaron, merlon, metope, modillion, monostyle, mullion, muntin(g), mutule, Norman, oeil-de-boeuf, ogee, opisthodomos, oriel, out-wall, ovolo, ox-eye, pagoda, pantile, pargret, patera, paternoster, patten, pediment, pilaster, pineapple, pinnacle, plafond, platband, plateresque, plinth, poppy-head, predella, propylaeum, propylon, prostyle, pylon, quatrefeuille, quatrefoil, queen-post, quirk, rear-arch, reglet, regula, rere-arch, retrochoir, reredos, revet, rocaille, rococo, Romanesque, rood-loft, rood-screen, rood-steeple, rood tower, roof, roof-tree, rosace, rose, rosette, rotunda, roughcast, sacristy, skew-back, socle, soffit, solidum, spandrel, strap-work, stria, string-course, subbasal, surbase, swag, systyle, tabernacle-work, table, telamon, terrazzo, tierceron, tondino, toroid, torsel, torus, trabeation, tracery, triforium, trumeau, tympanum, vault, vaultage, vaulted, vaulting, Venetian mosaic, vermiculate(d), vice, vitrail, vitrailled, Vitruvian, volute, voussoir, wainscot, wall-plate, water-joint, water-table, weathering, xystus.

art abstract, abstraction, action painting, anaglyph, anastasis, anastatic, anthemion, aquarelle, bas relief, Bauhaus, camaieu, cire perdue, dadaism, decal, decoupage, Der Blaue Reiter, diaglyph, Die Brücke, diptych, dry-point, duotone, écorché, enamel, encaustic, engraving, etch, etchant, faience, fashion-plate, Fauve, Fauvism, fête champêtre, figurine, filigree, flambé, flannelgraph, Flemish, flesh-tint, Florentine, free-hand, fresco, fret, frit, futurism, futurist, gadroon, genre, gesso, glyptics, glyptography, Gobelin, gouache, graphic, graphics, graphium, graticulation, gravure, grecque, grisaille, gumption, hachure, hatch, hatching, haut relief, herm(a), historiated, hound's-tooth, intaglio, linocut, literalism, litho, lithochromatic(s), lithchromy, lithograph, lithoprint, lost wax, mandorla, meander, monotint, monotype, morbidezza, Parian, paysage, phylactery, pietra-dura, piqué, pochoir, pompier, putto, quattrocento, relievo, repoussage, repoussé, reserved,

art *continued*

retroussage, rilievo, sculp(t), scumble, sea-piece, seascape, secco, serigraph, statuary, stipple, stylus, surrealism, symbolism, tachism(e), tempera, tenebrism, tessellated, tessera, tondo, trecento, triptych, ukiyo-e, velatura, Venetian mosaic, Venetian red, verditer, verism, vermiculate(d), versal, vitrail, vitraillist, vitrifacture, vitrine, vitro-di-trina, volute, vorticism, woodblock, wood-carving, woodcut, wood-engraving, xoanon, zoomorphic.

canonical hours compline, lauds, matins, none, orthros, prime, sext, terce, undern, vespers.

cattle breeds Africander, Alderney, Angus, Ankole, Ayrshire, Blonde d'Aquitaine, Brahman, Brown Swiss, cattabu, cattalo, Charol(l)ais, Chillingham, Devon, dexter, Durham, Friesian, Galloway, Guernsey, Hereford, Highland, Holstein, Jersey, Latvian, Limousin, Luing, Red Poll, Romagnola, Santa Gertrudis, short-horn, Simmenthaler, Teeswater, Ukrainian, Welsh Black.

cheeses Amsterdam, Bel Paese, Blarney, Bleu d'Auvergne, Blue Vinny, Boursin, Brie, Caboc, Caerphilly, Camembert, Carré, Cheddar, Cheshire, Chevrotin, Colwick, Coulommiers, Crowdie, Danish blue, Derby, Dolcelatte, Dorset Blue, double Gloucester, Dunlop, Edam, Emmental, Emment(h)al(er), Esrom, ewe-cheese, Feta, Fynbo, Gammelost, G(j)etost, Gloucester, Gorgonzola, Gouda, Grana, Grevé, Gruyère, Handkäse, Havarti, Herrgårdsost, Herve, Huntsman, Hushållsost, Islay, Jarlsberg, Killarney, Kryddost, Lancashire, Leicester, Limburg(er), Lymeswold, mouse-trap, mozzarella, Munster, Mysost, Neufchâtel, Parmesan, Petit Suisse, pipo creme, Pont-l'Éveque, Port(-du-)Salut, Prästost, Provolone, Pultost, Raclette, Red Windsor, Reggiano, ricotta, Romadur, Roquefort, sage Derby, Saint-Paulin, Samsø, sapsago, Stilton, stracchino, Tilsit(er), Vacherin, Wensleydale, Wexford.

chemical elements Actinium, Aluminum, Americium, Antimony, Argon, Arsenic, Astatine, Barium, Berkelium, Beryllium, Bismuth, Boron, Bromine, Cadmium, Calcium, Californium, Carbon, Cerium, Cesium, Chlorine, Chromium, Cobalt, Copper, Curium, Dysprosium, Einsteinium, Erbium, Europium, Fermium, Fluorine, Francium, Gadolinium, Gallium, Germanium, Gold, Hafnium, Hahnium, Helium, Holmium, Hydrogen, Indium, Iodine, Iridium, Iron, Krypton, Lanthanum, Lawrencium, Lead, Lithium, Lutetium, Magnesium, Manganese, Mendelevium, Mercury, Molybdenum, Neodymium, Neon, Neptunium, Nickel,

chemical elements *continued*

Niobium, Nitrogen, Nobelium, Osmium, Oxygen, Palladium, Phosphorus, Platinum, Plutonium, Polonium, Potassium, Praseodymium, Promethium, Protoactinium, Radium, Radon, Rhenium, Rhodium, Rubidium, Ruthenium, Rutherfordium, Samarium, Scandium, Selenium, Silicon, Silver, Sodium, Strontium, Sulfur, Tantalum, Technetium, Tellurium, Terbium, Thallium, Thorium, Thulium, Tin, Titanium, Tungsten, Uranium, Vanadium, Xenon, Ytterbium, Yttrium, Zinc, Zirconium.

cloths, fabrics

abaca, abb, alamonde, alepine, alpaca, American cloth, angora, armozine, armure, arrasene, astrakhan, atlas, baft, bagging, Balbriggan, baldachin, balzarine, barathea, barege, barracan, batiste, batting, bayadère, bearskin, beaver, beige, bengaline, Binca®, blanket, blanketing, blonde(e)-lace, bobbinet, bobbin-lace, bombasine, bone-lace, botany, bouclé, bolting cloth, box-cloth, broadcloth, brocade, brocatel(le), broché, Brussels lace, buckram, buckskin, budge, buff, bunting, Burberry, burlap, burnet, burrel, butter-cloth, butter-muslin, byssus, caddis, calamanco, calico, cambric, cameline, camlet, candlewick, canvas, carmelite, carpeting, casement-cloth, cashmere, cassimere, catgut, (cavalry) twill, challis, chamois, chantilly (lace), charmeuse, cheesecloth, damask, damassin, delaine, denim, devil's dust, dhoti, d(h)urrie, diamanté, diaper, dimity, doe-skin, doily, domett, dornick, dowlas, drab, drabbet, drap-de-Berry, dreadnought, drill, droguet, drugget, duchesse lace, duck, duffel, dungaree, dupion, durant, Dutch carpet, ecru, éolienne, façonné, faille, far(r)andine, fearnought, felt, ferret, filet, flannel, flannelette, foulard, foulé, frieze, frocking, fustian, gaberdine, galatea, galloon, gambroon, gauze, genappe, georgette, gingham, Gobelini(s), gold-cloth, gold-lace, grass cloth, grenadine, grogram, grosgrain, guipure, gunny, gurrah, habit-cloth, haircloth, harn, Hessian, hodden, holland, homespun, Honiton, hopsack, horsehair, huckaback, humhum, jaconet, Jaeger®, jamdani, jean, jeanette, jersey, kalamkari, karakul, kente cloth, kersey, kerseymere, khader, khaki, kid, kidskin, kilt, kincob, kip-skin, lamé, lampas, lawn, leather, leather-cloth, leatherette, leghorn, leno, levant, linen, linsey, linsey-woolsey, llama, lockram, loden, longcloth, lovat, Lurex®, luster, lustring, lutestring, mac(k)intosh, madras, mantling, marcella, marocain, maroquin, marquisette, mazarine, Mechlin, medley, melton, merino, Mexican, mignonette, mohair, moire, moleskin, monk's cloth, moreen, morocco, mourning-stuff, mousseline, mousseline-de-laine, mousseline-de-soie, Moygashel®, mull, mulmul(l), mungo, musk-rat, muslin, muslinet, musquash, nacarat, nainsook, nankeen, ninon, nitro-silk, nun's-veiling, nylon, oilcloth, organdie, organza, organzine, orleans, osnaburg, orris, ottoman, overcoating, paduasoy, paisley, panne, paper-cloth, paper-muslin, par(r)amatta, peau-de-soie, penistone, percale, percaline, perse, petersham, piña-cloth, pin-stripe, piqué, plaid,

cloths, fabrics *continued*

plush, point-lace, polycotton, poplin, poplinette, prunella, purple, quilting, rabanna, ratine(ratteen), raven('s)-duck, rep (repp), roan, russel, russel-cord, russet, sackcloth, sacking, sagathy, sail-cloth, samite, sarsenet, satara, sateen, satin, satinette, satin-sheeting, saxony, say, scarlet, schappe, scrim, seersucker, sendal, serge, shagreen, shalloon, shammy(-leather), shantung, sharkskin, sheepskin, Shetland wool, shoddy, Sicilian, sicilienne, silesia, silk, slipper satin, soneri, split, sponge-cloth, spun silk, stammel, strouding, suede, suedette, suiting, surah, surat, swansdown, swan-skin, tabaret, tabbinet, tabby, taffeta, tamin(e), tamise, tammy, tarlatan, tarpaulin, tartan, tat, Tattersall (check), T-cloth, tentage, tent-cloth, terry, Terylene®, thibet, thickset, thrown-silk, thunder-and-lightning, ticken, tick(ing), tiffany, toile, toilinet(te), torchon lace, toweling, tram, tricot, troll(e)y, tulle, tusser(-silk), tweed, union, Valenciennes, veiling, Velcro®, velour(s), veloutine, velveret, velvet, velveteen, velveting, vicuña, voile, wadmal, waistcoating, watchet, waterwork, waxcloth, webbing, whipcord, wigan, wild silk, wincey, winceyette, wire gauze, woolsey, worcester, worsted, zanella, zephyr.

coins, currencies agora, antoninianus, as, asper, aureus, baht, balboa, bawbee, bekah, belga, bezant, bit, bod(d)le, bolivar, boliviano, bonnet-piece, broad(piece), buck, cardecu(e), Carolus, cash, cent, centavo, centime, chiao, colon, conto, cordoba, couter, crown, crusado, cruzeiro, dam, daric, deaner, décime, denarius, denier, Deutschmark, didrachm(a), dime, dinar, dirham, doit, dollar, double, doubloon, drachma, ducat, dupondius, duro, eagle, écu, eighteen-penny piece, escudo, farthing, fen, fifty-pence piece, fifty-penny piece, five-pence piece, five-penny piece, florin, forint, franc, geordie, gerah, gourde, groat, groschen, guinea, gulden, haler, half-crown, half-dollar, halfpenny, half-sovereign, heller, jacobus, jane, jitney, joe, joey, jo(h)annes, kina, knife-money, koban(g), kopeck, koruna, kreutzer, krona, krone, Krugerrand, kwacha, kyat, lek, lepton, leu, lev, lion, lira, litre, livre, louis, louis-d'or, mag, maik, make, manch, mancus, maravedi, mark, mawpus, merk, mil, millième, millime, milreis, mina, mite, mna, mohur, moidore, mopus, naira, napoleon, (naya) paisa, (new) cedi, ngwee, nickel, obang, obol, obolus, öre, øre, Paduan, pagoda, paolo, para, patrick, paul, peseta, pesewa, peso, pfennig, piastre, picayune, pice, piece of eight, pine-tree money, pistareen, pistole, pistolet, plack, portague, portcullis, pound, punt, qintar, quetzal, quid, rag, rand, real, red, red cent, reichsmark, reis, rial, rider, riel, ringgit, rix-dollar, riyal, rose-noble, r(o)uble, royal, ruddock, ruddy, rupee, rupiah, ryal, saw-buck, sceat(t), schilling, scudo, semis, semuncia, sen, sequin, sesterce, sestertium, sextans, shekel, shilling, silverling, sixpence, skilling, smacker, sol, soldo, solidus, sou, sovereign, spade-guinea, spur-royal, stater, sterling, stiver, sucre, sword-dollar, sycee, tael, taka, talent, tanner, tenner, tenpence, ten-pence piece, ten-penny piece, tester(n),

coins, currencies *continued*

testo(o)n, testril(l), tetradrachm, thaler, thick'un, thin'un, three-farthings, three-halfpence, threepence, threepenny bit/piece, tical, tick(e)y, tizzy, toman, turner, twenty-pence piece, twenty-penny piece, two bits, twopence, two-pence piece, two-penny piece, unicorn, ure, vellon, wakiki, wampum, won, xerafin, yen, yuan, zack, zecchino, zimbi, zloty, zuz, zwanziger.

collective nouns

building of rooks, cast of hawks, cete of badgers, charm of goldfinches, chattering of choughs, clamor of rooks, clowder of cats, covert of coots, covey of partridges, down of hares, drift of swine, drove of cattle, dule of doves, exaltation of larks, fall of woodcock, fesnyng of ferrets, gaggle of geese, gam of whales, gang of elks, grist of bees, husk of hares, kindle of kittens, leap of leopards, leash of bucks, murder of crows, murmuration of starlings, muster of peacocks, mute of hounds, nide of pheasants, pace of asses, pod of seals, pride of lions, school of porpoises, siege (or sedge) of bitterns, skein of geese, skulk of foxes, sloth of bears, sounder of boars, spring of teals, stud of mares, team of ducks, tok of capercailzies, troop of kangaroos, walk of snipe, watch of nightingales.

collectors, enthusiasts

abolitionist, ailurophile, antiquary, antivaccinationist, antivivisectionist, arachnologist, arctophile, audiophil(e), balletomane, bibliolatrist, bibliomane, bibliopegist, bibliophagist, bibliophile, bibliophilist, bicameralist, campanologist, canophilist, cartophile, cartophilist, cheirographist, coleopterist, conservationist, cynophilist, Dantophilist, deltiologist, discophile, dog-fancier, ecclesiologist, egger, enophile, enophilist, entomologist, environmentalist, ephemerist, epicure, ex-librist, feminist, Francophile, Gallophile, gastronome, gemmologist, Germanophil(e), gourmet, herpetologist, hippophile, homoeopathist, iconophilist, incunabulist, Kremlinologist, lepidopterist, medallist, miscegenationist, monarchist, myrmecologist, negrophile, negrophilist, notaphilist, numismatist, ophiophilist, orchidomaniac, ornithologist, orthoepist, orthographist, ostreiculturist, pangrammatist, Panhellenist, panislamist, Pan-Slavist, paragrammatist, paroemographer, perfectionist, philanthrope, philatelist, philhellene, phillumenist, philogynist, philologist, philologue, prohibitionist, pteridophilist, reincarnationist, Russophile, Russophilist, scripophile, scripophilist, sericulturist, Sinophile, Slavophile, speleologist, steganographist, stegophilist, supernaturalist, tege(s)tologist, timbrologist, timbromaniac, timbrophilist, tulipomane, tulipomaniac, Turcophile, ufologist, ultramontanist, vexillologist, virtuoso, vulcanologist, xenophile, zoophile, zoophilist.

colors anthochlore, anthocyan(in), anthoxanthin, aquamarine, argent, aurora, avocado, badious, Berlin blue, beryl, biscuit, black, blae, blood-red, blue, bottle-green, brick-red, buff, canary, caramel, carmine, carnation, celadon, celeste, cerise, cerulean, cervine, cesious, champagne, charcoal, cobalt-blue, coral, cyan, dove, drab, dun, Dutch pink, dwale, eau de Nil, ebony, emerald, fawn, feldgrau, ferrugin(e)ous, filemot, flame, flavescent, flaxen, flesh-color, fulvous, fuscous, ginger, glaucous, gold, golden, gray, green, greige (grège), gridelin, griseous, grizzle(d), gules, guly, hoar, horse-flesh, hyacinth, hyacinthine, ianthine, icterine, icteritious, incarnadine, indigo, isabel, isabella, isabelline, jacinth, khaki, lake, lateritious, lemon, lilac, lovat, lurid, luteolous, luteous, lutescent, magenta, mahogany, maize, mandarin(e), maroon, mauve, mazarine, miniate, minium, modena, morel, mouse-color(ed), mous(e)y, mulberry, murrey, nacarat, Naples-yellow, nattier blue, Nile green, nut-brown, ochroleucous, off-white, orange, oxblood, Oxford blue, palatinate, pansy, peach, peach-bloom, peacock, peacock-blue, perse, philomot, piceous, pink, plum, plumbeous, pompadour, ponceau, pongee, porphyry, porraceous, puce, purple, purpure, pyrrhous, red, reseda, roan, rose, rose-colored, rose-pink, rose-red, rosy, rubicund, rubied, rubiginous, rubineous, rubious, ruby, ruby-red, ruddy, rufescent, rufous, russet, rust-colored, rusty, sable, saffron, sage, salmon, sand, sapphire, saxe blue, scarlet, sepia, siena, silver, sky, slate, smalt, straw, tan, taupe, tawny, tenné, Titian, tomato, tusser, Tyrian, ultramarine, vermeil, vermilion, vinous, violet, virescent, vitellary, vitreous, watchet, white, wine, xanthic, xanthous, yellow.

confections, dishes, foods angels-on-horseback, battalia pie, bir(i)yani, blanquette, Bombay duck, borsch(t), bouillabaisse, bubble-and-squeak, bummalo, burgoo, cannelloni, carbon(n)ade, cassoulet, cecils, charlotte russe, chilli con carné, chocolate vermicelli, chop-suey, chowder, chow-mein, cockaleekie, colcannon, consommé, Danish pastry, dariole, devil, devil's food cake, devils-on-horseback, Devonshire cream, diet-bread, dika-bread, dimsum, dough-boy, doughnut, dragée, drammock, duff, dumpling, dunderfunk, Eccles cake, éclair, Edinburgh rock, egg custard, enchilada, eryngo, escalope, escargot, faggot, fancy-bread, farle, fedelini, felafel, fettuc(c)ine, fishball, fishcake, fishfinger, flan, flapjack, floater, flummery, foie gras, fondant, fondue, forcemeat, fortune cookie, fraise, frankfurter, French bread, French dressing, French fry, French stick, French toast, fricandeau, fricassee, friedcake, fritter, fritto misto, friture, froise, fruit cocktail, fruit salad, fruitcake, frumenty, fu yung, fudge, fumado, galantine, game chips, garam masala, Garibaldi biscuit, gateau, gazpacho, gefilte fish, Genoa cake, ghee, ginger nut, gingerbread, gingersnap, gnocchi, gofer, goulash, graham bread, graham crackers, grits, gruel, guacamole, gumdrop, gundy, haberdine, haggis, halva(h), hamburger, hard sauce, hardbake, hardtack, hoe-cake, hominy, hoosh, hot dog, hot-cross-bun,

confections, dishes, food *continued*

hotpot, howtowdie, humbug, hummus, hundreds-and-thousands, hyson, jemmy, kedgeree, lardy-cake, laverbread, matelote, millefeuille(s), minestrone, mous(s)aka, na(a)n, navarin, olla-podrida, opsonium, paella, panada, pastrami, pavlova, pem(m)ican, pettitoes, pilaff, pilau, pinole, pirozhki, pizza, plowman's lunch, plum-duff, plum-porridge, plum-pudding, poi, polenta, polony, popover, pop(p)adum, porterhouse(-steak), pot-au-feu, prairie-oyster, profiterole, prosciutto, pumpernickel, queen of puddings, queen's pudding, quenelle, quiche, ragout, ramekin, ratatouille, ravioli, remoulade, risotto, roly-poly pudding, Sachertorte, salmagundi, salmi(s), saltimbocca, sauce hollandaise, sauerkraut, scampi, schnitzel, sch(t)chi, Scotch woodcock, shepherd's pie, smørbrød, smörgåsbord, soufflé, spaghetti (alla) bolognese, spotted dick, spring roll, stovies, stroganoff, succotash, sukiyaki, summer pudding, sundae, sup(p)awn, sushi, syllabub, Tabasco®, tablet, taco, tamal(e), tandoori, tapioca, taramasalata, tempura, timbale, toad-in-the-hole, torte, tortellini, tortilla, trifle, tsamba, turtle-soup, tutti-frutti, tzimmes, velouté sauce, vermicelli, vichyssoise, vienna loaf, vienna steak, vindaloo, vol-au-vent, wafer, waffle, warden pie, wastel-bread, water-biscuit, water-gruel, welsh rabbit (rarebit), white sauce, white-pot, white-pudding, Wiener schnitzel, Wimpy®, wine-biscuit, wonder, Worcestershire sauce, wurst, yoghurt, Yorkshire pudding, zabaglione, Zwieback.

dances allemande, beguine, belly-dance, bergamask, black bottom, bolero, bossanova, bourree, branle, breakdown, bunny-hug, cachucha, cakewalk, canary, cancan, carioca, carmagnole, carol, cha-cha, chaconne, Charleston, cinque-pace, Circassian, circle, clogdance, conga, coranto, corroboree, cotill(i)on, country-dance, courant, cracovienne, csárdás (czardas), dos-à-dos (dosi-do) dump, écossaise, egg-dance, fading, fado, fandango, farruca, figure-dance, flamenco, fling, flip-flap(-flop), forlana, fox-trot, galliard, gallopade, galop, gavotte, gigue, gopak, habanera, haka, halling, haymaker, hey (hay), hey-de-guy, Highland fling, hoedown, hoolachan, hula-hula, jig, jitterbug, jive, jota, juba, kolo, lancers, loure, malagueña, mambo, matachin, maxixe, mazurka, minuet, Moresco, morris-dance, musette, onestep, Paduan, paso doble, passacaglia, passepied, passy-measure, Paul Jones, pavan(e), petronella, planxty, polacca, polka, polo, polonaise, poule, poussette, quadrille, quickstep, redowa, reel, r(h)umba, rigadoon, ring-dance, romaika, roundel, roundelay, roundle, rumba, saltarello, samba, sand-dance, saraband, schottische, sequidilla, shimmy(-shake), siciliano, spring, square-dance, stomp, strathspey, sword-dance, tamborin, tango, tap-dance, tarantella, the twist, toe-dance, tripudium, turkey-trot, two-step, Tyrolienne, valeta, valse, varsovienne, volta, waltz, war dance, zapateado, ziganka.

dog-breeds affenpinscher, badger-dog, basenji, basset(-hound), Bedlington (terrier), Blenheim spaniel, boar-hound, Border terrier, borzoi, Boston terrier, Briard, Brussels griffon, bull mastiff, bulldog, bull-terrier, cairn terrier, Cavalier King Charles spaniel, chihuahua, chow, clumber spaniel, coach-dog, cocker spaniel, collie, corgi, dachshund, Dalmatian, Dandie Dinmont, Dane, deerhound, dhole, dingo, Doberman(n) pinscher, elkhound, Eskimo dog, foxhound, fox-terrier, German police dog, German Shepherd dog, Great Dane, greyhound, griffon, harlequin, (Irish) water-spaniel, Jack Russell, keeshond, King Charles spaniel, Labrador, laika, lhasa apso, lurcher, lyam-hound, malemute, Maltese, mastiff, peke, Pekin(g)ese, pinscher, pointer, Pomeranian, poodle, pug, pug-dog, retriever, Rottweiler, saluki, Samoyed(e), sausage-dog, schipperke, schnauzer, Scotch-terrier, Sealyham, setter, sheltie, Shetland sheepdog, shih tzu, shough, Skye (terrier), spaniel, Spartan, spitz, St Bernard, staghound, Sussex spaniel, talbot, teckel, terrier, vizsla, volpino, warragal, water-dog, Weimaraner, whippet, wire-hair(ed terrier), wolf-dog, wolf-hound, Yorkshire terrier, zorro.

drinks, alcoholic absinth(e), aguardiente, akvavit, amontillado, anisette, apple-jack, aqua-mirabilis, aquavit, aqua-vitae, arak, Armagnac, arrack, audit ale, ava, bacharach, badminton, barley-bree, Beaujolais, Beaune, Benedictine, bingo, bishop, black velvet, bloody Mary, blue ruin, bourbon, brandy-pawnee, bride-ale, Bristol-milk, bucellas, bumbo, burgundy, Calvados, Campari, canary, catawba, Chablis, chain-lightning, Chambertin, Champagne, Chartreuse, cherry brandy, cherry-bounce, Chianti, chicha, cider, claret, claret-cup, cobbler, cobbler's punch, Cognac, Cointreau®, cold-without, Constantia, cool-tankard, cooper, cordial, corn-brandy, daiquiri, demerara, dog's nose, dop, eau de vie, eau des creoles, egg-flap, eggnog, enamel, enzian, fine, fino, four-ale, geneva, genevrette, geropiga, gimlet, gin, gin and it, gin-fizz, ginger wine, ginsling, glogg, gooseberry wine, grappa, Graves, grog, haoma, heavy wet, herb-beer, hermitage, hippocras, hock, hollands, hoo(t)ch, it, Johannisberger, John Barleycorn, John Collins, kaoliang, kava, kefir, kirsch, kirschwasser, k(o)umiss, kümmel, kvass, London particular, manzanilla, maraschino, marc brandy, Marcobrunner, Marsala, Martini®, Médoc, metheglin, mirabelle, mobbie, Moselle, mountain, mountain dew, muscat, muscatel, negus, Nipa, noyau, Old Tom, oloroso, olykoek, Orvieto, ouzo, pastis, peach-brandy, Pernod®, perry, persico(t), Peter-see-me, pils(e)ner, plottie, pombe, port, pot(h)een, pousse-café, pulque, punch, purl, quetsch, ratafia, resinata, retsina, Rhine-wine, Riesling, Rioja, rosé, Rudesheimer, Rüdesheimer, rum, rumbo, rumfustian, rum-punch, rum-shrub, rye, rye-whisky, sack, sack-posset, sake, samshoo, sangaree, sangria, Sauterne(s), schiedam, schnapps, Scotch, shandy, sherry, sherry-cobbler, shrub, sidecar, Sillery, sling, slivovitz, sloe-gin, small beer, small-ale, sour, spruce-beer, St Julien, Steinberger, stengah, stinger, stingo, swipes, swizzle, tafia,

drinks, alcoholic *continued*
Tarragona, tent, tequil(l)a, tipper, toddy, Tokay, Tom Collins, Tom-and-Jerry, twankay, twopenny, usquebaugh, vermouth, vin blanc, vin ordinaire, vin rosé, vinho verde, vodka, wassail, water-brose, whisk(e)y, whisky toddy, white wine, white-ale, Xeres, zythum.

French Revolutionary calendar Brumaire, Floréal, Frimaire, Fructidor, Germinal, Messidor, Nivôse, Pluviôse, Prairiel, Thermidor, Vendémiaire, Ventôse.

furniture, furnishings andiron, banquette, basket-chair, basketwork, bergama, bergamot, bolster, bonheur-du-jour, box-bed, bracket clock, brise-soleil, buffet, buhl, bureau, cabriolet, camp-bed, canterbury, chair-bed, chaise-longue, chesterfield, cheval-glass, chiffonier, coaster, commode, continental quilt, credence (table/shelf), credenza, davenport, day-bed, desk, dinner-table, dinner-wagon, divan, dos-à-dos, drape, drawer, drawing-table, draw-leaf table, dresser, dressing-table, dumb-waiter, easy-chair, elbow-chair, electrolier, encoignure, escritoire, étagere, faldstool, fauteuil, fender, fender-stool, festoon-blind, fire-dog, fireguard, firescreen, four-poster, gasalier, girandole, girnel, guéridon, hallstand, hassock, hearth-rug, highboy, high-chair, hip-bath, humpty, jardinière, lectern, looking-glass, lounge, lounger, love-seat, lowboy, lug-chair, mirror, mobile, ottoman, overmantel, pelmet, pembroke (table), picture rail, piecrust table, pier-glass, pier-table, plaque, plenishings, pouf(fe), prie-dieu, pulpit, pulvinar, radiator, rocking chair, sag-bag, scatter rug/cushion, sconce, secretaire, settee, settle, settle-bed, sideboard, side-table, sofa, sofa-bed, sofa-table, squab, standard lamp, studio couch, swivel-chair, table, tallboy, tapestry, tatami, teapoy, tea-service, tea-set, tea-table, tea-tray, tea-trolley, tent-bed, tête-à-tête, toilet-table, toilet(te), torchère, tridarn, tringle, umbrella-stand, Vanitory®, vanity unit, vargueño, veilleuse, vis-à-vis, vitrine, wall-unit, wardrobe, washhand-stand, wash-stand, water bed, Welsh dresser, whatnot, writing-desk, writing-table.

garments, vestments aba, abaya, abba, abolla, achkan, acton, Afghan, alb, alpargata, amice, anorak, antigropelo(e)s, babouche, babushka, balaclava, Balbriggan, balibuntal, balmoral, bandan(n)a, bania(n), barret, basher, bashlyk, basinet, basque, basquine, bathing-costume, bauchle, beanie, bearskin, beaver, bed-jacket, bedsocks, beetle-crushers, belcher, benjamin, Bermuda shorts, Bermudas, bertha, bikini, billycock, biretta, blanket, blouson, blucher, boa, boater, bobbysock, bodice, body stocking, bolero, bomber jacket, bongrace, bonnet, bonnet-rouge, boob-tube, bootee, bottine, box-coat, bow-tie, bra, brassière,

garments, vestments *continued*

breeches, breeks, breton, broad-brim, brogue(s), buckskins, buff, buffalo-robe, buff-coat, buff-jerkin, bumfreezer, Burberry, burdash, burk(h)a, burnous(e), busby, bush jacket, bush shirt, buskin, bustle, bustle, bycoket, caftan, cagoul(e), calamanco, calash, calceamentum, calotte, calyptra, camiknickers, camise, camisole, capa, cape, capel(l)ine, capote, capuche, capuchin, carcanet, car-coat, cardigan, cardinal, carmagnole, cashmere, casque, cassock, casuals, catsuit, caul, cere-cloth, cerement, chadar, chaparajos, chapeau, chapeau-bras, chaperone, chapka, chaplet, chaps, chasuble, collar of esses, corset, corslet, cummerbund, dalmahoy, Dalmatic, décolletage, derby, diadem, diaper, dick(e)y, dinner-gown, dinner-jacket, dirndl, dishabille, dittos, divided skirt, djellaba(h), djibbah, dog-collar, Dolly Varden, dolman, donkey jacket, doublet, drainpipes, drapesuit, drawers, dreadnought, dress uniform, dress-coat, dress-improver, dressing-gown, dressing-jacket, dressing-sack, dress-shirt, dress-suit, dress-tie, duffel coat, dungarees, earmuffs, encolpion, epaulet(te), ephod, epitrachelion, espadrille, Eton collar, Eton jacket, Etons, evening dress, evening-dress, exomis, faldetta, falling band, fannel(l), fanon, farthingale, fascinator, fatigues, fedora, ferronnière, fez, fibula, fichu, filibeg, fillet, finnesko, flat-cap, flip-flop, fob, fontange, fore-and-after, fraise, French knickers, frock, frock-coat, frog, frontlet, fustanella, gaberdine, gaiter, galligaskins, galoshes, gamash, gambeson, garibaldi, gauchos, gay deceivers, gee-string (G-string), geneva bands, geta, gibus, gi(e), gilet, girandole, gizz, grego, gremial, g-suit, guernsey, gumboot, gum(shoe), habergeon, hacqueton, haik, hair-net, hair-piece, half-boot, hat, hatband, hatpin, hattock, hauberk, havelock, headcloth, head-hugger, headsquare, himation, hip-huggers, hipsters, hogger, Homburg, hood, hotpants, housecoat, hug-me-tight, humeral veil, hummel, hunting cap, ihram, indescribables, jabot, jacket, Jap-silk, jeans, jersey, jiz, jubbah (djibbah), jumper, jump-suit, jupon, kabaya, kaffiyeh, kaftan, kagoul, kalpak, kalyptra, kamees, kanzu, kell, kerchief, k(h)anga, k(h)urta, Kilmarnock, Kilmarnock cowl, kimono, kirtle, kiss-me, kiss-me-quick, knickerbockers, knickers, lammy, lava-lava, lederhosen, leggings, leghorn, leg-warmers, leotard, Levis®, liberty bodice, lingerie, loden, lounger, lounge-suit, lungi, mac(k), mackinaw, mac(k)intosh, madras, manta, manteau, mantilla, mantle, mantlet, manto, matinee, matinee jacket/coat, maud, mazarine, mazarine hood, middy (blouse), mink, miter, mitt, mitten, mob, mob-cap, mode, modius, mohair, moleskins, monkey-jacket, monteith, montero, montero-cap, morning-dress, morning-gown, mortar-board, Mother Hubbard, mourning-cloak, mousquetaire, moz(z)etta, muff, muffin-cap, muffler, mutch, muu-muu, netherstock, newmarket, nightingale, Nithsdale, Norfolk jacket, nubia, obi, omophorion, orarion, orarium, overcoat, overgarment, Oxonian, paduasoy, paenula, pagri, paletot, pall, palla, pallium, paludament, pantable, pantalets, pantaloons, panties, pantihose, pantof(f)le, panton, pantoufle, pants, pants suit, pea-coat, pea-jacket, pearlies, pectoral, pedal-

garments, vestments *continued*

pushers, pelerine, pelisse, pencil skirt, penitentials, peplos, peplum, petasos, petersham, petticoat, petticoat, petticoat-breeches, ph(a)elonion, Phrygian cap, picture-hat, pierrot, pilch, pileus, pill-box, pinafore, pinafore-dress, pinafore-skirt, pinner, pixie-hood, plaid, plimsoll, plus-fours, plushes, pneumonia-blouse, poke-bonnet, polonaise, polo-neck, poncho, pontificals, pos(h)teen, powdering-gown, pressure-helmet, pressure-suit, pressure-waistcoat, princess(e), pumps, puttee, rabato, raglan, raincoat, rami(e), Ramil(l)ie(s), ra-ra skirt, rat-catcher, rational, rationals, rebater, rebato, redingote, reefer, reefing-jacket, riding-breeches, riding-cloak, riding-clothes, riding-coat, riding-glove, riding-habit, riding-hood, riding-robe, riding-skirt, riding-suit, robe, robe-de-chambre, rochet, roll-neck sweater, roll-on, rompers, romper-suit, roquelaure, ruff, rug-gown, sabot, sack, sack-coat, safari jacket, safari suit, sagum, sailor-hat, sakkos, salopette, samfoo, sanbenito, sandal, sarafan, sari, sarong, sash, sayon, scapular, scarf, scarpetto, schema, scotch bonnet, screen, sea-boots, sealskin, semmit, separates, shako, shaps, shauchle, shawl, shawl-waistcoat, shift, shirt, shirt dress, shirtwaist, shirtwaister, shoe, shooting-jacket, short-clothes, short-coats, shortgown, shorts, shovel-hat, silk-hat, silly-how, singlet, siren suit, skeleton suit, skin-tights, skirt, skullcap, slacks, slicker, sling-back, slip, slip-over, slipper(s), slipslop, sloppy Joe, slop(s), slouch(-hat), small-clothes, smalls, smicket, smock, smock-frock, smoking cap, smoking jacket, sneaker(s), snood, snow-boots, snow-shoe(s), sock, sola(r) topi/helmet, solitaire, solleret, sombrero, sontag, soubise, soutane, sou'-wester, space-suit, spat, spattee, spatterdash, spencer, sphendone, sponge-bags, sporran, sports jacket, sports shirt, start-up, stays, steenkirk, steeple-crown, steeple-hat, stephane, step-in, Stetson, sticharion, stock, stockinet(te), stockingette, stocking(s), stola, stole, stomacher, stovepipe (hat), strait-jacket, strait-waistcoat, straw (hat), string vest, string-tie, strip, stuff-gown, subfusc, subucula, succinctorium, sun-bonnet, sundown, sun-dress, sunhat, sunsuit, superhumeral, surcingle, surcoat, surplice, surtout, suspender-belt, suspenders, swaddling-band/cloth/clothes, swagger-coat, swallow-tail, sweat band, sweat suit, sweater, sweat-shirt, swimming costume, swimsuit, swimwear, sword-belt, tabard, taglioni, tail-coat, tails, taj, talar, talaria, tall hat, tallith, talma, tam, Tam O'Shanter, tammy, tanga, tank top, tarboosh, tarpaulin, tasse, tawdry-lace, tea-gown, Teddy suit, tee-shirt, ten-gallon hat, terai, thrum-cap, tiar(a), tie, tights, tile(-hat), tippet, toga, tonnag, top-boots, topcoat, topee, topi, topper, tops, toque, toreador pants, tournure, tower, toy, tozie, track shoe, track suit, trenchard, trench-coat, trencher-cap, trews, tricorn(e), trilby, trollopee, trot-cozy, trouser suit, trousers, trouse(s), trunk-breeches, trunk-hose, trunks, truss(es), trusty, T-shirt, tube-skirt, tunic, tunicle, tuque, turban, turtle-neck, tuxedo, twin-set, ugly, ulster, ulsterette, undercoat, underpants, undershorts, undervest, upper-stock, Vandyke (collar), vareuse, veil, veld(-)schoen, vest, victorine, visite, vitta, volet, waistcloth, waistcoat, wam(p)us, war bonnet, warm,

garments, vestments *continued*

watch cap, watch chain, Watteau bodice, weeper, wellie, wellington, wet-suit, whisk, white tie, wide-awake, wig, wimple, windcheater, windjammer, wing collar, winkle-pickers, woggle, wrap, wraparound, wrapover, wrapper, wrap-rascal, wristlet, wylie-coat, yarmulka, yashmak, Y-fronts, zamarra, zoot suit, zoster, zucchetto.

heraldry abatement, addorsed, affrontee, Albany Herald, allusive, annulet, armorist, assurgent, augmentation, baton-sinister, bendlet, bend-sinister, bendwise, bendy, bezant, bicorporate, billet, bordure, botoné, brisure, caboched, cabré, cadency, canting, canton, catherine-wheel, champ, chequy, chevron, chevrony, chief, coupé, debased, debruised, declinant, delf, device, dexter, difference, dimidiate, dismembered, displayed, dormant, double, doubling, dragonné, dwale, eightfoil, embattled, emblaze, emblazon, emblazoner, emblazonment, emblazonry, enarched, enarmed, engouled, engrail, engrailed, engrailment, enveloped, escrol(l), escutcheon, extendant, fess(e), fesse-point, fetterlock, field, fimbriate, fitché(e), flanch, flanched, flotant, fracted, fret, fructed, fur, fusil, gale, gamb, garb(e), gemel, gerbe, golp(e), gorged, grieced, g(u)ardant, gules, gyron, gyronny, hatchment, haurient, herisson, honor-point, impale, impalement, increscent, inescutcheon, interfretted, invected, jessant, langued, lioncel, lis, lozenge, lozengy, manche, mantling, martlet, mascle, mascled, masculy, moline, morné, morned, mounted, mullet, naiant, naissant, nombril, nowed, nowy, opinicus, or, orle, palewise, pall, passant, patonce, patté(e), pean, percussant, pheon, pile, point, pommelé, pommeled, pommetty, portate, portcullis, posé, potencé, potent, primrose, quarter, quartering, quarterly, queue, ragged staff, raguled, raguly, rampant, raping, rebate, regardant, respect, respectant, roundel, rustre, saltire, sans nombre, satyral, scarp, segreant, sej(e)ant, semé(e), square-pierced, statant, tenné, trangle, tressure, trippant, umbrated, undee, undifferenced, unguled, urinant, vair, vairé, verdoy, vert, voided, vol, volant, vorant, vuln, vulned, waved, weel, wivern, woodwose (wood-house).

herbs, spices amaracus, basil thyme, caraway seeds, cardamom, cassia, cayenne, chervil, chilli, chive, cinnamon, cloves, coriander, cum(m)in, dill, dittany, endive, eyebright, fennel, fenugreek, finoc(c)hio, galega, garlic, gentian, ginger, groundsel, hellebore, henbane, horehound, horseradish, Hyoscyamus, hyssop, isatis, juniper, lemon thyme, licorice, lovage, lungwort, mace, marjoram, mint, motherwort, mustard, myrrh, nutmeg, oregano, orpine, paprika, parsley, peppermint, purslane, rampion, rape, rosemary, rue, saffron, sage, savory, stacte, tarragon, thyme, turmeric, vanilla, verbena, watercress, wintergreen, wormwood, woundwort, yerba.

jewels, gems agate, amber, amethyst, aquamarine, asteria, balas ruby, baroque, beryl, bloodstone, brilliant, cairngorm, cameo, carbuncle, chalcedony, chrysolite, coral, cornelian, crystal, diamond, draconites, emerald, fire-opal, garnet, girasol(e), grossular(ite), heliodor, hyacinth, hyalite, hydrophane, intaglio, jacinth, jade, jango(o)n, jasper, jet, lapis lazuli, ligure, marcasite, marquise, Mocha stone, moonstone, morganite, mother-of-pearl, nacre, olivet, olivine, onyx, opal, oriental amethyst, paragon, pearl, peridot(e), pyreneite, pyrope, Rhinestone, rhodolite, rose, rose-cut, rose-diamond, ruby, sapphire, sard, sardine, sardonyx, smaragd, topaz, tourmaline, turquoise, water-sapphire, wood-opal, yu, yu-stone, zircon.

Jewish calendar Ab, Abib, Adar, Adar Sheni, Elul, Hes(h)van, Iy(y)ar, Kislev, Nisan, S(h)ebat, Sivan, Tammuz, Tebet(h), Tis(h)ri, Veadar.

languages Aeolic, Afghan, Afrikaans, Akkadian, Albanian, Alemannic, Algonki(a)n, Altaic, Ameslan, Amharic, Anatolian, Anglo-Saxon, Arabic, Aramaic, Armenian, Armoric, Aryan, Assyrian, Attic, Austric, Austroasiatic, Austronesian, Avestan, Bahasa Indonesia, Balinese, Baltoslav(on)ic, Baluch(i), Bantu, Basque, Basuto, Bengali, Berber, Bohemian, bohunk, Breton, Brezonek, British, Brythonic, Bulgarian, Bulgaric, Burmese, B(y)elorussian, Cajun, Carib, Catalan, Celtic, Chaldaic, Cherokee, Chinese, Choctaw, Circassian, Cornish, creole, Croat(ian), Cushitic, Czech, Danish, Dardic, Doric, Dravidian, Dutch, Early English, English, Erse, Eskimo, Esperanto, Est(h)onian, Ethiopic, Etruscan, Euskarian, Fanti, Farsi, Finnish, Finno-Ugric(-Ugrian), Flemish, Franglais, French, Frisian, Gadhelic (Goidelic), Gaelic, Gaulish, Geëz (Giz), Gentoo, Georgian, German, Germanic, Greek, Guarani, Gujarat(h)i, Gullah, Hausa, Hawaiian, Hebrew, Hellenic, Herero, High German, Hindi, Hindustani, Hittite, Hottentot, Hungarian, Icelandic, Idiom Neutral, Ido, I(g)bo, Indian, Indic, Indo-European, Indo-Germanic, In(n)uit, Interlingua, Ionic, Iranian, Iraqi, Irish, Iroquoian, Italian, Italic, Japanese, Kalmuck, Kanarese, Kannada, Karen, Kennick, Khmer, Koine, Kolarian, Kuo-yü, Kurdish, Ladin, Ladino, Lallans, Landsmaal, Langue d'oc, Langue d'oil, Langue d'oui, Laplandish, Lapp, Lappish, Latin, Latvian, Lettic, Lettish, lingua franca, lingua geral, Lithuanian, Low German, Magyar, Malagasy, Malay, Malayala(a)m, Maltese, Manchu, Mandaean, Mandarin, Mandingo, Manx, Maori, Marathi, Median, Melanesian, Mexican, Micmac, Middle English, Moeso-gothic, Mohawk, Mohican, Mon, Mongolian, Munda, Nahuati, Neo, Newspeak, Norwegian, Novial, Nynorsk, Old English, Old Norse, Oriya, Oscan, Ostyak, Pali, Pawnee, Pehlevi, Pekin(g)ese, Pennsylvania Dutch, Persian, Persic, Phoenician, Pictish, pig Latin, Pilipino, Platt-Deutsch, Polabian, Polish, Portuguese, Prakrit, Provençal Provinçal, Prussian, Punic, Punjabi, Pushtu, Quechua, Rabbinic, Rhaetic, Rhaeto-Romance,

languages *continued*

Rhaeto-Romanic, Rock English, rogues' Latin, Romaic, Romance, Romanes,
Romanic, Roman(n)y, Romans(c)h, Rumanian, Russian, Russniak, Ruthenian,
Sakai, Samnite, Samoyed(e), Sanskrit, Saxon, Scots, Scythian, Semitic, Serb(ian),
Serbo-Croat(ian), Shan, Shona, Siamese, Sinhalese, Siouan, Slavonic, Slovak,
Slovenian, Somali, Sorbian, Sorbish, Spanish, Sudanic, Sumerian, Suomi, Swahili,
Swedish, Swiss, Syriac, Taal, Tagálog, Taino, Tamil, Tataric, Telugu, Teutonic,
Thai, Tibetan, Tocharian, Tswana, Tuareg, Tungus(ian), Tupi, Turki, Turkish,
Twi, Ugrian, Ugro-finnic, Ukrainian, Umbrian, Uralic, Urdu, Uzbeg, Vaudois,
Vietnamese, Volapük, Volga-Baltic, Volscian, Welsh, Wendic, Wendish, West-Saxon,
Wolof, Xhosa, Yakut, Yiddish, Yoruba, Zulu.

legal abate, abatement, absolvitor, abstract of title, acceptilation, accession,
accessory, accessory after the fact, accessory before the fact, Acts of Adjournal,
(ad)avizandum, adeem, adhere, adjudication, adminicle, administrator, afforce,
alienee, alienor, allenarly, allodial, amicus curiae, amove, appointer, apprize,
apprizer, assumpsit, attorn, back-bond, bairn's-part, capias, certiorari, chaud-
mellé, cognosce, cognovit, compear, compulsitor, copyhold, cross-examine, decree
absolute, decree nisi, decreet, decretals, decretist, dedimus, deed, deed of accession,
defalcate, defeasance, defeasanced, defeasible, defendant, defender, deforce,
deforcement, deforciant, delapidation, delate, delation, delator, delict, demurrer,
deodand, detainer, detinue, devastavit, devest, diet, dimissory, disapply, disbar,
disbench, discovert, discoverture, disentail, disgavel, disinherison, dispone,
disponee, disposition, disseise, disseisin, disseisor, distinguish, distrain, distrainee,
distrainer, distrainment, distrainor, distraint, distress, distringas, dittay, dole,
donatary, droit, droit du Seigneur, duplicand, duply, dying declaration, easement,
ejectment, embracer, embracery, emendals, emphyteusis, en ventre sa mère,
enfeoff, enfeoffment, enjoin, enlevé, enlevement, entry, eric, escheat, escrow
(escroll), escuage, esnecy, esrepe, essoin, estate, estop, estoppel, estover, estray,
estreat, estrepement, examination, excamb, excambion, excambium, executry,
exemplify, expromission, extend, extent, extinguishment, extract, extradition,
facile, facility, factorize, faldage, felo de se, felony, feme, feme covert, feme sole,
feoff, feoffee, feoffer (feoffor), feoffment, feu, feuar, fief, filacer, fire-bote, fiscal,
folio, force and fear, force majeure, foreclose, foreclosure, forinsec, forisfamiliate,
forjudge, frankalmoign, french-bench, frontager, fugitation, fungibles, garnishee,
garnisheement, garnisher, gavelkind, gavelman, granter (grantor), grassum,
hamesucken, hedge-bote, hide, homologation, horning, house-bote, hypothec,
hypothecary, hypothecate, hypothecation, improbation, indenture, indict, indictee,
indictment, induciae, infangthief, infeft, inquirendo, institorial, insucken,
interlocutor, interplead, interpleader, interpose, irrepleviable, irreplevisable, ish,

legal *continued*

John Doe and Richard Roe, joinder, jointure, jus primae noctis, laches, law-agent, law-burrows, legitim, lenocinium, letters of administration, lien, life-rent, malfeasance, mens rea, mesne, messuage, misdemeanant, misfeasance, misfeasor, misprison, mittimus, mora, mortmain, multiplepoinding, nolle prosequi, nolo contendere, non-access, nonage, non-compearance, non-entry, nonsuit, non-user, notour, novalia, noverint, novodamus, noxal, obligant, obligation, obligor, obreption, onus probandi, ouster, outfangthief, overt act, owelty, oyer, pactum nudum, Pandect, panel, pernancy, personalty, pickery, plaint, plaintiff, porteous roll, portioner, practic, prima facie, privy, prorogate, pupil, quadruply, realty, recaption, recusation, reddendo, relator, relaxation, remise, replevin, replevy, repone, reprobator, res gestae, retour, retroact, retroactive, reverser, right of drip, rout, scutage, stillicide, supersedeas, supplicavit, surrebut, surrebuttal, surrebutter, surrejoin, surrejoinder, terminer, tolt, tort, tortfeasor, tortious, udal, udaller, ultimus haeres, unlaw, uses, usucapient, usucapion (usucaption), usucapt, usucaptible, usufruct, usufructuary, ultimogeniture, vacatur, venire (facias), venter, venue, vert, vest, vested, visne, voidable, voir dire, volunteer, wage, waive, waste, watch, watching brief, water-privilege, wit.

minerals adularia, aegirine, aegirite, alabandine, almandine, alum-shale, alum-slate, alum-stone, alunite, amazonite, amazon-stone, amianthus, amphibole, analcime, anatase, andesine, argil, arkose, asbestos, asparagus-stone, asphalt(um), aventurine, baetyl, balas, Barbados earth, barilla, baryta, barytes, basalt, Bath stone, bath-brick, bezoar, bitter-earth, bitter-spar, bitumen, blackjack, blacklead, blaes, blende, bloodstone, blue ground, blue John, blue vitriol, bluestone, Bologna phosphorous, borane, borax, borazon, boride, bornite, boulder-clay, breccia, Bristol-brick, Bristol-diamond, brown spar, brownstone, buhrstone, cacholong, caen-stone, cairngorm, calamine, calc-sinter, calcspar, calc-tuff, caliche, calp, Carborundum®, cat's-eye, cat-silver, cauk, celestine, cement-stone, ceruse, chalcedony, chalcedonyx, chalk, chert, Chile saltpeter, china clay, china stone, chrome-alum, chrome-spinel, chrysoberyl, chrysocolla, chrysoprase, chrysotile, cinnabar, cinnamon-stone, cipollino, corundum, cryolite, cymophane, dacite, dendrite, Derbyshire spar, diabase, diallage, dialogite, diaspore, diatomite, dice-coal, diopside, dioptase, diorite, dogger, dogtooth-spar, dolerite, dolomite, dopplerite, dropstone, dunite, dyscrasite, dysodyle, eagle-stone, earthflax, earthwax, eclogite, electric calamine, elvan, emery, encrinite, enhydrite, enhydros, epidiorite, epidosite, epidote, epistilbite, epsomite, erinite, erubescite, erythrite, euclase, eucrite, eudialyte, eutaxite, euxenite, fahlerz, fahlore, fakes, fayalite, fel(d)spar, felsite, felstone, flint, fluorite, fluorspar, franklinite, French chalk, fuchsite, fulgurite, fuller's earth, gabbro, gadolinite, gahnite, galena, galenite,

minerals *continued*

gangue, gan(n)ister, garnet-rock, gibbsite, glance, glauberite, glauconite, glimmer, gmelinite, gneiss, goldstone, goslarite, gossan, göthite, granite, granitite, granodiorite, granophyre, granulite, graphic granite, graphite, green earth, greenockite, greensand, greenstone, greisen, greywacke, gummite, gypsum, hälleflinta, halloysite, harmotome, hatchettite, haüyne, heavy spar, hedyphane, hematite, hemimorphite, hepatite, hercynite, (h)essonite, heulandite, hiddenite, honey-stone, hornblende, hornfels, hornstone, horseflesh ore, humite, hyacinth, hyalophane, hypersthene, ice-spar, ice-stone, idocrase, ironstone, jacinth, keratophyre, kermes, kermesite, kieselguhr, kunkur, kupferschiefer, lamprophyre, lapis lazuli, lepidomelane, limestone, lithomarge, marlstone, meerschaum, mellite, mica, microlite, microlith, mispickel, morion, moss-agate, mundic, nail-head-spar, needle-tin, nepheline, nickel-bloom, nickel-ocher, Norway saltpeter, nosean, noselite, obsidian, omphacite, onyx, onyx-marble, orthoclase, orthophyre, ottrelite, ozokerite, peacock-ore, pencil-ore, pencil-stone, peperino, periclase, pericline, petuntse, pipeclay, pipestone, plagioclose, pleonaste, porphyry, potstone, prase, protogine, pyrites, quartz, realgar, rock-oil, rubicelle, ruby-spinel, rutile, saltpeter, sandstone, sanidine, sapphire, sapphire-quartz, sapphirine, sard, sardonyx, satin-, spar, satin-stone, scaglia, schalstein, schiller-spar, schist, schorl, serpentine, serpentine(-rock), shale, shell-limestone, shell-marl, silica, silver-glance, sinter, slate, soapstone, spar, speiss-cobalt, spelter, sphene, spiegeleisen, spinel, spinel-ruby, spodumene, stinkstone, sunstone, surturbrand, swinestone, sylvine, tabular spar, tachylite, talc, talc-schist, terne, terpene, terpineol, terra alba, terracotta, terra-japonica, terramara, terra-rossa, terra-sigillata, terts, thulia, tiger(s)-eye, till, tin-stone, toad-stone, tombac, touchstone, tourmaline, trass, travertin(e), tripoli, troutstone, tufa, tuff, Turkey hone, Turkey stone, turquoise, tutty, uinta(h)ite, umber, Uralian emerald, uralite, uraninite, uranite, uvarovite, vanadinite, variolite, variscite, veinstone, veinstuff, Venice talc, verd-antique, vesuvianite, vitrain, vivianite, vulpinite, wacke, wad(d), wallsend, wavellite, Wernerite, whet-slate, whewellite, whinstone, white pyrites, willemite, witherite, wolfram, wollastonite, wood-coal, wulfenite, wurtzite, zaratite, zarnich, zeolite, zeuxite, zinkenite, zircon, zoisite, zorgite.

musical instruments aeolian harp, aerophone, alpenhorn, alphorn, althorn, alto, Amati, American organ, apollonicon, archlute, arpeggione, atabal, autoharp, balalaika, bandore, banjulele, baryton(e), bass clarinet, bass drum, bass fiddle, bass horn, bass tuba, bass viol, basset horn, bazooka, bombard, bombardon, bongo (drum), bouzouki, buccina, bugle, buglet, bull fiddle, calliope, castanets, celeste, cello, cembalo, chair-organ, chalumeau, chamber organ, chikara, Chinese pavilion, chitarrone, chordophone, cinema-organ, cithara, cither(n), citole, cittern,

musical instruments *continued*

clarichord, clarinet, clarion, clarsach, clave, clavichord, crwth, cymbal, cymbalo, decachord, dichord, didgeridoo, digitorium, double bass, drum, dulcimer, Dulcitone®, dumb-piano, echo, electric guitar, electric organ, euphonium, fagotto, fife, fipple-flute, flageolet, flügel, flügelhorn, flute, flûte-à-bec, flutina, French horn, gamelan, German flute, gimbard, gittern, glass harmonica, glockenspiel, grand piano, gu, guitar, gusla, Hammerklavier, hand-horn, hand-organ, harmonica, harmonicon, harmoniphone, harmonium, harp, harpsichord, hautboy, heckelphone, heptachord, horn, hornpipe, humstrum, hunting-horn, hurdy-gurdy, idiophone, jingling Johnny, kazoo, kent-bugle, keyboard(s), keybugle, klavier, koto, krummhorn, Kuh-horn, langsp(i)el, lituus, lur(e), lyra-viol, lyre, mandola, mandolin(e), mandora, maraca, marimba, marine trumpet, melodeon, metallophone, mirliton, monochord, Moog synthesizer, mouth-harp, mouth-organ, musette, musical glasses, naker, nose-flute, nun's-fiddle, oboe, oboe d'amore, oboe di caccia, ocarina, octachord, octave-flute, ophicleide, organ-harmonium, orpharion, orpheorion, pandora, panharmonicon, Pan-pipes, Pan's pipes, pantaleon, pianette, pianino, piano, piano-accordion, pianoforte, Pianola®, piano-organ, piffero, pipe, pipeless organ, pipe-organ, player piano, polyphon(e), posaune, psaltery, pyrophone, quint(e), racket(t), rebec(k), regal, rote, sackbut, salpinx, sambuca, sancho, sang, santir, sarangi, sarrusophone, sausage-bassoon, saxhorn, saxophone, seraphine, serinette, serpent, s(h)amisen, shawm, side-drum, sitar, small-pipes, sourdeline, sousaphone, spinet(te), squeeze-box, squiffer, steel drum, sticcado, stock-and-horn, strad, Stradivari(us), string bass, sultana, symphonion, symphony, synthesizer, syrinx, tabla, tabor, tabo(u)rin, tabret, tambour, tamboura, tambourine, tam-tam, testudo, tetrachord, theater organ, theorbo, timbal, timbrel, timpano, tin whistle, traps, triangle, trichord, tromba marina, trombone, trump, trumpet, trumpet marine, tuba, tubular bells, tympan, uillean pipes, ukulele, vibraharp, vibraphone, vielle, vihuela, vina, viol, viola, viola da braccio, (viola da) gamba, viola da gamba, viola da spalla, viola d'amore, violin, violoncello, violone, virginal(s), vocalion, waldflute, waldhorn, Welsh harp, xylophone, zambomba, zampogna, zanze, zel, zinke, zither, zufolo.

parliaments Althing (Iceland), Congress (USA), Cortes (Spain, Portugal), Dáil (Ireland), d(o)uma (Russia), ecclesia (Athens), Folketing (Denmark), House of Commons (UK), House of Keys (Isle of Man), House of Lords (UK), Knesset (Israel), Lagt(h)ing (Norway), Lagting (Norway), Landst(h)ing (Denmark), Landtag (Germany), Lok Sabha (India), Majlis (Iran), Odelst(h)ing (Norway), Oireachtas (Ireland), Parliament (UK), Pnyx (Athens), Porte (Turkey), Rajya Sabha (India), Reichsrat(h) (Austria), Reichstag (Germany), Rigsdag (Denmark), Riksdag (Sweden), Seanad (Ireland), Senate (Rome, USA, etc.), Skupshtina

Parliaments *continued*
(Yugoslavia), Sobranje (Bulgaria), Stort(h)ing (Norway), Tynwald (Isle of Man), witenagemot (England).

prosody Alcaic, alexandrine, amphibrach, amphibrachic, amphimacer, Anacreontic, anacrusis, anacrustic, anapaest, anapaestic, antibacchius, antispast, antispastic, antistrophe, Archilochian, arsis, Asclepiad, asynartete, atonic, bacchius, catalectic, choliamb, choree, choriamb, cinquain, cretic, dactyl, decastich, decasyllabic, decasyllable, dipody, dispondaic, dispondee, distich, disyllable, ditrochean, ditrochee, dizain, dochmiac, dochmius, dodecasyllabic, dodecasyllable, dolichurus, duan, ectasis, ecthlipsis, elide, elision, enjamb(e)ment, envoy, epic, epirrhema, epistrophe, epitrite, epode, epopee, epopoeia, epos, epyllion, extrametrical, eye-rhyme, false quantity, feminine caesura, feminine ending, feminine rhyme, fifteener, free verse, galliambic, g(h)azal, glyconic, gradus, haiku, head-rhyme, hendecasyllabic, hendecasyllable, hephthemimer, heptameter, heptapody, heptasyllabic, heterostrophic, heterostrophy, hexameter, hexametric(al), hexapody, hexastich, Hudibrastic, huitain, hypercatalectic, hypercatalexis, hypermetrical, iamb, iambus, ictus, Ionic, irrational, kyrielle, laisse, Leonine, limerick, limma, linked verse, logaoedic, long-measure, macaronic(s), masculine ending, masculine rhyme, meliboean, miurus, monometer, monorhyme, monostich, monostrophic, mora, outride, oxytone, pantoum, pentameter, pentastich, penthemimer, Pherecratean, Pherecratic, Pindaric, poulters' measure, proceleusmatic, pyrrhic, Pythian, quatorzain, quatrain, reported verses, rhopalic, rhyme-royal, rich rhyme, riding-rhyme, rime riche, rime suffisante, rondeau, rondel, rove-over, rubaiyat, run-on, Sapphics, scazon, semeion, senarius, septenarius, sestina, spondee, strophe, synaphe(i)a, tetrameter, tetrapody, tetrasemic, tetrastich, thesis, tirade, tribrach, trimeter, tripody, triseme, trochee, villanelle, virelay.

ranks in armed forces able seaman, acting sub-lieutenant, admiral, admiral of the fleet, air chief marshal, air commandant, air commodore, air vice marshal, aircraftsman, air-marshal, brigadier, captain, chief officer, chief petty officer, chief technician, colonel, commandant, commander, commodore, corporal, field marshal, first officer, fleet chief petty officer, flight lieutenant, flight officer, flight sergeant, flying officer, general, group captain, group officer, junior seaman, junior technician, lance-corporal, lance-jack, lance-sergeant, leading aircraftsman, leading seaman, lieutenant, lieutenant-colonel, lieutenant-commander, lieutenant-general, major, major-general, marshal, marshal of the Royal Air Force, master-at-arms, midshipman, ordinary seaman, petty officer, pilot officer, post-captain, private, purser, quartermaster, quartermaster-general, quartermaster-sergeant,

ranks in armed forces *continued*
    quartermistress, rear-admiral, risaldar, ritt-master, second lieutenant, second
    officer, senior aircraftsman, sergeant, sergeant-major, squadron leader, squadron
    officer, staff sergeant, sub-lieutenant, superintendent, third officer, vice admiral,
    warrant officer, wing commander, wing officer.

rhetoric abscission, alliteration, amoebaean, anacoluthia, anacoluthon, anadiplosis,
    anaphora, anaphoric, anastrophe, antimetabole, antimetathesis, antiphrasis,
    antiphrastic(al), antithesis, antithetic(al), antonomasia, aporia, asteism, asyndeton,
    auxesis, catachresis, chiasmus, climax, diallage, diegesis, dissimile, double entendre,
    dramatic irony, dysphemism, ecbole, echoic, ecphonesis, ellipsis, enallage,
    enantiosis, enumeration, epanadiplosis, epanalepsis, epanaphora, epanodos,
    epanorthosis, epexegesis, epiphonema, epizeuxis, erotema, erotetic, figure, flower,
    head-rhyme, hendiadys, holophrase, hypallage, hyperbaton, hyperbole, hypobole,
    hypostrophe, hypotyposis, hysteron-proteron, increment, irony, litotes, meiosis,
    metalepsis, metaphor, metonym, metonymy, mixed metaphor, onomatopoeia,
    oxymoron, parabole, paral(e)ipsis, parenthesis, prolepsis, simile, syllepsis, symploce,
    synchoresis, synchysis, synedoche, synoeciosis, trope, vicious circle, zeugma.

titles of rulers abuna, adelantado, ag(h)a, alderman, amir, amman, amtman, ard-
    ri(gh), atabeg, atabek, ataman, atheling, ayatollah, Ban, beglerbeg, begum, bey,
    boyar, burgrave, caboceer, cacique, caliph, caudillo, Cid, Dan, Dauphin, Dauphine,
    Dauphiness, dey, diadochus, doge, duce, duke, ealdorman, elector, emir, emperor,
    empress, ethnarch, exarch, gospodar, Graf, Gräfin, grave, Great Mogul, harmost,
    heptarch, hospodar, huzoor, imperator, Inca, infanta, infante, jarl, kaid, kaiser,
    kalif, khan, khedive, king, kinglet, kingling, landgrave, landgravine, maharaja(h),
    maharani, mandarin, marchesa, marchese, marchioness, margrave, margravine,
    marquess, marquis, marquise, mikado, Mirza, Monseigneur, monsieur, Monsignor,
    Monsignore, mormaor, mpret, nabob, naik, nawab, nizam, nomarch, omrah,
    padishah, palatine, palsgrave, pasha, pendragon, pentarch, pharaoh, prince, prince-
    bishop, prince-imperial, princess, raja(h), rajpramukh, rana, rani, Rhinegrave,
    Rhinegravine, sachem, sagamore, satrap, shah, sheik(h), sherif, shogun, sirdar,
    sovereign, stad(t)holder, starosta, suba(h)dar, sultan, suzerain, taoiseach, theocrat,
    toiseach, toparch, tsar, tuchun, voivode, waldgrave.

tools about-sledge, aiguille, auger, auger-bit, awl, boaster, bodkin, bolster, bradawl,
    broach, bucksaw, burin, burr, buzz-saw, card, caschrom, caulking-iron, celt,
    center-bit, chaser, chisel, chopper, clamp, cleaver, cold-chisel, cradle-scythe,

tolls *continued*

crosscut-saw, crown-saw, diamond-drill, dibble, dividers, dolly, drawing-knife, draw-knife, drill, drove, els(h)in, extirpator, fillister, float, forceps, forfex, fork, fraise, frame-saw, fretsaw, gad, gang-saw, gavelock, gimlet, gouge, grapnel, grapple, graver, gurlet, hacksaw, hammer, handsaw, hawk, hay fork, hay knife, helve-hammer, hod, hoe, holing-axe, jackhammer, jack-plane, jointer, laster, level, leveling rod, leveling staff, loy, mace, madge, maker, mall, mallet, mattock, maul, monkey, moon-knife, mortar, muller, oliver, oustiti, pachymeter, pad-saw, palstave, panel saw, panga, paper-cutter, paper-knife, pattle, pecker, peel, pestle, pick, pickaxe, pincers, pinch, pinking-shears, piolet, pitchfork, plane, planer, plessor, plexor, pliers, plow, plugger, plumb, plumb-line, plumb-rule, plummet, pocket-knife, pointel, pricker, priest, priming-iron, priming-wire, probang, probe, probing-scissors, prod, prog, pruning-bill, pruning-hook, pruning-knife, pruning-shears, prunt, punch, puncheon, punty, quadrant, quannet, rabble, rake, raspatory, reed-knife, repositor, retractor, ricker, rickstick, riddle, riffle, ripper, ripping-saw, ripple, rip-saw, risp, router, rule, ruler, sash-tool, saw, sax, scalpel, scauper, scissors, scoop, scooper, scorper, scraper, screwdriver, screwjack, screw-wrench, scribe(r), scutch(er), scythe, seam-set, serving-mallet, shave, shears, shovel, sickle, slane, slate-axe, slater, slicker, smoother, snap, snarling-iron, snarling-rod, snips, soldering-bolt, soldering-iron, spade, spanner, spider, spokeshave, spud, squeegee, stadda, stake, stapler, stapling-machine, steel, stithy, stone-hammer, stretching-iron, strickle, strigil, stubble-rake, style, stylet, swage, swingle(-hand), switch, tedder, tenon-saw, threshel, thresher, thrust-hoe, tint-tool, tongs, trepan, trowel, T-square, turfing-iron, turf-spade, turning-saw, tweezers, twist drill, upright, van, vice, vulsella, waster, whip-saw, widener, wimble, wood-shears, wortle, xyster, Y-level.

units of measurement acre, ampere, angstrom, anker, ardeb, are, arpent, arroba, arshin, as, bar, barleycorn, barn, barrel, bath, baud, becquerel, bel, bigha, bit, board-foot, boll, bolt, braccio, bushel, butt, cab, cable, calorie, candela, candle, candy, carat, catty, cell, cental, centner, chain, chalder, chaldron, chenix, chopin, chronon, clove, co(o)mb, cor, cord, coss, coulumb, cran, crith, cubit, cumec, curie, cusec, cyathus, daraf, Debye (unit), degree, demy, dessiatine, digit, dirham, dra(ch)m, dyne, ell, em, en, epha(h), erg, farad, faraday, fathom, fermium, firkin, firlot, foot, fother, fou, furlong, gal, gallon, gerah, gilbert, gill, grain, gram, hectare, henry, hertz, hin, hogshead, homer, hoppus foot, hundredweight, inch, joule, kaneh, kantar, kelvin, k(h)at, kilderkin, kin, knot, league, leaguer, li, liang, liard, ligne, link, lippy, lire lisp(o)und, liter, log, lux, maneh, maund, meter, mho, micrometer, micron, mile, mil(l), mina, minim, minute, mna, modius, mole, morgen, muid, mutchkin, nail, neper, nepit, newton, nit (information), nit

units of measurement *continued*

(luminance), noggin, obol, oersted, ohm, oke, omer, ounce, oxgang, parasang, pascal, peck, perch, picul, pin, pint, pipe, poise, pole, pood, pound, poundal, quart, quarter, quartern, quintal, quire, radian, ream, rem, rod, rood, rote, rotolo, run(d)let, rutherford, sabin, s(a)eculum, sazhen, scruple, second, seer, semuncia, shekel, shippound, siemens, sievert, sone, span, square, stadium, steradian, stere, stilb, stoke(s), stone, tael, talent, tare, tesla, therm, tical, tierce, tod, toise, tola, ton, tonne, tonneau, tor, truss, tun, vara, verst, virgate, volt, watt, weber, wey, yard, yardland, yojan.

vehicles aerotrain, air-car, amtrack, araba, arba, aroba, automobile, barouche, Bath chair, berlin(e), bicycle, biga, bobsled, bobsleigh, bogie, boneshaker, brake, britzka, brougham, bubble-car, buckboard, buckcart, buck-wagon, buggy, bus, cab, caboose, cabriolet, caisson, calash, camper, caravan, caravanette, caroche, car(r)iole, carry-all, catafalque, chair, chaise, chaise-cart, chapel cart, charabanc, chariot, clarence, coach, convertible, conveyance, cycle, dandy-cart, dandy-horse, dennet, désobligeante, dhooly, diesel, diligence, dilly, Dodgem(s)®, dog-cart, dogcart, dolly, doolie, dormitory-car, drag, dray, dros(h)ky, duck, ekka, fiacre, fly, fork-lift truck, four-in-hand, gharri, gig, glass-coach, go-kart, Green Goddess, gyrocar, gyrodyne, hack, hackery, hackney-carriage/coach, hatchback, herdic, honey-cart, honey-wagon, hurley-hacket, ice-yacht, inside-car, jeep, jingle, jinricksha(w), jitney, juggernaut, kago, kajawah, kart, kibitka, landau, landaulet(te), limousine, litter, lorry, mail-cart, minibus, monorail, motor caravan, motor-bicycle, motor-bike, motor-bus, motor-car, motor-coach, motor-cycle, motor-lorry, motor-scooter, norimon, omnibus, outside-car, palanquin (palankeen), palki, pantechnicon, pedal cycle, pedicab, people mover, phaeton, pick-up, pill-box, pincers, post-chaise, prairie schooner, pulka, quadriga, rail-bus, rail-car, rail-motor, ricksha(w), roadster, rockaway, runabout, safety bicycle, saloon-car, saloon-carriage, scooter, sedan, sedan-chair, shandry(dan), shooting-brake, sidecar, single-decker, skateboard, ski-bob, sled, sledge, sleeper, sleeping-car, sleeping-carriage, sleeping-coach, sleigh, slip-carriage, slip-coach, slipe, snowmobile, snow-plow, sociable, solo, speedster, spider, spring-carriage, spring-cart, squad car, stage-coach, stage-wagon, stanhope, station-wagon, steam-car, steam-carriage, steamer, steam-roller, stillage, stone boat, straddle carrier, street-car, sulky, surrey, tally-ho, tandem, tank, tank-car, tank-engine, tanker, tank-wagon, tarantas(s), tartana, tax(ed)-cart, taxi, taxicab, T-cart, telega, telpher, tender, thoroughbrace, through-train, tilbury, tim-whisk(e)y, tin Lizzie, tip, tip-cart, tipper, toboggan, tonga, tourer, touring-car, tractor, trailer, train, tram, tramway-car, transporter, transport-rider, trap, tricar, tricycle, trike, triplet, trishaw, troika, trolley, trolley-bus, trolley-car, troop-carrier, truck, tube, tumble-car(t), tumbrel, turbocar, two-

vehicles *continued*
    decker, twoseater, two-wheeler, velocipede, vettura, victoria, village cart, vis-à-vis, volante, wagon, wagonette, wagon-lit, wain, water-cart, water-wagon, weasel, wheelbarrow, wheel-chair, whisk(e)y, Whitechapel cart.

vessels, ships argosy, barca, barque, barquentine, bateau, bawley, Berthon-boat, bilander, billyboy, bireme, birlinn, boat, bomb-ketch, bomb-vessel, brig, brigantine, Bucentaur, budgerow, bum-boat, buss, butty, cabin cruiser, caique, canal-boat, canoe, caravel, Carley float, carrack, casco, cat, catamaran, catboat, clipper, coaster, cob(b)le, cockboat, cockleshell, cog, collier, commodore, coracle, corocore, corvette, cot, crare, crayer, currach, cutter, dandy, deep-sinker, destroyer, d(h)ow, dinghy, diving-bell, dogger, drake, dreadnought, dredger, drog(h)er, dromond, dugout, East-Indiaman, E-boat, faltboat, felucca, flatboat, floating battery, flyboat, flying bridge, fore-and-after, frigate, frigatoon, funny, gabbart, galleass, galleon, galley, gal(l)iot, gallivat, gay-you, geordie, gondola, grab, hatch-boat, herringer, hooker, hovercraft, hoy, hydrofoil, hydroplane, hydrovane, ice-boat, Indiaman, iron-clad, jigger, jollyboat, junk, kayak, ketch, koff, laker, landing-craft, lapstreak, launch, liberty-ship, lighter, line-of-battle-ship, liner, long-boat, longship, lorcha, lugger, lymphad, mackinaw, masoolah, merchantman, mistico, monitor, monkey-boat, monohull, monoxylon, montaria, motor-boat, motor-launch, motor-ship, motoscafo, mud-boat, mudscow, multihull, nacelle, nuggar, outrigger, packet, packet-boat, packet-ship, pair-oar, patamar, pedalo, penteconter, periagua, peter-boat, pink, pinkie, pinky, pinnace, piragua, pirogue, pleasure-boat, pocket battleship, polacca, polacre, pontoon, powerboat, praam, pra(h)u, pram, privateer, puffer, pulwar, punt, puteli, quadrireme, quinquereme, randan, razee, river-boat, river-craft, row-barge, row-boat, rowing-boat, saic, sail-boat, sailing-boat, sailing-ship, salmon-coble, sampan, schooner, schuit, scooter, scow, scull, sculler, sea-boat, seaplane-carrier, settee, shallop, ship, ship-of-the-line, shore-boat, show-boat, skiff, sloop, sloop-of-war, smack, smuggler, snow, speed-boat, speedster, square rigger, steamboat, steamer, steam-launch, steam-packet, steamship, steam-tug, steam-vessel, steam-yacht, stern-wheeler, stew-can, sub, submarine, super-Dreadnought, supertanker, surface-craft, surf-board, surf-boat, surf-canoe, surfing-board, swamp boat, tanker, tartane(e), tender, tern, three-decker, three-master, tilt-boat, torpedo-boat, torpedo-boat destroyer, track-boat, tracker, trader, train ferry, tramp, transport-ship, trawler, trek-schuit, triaconter, trimaran, trireme, troop-carrier, trooper, troop-ship, tub, tug, tug-boat, turbine-steamer, turret-ship, two-decker, two-master, U-boat, umiak, vaporetto, vedette(-boat), vessel, wager-boat, warship, water-bus, well-boat, well-smack, whaleboat, whaler, wherry, whiff, windjammer, xebec, yacht, yawl, zabra.

weapons, armor A-bomb, ack-ack, aerodart, ailette, air rifle, amusette, an(e)lace, arbalest, arblast, Archibald, Archie, arcubalist, armet, arquebus(e), baldric(k), ballista, ballistic missile, bandolier, Bangalore torpedo, basilisk, baton gun, bazooka, beaver, bill, Biscayan, blackjack, blowgun, blowpipe, bludgeon, blunderbuss, boarding-pike, bodkin, Bofors gun, bolas, bomb, bombard, boomerang, bowie knife, brassard, breastplate, breech-loader, Bren(gun), bricole, brigandine, broadsword, brown Bess, brown bill, buckler, buckshot, bulldog, bullet, bundook, burganet, byrnie, caltrop, cannon, carbine, carronade, casque, cataphract, catapult, chain-armor, chain-mail, chamfrain, Chassepot, chausses, cheval-de-frise, chokebore, claymore, cluster-bomb, coal-box, co(e)horn, Colt, Congreve, corium, dag, dagger, dah, Damascus blade, Damascus sword, demi-cannon, demi-culverin, demi-lance, depth-bomb, depth-charge, dirk, dragoon, elephant gun, épée, escopette, Exocet®, express rifle, falchion, falconet, field gun, fire-arm, fire-arrow, firebomb, firelock, firepot, fission bomb, flail, flame-thrower, flick-knife, flintlock, foil, fougade, fougasse, four-pounder, fusee, fusil, Garand rifle, gatling-gun, gavelock, genouillère, gisarme, gladius, gorget, grapeshot, greave, Greek fire, grenade, gun, habergeon, hackbut, hacqueton, hailshot, halberd, half-pike, hand-grenade, hand-gun, han(d)jar, handstaff, harquebus, hauberk, H-bomb, heaume, helm, helmet, hielaman, howitzer, jack, jamb(e), jazerant, jesserant, Jethart staff, kris, lamboys, lame, lance, Lochaber-axe, Long Tom, machete, machine-gun, mangonel, martel, Martini(-Henry), matchlock, Mauser, Maxim(-gun), mesail, Mills bomb, Mills grenade, mine, mine-thrower, mini-rocket launcher, minnie, mitrailleur, mitrailleuse, morgenstern, morglay, morning-star, mor(r)ion, mortar, musket, musketoon, nulla-nulla, oerlikon, panga, partisan, pauldron, pavis(e), peasecod-cuirass, pederero, pelican, pelta, perrier, petrary, petronel, pickelhaube, pike, pilum, pistol, pistolet, placket, plastron, plate-armor, pocket-pistol, poitrel, pole-ax(e), poleyn, pompom, poniard, potgun, quarter-staff, queen's-arm, rapier, rerebrace, rest, revolver, rifle, rifle-grenade, sabaton, saber, saker, sallet, saloon-pistol, saloon-rifle, sap, sarbacane, schiavone, schläger, scimitar, scorpion, scutum, serpentine, sharp, shell, shield, shillela(g)h, shortsword, shotgun, shrapnel, siege-artillery, siege-gun, siege-piece, singlestick, six-gun, six-shooter, skean(dhu), sling, slung-shot, small-arm, small-sword, smoke-ball, smoke-bomb, snickersnee, spadroon, sparth(e), spear, spear gun, splint-armor, spontoon, spring-gun, squid, steel, sten gun, Sterling, stern-chaser, stiletto, stone axe, stone-bow, stylet, submachine-gun, sumpit(an), switch-blade (knife), swivel-gun, sword, sword bayonet, sword-cane, sword-stick, tace, targe, target, taslet, tasse, tasset, testudo, three-pounder, threshel, throw-stick, time-bomb, toc emma, toggle-iron, tomahawk, tomboc, tommy-gun, tormentum, torpedo, tortoise, trecento, trench-mortar, trident, truncheon, tuille, tuillette, tulwar, turret-gun, twibill, vambrace, vamplate, V-bomb, visor, vou(l)ge, war-wolf, waster, water-cannon, water-pistol, Welsh hook, white-arm, Winchester (rifle), wind-gun, wo(o)mera(ng), yatag(h)an, zumbooruk.

wine-bottle sizes baby, balthasar, jeroboam, magnum, Methuselah, nebuchadnezzar, nip, rehoboam, Salmanazar.

zodiac signs Aquarius, Aries, Cancer, Capricorn, Gemini, Leo, Libra, Pisces, Sagittarius, Scorpio, Taurus, Virgo.

Words listed by suffix

-**ast** chiliast, diaskeuast, dicast, dikast, dynast, ecclesiast, ecdysiast, elegiast, encomiast, enthusiast, fantast, gymnasiast, gymnast, Hesychast, hypochondriast, iconoclast, idoloclast, metaphrast, orgiast, pancratiast, paraphrast, pederast, peltast, phantasiast, pleonast, scholiast, utopiast.

-**aster** criticaster, grammaticaster, medicaster, philosophaster, poetaster, politicaster, theologaster.

-**cide** aborticide, acaricide, algicide, aphicide, aphidicide, bacillicide, bactericide, biocide, deicide, ecocide, ethnocide, feticide, filicide, foeticide, fratricide, fungicide, genocide, germicide, giganticide, herbicide, homicide, infanticide, insecticide, larvicide, liberticide, matricide, menticide, molluscicide, ovicide, parasiticide, parasuicide, parricide, patricide, pesticide, prolicide, regicide, rodenticide, sororicide, spermicide, suicide, taeniacide, trypanocide, tyrannicide, uxoricide, vaticide, verbicide, vermicide, viricide, viticide, vulpicide, weedicide,

-**cracy** aristocracy, autocracy, bureaucracy, chrysocracy, cottonocracy, democracy, demonocracy, despotocracy, dollarocracy, doulocracy, dulocracy, ergatocracy, Eurocracy, gerontocracy, gynecocracy, hagiocracy, hierocracy, isocracy, kakistocracy, meritocracy, millocracy, mobocracy, monocracy, nomocracy, ochlocracy, pantisocracy, pedantocracy, physiocracy, plantocracy, plutocracy, plutodemocracy, pornocracy, ptochocracy, slavocracy, snobocracy, squattocracy, stratocracy, technocracy, thalassocracy, thalattocracy, theocracy, timocracy.

-**crat** aristocrat, autocrat, bureaucrat, cosmocrat, democrat, hierocrat, meritocrat, millocrat, mobocrat, monocrat, ochlocrat, pantisocrat, pedantocrat, physiocrat, plutocrat, slavocrat, stratocrat, technocrat, theocrat.

-cratic aristocratic, autocratic, bureaucratic, cosmocratic, democratic, Eurocratic, gerontocratic, gynecocratic, hierocratic, isocratic, meritocratic, mobocratic, monocratic, ochlocratic, pancratic, pantisocratic, pedantocratic, physiocratic, plutocratic, stratocratic, technocratic, theocratic, timocratic, undemocratic.

-cultural accultural, agricultural, arboricultural, crinicultural, cultural, floricultural, horticultural, piscicultural, subcultural, vinicultural, vocicultural.

-culture agriculture, apiculture, aquaculture, aquiculture, arboriculture, aviculture, culture, electroculture, floriculture, horticulture, mariculture, monoculture, ostreiculture, pisciculture, pomiculture, self-culture, sericiculture, sericulture, silviculture, stirpiculture, subculture, sylviculture, viniculture, viticulture, water-culture, zooculture.

-cyte athrocyte, cyte, erythrocyte, fibrocyte, gonocyte, granulocyte, hemocyte, leucocyte, lymphocyte, macrocyte, microcyte, oocyte, phagocyte, poikilocyte, spermatocyte, thrombocyte, thymocyte.

-dom Anglo-Saxondom, apedom, archdukedom, attorneydom, babeldom, babudom, bachelordom, beadledom, beggardom, birthdom, bishopdom, boredom, Bumbledom, chiefdom, Christendom, clerkdom, cockneydom, crippledom, cuckoldom, czardom, demirepdom, devildom, Dogberrydom, dolldom, dufferdom, dukedom, dancedom, earldom, enthraldom, fairydom, fandom, filmdom, flunkeydom, fogydom, freedom, fresherdom, Greekdom, gypsydom, halidom, heathendom, heirdom, hobbledehoydom, hobodom, junkerdom, kaiserdom, kingdom, kitchendom, leechdom, liegedom, mandom, martyrdom, masterdom, newspaperdom, noodledom, noveldom, officialdom, overfreedom, penny-wisdom, popedom, princedom, puppydom, puzzledom, Quakerdom, queendom, queerdom, rascaldom, rebeldom, sachemdom, saintdom, savagedom, Saxondom, scoundreldom, serfdom, sheikdom, sheikhdom, sheriffdom, Slavdom, spinsterdom, squiredom, stardom, subkingdom, swelldom, thanedom, thraldom, thralldom, topsyturvydom, tsardom, underkingdom, unwisdom, villadom, whoredom, wisdom, Yankeedom.

-ferous aluminiferous, amentiferous, antenniferous, argentiferous, auriferous, bacciferous, balsamiferous, bulbiferous, calciferous, carboniferous, celliferous,

-ferous *continued*

celluliferous, cheliferous, cobaltiferous, conchiferous, coniferous, coralliferous, corniferous, cruciferous, culmiferous, cupriferous, cupuliferous, diamantiferous, diamondiferous, doloriferous, dorsiferous, ferriferous, flagelliferous, flammiferous, floriferous, foraminiferous, fossiliferous, frondiferous, fructiferous, frugiferous, furciferous, garnetiferous, gemmiferous, glandiferous, glanduliferous, globuliferous, glumiferous, granuliferous, guaniferous, gummiferous, guttiferous, lactiferous, laniferous, laticiferous, lethiferous, luciferous, luminiferous, mammaliferous, mammiferous, manganiferous, manniferous, margaritiferous, melliferous, metalliferous, morbiferous, mortiferous, moschiferous, muciferous, nectariferous, nickeliferous, nubiferous, nuciferous, odoriferous, oleiferous, omniferous, ossiferous, oviferous, ovuliferous, ozoniferous, papilliferous, papuliferous, Permo-Carboniferous, pestiferous, petaliferous, petroliferous, piliferous, platiniferous, plumbiferous, polliniferous, pomiferous, poriferous, proliferous, pyritiferous, quartziferous, reptiliferous, resiniferous, rotiferous, sacchariferous, saliferous, salutiferous, sanguiferous, sebiferous, seminiferous, septiferous, siliciferous, soboliferous, somniferous, soporiferous, spiniferous, spinuliferous, splendiferous, staminiferous, stanniferous, stelliferous, stigmatiferous, stoloniferous, strombuliferous, styliferous, sudoriferous, tentaculiferous, thuriferous, titaniferous, tuberiferous, umbelliferous, umbriferous, unfossiliferous, uriniferous, vitiferous, vociferous, yttriferous, zinciferous, zinkiferous.

-gamy allogamy, apogamy, autogamy, bigamy, chalazogamy, chasmogamy, cleistogamy, clistogamy, cryptogamy, deuterogamy, dichogamy, digamy, endogamy, exogamy, geitonogamy, hercogamy, herkogamy, heterogamy, homogamy, hypergamy, isogamy, misogamy, monogamy, oogamy, pangamy, pantagamy, plasmogamy, plastogamy, polygamy, porogamy, siphonogamy, syngamy, trigamy, xenogamy, zoogamy.

-genesis abiogenesis, agamogenesis, anthropogenesis, autogenesis, biogenesis, blastogenesis, carcinogenesis, chondrogenesis, cytogenesis, diagenesis, diplogenesis, dynamogenesis, ectogenesis, electrogenesis, embryogenesis, epeirogenesis, epigenesis, gametogenesis, gamogenesis, hematogenesis, heterogenesis, histogenesis, homogenesis, hylogenesis, hypogenesis, merogenesis, metagenesis, monogenesis, morphogenesis, mythogenesis, neogenesis, noogenesis, ontogenesis, oogenesis, organogenesis, orogenesis, orthogenesis, osteogenesis, palingenesis, pangenesis, paragenesis, parthenogenesis, pathogenesis, pedogenesis, perigenesis, petrogenesis, phylogenesis, phytogenesis, polygenesis, psychogenesis, pyogenesis, schizogenesis,

-genesis *continued*
spermatogenesis, sporogenesis, syngenesis, thermogenesis, xenogenesis.

-genic aesthesiogenic, allergenic, androgenic, anthropogenic, antigenic, biogenic, blastogenic, carcinogenic, cariogenic, cryogenic, dysgenic, ectogenic, electrogenic, endogenic, epeirogenic, erogenic, erotogenic, eugenic, genic, glycogenic, hallucinogenic, histogenic, hypnogenic, hysterogenic, iatrogenic, lactogenic, lysigenic, mammogenic, mutagenic, myogenic, neurogenic, odontogenic, oestrogenic, oncogenic, ontogenic, orogenic, orthogenic, osteogenic, pathogenic, photogenic, phytogenic, polygenic, psychogenic, pyogenic, pyrogenic, pythogenic, radiogenic, rhizogenic, saprogenic, schizogenic, somatogenic, spermatogenic, telegenic, teratogenic, thermogenic, tumorgenic, tumorigenic, visiogenic, zoogenic, zymogenic.

-gon chiliagon, decagon, dodecagon, endecagon, enneagon, hendecagon, heptagon, hexagon, isogon, nonagon, octagon, pentagon, perigon, polygon, tetragon, trigon.

-gram airgram, anagram, anemogram, angiogram, audiogram, ballistocardiogram, barogram, cablegram, calligram, cardiogram, cartogram, centigram, centimeter-gram, chromatogram, chromogram, chronogram, cryptogram, dactylogram, decagram, decigram, dendrogram, diagram, echogram, electrocardiogram, electroencephalogram, encephalogram, engram, epigram, ergogram, ferrogram, harmonogram, hectogram, hexagram, hierogram, histogram, hologram, ideogram, indicator-diagram, isogram, kilogram, lexigram, lipogram, logogram, lymphogram, marconigram, marigram, meteorogram, microgram, monogram, myogram, nanogram, nephogram, neurogram, nomogram, organogram, oscillogram, pangram, paragram, parallelogram, pentagram, phonogram, photogram, phraseogram, pictogram, program, psychogram, pyelogram, radiogram, radiotelegram, röntgenogram, scintigram, seismogram, sialogram, skiagram, sociogram, spectrogram, spectroheliogram, sphenogram, sphymogram, steganogram, stereogram, tachogram, telegram, tephigram, tetragram, thermogram, tomogram, trigram.

-graph Addressograph®, airgraph, allograph, anemograph, apograph, audiograph, autograph, autoradiograph, ballistocardiograph, bar-graph, barograph, biograph, cardiograph, cathodograph, cerograph, chirograph, choreograph, chromatograph, chromolithograph, chromoxylograph, chronograph, cinematograph, coronagraph,

-graph *continued*

coronograph, cryptograph, cyclograph, cymagraph, cymograph, diagraph, Dictograph®, digraph, dynamograph, eidograph, electrocardiograph, electroencephalograph, electrograph, electromyograph, ellipsograph, encephalograph, epigraph, ergograph, evaporograph, flannelgraph, glyphograph, harmonograph, hectograph, helicograph, heliograph, hierograph, hodograph, holograph, homograph, hydrograph, hyetograph, hyetometrograph, hygrograph, ideograph, idiograph, jellygraph, keraunograph, kinematograph, kinetograph, kymograph, lithograph, logograph, magnetograph, marconigraph, marigraph, meteorograph, micrograph, microphotograph, microseismograph, mimeograph, monograph, myograph, nephograph, nomograph, odograph, odontograph, oleograph, opisthograph, orthograph, oscillograph, pantograph, paragraph, pentagraph, phonautograph, phonograph, photograph, photolithograph, photomicrograph, phototelegraph, photozincograph, phraseograph, pictograph, planigraph, plethysmograph, polygraph, pseudograph, psychograph, pyrophotograph, radioautograph, radiograph, radiometeorograph, radiotelegraph, rotograph, seismograph, salenograph, serigraph, shadowgraph, skiagraph, spectrograph, spectroheliograph, sphygmograph, spirograph, steganograph, stenograph, stereograph, Stevengraph, stylograph, syngraph, tachograph, tachygraph, Telautograph®, telegraph, telephotograph, thermograph, thermometrograph, tomograph, torsiograph, trigraph, vectograph, vibrograph, xylograph, zincograph.

-graphy

aerography, ampelography, angiography, anthropogeography, anthropography, areography, autobiography, autography, autoradiography, autotypography, ballistocardiography, bibliography, biogeography, biography, brachygraphy, cacography, calligraphy, cardiography, cartography, cathodography, ceramography, cerography, chalcography, chartography, chirography, cholangiography, choregraphy, choreography, chorography, chromatography, chromolithography, chromotypography, chromoxylography, chronography, cinematography, cinemicrography, climatography, cometography, cosmography, cryptography, crystallography, dactyliography, dactylography, demography, dermatography, dermography, discography, dittography, doxography, echocardiography, ectypography, electrocardiography, electroencephalography, electrography, electromyography, electrophotography, encephalography, enigmatography, epigraphy, epistolography, ethnography, ferrography, filmography, geography, glossography, glyphography, glyptography, hagiography, haplography, heliography, heresiography, hierography, historiography, holography, horography, hydrography, hyetography, hymnography, hypsography, ichnography, ichthyography, iconography, ideography, lexicography, lexigraphy, lipography,

-graphy *continued*

lithography, logography, lymphography, mammography, metallography, microcosmography, micrography, microphotography, mimography, monography, morphography, myography, mythography, nomography, nosography, oceanography, odontography, oleography, opisthography, orchesography, oreography, organography, orography, orthography, osteography, paleogeography, paleography, paleontography, pantography, paroemiography, pasigraphy, pathography, petrography, phonography, photography, photolithography, photomicrography, phototelegraphy, photoxylography, photozincography, physiography, phytogeography, phytography, pictography, polarography, polygraphy, pornography, prosopography, pseudepigraphy, pseudography, psychobiography, psychography, pterylography, pyelography, pyrography, pyrophotography, radiography, radiotelegraphy, reprography, rhyparography, röntgenography, scenography, scintigraphy, seismography, selenography, serigraphy, sialography, snobography, spectrography, sphygmography, steganography, stenography, stereography, stratigraphy, stylography, symbolography, tachygraphy, telautography, telegraphy, telephotography, thalassography, thanatography, thaumatography, thermography, tomography, topography, typography, ultrasonography, uranography, urography, ventriculography, xerography, xeroradiography, xylography, xylopyrography, xylotypography, zincography, zoogeography, zoography.

-graphical autobiographical, bathygraphical, bathyorographical, bibliographical, biobibliographical, biogeographical, biographical, cacographical, calligraphical, cartographical, cerographical, chorographical, cinematographical, climatographical, cosmographical, geographical, glossographical, graphical, hagiographical, hierographical, historiographical, hydrographical, hyetographical, hygrographical, ichnographical, ideographical, lexicographical, lexigraphical, lithographical, logographical, monographical, myographical, oceanographical, oreographical, orographical, orthographical, paleographical, paleontographical, pantographical, paragraphical, pasigraphical, petrographical, photographical, physiographical, prosopographical, pseudepigraphical, psychobiographical, psychographical, pterylographical, seismographical, selenographical, spectrographical, stenographical, stereographical, stratigraphical, tachygraphical, topographical, typographical, xylographical, zincographical, zoogeographical, zoographical.

-hedron chiliahedron, decahedron, dihedron, dodecahedron, enneahedron, hemihedron, hexahedron, holohedron, icosahedron, icositetrahedron,

-hedron *continued*

leucitohedron, octahedron, octohedron, pentahedron, polyhedron, pyritohedron, rhombohedron, scalenohedron, tetrahedron, tetrakishexahedron, trapezohedron, triakisoctahedron, trihedron, trisoctahedron.

-hood adulthood, angelhood, apehood, apprenticehood, babyhood, bachelorhood, beadlehood, beasthood, bountihood, boyhood, brotherhood, cathood, childhood, Christhood, companionhood, cousinhood, cubhood, deaconhood, dollhood, drearihood, elfhood, fairyhood, falsehood, fatherhood, flapperhood, flesh-hood, gawkihood, gentlehood, gentlemanhood, gianthood, girlhood, godhood, hardihood, high-priesthood, hobbledehoyhood, hoghood, hoydenhood, idlehood, invalidhood, jealoshood, kinghood, kinglihood, knighthood, ladyhood, likelihood, livelihood, lustihood, maidenhood, maidhood, manhood, masterhood, matronhood, misshood, monkhood, motherhood, nationhood, needy-hood, neighborhood, novicehood, nunhood, old-maidhood, orphanhood, pagehood, parenthood, popehood, priesthood, princehood, prophethood, puppyhood, queenhood, sainthood, selfhood, serfhood, sisterhood, spinsterhood, squirehood, statehood, swinehood, tabbyhood, thanehood, thinghood, traitorhood, unlikelihood, virginhood, waiterhood, widowerhood, widowhood, wifehood, wivehood, womanhood, youthhood.

-iac ammoniac, amnesiac, anaphrodisiac, anglomaniac, Anglophobiac, antaphrodisiac, anthomaniac, aphasiac, aphrodisiac, archgenethliac, bacchiac, bibliomaniac, cardiac, celiac, Cluniac, coprolaliac, demoniac, dextrocardiac, Dionysiac, dipsomaniac, dochmiac, dysthymiac, egomaniac, elegiac, endocardiac, erotomaniac, etheromaniac, Genesiac, genethliac, hebephreniac, heliac, hemophiliac, hypochondriac, iliac, insomniac, intracardiac, Isiac, kleptomaniac, maniac, megalomaniac, meloncholiac, melomaniac, monomaniac, morphinomaniac, mythomaniac, necrophiliac, neurastheniac, nymphomaniac, opsomaniac, orchidomaniac, Pandemoniac, paradisiac, paranoiac, paraphiliac, paroemiac, pedophiliac, pericardiac, phrenesiac, pyromaniac, sacroiliac, scopophiliac, scoriac, simoniac, symposiac, Syriac, theomaniac, theriac, timbromaniac, toxiphobiac, zodiac, zygocardiac.

-iatric chemiatric, chemopsychiatric, geriatric, hippiatric, kinesiatric, pediatric, psychiatric, psychogeriatric.

-iatry chemopsychiatry, geriatry, hippiatry, neuropsychiatry, orthopsychiatry, pediatry, podiatry, psychiatry.

-ician academician, acoustician, aeroelastician, aesthetician, arithmetician, audiometrician, beautician, biometrician, clinician, cosmetician, diagnostician, dialectician, dietician, econometrician, ekistician, electrician, geometrician, geopolitician, geriatrician, informatician, linguistician, logician, logistician, magician, magnetician, mathematician, mechanician, metaphysician, metrician, mortician, musician, obstetrician, optician, pediatrician, patrician, Paulician, phonetician, physician, politician, practician, psychogeriatrician, psychometrician, rhetorician, rubrician, statistician, systematician, tactician, technician, theoretician.

-ics acoustics, acrobatics, aerobatics, aerobics, aerodynamics, aeronautics, aerostatics, aesthetics, agogics, agnostics, ambisonics, apologetics, aquabatics, aquanautics, astrodynamics, astronautics, astrophysics, athletics, atmospherics, autonomics, avionics, axiomatics, ballistics, bioastronautics, biodynamics, bioethics, biomathematics, biomechanics, biometrics, bionics, bionomics, biophysics, biorhythmics, biosystematics, cacogenics, calisthenics, callisthenics, catacoustics, catallactics, cataphonics, catechetics, catoptrics, ceroplastics, chemotherapeutics, chrematics, chromatics, civics, cliometrics, conics, cosmonautics, cosmopolitics, cryogenics, cryonics, cryophysics, cybernetics, cytogenetics, deontics, dermatoglyphics, diacoustics, diagnostics, dialectics, dianetics, didactics, dietetics, dioptrics, dogmatics, dramatics, dynamics, dysgenics, eclectics, econometrics, economics, ecumenics, ekistics, electrodynamics, electrokinetics, electromechanics, electronics, electrostatics, electrotechnics, electrotherapeutics, electrothermics, energetics, entoptics, environics, epigenetics, epistemics, epizootics, ergonomics, ethics, ethnolinguistics, eudaemonics, eudemonics, eugenics, eurhythmics, euthenics, exegetics, floristics, fluidics, forensics, genetics, geodetics, geodynamics, geophysics, geopolitics, geoponics, geostatics, geotectonics, geriatrics, gerontotherapeutics, glyptics, gnomonics, gnotobiotics, graphemics, graphics, gyrostatics, halieutics, haptics, harmonics, hedonics, hermeneutics, hermetics, hippiatrics, histrionics, homiletics, hydraulics, hydrodynamics, hydrokinetics, hydromagnetics, hydromechanics, hydroponics, hydrostatics, hydrotherapeutics, hygienics, hypersonics, hysterics, informatics, irenics, isagogics, isometrics, kinematics, kinesics, kinetics, linguistics, lithochromatics, liturgics, logistics, loxodromics, macrobiotics, macroeconomics, magnetics, magneto-hydrodynamics, magneto-optics, maieutics, mathematics, mechanics, melodics, metalinguistics, metamathematics, metaphysics, metapsychics, meteoritics, microeconomics, microelectronics, microphysics, mnemotechnics, mole-electronics, monostrophics, morphemics, morphophonemics, nautics, nucleonics, numismatics, obstetrics, olympics, onomastics, optics, optoelectronics, orchestics, orthodontics, orthodromics, orthogenics, orthopedics,

-ics *continued*

orthoptics, orthotics, paideutics, pantopragmatics, paralinguistics, party-politics, pataphysics, patristics, pedagogics, pedentics, pediatrics, pedodontics, peptics, periodontics, pharmaceutics, pharmacodynamics, pharmacokinetics, phelloplastics, phonemics, phonetics, phonics, phonocamptics, phonotactics, photics, photochromics, photoelectronics, phototherapeutics, photovoltaics, physics, physiotherapeutics, plastics, pneumatics, pneumodynamics, polemics, politico-economics, politics, power-politics, problematics, prosthetics, prosthodontics, psychics, psychodynamics, psychogeriatrics, psycholinguistics, psychometrics, psychonomics, psychophysics, psychosomatics, psychotherapeutics, pyrotechnics, quadraphonics, quadrophonics, radionics, radiophonics, radiotherapeutics, rhythmics, robotics, semantics, semeiotics, semiotics, Semitics, sferics, significs, sociolinguistics, sonics, sophistics, spherics, sphragistics, statics, stereoptics, strategics, stylistics, subatomics, subtropics, syllabics, symbolics, synectics, systematics, tactics, technics, tectonics, telearchics, thaumaturgics, theatrics, therapeutics, thermionics, thermodynamics, thermotics, toponymics, toreutics, transonics, transsonics, ultrasonics, vitrics, zoiatrics, zootechnics, zymotechnics.

-iform

aciform, acinaciform, aciniform, aeriform, alphabetiform, amoebiform, anguiform, anguilliform, antenniform, asbestiform, auriform, aviform, bacciform, bacilliform, biform, bursiform, cactiform, calcariform, calceiform, calyciform, cambiform, campaniform, campodeiform, cancriform, capriform, cauliform, cerebriform, cirriform, claviform, clypeiform, cobriform, cochleariform, coliform, colubriform, conchiform, coniform, coralliform, cordiform, corniform, corolliform, cotyliform, crateiform, cribriform, cristiform, cruciform, cteniform, cubiform, cucumiform, culiciform, cultriform, cumuliform, cuneiform, curviform, cyathiform, cylindriform, cymbiform, cystiform, deiform, dendriform, dentiform, digitiform, dolabriform, elytriform, ensiform, equisetiform, eruciform, falciform, fibriform, filiform, flabelliform, flagelliform, floriform, fringilliform, fungiform, fusiform, gangliform, gasiform, glandiform, granitiform, granuliform, hydatidiform, incisiform, infundibuliform, insectiform, janiform, jelliform, lamelliform, lanciform, lapilliform, larviform, lentiform, limaciform, linguiform, lumbriciform, lyriform, malleiform, mamilliform, mammiform, maniform, medusiform, mitriform, monadiform, moniliform, morbilliform, multiform, mummiform, muriform, mytiliform,, napiform, natiform, naupliiform, nubiform, omniform, oviform, paliform, panduriform, papilliform, patelliform, pelviform, penicilliform, penniform, perciform, phialiform, piliform, pisciform, pisiform, placentiform, planuliform, plexiform, poculiform, proteiform, pulvilliform, pyriform, quadriform, radiciform, raduliform, raniform, reniform, restiform, retiform, sacciform, sagittiform, salpiform, scalariform, scalpelliform, scalpriform,

140

-iform *continued*

scoleciform, scolopendriform, scutiform, scyphiform, securiform, septiform, serpentiform, spiniform, spongiform, squamiform, stalactiform, stalactitiform, stelliform, stratiform, strigiform, strobiliform, strombuliform, styliform, tauriform, tectiform, telescopiform, thalliform, triform, tuberiform, tubiform, tympaniform, umbraculiform, unciform,unguiform, uniform, vaporiform, variform, vasculiform, vasiform, vermiform, verruciform, versiform, villiform, viperiform, vitriform, vulviform, ypsiliform, zeolitiform.

-ism abnormalism, abolitionism, aboriginalism, absenteeism, absolutism, academicalism, academicism, accidentalism, achromatism, acosmism, acrobatism, acotism, actinism, activism, Adamitism, adiaphorism, adoptianism, Adopttionism, adventurism, aeroembolism, aerotropism, aestheticism, Africanism, ageism, agnosticism, agrarianism, Albigensianism, albinism, albinoism, alcoholism, algorism, alienism, allelomorphism, allotropism, alpinism, altruism, amateurism, Americanism, ametabolism, amoralism, amorism, amorphism, anabaptism, anabolism, anachronism, anagrammatism, anarchism, anastigmatism, androdioecism, andromonoecism, aneurism, Anglicanism, anglicism, Anglo-Catholicism, aniconism, animalism, animatism, animism, annihilationism, antagonism, anthropomorphism, anthropomorphitism, anthropopathism, anthropophuism, anthropopsychism, antichristianism, anticivism, anticlericalism, antidisestablishmentarianism, anti-federalism, anti-Gallicanism, anti-Jacobinism, antinomianism, antiochianism, antiquarianism, anti-Semitism, antisepticism, antisocialism, antitheism, antitrinitarianism, antivaccinationism, antivivisectionism, anythingarianism, apheliotropism, aphorism, apism, aplanatism, apochromatism, apogeotropism, apoliticism, Apollinarianism, apostolicism, apriorism, Arabism, Aramaism, Arcadianism, archaicism, archaism, Arianism, aristocratism, Aristotelianism, Aristotelism, Arminianism, asceticism, asepticism, Asiaticism, aspheterism, asteism, asterism, astigmatism, asynchronism, asystolism, atavism, atheism, athleticism, Atlanticism, atomism, atonalism, atropism, Atticism, attorneyism, Augustinianism, Australianism, authorism, authoritarianism, autism, autochthonism, autoeroticism, autoerotism, automatism, automobilism, automorphism, autotheism, avant-gardism, Averrhoism, Averroism, Baalism, Baathism, Ba'athism, Babbitism, Babeeism, babelism, Babiism, Babism, babuism, bacchanalianism, bachelorism, Baconianism, Bahaism, bantingism, baptism, barbarism, bashawism, bastardism, bathmism, bedlamism, behaviorism, Benthamism, Bergsonism, Berkeleianism, bestialism, betacism, biblicism, bibliophilism, bilateralism, bilingualism, bimetallism, bipedalism, blackguardism, blepharism, bogeyism, bogyism, Bohemianism, bolshevism, Bonapartism, bonism, boobyism, Boswellism, botulism, Bourbonism, bowdlerism, bradyseism,

-ism *continued*

braggartism, Brahmanism, Brahminism, Braidism, Briticism, Britishism, Brownism, bruxism, Buchmanism, Buddhism, bullyism, Burschenism, Byronism, Byzantinism, cabalism, cabbalism, Caesarism, caesaropapism, caffeinism, caffeism, Calvinism, cambism, Camorrism, cannibalism, capitalism, Carbonarism, careerism, Carlism, Carlylism, carnalism, Cartesianism, casualism, catabolism, catastrophism, catechism, catechumenism, Catharism, catheterism, catholicism, causationism, cauterism, cavalierism, Celticism, cenobitism, centenarianism, centralism, centripetalism, centrism, cerebralism, ceremonialism, chaldaism, characterism, charism, charlatanism, chartism, Chasidism, Chassidism, Chaucerism, chauvinism, chemism, chemotropism, chloralism, Christianism, chromaticism, churchism, Ciceronianism, cicisbeism, cinchonism, civisim, classicism, clericalism, cliquism, clubbism, coalitionism, Cobdenism, cocainism, cockneyism, collectivism, collegialism, colloquialism, colonialism, commensalism, commercialism, communalism, communism, compatriotism, comstockism, Comtism, conacreism, conceptualism, concettism, concretism, confessionalism, confrontationism, Confucianism, Congregationalism, conservatism, consortism, constitutionalism, constructionism, constructivism, consubstantialism, consumerism, contact-metamorphism, continentalism, contortionism, contrabandism, conventionalism, conversationism, convictism, copyism, corporatism, corporealism, corybantism, cosmeticism, cosmism, cosmopolitanism, cosmopolitism, cosmotheism, cottierism, Couéism, courtierism, creatianism, creationism, cretinism, cretism, criticism, crotalism, cubism, cultism, curialism, cyclicism, cynicism, czarism, Dadaism, Daltonism, dandyism, Darwinism, deaf-mutism, decimalism, defeatism, deism, demagogism, demagoguism, demoniacism, demonianism, demonism, denominationalism, departmentalism, descriptivism, depotism, deteriorism, determinism, deviationism, devilism, diabolism, diachronism, diageotropism, diaheliotropism, dialecticism, diamagnetism, diaphototropism, diastrophism, diatropism, dichroism, dichromatism, dichromism, diclinism, dicrotism, didacticism, diffusionism, dilettanteism, dilettantism, dimerism, dimorphism, diocism, diorism, diothelism, diphysitism, dirigism, dissenterism, dissolutionism, disyllabism, ditheism, ditheletism, dithelism, dithelitism, divisionism, Docetism, doctrinairism, doctrinarianism, Dogberryism, dogmatism, do-goodism, dolichocephalism, donatism, donnism, do-nothingism, Doricism, Dorism, dowdyism, draconism, dragonism, dramaticism, drudgism, druidism, dualism, dudism, dufferism, dunderheadism, dynamism, dyotheletism, dyothelism, dysphemism, ebionism, ebionitism, echoism, eclecticism, ecumenicalism, ecumenicism, ecumenism, Edwardianism, egalitarianism, egoism, egotheism, egotism, electromagnetism, electromerism, elementalism, elitism, Elizabethanism, embolism, emotionalism, empiricism, enantiomorphism, Encratism, encyclopedism, endemism, Englishism, entrism, environmentalism,

-ism *continued*

eonism, epicism, Epicureanism, epicurism, epiphenomenalism, epiphytism,
epipolism, episcopalianism, episcopalism, equalitarianism, equestrianism,
Erastianism, eremitism, erethism, ergotism, eroticism, erotism, erythrism,
escapism, esotericism, esoterism, Essenism, essentialism, etacism, etherism,
ethicism, ethnicism, ethnocentrism, eudemonism, eugenism, euhemerism,
eumerism, eunuchism, eunuchoidism, euphemism, euphuism, Eurocommunism,
Europeanism, evangelicalism, evangelicism, evangelism, evolutionism,
exclusionism, exclusivism, exhibitionism, existentialism, ex-librism, exorcism,
exotericism, exoticism, expansionism, experientialism, experimentalism,
expressionism, extensionalism, externalism, extremism, Fabianism, factionalism,
faddism, fairyism, fakirism, falangism, familism, fanaticism, fantasticism,
faradism, fascism, fatalism, Fauvism, favism, favoritism, Febronianism, federalism,
femininism, feminism, Fenianism, fetichism, fetishism, feudalism, feuilletonism,
fideism, fifth-monarchism, filibusterism, finalism, fissiparism, flagellantism,
flunkeyism, fogyism, formalism, fortuitism, Fourierism, fractionalism, Froebelism,
functionalism, fundamentalism, fusionism, futurism, gaelicism, Galenism,
Gallicanism, gallicism, galvanism, gamotropism, ganderism, gangsterism,
Gargantuism, gargarism, gargoylism, Gasconism, Gaullism, generationism,
Genevanism, genteelism, gentilism, geocentricism, geomagnetism, geophagism,
geotropism, Germanism, giantism, gigantism, Girondism, Gnosticism, Gongorism,
gormandism, Gothicism, gradualism, Graecism, grammaticism, Grangerism,
Grecism, gregarianism, griffinism, Grobianism, Grundyism, gynandrism,
gynandromophism, gynodioecism, gynomonoecism, gypsyism, gyromagnetism,
haptotropism, Hasidism, Hassidism, heathenism, Hebraicism, Hebrewism,
hectorism, hedonism, Hegelianism, hegemonism, heliotropism, Hellenism,
helotism, hemihedrism, hemimorphism, henotheism, hermaphroditism, heroism,
hetaerism, hetairism, heterochronism, heteroecism, heteromorphism, heterostylism,
heterothallism, heurism, Hibernianism, Hibernicism, hidalgoism, hierarchism,
highbrowism, High-Churchism, Hildebrandism, Hinduism, Hippocratism,
hispanicism, historicism, historism, histrionicism, histrionism, Hitlerism,
Hobbesianism, Hobbianism, Hobbism, hobbledehoyism, hobbyism, hobgoblinism,
hoboism, holism, holohedrism, holometabolism, holophytism, homeomorphism,
homoeroticism, homoerotism, homomorphism, homothallism, hooliganism,
hoydenism, humanism, humanitarianism, Humism, humoralism, hybridism,
hydrargyrism, hydrotropism, hylicism, hylism, hylomorphism, hylopathism,
hylotheism, hylozoism, hyperadrenalism, hyperbolism, hypercriticism,
hyperthyroidism, hyphenism, hypnotism, hypochondriacism, hypocorism,
hypognathism, hypothyroidism, Ibsenism, iconomaticism, iconophilism, idealism,
idiotism, idolism, illuminism, illusionism, imagism, immanentism, immaterialism,
immediatism, immersionism, immobilism, immoralism, imperialism, impossibilism,

-ism *continued*

impressionism, incendiarism, incivism, incorporealism, indeterminism, indifferentism, individualism, industrialism, infallibilism, infantilism, inflationism, Infralapsarianism, inquilinism, inspirationism, institutionalism, instrumentalism, insularism, insurrectionism, intellectualism, interactionism, internationalism, interventionism, intimism, intransigentism, intuitionalism, intuitionism, intuitivism, invalidism, iodism, Ionism, iotacism, irenicism, Irishism, irrationalism, irredentism, Irvingism, Islamism, ism, Ismailism, isochronism, isodimorphism, isolationism, isomerism, isomorphism, isotropism, itacism, Italianism, italicism, Jacobinism, Jacobitism, Jainism, Jansenism, Jesuitism, jingoism, jockeyism, Johnsonianism, Johnsonism, journalism, Judaism, junkerism, kaiserism, Kantianism, Kantism, katabolism, Kelticism, Keynesianism, klephtism, know-nothingism, Krishnaism, labdacism, labialism, laborism, laconicism, laconism, ladyism, Lamaism, Lamarckianism, Lamarckism, lambdacism, landlordism, Laodiceanism, larrikinism, lathyrism, Latinism, latitudinarianism, laxism, leftism, legalism, leggism, Leibnitzianism, Leibnizianism, Leninism, lesbianism, liberalism, liberationism, libertarianism, libertinism, lichenism, lionism, lipogrammatism, Listerism, literalism, literaryism, localism, Lollardism, Londonism, Low-Churchism, Luddism, luminarism, Lutheranism, Lutherism, lyricism, lyrism, Lysenkoism, macarism, Machiavellianism, Machiavellism, Magianism, Magism, magnetism, Magyarism, Mahdiism, Mahdism, maidism, malapropism, Malthusianism, mammonism, Manichaeism, Manicheanism, Manicheism, mannerism, Maoism, Marcionitism, Marinism, martialism, martinetism, Marxianism, Marxism, masochism, materialism, mathematicism, matriarchalism, maudlinism, Mazdaism, Mazdeism, McCarthyism, mechanism, medievalism, Medism, melanism, meliorism, memoirism, Mendelism, mentalism, mephitism, mercantilism, mercenarism, mercurialism, merism, merycism, mescalism, mesmerism, mesocephalism, mesomerism, Messianism, metabolism, metachronism, metamerism, metamorphism, metasomatism, metempiricism, meteorism, methodism, metopism, Micawberism, Michurinism, micro-organism, microseism, militarism, millenarianism, millenarism, millennianism, millenniarism, Miltonism, minimalism, minimism, misoneism, Mithraicism, Mithraism, mithridatism, modalism, moderatism, modernism, Mohammedanism, Mohammedism, Molinism, monachism, monadism, monarchianism, monarchism, monasticism, monergism, monetarism, mongolism, mongrelism, monism, monkeyism, monochromatism, monoecism, monogenism, monolingualism, monometallism, monophysitism, monorchism, monosyllabism, monotheism, monotheletism, monothelism, monothelitism, Monroeism, Montanism, moralism, Moravianism, Morisonianism, Mormonism, morphinism, mosaicism, Mosaism, Moslemism, mountebankism, multiracialism, Munichism, municipalism, Muslimism, mutism, mutualism, myalism, mysticism, mythicism, mythism, namby-pambyism, nanism,

-ism *continued*

Napoleonism, narcissism, narcotism, nationalism, nativism, naturalism, naturism, navalism, Nazaritism, Naziism, Nazism, necessarianism, necessitarianism, necrophilism, negativism, negroism, negrophilism, neoclassicism, neocolonialism, Neo-Darwinism, Neofascism, Neohellenism, Neo-Impressionism, Neo-Kantianism, Neo-Lamarckism, neologism, Neo-Malthusianism, neo-Nazism, neonomianism, neopaganism, neoplasticism, Neo-Plasticism, Neoplatonism, Neopythagoreanism, neoterism, neovitalism, nephalism, Nestorianism, neuroticism, neutralism, newspaperism, nicotinism, Nietzscheanism, nihilism, noctambulism, Noetianism, nomadism, nominalism, nomism, northernism, notaphilism, nothingarianism, nothingism, Novatianism, novelism, nudism, nyctitropism, obeahism, obeism, obiism, objectivism, obscurantism, obsoletism, Occamism, occasionalism, Occidentalism, occultism, Ockhamism, odism, odylism, officialism, old-maidism, onanism, onirocriticism, Ophism, Ophitism, opportunism, optimism, Orangeism, Orangism, organicism, organism, Orientalism, Origenism, Orleanism, orphanism, Orphism, orthognathism, orthotropism, ostracism, ostrichism, Owenism, pacificism, pacifism, Paddyism, paganism, paleomagnetism, palladianism, paludism, panaesthetism, Pan-Africanism, Pan-Americanism, Pan-Arabian, panchromatism, pancosmism, panderism, panegoism, Pan-Germanism, Panhellenism, panislamism, panlogism, panpsychism, pansexualism, Pan-Slavism, pansophism, panspermatism, panspermism, Pantagruelism, pantheism, papalism, papism, parabaptism, parachronism, paragnathism, paraheliotropism, parallelism, paralogism, paramagnetism, paramorphism, parapsychism, parasitism, Parkinsonism, parliamentarism, Parnassianism, Parnellism, parochialism, Parseeism, Parsiism, Parsism, partialism, particularism, partyism, passivism, pasteurism, pastoralism, paternalism, patrialism, patriarchalism, patriarchism, patriotism, Patripassianism, patristicism, Paulinism, pauperism, pedagogism, pedagoguism, pedanticism, pedantism, pedestrianism, pedobaptism, pedomorphism, Pelagianism, pelmanism, pelorism, pennalism, penny-a-linerism, pentadactylism, pentamerism, pentaprism, peonism, perfectibilism, perfectionism, peripateticism, perpetualism, Persism, personalism, perspectivism, pessmism, petalism, Petrarchianism, Petrarchism, Petrinism, phagocytism, phalansterianism, phalansterism, phallicism, phallism, pharisaism, phariseeism, pheism, phenakism, phenomenalism, phenomenism, philhellenism, philistinism, philosophism, phobism, phoneticism, phonetism, phosphorism, photism, photochromism, photoperiodism, phototropism, physicalism, physicism, physitheism, pianism, pietism, piezomagnetism, Pindarism, Pittism, plagiarism, plagiotropism, Platonicism, Platonism, plebeianism, pleiotropism, pleochroism, pleomorphism, plumbism, pluralism, Plutonism, Plymouthism, pococuranteism, pococurantism, poeticism, pointillism, polonism, polychroism, polycrotism, polydactylism, polygenism, polymastism, polymerism, polymorphism, polynomialism, polysyllabicism,

-ism *continued*

polysynthetism, polytheism, Pooterism, populism, porism, Porphyrogenitism, positivism, possibilism, Post-Impressionism, post-millennialism, Poujadism, Powellism, practicalism, pragmatism, precisianism, predestinarianism, predeterminism, preferentialism, preformationism, prelatism, premillenarianism, premillennialism, Pre-Raphaelism, Pre-Raphaelitism, Presbyterianism, presentationism, preternaturalism, prettyism, priapism, priggism, primitivism, primordialism, probabiliorism, probablism, prochronism, professionalism, prognathism, progressionism, progressism, progressivism, prohibitionism, proletarianism, propagandism, prophetism, prosaicism, prosaism, proselytism, prostatism, prosyllogism, protectionism, Protestantism, proverbialism, provincialism, prudentialism, Prussianism, psellism, psephism, pseudo-archaism, pseudoclassicism, pseudomorphism, psilanthropism, psychism, psychologism, psychopannychism, psychoticism, ptyalism, puerilism, pugilism, puppyism, purism, puritanism, Puseyism, pyrrhonism, Pythagoreanism, Pythagorism, Quakerism, quattrocentism, quietism, quixotism, rabbinism, Rabaelaisianism, racemism, Rachmanism, racialism, racism, radicalism, Ramism, ranterism, rascalism, rationalism, reactionarism, realism, rebaptism, Rebeccaism, Rechabitism, recidivism, red-tapism, reductionism, reformism, regalism, regionalism, reincarnationism, relationism, relativism, religionism, Rembrandtism, representationalism, representationism, republicanism, restitutionism, restorationism, resurrectionism, reunionism, revanchism, revisionism, revivalism, revolutionism, rheotropism, rheumatism, rhopalism, rhotacism, Ribbonism, rigorism, ritualism, Romanism, romanticism, Rosicrucianism, Rosminianism, Rotarianism, routinism, rowdyism, royalism, ruffianism, ruralism, Russianism, Russophilism, Sabaism, Sabbatarianism, sabbatism, Sabellianism, Sabianism, sacerdotalism, sacramentalism, sacramentarianism, Sadduceeism, Sadducism, sadism, sado-masochism, saintism, Saint-Simonianism, Saint-Simonism, Saivism, Saktism, salvationism, Samaritanism, sanitarianism, sansculottism, sapphism, saprophytism, Saracenism, satanism, saturnism, Saxonism, schematism, scholasticism, scientism, sciolism, Scotism, Scotticism, scoundrelism, scribism, scripturalism, scripturism, secessionism, sectarianism, sectionalism, secularism, self-criticism, self-hypnotism, selfism, semi-Arianism, semi-barbarism, Semi-Pelagianism, Semitism, sensationalism, sensationism, sensism, sensualism, sensuism, sentimentalism, separatism, serialism, servilism, servo-mechanism, sesquipedalianism, sexism, sexualism, Shaivism, shakerism, Shaktism, shamanism, shamateurism, Shiism, Shintoism, Shivaism, shunamitism, sigmatism, Sikhism, simplism, sinapism, sinecurism, singularism, Sinicism, Sinophilism, Sivaism, skepticism, Slavism, snobbism, socialism, Socinianism, sociologism, Sofism, solarism, solecism, sol-faism, solidarism, solidism, solifidianism, solipsism, somatism, somnambulism, somniloquism, sophism, southernism, sovietism,

-ism *continued*

specialism, speciesism, Spencerianism, Spinozism, spiritism, spiritualism, spoonerism, spread-eagleism, Stahlianism, Stahlism, Stakhanovism, Stalinism, stand-pattism, statism, stercoranism, stereoisomerism, stereotropism, stibialism, stigmatism, stoicism, strabism, structuralism, strychninism, strychnism, Stundism, subjectivism, sublapsarianism, subordinationism, substantialism, suburbanism, suffragism, Sufiism, Sufism, suggestionism, supernationalism, supernaturalism, superrealism, Supralapsarianism, supremacism, suprematism, surrealism, sutteeism, Swadeshism, swarajism, Swedenborgianism, swingism, sybaritism, sybotism, syllabism, syllogism, symbolism, symphilism, synaposematism, synchronism, syncretism, syndactylism, syndicalism, synecdochism, synergism, synoecism, syntheticism, Syriarcism, Syrianism, systematism, tachism, tactism, Tammanyism, tantalism, Tantrism, Taoism, tarantism, Tartuffism, Tartufism, tautochronism, tautologism, tautomerism, teetotalism, teleologism, tenebrism, teratism, terminism, territorialism, terrorism, tetramerism, tetratheism, Teutonicism, Teutonism, textualism, thanatism, thaumaturgism, theanthropism, theatricalism, theatricism, theism, theomorphism, Theopaschitism, theophilanthropism, theosophism, therianthropism, theriomorphism, thermotropism, thigmotropism, Thomism, thrombo-embolism, thuggism, tigerism, Timonism, Titanism, Titoism, toadyism, tokenism, Toryism, totalitarianism, totemism, tourism, tractarianism, trade-unionism, traditionalism, Traducianism, traitorism, transcendentalism, transformism, transmigrationism, transsexualism, tranvestism, tranvestitism, traumatism, trialism, tribadism, tribalism, trichroism, trichromatism, tricrotism, triliteralism, trimorphism, Trinitarianism, trinomialism, tripersonalism, tritheism, triticism, trituberculism, trivialism, troglodytism, troilism, trophotropism, tropism, Trotskyism, truism, tsarism, tuism, Turcophilism, tutiorism, tutorism, tychism, ultra-Conservatism, ultraism, ultramontanism, undenominationalism, unicameralism, unidealism, uniformitarianism, unilateralism, unionism, unitarianism, unversalism, unrealism, unsectarianism, unsocialism, untuism, uranism, utilitarianism, utopianism, utopism, Utraquism, vagabondism, Valentinianism, valetudinarianism, vampirism, vandalism, Vansittartism, Vaticanism, Vedism, veganism, vegetarianism, ventriloquism, verbalism, verism, vernacularism, Victorianism, vigilantism, vikingism, virilism, virtualism, vitalism, viviparism, vocalism, vocationalism, volcanism, Voltaireanism, Voltairianism, Voltairism, voltaism, voltinism, voluntarism, voluntaryism, voodooism, vorticism, voyeurism, vulcanism, vulgarism, vulpinism, vulturism, Wagnerianism, Wagnerism, Wahabiism, Wahabism, welfarism, werewolfism, Wertherism, werwolfism, Wesleyanism, westernism, Whiggism, wholism, witticism, Wodenism, Wolfianism, xanthochroism, Yankeeism, yogism, zanyism, Zarathustrianism, Zarathustrism, zealotism, Zionism, Zoilism, zoism, Zolaism, zombiism, zoomagnetism, zoomorphism, zoophilism, zootheism, Zoroastrianism, Zwinglianism, zygodactylism, zygomorphism.

-itis adenitis, antiaditis, aortitis, appendicitis, arteritis, arthritis, balanitis, blepharitis, bronchitis, bursitis, carditis, cellulitis, cephalitis, ceratitis, cerebritis, cholecystitis, colitis, conchitis, conjunctivitis, crystallitis, cystitis, dermatitis, diaphragmatitis, diphtheritis, diverticulitis, duodenitis, encephalitis, endocarditis, endometritis, enteritis, fibrositis, gastritis, gastroenteritis, gingivitis, glossitis, hamarthritis, hepatitis, hysteritis, ileitis, iritis, keratitis, labyrinthitis, laminitis, laryngitis, lymphangitis, mastitis, mastoiditis, meningitis, metritis, myelitis, myocarditis, myositis, myringitis, nephritis, neuritis, onychitis, oophoritis, ophthalmitis, orchitis, osteitis, osteo-arthritis, osteomyelitis, otitis, ovaritis, panarthritis, pancreatitis, panophthalmitis, papillitis, parotiditis, parotitis, pericarditis, perigastritis, perihepatitis, perinephritis, perineuritis, periostitis, peritonitis, perityphlitis, pharnygitis, phlebitis, phrenitis, pleuritis, pneumonitis, poliomyelitis, polyneuritis, proctitis, prostatitis, pyelitis, pyelonephritis, rachitis, rectitis, retinitis, rhachitis, rhinitis, rhinopharyngitis, salpingitis, scleritis, sclerotitis, sinuitis, splenitis, spondylitis, staphylitis, stomatitis, strumitis, synovitis, syringitis, thrombo-phlebitis, thyroiditis, tonsilitis, tonsillitis, tracheitis, trachitis, tympanitis, typhlitis, ulitis, ureteritis, urethritis, uteritis, uveitis, uvulitis, vaginitis, valvulitis, vulvitis.

-latrous bibliolatrous, heliolatrous, ichthyolatrous, idolatrous, litholatrous, Mariolatrous, Maryolatrous, monolatrous, ophiolatrous, zoolatrous.

-latry angelolatry, anthropolatry, astrolatry, autolatry, bardolatry, bibliolatry, Christolatry, cosmolatry, demonolatry, dendrolatry, ecclesiolatry, epeolatry, geolatry, hagiolatry, heliolatry, hierolatry, ichthyolatry, iconolatry, idolatry, litholatry, lordolatry, Mariolatry, Maryolatry, monolatry, necrolatry, ophiolatry, physiolatry, plutolatry, pylolatry, symbololatry, thaumatolatry, theriolatry, zoolatry.

-logical aerobiological, aerological, aetiological, agrobiological, agrological, agrostological, algological, alogical, amphibological, analogical, anthropological, arachnological, archaeological, astrological, atheological, audiological, autecological, axiological, bacteriological, batological, battological, biological, bryological, campanological, carcinological, cartological, chorological, Christological, chronological, climatological, codicological, conchological, cosmological, craniological, cryobiological, cryptological, cytological, demonological, dendrological, deontological, dermatological, dysteleological, ecclesiological, ecological, Egyptological, electrophysiological, embryological, enological, entomological, epidemiological, epistemological, eschatological,

-logical *continued*

ethnological, ethological, etymological, futurological, gastrological, gemmological, gemological, genealogical, genethlialogical, geochronological, geological, geomorphological, gerontological, glaciological, glossological, gnotobiological, graphological, gynecological, hagiological, helminthological, hepaticological, herpetological, histological, histopathological, homological, horological, hydrobiological, hydrological, ichthyological, ideological, illogical, immunological, laryngological, limnological, lithological, logical, malacological, mammalogical, martyrological, metapsychological, meteorological, micrological, mineralogical, monological, morphological, musicological, mycological, myological, myrmecological, mythological, necrological, neological, nephological, nephrological, neurological, nomological, nosological, nostological, oceanological, odontological, ontological, ophiological, ophthalmological, oreological, ornithological, orological, osteological, paleontological, paleozoological, palynological, parapsychological, pathological, pedological, penological, pestological, petrological, phenological, phenomenological, philological, phonological, phraseological, phrenological, phycological, physiological, phytological, phytopathological, pneumatological, pomological, posological, potamological, protozoological, psephological, psychobiological, psychological, radiological, reflexological, rheumatological, rhinological, scatological, sedimentological, seismological, selenological, serological, Sinological, sociobiological, sociological, somatological, soteriological, Sovietological, spectrological, speleological, stoechiological, stoicheiological, stoichiological, synecological, tautological,technological, teleological, teratological, terminological, theological, topological, toxicological, traumatological, trichological, tropological, typological, unlogical, untheological, urological, virological, volcanological, vulcanological, zoological, zoophytological, zymological.

-logous analogous, antilogous, dendrologous, heterologous, homologous, isologous, tautologous.

-logue apologue, collogue, decalogue, dialogue, duologue, eclogue, epilogue, grammalogue, homologue, idealogue, ideologue, isologue, monologue, philologue, prologue, Sinologue, theologue, travelogue, trialogue.

-logy acarology, aerobiology, aerolithology, aerology, aetiology, agriology, agrobiology, agrology, agrostology, algology, amphibology, anesthesiology, analogy, andrology, anemology, angelology, anthology, anthropobiology, anthropology,

149

-logy *continued*

antilogy, apology, arachnology, archaeology, archology, aristology, Assyriology, astrogeology, astrology, atheology, atmology, audiology, autecology, autology, axiology, bacteriology, balneology, batology, battology, bibliology, bioecology, biology, biotechnology, brachylogy, bryology, bumpology, cacology, caliology, campanology, carcinology, cardiology, carphology, cartology, cetology, cheirology, chirology, choreology, chorology, Christology, chronobiology, chronology, cine-biology, climatology, codicology, cometology, conchology, coprology, cosmetology, cosmology, craniology, criminology, cryobiology, cryptology, cytology, dactyliology, dactylology, deltiology, demology, demonology, dendrochronology, dendrology, deontology, dermatology, diabology, diabolology, dialectology, diplomatology, dittology, docimology, dogmatology, dosiology, dosology, doxology, dyslogy, dysteleology, ecclesiology, eccrinology, ecology, edaphology, Egyptology, electrobiology, electrology, electrophysiology, electrotechnology, elogy, embyology, emmenology, endemiology, endocrinology, enology, entomology, enzymology, epidemiology, epistemology, escapology, eschatology, ethnology, ethnomusicology, ethology, Etruscology, etymology, euchology, eulogy, exobiology, festilogy, festology, folk-etymology, futurology, gastroenterology, gastrology, gemmology, gemology, genealogy, genethlialogy, geochronology, geology, geomorphology, gerontology, gigantology, glaciology, glossology, glottology, gnomonology, gnoseology, gnosiology, gnotobiology, graphology, gynecology, hematology, hagiology, hamartiology, haplology, heliology, helminthology, heorology, hepaticology, hepatology, heresiology, herpetology, heterology, hierology, hippology, histiology, histology, histopathology, historiology, homology, hoplology, horology, hydrobiology, hydrogeology, hydrology, hydrometeorology, hyetology, hygrology, hymnology, hypnology, ichnology, ichthyology, iconology, ideology, immunology, insectology, irenology, kidology, kinesiology, koniology, Kremlinology, laryngology, lepidopterology, lexicology, lichenology, limnology, lithology, liturgiology, macrology, malacology, malariology, mammalogy, Mariology, martyrology, Maryology, Mayology, menology, metapsychology, meteorology, methodology, microbiology, microclimatology, micrology, micro-meteorology, microtechnology, mineralogy, misology, monadology, monology, morphology, muscology, museology, musicology, mycetology, mycology, myology, myrmecology, mythology, necrology, nematology, neology, nephology, nephrology, neurobiology, neurohypnology, neurology, neuropathology, neurophysiology, neuroradiology, neurypnology, nomology, noology, nosology, nostology, numerology, numisatology, oceanology, odontology, olfactology, oncology, onirology, ontology, oology, ophiology, ophthalmology, optology, orchidology, oreology, ornithology, orology, orthopterology, oryctology, osteology, otolaryngology, otology, otorhinolaryngology, ourology, paleanthropology, paleethnology, paleichthyology, paleoclimatology, paleolimnology, paleontology, paleopelology, paleophytology, paleozoology,

-logy *continued*

palillogy, palynology, pantheology, papyrology, paradoxology, paralogy, parapsychology, parasitology, paroemiology, pathology, patrology, pedology, pelology, penology, periodontology, perissology, pestology, petrology, phenology, pharmacology, pharyngology, phenology, phenomenology, philology, phonology, photobiology, photogeology, phraseology, phrenology, phycology, physiology, phytology, phytopathology, planetology, plutology, pneumatology, prodology, pomology, ponerology, posology, potamology, primatology, protistology, protozoology, psephology, pseudology, psychobiology, psychology, psychopathology, psychophysiology, pteridology, pyretology, pyroballogy, radiobiology, radiology, reflexology, rheology, rheumatology, rhinology, röntgenology, sacrology, satanology, scatology, Scientology, sedimentology, seismology, selenology, selenomorphology, semasiology, semeiology, semiology, serology, sexology, sindonology, Sinology, sitiology, sitology, skatology, sociobiology, sociology, somatology, soteriology, spectrology, speleology, sphagnology, sphygmology, spongology, stichology, stoechiology, stoichiology, stomatology, storiology, symbology, symbolology, symptomatology, synchronology, synecology, syphilology, systematology, tautology, technology, teleology, teratology, terminology, terotechnology, tetralogy, thanatology, theology, thermology, therology, thremmatology, timbrology, tocology, tokology, topology, toxicology, traumatology, tribology, trichology, trilogy, trophology, tropology, typhlology, typology, ufology, uranology, urbanology, urinology, urology, venereology, vexillology, victimology, vinology, virology, volcanology, vulcanology, xylology, zoopathology, zoophytology, zoopsychology, zymology.

-lysis analysis, atmolysis, autocatalysis, autolysis, bacteriolysis, catalysis, cryptanalysis, cytolysis, dialysis, electroanalysis, electrolysis, hematolysis, hemodialysis, hemolysis, histolysis, hydrolysis, hypno-analysis, leucocytolysis, microanalysis, nacro-analysis, neurolysis, paralysis, photolysis, plasmolysis, pneumatolysis, proteolysis, psephoanalysis, psychoanalysis, pyrolysis, radiolysis, thermolysis, uranalysis, urinalysis, zincolysis, zymolysis.

-lytic analytic, anxiolytic, autocatalytic, autolytic, bacteriolytic, catalytic, dialytic, electrolytic, hemolytic, histolytic, hydrolytic, paralytic, photolytic, plasmolytic, pneumatolytic, proteolytic, psychoanalytic, pyrolytic, sympatholytic, tachylytic, thermolytic, unanalytic.

-mania acronymania, anglomania, anthomania, balletomania, bibliomania, Celtomania, demonomania, dipsomania, egomania, enomania, erotomania, etheromania, francomania, gallomania, hydromania, hypomania, hysteromania, Keltomania, kleptomania, mania, megalomania, melomania, methomania, metromania, monomania, morphinomania, mythomania, nostomania, nymphomania, opsomania, orchidomania, petalomania, phyllomania, potichomania, pteridomania, pyromania, squandermania, theatromania, theomania, timbromania, toxicomania, tulipomania, typomania, xenomania.

-mancy aeromancy, axinomancy, belomancy, bibliomancy, botanomancy, capnomancy, cartomancy, ceromancy, chiromancy, cleromancy, coscinomancy, crithomancy, crystallomancy, dactyliomancy, enomancy, gastromancy, geomancy, gyromancy, hieromancy, hydromancy, lampadomancy, lithomancy, myomancy, necromancy, nigromancy, omphalomancy, oniromancy, onychomancy, ornithomancy, pyromancy, rhabdomancy, scapulimancy, spodomancy, tephromancy, theomancy, zoomancy.

-mantic chiromantic, geomantic, hydromantic, myomantic, necromantic, ornithomantic, pyromantic, scapulimantic, spodomantic, theomantic, zoomantic.

-mathic chrestomathic, philomathic, polymathic.

-mathy chrestomathy, opsimathy, philomathy, polymathy.

-meter absorptiometer, accelerometer, acidimeter, actinometer, aerometer, alcoholometer, alkalimeter, altimeter, ammeter, anemometer, areometer, arithmometer, atmometer, audiometer, auxanometer, auxometer, barometer, bathometer, bathymeter, bolometer, bomb-calorimeter, calorimeter, cathetometer, centimeter, chlorimeter, chlorometer, chronometer, clinometer, colorimeter, Comptometer®, coulombmeter, coulometer, craniometer, cryometer, cyanometer, cyclometer, decelerometer, declinometer, dendrometer, densimeter, densitometer, diagometer, diameter, diaphanometer, diffractometer, dimeter, dose-meter, dosimeter, drosometer, dynamometer, effusiometer, electrodynamometer, electrometer, endosmometer, enometer, ergometer, eriometer, evaporimeter, extensimeter, extensometer, fathometer, flowmeter, fluorimeter, fluorometer, focimeter, galactometer, galvanometer, gas-meter, gasometer, geometer,

-meter *continued*

geothermometer, goniometer, gradiometer, gravimeter, harmonometer, heliometer, heptameter, hexameter, hodometer, hydrometer, hyetometer, hygrometer, hypsometer, iconometer, inclinometer, interferometer, isoperimeter, katathermometer, konimeter, kryometer, lactometer, luxmeter, lysimeter, machmeter, magnetometer, manometer, mekometer, meter, micrometer, microseismometer, mileometer, milometer, monometer, nephelometer, Nilometer, nitrometer, octameter, odometer, ohmmeter, ombrometer, oncometer, ophthalmometer, opisometer, opsiometer, optometer, osmometer, oximeter, pachymeter, parameter, passimeter, pedometer, pelvimeter, pentameter, perimeter, permeameter, phonmeter, phonometer, photometer, piezometer, planimeter, planometer, plessimeter, pleximeter, pluviometer, pneumatometer, polarimeter, potentiometer, potometer, psychometer, psychrometer, pulsimeter, pulsometer, pycnometer, pyknometer, pyrheliometer, pyrometer, quantometer, radiogoniometer, radiometer, radiotelemeter, refractometer, rheometer, rhythmometer, saccharimeter, saccharometer, salimeter, salinometer, scintillometer, sclerometer, seismometer, semi-diameter, semiperimeter, sensitometer, slot-meter, solarimeter, spectrophotometer, speedometer, spherometer, sphygmomanometer, sphygmometer, stactometer, stalagometer, stereometer, strabismometer, strabometer, swingometer, sympiesometer, tacheometer, tachometer, tachymeter, taseometer, tasimeter, taximeter, telemeter, tellurometer, tetrameter, thermometer, Tintometer®, tonometer, torque-meter, tribometer, trigonometer, trimeter, trocheameter, trochometer, tromometer, udometer, urinometer, vaporimeter, variometer, viameter, vibrometer, viscometer, viscosimeter, voltameter, voltmeter, volumenometer, volumeter, volumometer, water-barometer, water-meter, water-thermometer, wattmeter, wavemeter, weathermeter, xylometer, zymometer, zymosimeter.

-metry acidimetry, aerometry, alcoholometry, alkalimetry, anemometry, anthropometry, areometry, asymmetry, barometry, bathymetry, biometry, bolometry, calorimetry, chlorimetry, chlorometry, chronometry, clinometry, colorimetry, coulometry, craniometry, densimetry, densitometry, dissymmetry, dosimetry, dynamometry, electrometry, galvanometry, gasometry, geometry, goniometry, gravimetry, hodometry, horometry, hydrometry, hygometry, hypsometry, iconometry, interferometry, isometry, isoperimetry, micrometry, microseismometry, nephelometry, noometry, odometry, ophthalometry, optometry, pelvimetry, perimetry, photometry, planimetry, plessimetry, pleximetry, polarimetry, pseudosymmetry, psychometry, psychrometry, pyrometry, saccharimetry, seismometry, sociometry, spectrometry, spectrophotometry, spirometry, stalagmometry, stereometry, stichometry, stoechiometry,

-metry *continued*
stoichiometry,symmetry, tacheometry, tachometry, tachymetry, telemetry, tensiometry, thermometry, trigonometry, unsymmetry, uranometry, viscometry, viscosimetry, zoometry.

-monger balladmonger, barber-monger, borough-monger, carpetmonger, cheese-monger, costardmonger, costermonger, fellmonger, fishmonger, flesh-monger, gossip-monger, ironmonger, lawmonger, love-monger, maxim-monger, meal-monger, miracle-monger, mystery-monger, newsmonger, panic-monger, peace-monger, pearmonger, peltmonger, phrasemonger, place-monger, prayer-monger, relic-monger, scandalmonger, scaremonger, sensation-monger, species-monger, starmonger, state-monger,
system-monger, verse-monger, warmonger, whoremonger, wit-monger, wonder-monger.

-morphic actinomorphic, allelomorphic, allotriomorphic, anamorphic, anthropomorphic, automorphic, biomorphic, dimorphic, ectomorphic, enantiomorphic, endomorphic, ergatomorphic, gynandromorphic, hemimorphic, heteromorphic, homeomorphic, homomorphic, hylomorphic, idiomorphic, isodimorphic, isomorphic, lagomorphic, mesomorphic, metamorphic, monomorphic, morphic, ophiomorphic, ornithomorphic, paramorphic, pedomorphic, perimorphic, pleomorphic, polymorphic, protomorphic, pseudomorphic, tetramorphic, theomorphic, theriomorphic, trimorphic, xenomorphic, xeromorphic, zoomorphic, zygomorphic.

-morphous amorphous, anamorphous, anthropomorphous, dimorphous, enantiomorphous, gynandromorphous, heteromorphous, homeomorphous, homomorphous, isodimorphous, isomorphous, lagomorphous, mesomorphous, monomorphous, ophiomorphous, perimorphous, pleomorphous, polymorphous, pseudomorphous, rhizomorphous, tauromorphous, theriomorphous, trimorphous, xeromorphous, zygomorphous.

-onym acronym, anonym, antonym, autonym, cryptonym, eponym, exonym, heteronym, homonym, metonym, paronym, polyonym, pseudonym, synonym, tautonym, toponym, trionym.

onymic acronymic, Hieronymic, homonymic, matronymic, metonymic, metronymic, patronymic, polyonymic, synonymic, toponymic.

osis abiosis, acidosis, actinobacillosis, actinomycosis, aerobiosis, aeroneurosis, alkalosis, amaurosis, amitosis, anabiosis, anadiplosis, anamorphosis, anaplerosis, anastomosis, anchylosis, anerobiosis, ankylosis, anthracosis, anthropomorphosis, antibiosis, apodosis, aponeurosis, apotheosis, arteriosclerosis, arthrosis, asbestosis, aspergillosis, ateleiosis, atherosclerosis, athetosis, autohypnosis, avitaminosis, bacteriosis, bagassosis, bilharziosis, biocoenosis, bromhidrosis, bromidrosis, brucellosis, byssinosis, carcinomatosis, carcinosis, chlorosis, cirrhosis, coccidiosis, cyanosis, cyclosis, dermatosis, diarthrosis, diorthosis, diverticulosis, dulosis, ecchymosis, enantiosis, enarthrosis, endometriosis, endosmosis, enosis, enteroptosis, epanadiplosis, epanorthosis, exosmosis, exostosis, fibrosis, fluorosis, furunculosis, gliomatosis, gnotobiosis, gomphosis, gummosis, halitosis, hallucinosis, heliosis, hematosis, heterosis, hidrosis, homeosis, homomorphosis, homozygosis, hydronephrosis, hyperhidrosis, hyperidrosis, hyperinosis, hypersacosis, hypervitaminosis, hypinosis, hypnosis, hypotyposis, ichthyosis, kenosis, keratosis, ketosis, kurtosis, kyllosis, kyphosis, leishmaniosis, leptospirosis, leucocytosis, limosis, lipomatosis, lordosis, madarosis, marmarosis, meiosis, melanosis, metachrosis, metamorphosis, metempsychosis, miosis, mitosis, molybdosis, mononucleosis, monosis, morphosis, mucoviscidosis, mycosis, mycotoxicosis, myosis, myxomatosis, narcohypnosis, narcosis, necrobiosis, necrosis, nephroptosis, nephrosis, neurosis, onychocryptosis, ornithosis, osmidrosis, osmosis, osteoarthrosis, osteoporosis, otosclerosis, parabiosis, paraphimosis, parapsychosis, parasitosis, pedamorphosis, pediculosis, phagocytosis, phimosis, pholidosis, phytosis, pneumoconiosis, pneumokoniosis, pneumonokoniosis, pneumonoultramicroscopicsilicovolcanoconiosis, pollenosis, polyposis, porosis, proptosis, psilosis, psittacosis, psychoneurosis, psychosis, pterylosis, ptilosis, ptosis, pyrosis, resinosis, salmonellosis, sarcoidosis, sarcomatosis, sclerosis, scoliosis, self-hypnosis, siderosis, silicosis, sorosis, spirillosis, spirochetosis, steatosis, stegnosis, stenosis, strongylosis, sycosis, symbiosis, symptosis, synarthrosis, synchrondrosis, syndesmosis, synociosis, synostosis, syntenosis, syssarcosis, thanatosis, theriomorphosis, thrombosis, thylosis, thyrotoxicosis, torulosis, toxoplasmosis, trichinosis, trichophytosis, trichosis, trophobiosis, trophoneurosis, tuberculosis, tylosis, ulosis, urosis, virosis, visceroptosis, xerosis, zoonosis, zygosis, zymosis.

path allopath, homeopath, kinesipath, naturopath, neuropath, osteopath, psychopath, sociopath, telepath.

-pathic allopathic, anthropopathic, antipathic, empathic, homoeopathic, hydropathic, idiopathic, kinesipathic, naturopathic, neuropathic, osteopathic, protopathic, psychopathic, sociopathic, telepathic.

-pathy allopathy, anthropopathy, antipathy, apathy, cardiomyopathy, dyspathy, empathy, enantiopathy, homeopathy, hydropathy, idiopathy, kinesipathy, myocardiopathy, naturopathy, neuropathy, nostopathy, osteopathy, psychopathy, sociopathy, sympathy, telepathy, theopathy, zoopathy.

-phage bacteriophage, macrophage, ostreophage, xylophage.

-phagous anthropophagous, autophagous, carpophagous, coprophagous, creophagous, endophagous, entomophagous, exophagous, geophagous, hippophagous, hylophagous, ichthyophagous, lithophagous, mallophagous, meliphagous, monophagous, myrmecophagous, necrophagous, omophagous ophiophagous, ostreophagous, pantophagous, phyllophagous, phytophagous, polyphagous, rhizophagous, saprophagous, sarcophagous, scatophagous, theophagous, toxicophagous, toxiphagous, xylophagous, zoophagous.

-phagy anthropophagy, autophagy, coprophagy, dysphagy, endophagy, entomophagy, exophagy, hippophagy, ichthyophagy, monophagy, mycophagy, omophagy, ostreophagy, pantophagy, polyphagy, sacrophagy, scatophagy, theophagy, xerophagy.

-phile ailurophile, arctophile, audiophile, bibliophile, cartophile, discophile, enophile francophile, gallophile, Germanophile, gerontophile, halophile, hippophile, homophile, iodophile, lyophile, myrmecophile, necrophile, negrophile, ombrophile, pedophile, psammophile, Russophile, scripophile, Sinophile, Slavophile, spermophile, thermophile, Turcophile, xenophile, zoophile.

-philia ailurophilia, anglophilia, canophilia, coprophilia, ephebophilia, Germanophilia, gerontophilia, hemophilia, necrophilia, paraphilia, pedophilia, scopophilia, scoptophilia, zoophilia.

-philist bibliophilist, canophilist, cartophilist, Dantophilist, enophilist, iconophilist, negrophilist, notaphilist, ophiophilist, pteridophilist, Russophilist, scripophilist, stegophilist, timbrophilist, zoophilist.

-phily acarophily, anemophily, bibliophily, cartophily, enophily, entomophily, halophily, hydrophily, myrmecophily, necrophily, notaphily, ornithophily, photophily, scripophily, Sinophily, symphily, timbrophily, toxophily, xerophily.

-phobe ailurophobe, anglophobe, francophobe, gallophobe, Germanophobe, hippophobe, hygrophobe, lyophobe, negrophobe, ombrophobe, photophobe, Russophobe, Slavophobe, Turcophobe, xenophobe.

-phobia acrophobia, aerophobia, agoraphobia, ailurophobia, algophobia, anglophobia, astraphobia, astrapophobia, bathophobia, bibliophobia, canophobia, claustrophobia, cynophobia, dromophobia, ecophobia, ergophobia, gallophobia, hydrophobia, hypsophobia, monophobia, mysophobia, necrophobia, negrophobia, neophobia, nosophobia, nyctophobia, ochlophobia, panophobia, pantophobia, pathophobia, phonophobia, photophobia, Russophobia, satanophobia, scopophobia, sitiophobia, sitophobia, symmetrophobia, syphilophobia, taphephobia, taphophobia, thanatophobia, theophobia, toxicophobia, toxiphobia, triskaidecaphobia, triskaidekaphobia, xenophobia, zoophobia.

-phobic aerophobic, agoraphobic, anglophobic, claustrophobic, heliophobic, hydrophobic, lyophobic, monophobic, phobic, photophobic.

-phone aerophone, allophone, anglophone, Ansaphone®, audiphone, chordophone, detectophone, diaphone, dictaphone, diphone, earphone, Entryphone®, francophone, geophone, gramophone, harmoniphone, headphone, heckelphone, homophone, hydrophone, idiophone, interphone, kaleidophone, megaphone, metallophone, microphone, monotelephone, optophone, phone, photophone, Picturephone®, polyphone, pyrophone, radiogramophone, radiophone, radiotelephone, sarrusophone, saxophone, sousaphone, speakerphone, sphygmophone, stentorphone, telephone, theatrophone, triphone, vibraphone, videophone, videotelephone, viewphone, zylophone.

-phonic acrophonic, allophonic, anglophonic, antiphonic, aphonic, cacophonic, cataphonic, chordophonic, dodecaphonic, dysphonic, euphonic, gramophonic, homophonic, microphonic, monophonic, paraphonic, photophonic, quadraphonic, quadrophonic, radiophonic, stentorophonic, stereophonic, symphonic, telephonic, xylophonic.

-phony acrophony, antiphony, aphony, autophony, cacophony, colophony, dodecaphony, euphony, gramophony, homophony, laryngophony, monophony, photophony, polyphony, quadraphony, quadrophony, radiophony, radiotelephony, stereophony, symphony, tautophony, telephony.

-phorous discophorous, Eriophorous, galactophorous, hypophosphorous, mastigophorous, necrophorous, odontophorous, phosphorous, pyrophorous, rhynchophorous, sporophorous.

-phyte aerophyte, bryophyte, cormophyte, dermatophyte, ectophyte, endophyte, entophyte, epiphyte, gametophyte, geophyte, halophyte, heliophyte, heliosciophyte, holophyte, hydrophyte, hygrophyte, hylophyte, lithophyte, mesophyte, microphyte, neophyte, oophyte, osteophyte, phanerophyte, phreatophyte, protophyte, psammophyte, pteridophyte, saprophyte, schizophyte, spermaphyte, spermatophyte, spermophyte, sporophyte, thallophyte, tropophyte, xerophyte, zoophyte, zygophyte.

-saurus Allosaurus, Ankylosaurus, Apatosaurus, Atlantosaurus, brachiosaurus, brontosaurus, Ceteosaurus, Dolichosaurus, Ichthyosaurus, megalosaurus, Plesiosaurus, Stegosaurus, Teleosaurus, Titanosaurus, tyrannosaurus.

-scope aethrioscope, auriscope, baroscope, bathyscope, benthoscope, bioscope, bronchoscope, chromoscope, chronoscope, colposcope, cryoscope, cystoscope, dichrooscope, dichroscope, dipleidoscope, ebullioscope, electroscope, endoscope, engiscope, engyscope, epidiascope, episcope, fluoroscope, galvanoscope, gastroscope, gyroscope, hagioscope, helioscope, hodoscope, horoscope, hydroscope, hygroscope, iconoscope, iriscope, kaleidoscope, kinetoscope, koniscope, lactoscope, laparoscope, laryngoscope, lychnoscope, megascope, microscope, mutoscope, myringoscope, myrioscope, nephoscope, opeidoscope, ophthalmoscope, oscilloscope otoscope, pantoscope, periscope, pharyngoscope, phenakistoscope, phonendoscope,

-scope *continued*

polariscope, poroscope, praxinoscope, proctoscope, pseudoscope, pyroscope, radarscope, radioscope, rhinoscope, scintilloscope, scope, seismoscope, sigmoidoscope, somascope, spectrohelioscope, spectroscope, sphygmoscope, spinthariscope, statoscope, stereofluoroscope, stereoscope, stethoscope, stroboscope, tachistoscope, teinoscope, telescope, thermoscope, triniscope, ultramicroscope, vectorscope, Vertoscope®, vitascope.

-scopic autoscopic, bronchoscopic, cryoscopic, deuteroscopic, dichroscopic, ebullioscopic, electroscopic, endoscopic, gyroscopic, hagioscopic, helioscopic, horoscopic, hygroscopic, kaleidoscopic, laryngoscopic, macroscopic, megascopic, metoscopic, microscopic, necroscopic, ophthalmoscopic, orthoscopic, pantoscopic, periscopic, poroscopic, rhinoscopic, seismoscopic, spectroscopic, stethoscopic, stroboscopic, submicroscopic, tachistoscopic, telescopic, thermoscopic, ultramicroscopic, zooscopic.

-scopy autoscopy, bronchoscopy, colposcopy, cranioscopy, cryoscopy, cystoscopy, dactyloscopy, deuteroscopy, ebullioscopy, endoscopy, episcopy, fluoroscopy, hepatoscopy, hieroscopy, horoscopy, laparoscopy, laryngoscopy, metoposcopy, microscopy, necroscopy, omoplatoscopy, oniroscopy, ophthalmoscopy, ornithoscopy, ouroscopy, pharyngoscopy, poroscopy, proctoscopy, radioscopy, retinoscopy, rhinoscopy, röntgenoscopy, skiascopy, spectroscopy, stereoscopy, stethoscopy, telescopy, tracheoscopy, ultramicroscopy, urinoscopy, uroscopy, zooscopy.

-ship abbotship, accountantship, acquaintanceship, administratorship, admiralship, advisership, aedileship, airmanship, aldermanship, amateurship, ambassadorship, apostleship, apprenticeship, archonship, assessorship, associateship, attorneyship, auditorship, augurship, authorship, bachelorship, bailieship, baillieship, bardship, barristership, bashawship, batmanship, beadleship, bedellship, bedelship, benchership, bondmanship, brinkmanship, bursarship, bushmanship, butlership, cadetship, Caesarship, candidateship, captainship, cardinalship, catechumenship, censorship, chairmanship, chamberlainship, championship, chancellorship, chaplainship, chelaship, chiefship, chieftainship, citizenship, clanship, clerkship, clientship, clownship, coadjutorship, colleagueship, collectorship, colonelship, commandantship, commandership, commissaryship, commissionership, committeeship, companionship, compotationship, comradeship, conductorship, confessorship, connoisseurship, conservatorship, constableship, consulship, controllership, copartnership, co-rivalship, corporalship, counsellorship, countship,

-ship *continued*

courtship, cousinship, cowardship, craftmanship, craftsmanship, creatorship, creatureship, curateship, curatorship, custodianship, deaconship, dealership, deanship, demyship, denizenship, devilship, dictatorship, directorship, discipleship, disfellowship, doctorship, dogeship, dogship, dollarship, donship, draftsmanship, dukeship, editorship, eldership, electorship, emperorship, endship, ensignship, entrepreneurship, envoyship, executorship, factorship, fathership, fellowship, foxship, freshmanship, friendship, gamesmanship, generalship, gentlemanship, giantship, gladiatorship, goddess-ship, godship, good-fellowship, governor-generalship, governorship, grandeeship, guardianship, guideship, hardship, headship, hectorship, heirship, heraldship, heroship, hership, hetmanship, horsemanship, hostess-ship, housewifeship, huntsmanship, inspectorship, interpretership, interrelationship, janitorship, jockeyship, judgeship, justiceship, kaisership, keepership, kindredship, kingship, kinship, knaveship, ladyship, lairdship, land-ownership, laureateship, leadership, lectorship, lectureship, legateship, legislatorship, librarianship, lieutenant-commandership, lieutenant-generalship, lieutenant-governorship, lieutenantship, lifemanship, logship, lordship, ludship, mageship, major-generalship, majorship, managership, marshalship, mastership, matronship, mayorship, mediatorship, membership, Messiahship, milk-kinship, minorship, mistress-ship, moderatorship, monitorship, multi-ownership, musicianship, noviceship, nunship, oarsmanship, one-upmanship, overlordship, ownership, partisanship, partnership, pastorship, patroonship, peatship, pendragonship, penmanship, physicianship, poetship, popeship, possessorship, postmastership, praetorship, preachership, precentorship, perfectship, prelateship, premiership, prenticeship, presbytership, presidentship, pretendership, priestship, primateship, primogenitureship, principalship, priorship, probationership, proconsulship, proctorship, procuratorship, professorship, progenitorship, prolocutorship, prophetship, proprietorship, prosectorship, protectorship, provostship, pursership, quaestorship, queenship, rajahship, rajaship, rangership, readership, recordership, rectorship, regentship, registrarship, relationship, residentiaryship, residentship, retainership, rivalship, rogueship, rulership, sachemship, saintship, salesmanship, scholarship, school-friendship, schoolmastership, scrivenership, seamanship, secretaryship, seigniorship, sempstress-ship, senatorship, seneschalship, serfship, sergeantship, serjeantship, servantship, servitorship, sextonship, sheriffship, showmanship, sibship, sizarship, soldiership, solicitorship, sonship, speakership, spectatorship, spinstership, sponsorship, sportsmanship, squireship, statesmanship, stewardship, studentship, subahship, subdeaconship, subeditorship, subinspectorship, subjectship, successorship, suffraganship, sultanship, superintendentship, superiorship, supervisorship, suretyship, surgeonship, surrogateship, surveyorship, survivorship, swordsmanship, teachership, tellership, tenantship, thaneship, thwartship, tide-

-ship *continued*

waitership, township, traineeship, traitorship, treasurership, treeship, tribuneship, truantship, trusteeship, tutorship, twinship, umpireship, uncleship, under-clerkship, undergraduateship, under-secretaryship, unfriendship, ushership, vaivodeship, vergership, vicarship, vice-chairmanship, vice-chancellorship, vice-consulship, viceroyship, virtuosoship, viscountship, viziership, vizirship, voivodeship, waivodeship, wardenship, wardship, watermanship, Whigship, workmanship, worship, wranglership, writership, yachtsmanship.

-sophy anthroposophy, gastrosophy, gymnosophy, pansophy, philosophy, sciosophy, theosophy.

-stat aerostat, antistat, appestat, bacteriostat, barostat, celostat, chemostat, coccidiostat, cryostat, gyrostat, heliostat, hemostat, humidistat, hydrostat, hygrostat, klinostat, pyrostat, rheostat, siderostat, thermostat.

-therapy actinotherapy, balneotherapy, chemotherapy, cryotherapy, curietherapy, electrotherapy, heliotherapy, hydrotherapy, hypnotherapy, immunotherapy, kinesitherapy, musicotherapy, narcotherapy, opotherapy, organotherapy, pelotherapy, phototherapy, physiotherapy, psychotherapy, pyretotherapy, radiotherapy, röntgenotherapy, serotherapy, serum-therapy, zootherapy.

-tomy adenectomy, adenoidectomy, anatomy, anthropotomy, appendectomy, appendicectomy, arteriotomy, autotomy, cephalotomy, cholecystectomy, cholecystotomy, colotomy, cordotomy, craniectomy, craniotomy, cystotomy, dichotomy, duodenectomy, embryotomy, encephalotomy, enterectomy, enterotomy, gastrectomy, gastrotomy, gingivectomy, glossectomy, hepatectomy, herniotomy, hysterectomy, hysterotomy, iridectomy, iridotomy, laparotomy, laryngectomy, laryngotomy, leucotomy, lipectomy, lithotomy, lobectomy, lobotomy, lumpectomy, mastectomy, microtomy, myringotomy, necrotomy, nephrectomy, nephrotomy, neurectomy, neuroanatomy, neurotomy, oophorectomy, orchidectomy, orchiectomy, osteotomy, ovariotomy, pharyngotomy, phlebotomy, phytotomy, pleurotomy, pneumonectomy, pogonotomy, prostatectomy, rhytidectomy, salpingectomy, sclerotomy, splenectomy, stapedectomy, stereotomy, strabotomy, sympathectomy, symphyseotomy, symphsiotomy, syringotomy, tenotomy, tetrachotomy, thymectomy, tonsillectomy, tonsillotomy, topectomy, tracheotomy, trichotomy, tubectomy, ultramicrotomy, uterectomy, uterotomy, varicotomy, vasectomy, zootomy.

-urgy chemurgy, dramaturgy, electrometallurgy, hierurgy, hydrometallurgy, liturgy, metallurgy, micrurgy, theurgy, zymurgy.

-vorous apivorous, baccivorous, carnivorous, fructivorous, frugivorous, graminivorous, granivorous, herbivorous, insectivorous, lignivorous, mellivorous, myristicivorous, nucivorous, omnivorous, ossivorous, piscivorous, radicivorous, ranivorous, sanguinivorous, sanguivorous, vermivorous.

WEIGHTS AND MEASURES

Measurement of mass or weight

avoirdupois		metric equivalent
	1 grain (gr)	= 64.8 mg
	1 dram (dr)	= 1.772 g
16 drams	= 1 ounce (oz.)	= 28.3495 g
16 oz (=7000 gr.)	= 1 pound (lb)	= 0.4536 kg
100 lb	= 1 short hundredweight	= 45.3592 kg
112 lb	= 1 long hundredweight	= 50.8024 kg
2,000 lb	= 1 short ton	= 0.9072 tonnes
2,240 lb	= 1 long ton	= 1.01605 tonnes

metric		avoirdupois equivalent
	1 milligram (mg)	= 0.015 gr
10 mg	= 1 centigram (cg)	= 0.154 gr
10 cg	= 1 decigram (dg)	= 1.543 gr
10 dg	= 1 gram (g)	= 15.43 gr = 0.035 oz
10 g	= 1 decagram (dag)	= 0.353 oz
10 dag	= 1 hectogram (hg)	= 3.527 oz
10 hg	= 1 kilogram (kg)	= 2.205 lb
1000 kg	= 1 tonne (metric ton)	= 0.984 (long) ton
		= 2204.62 lb

Troy weight

		metric equivalent
	1 grain	= 0.065 g
4 grains	= 1 carat of gold or silver	= 0.2592 g
6 carats	= 1 pennyweight (dwt)	= 1.5552 g
20 dwt	= 1 ounce (oz)	= 31.1035 g
12 oz	= 1 pound (lb)	= 373.242 g
25 lb	= 1 quarter (qr)	= 9.331 kg
100 lb	= 1 hundredweight (cwt)	= 37.324 kg
20 cwt	= 1 ton of gold or silver	= 746.48 kg

Note: the grain troy is the same as the grain avoirdupois, but the pound troy contains 5760 grains, the pound avoirdupois 7000 grains. Jewels are not weighed by this measure.

Linear measure

		metric equivalent
	1 inch (in)	= 25.4 mm
12 in	= 1 foot (ft)	= 0.305 m
3 ft	= 1 yard (yd)	= 0.914 m
2 yds	= 6 ft = 1 fathom (fm)	= 1.829 m
5.5 yds	= 16.5 ft = 1 rod	= 5.029 m
4 rod	= 22 yds = 66 ft = 1 chain	= 20.12 m
10 chain	= 220 yds = 660 ft = 1 furlong (fur.)	= 0.201 km
8 fur.	= 1760 yds = 5280 ft = 1 (statute) mile (mi)	= 1.609 km
3 mi	= 1 league	= 4.827 km

metric		U. S. equivalent
	1 millimeter (mm)	= 0.0394 in
10 mm	= 1 centimeter (cm)	= 0.3937 in
10 cm	= 1 decimeter (dm)	= 3.937 in
10 dm	= 1 meter (m)	= 39.37 in
10 m	= 1 decameter (dam)	= 10.94 yds
10 dam	= 1 hectometer (hm)	= 109.4 yds
10 hm	= 1 kilometer (km)	= 0.621 mi

Surveyor's measure

Surveyor's linear units

		metric equivalent
1 link	= 7.92 in	= 20.117 cm
25 links = 1 rod	= 5.50 yds	= 5.029 m
100 links = 1 chain	= 22 yds	= 20.12 m
10 chains = 1 furlong (fur.)	= 220 yds	= 0.201 m
80 chains = 8 fur.	= 1 mile (mi)	= 1.609 km

Surveyor's square units

		metric equivalent
100 x 100 links or 10,000 sq. links	= 1 sq. chain = 484 sq. yds	= 404.7 m²
4 x 4 poles or 16 sq. poles	= 1 sq. chain	
22 x 22 yds or 484 sq. yds	= 1 sq. chain	
100,000 sq. links or 10 sq. chains	= 1 acre = 4840 sq. yds.	= 0.4047 ha.

Square measure

		metric equivalent
	1 square inch (sq. in)	= 6.4516 cm^2
144 sq. in.	= 1 square foot (sq. ft)	= 0.0929 m^2
9 sq. ft.	= 1 square yard (sq. yd)	= 0.8361 m^2
30 $^1/_4$ sq. yds.	= 1 square perch	= 25.29 m^2
40 sq. perch	= 1 rood	= 0.1012 ha
4 roods or 4840 sq. yds	= 1 acre	= 04.047 ha
640 acres	= 1 square mile (sq. mi)	= 2.5900 km^2
metric units		*U. S. equivalent*
	1 square millimeter (mm^2)	= 0.0016 sq. in
100 mm^2	= 1 square centimeter (cm^2)	= 0.1550 sq. in
100 cm^2	= 1 square decimeter (dm^2)	= 15.5000.sq. in
100 dm^2	= 1 square meter (m^2)	= 10.7639 sq. ft
		(=1.1959 sq. yds)
100m^2	= 1 square decameter (dam^2)	= 1076.3910 sq. ft
100 dam^2	= 1 square hectometer (hm^2)	= 0.0039 sq. mi
100 hm^2	= 1 square kilometer (km^2)	= 0.3861 sq. mi

*Note: The square hectometer is also known as a *hectare* (ha.).

The hectare can be sub-divided into *ares:*

metric units		
100 m^2	= 1 are	= 119.59 sq. yds
1000 m^2	= 10 ares = 1 dekare	= 1195.9 sq. yds
10,000 m^2	= 100 ares = 1 hectare	= 2.471 acres

Cubic measure

		metric equivalent
	1 cubic inch (cu. in)	= 16.39 cm^3
1728 cu. in	= 1 cubic foot (cu. ft)	= 0.0283 m^3
27 cu. ft	= 1 cubic yard (cu. yd)	= 0.7646 m^3
		metric units
1000 cubic millimeters (mm^3)	= 1 cubic centimeter (cm^3)	= 0.0610 cu. in
1000 cubic centimeters (cm^3)	= 1 cubic decimeter (dm^3)	= 610 cu. in
1000 cubic decimeters (dm^3)	= 1 cubic meter (m^3)	= 35.3147 cu. ft

The *stere* is also used, in particular as a unit of measurement for timber:

1 cubic meter	= 1 stere	= 35.3147 cu. ft
10 decisteres	= 1 stere	= 35.3147 cu. ft
10 steres	= 1 decastere	= 353.1467 cu. ft
		(= 13.0795 cu. yds)

Liquid measure

		metric equivalent
	1 fluid ounce (fl. oz)	= 29.573 ml
4 fl. oz	= 1 gill	= 118.291 ml
4 gills	= 1 pint (pt)	= 473.163 ml
2 pt	= 1 quart (qt)	= 0.9461
4 qt	= 1 gallon (gal)	= 3.7851

U.S. and British equivalents

U.S.	British
1 fluid ounce	1.0408 fl oz
1 pint	0.8327 pt
1 gallon	0.8327 gal

metric units

10 milliliters (ml)	= 1 centiliter (cl)	= 0.0211 pt
10 cl	= 1 deciliter (dl)	= 0.211 pt
10 dl	= 1 liter (l)	= 2.11 pt
		(= 0.264 gal)
10 l	= 1 decaliter (dal)	= 2.64 gal
10 dal	= 1 hectoliter (hl)	= 26.4 gal
10 hl	= 1 kiloliter (kl)	= 264.0 gal

Temperature

Equations for conversion

$$°\text{Fahrenheit} = (9/5 \times x°\text{C}) + 32 \qquad °\text{Centigrade} = 5/9 \times (x°\text{F} - 32)$$

$$°\text{Kelvin} = x°\text{C} + 273.15$$

Some equivalents

	Centigrade	Fahrenheit
Normal temperature of the human body	36.9°C	98.4°F
Freezing point	0°C	32°F
Boiling point	100°C	212°F

Table of equivalents

Fahrenheit	Centigrade	Centigrade	Fahrenheit
100°C	212°F	30°C	86°F
90°C	194°F	20°C	68°F
80°C	176°F	10°C	50°F
70°C	158°F	0°C	32°F
60°C	140°F	-10°C	14°F
50°C	122°F	-20°C	4°F
40°C	104°F	-30°C	-22°F

Approximate oven temperatures

	Electric		
Description	°C	°F	Gas no. (equiv. °F)
very cool	107°	225°	1/4 (240°)
	121°	250°	1/2 (265°)
cool	135°	275°	1 (290°)
	149°	300°	2 (310°)
warm	163°	325°	3 (335°)
moderate	177°	350°	4 (355°)
fairly hot	191°	375°	5 (375°)
	204°	400°	6 (400°)
hot	218°	425°	7 (425°)
very hot	232°	450°	8 (450°)
	246°	475°	9 (470°)

Calorific value of foods

Portion	Calories
Apple (1) 142g (5oz)	70
Bacon (fried) 57g (2oz)	250-320
Banana (1) 142g (5oz)	110
Beans, green (boiled) 113g (4oz)	10
Beef (roast) 85g (3oz)	325
Beef steak (grilled) 170g (6oz)	520
Beer (bitter) 0.561 (1 pint)	180
Bread (white, 1 slice) 28g (1oz)	73
Bread (wholewheat, 1 slice) 28g (1oz)	65
Butter 14 g (1/2oz)	110
Cabbage (boiled) 142g (5oz)	15
Carrots(boiled) 113g (4oz)	24
Celery (raw) 113g (4oz)	8
Cheese (cheddar) 28g (1oz)	112
Cheese (cottage) 28g (1oz)	29
Chicken (roast) 113g (4oz)	220
Chocolate (milk) 57g (2oz)	300
Cod (grilled) 113g (4oz)	170
Coffee (white, no sugar) 170 ml (6 fl.oz)	25
Cornflakes 28g (1oz)	100
Cream (double) 14g (1/2oz)	64

Portion	Calories
Egg (boiled 1) 57g (2oz)	90
Grapefruit (1/2) 198 g (7oz)	42
Honey 14g (1/2oz)	41
Lamb (roast) 85g (3oz)	250
Lettuce 57g (2oz)	5
Margarine 14g (1/2oz)	110
Melon (1 slice) 142g (5oz)	30
Milk (cup) 170ml (6 fl. oz)	110
Orange (1) 170g (6oz)	60
Peanuts 57g (2oz)	330
Potatoes (fried) 113g (4oz)	270
(boiled, baked) 113g (4oz)	90
Rice (boiled) 170g (6oz)	600
Sardines (tinned) 85g (3oz)	240
Sausages (pork, 2) 113g (4oz)	400
Spinach (boiled) 43g (1 1/2oz)	10
Spirits (measure) 28 ml (1 fl.oz)	63
Strawberries 142g (5oz)	35
Sugar 57g (2oz)	215
1 teaspoon	25
Tea (cup, no sugar) 170ml (6 fl.oz)	15
Tomato (1) 85g (3oz)	12
Wine, dry (glass) 114ml (4 fl.oz)	84
sweet (glass) 114ml (4 fl.oz)	128

Numeration

Arabic	Roman	Ordinal	Binary
1	I	1st first	1
2	II	2nd second	10
3	III	3rd third	II
4	IV	4th fourth	100
5	V	5th fifth	101
6	VI	6th sixth	110
7	VII	7th seventh	111
8	VIII	8th eighth	1000
9	IX	9th ninth	1001
10	X	10th tenth	1010
11	XI	11th eleventh	1011
12	XII	12th twelfth	1100
13	XIII	13th thirteenth	1101
14	XIV	14th fourteenth	1110
15	XV	15th fifteenth	1111
16	XVI	16th sixteenth	10000
17	XVII	17th seventeenth	10001
18	XVIII	18th eighteenth	10010
19	XIX	19th nineteenth	10011
20	XX	20th twentieth	10100
21	XXI	21st twenty-first	10101
29	XXIX	29th twenty-ninth	11101
30	XXX	30th thirtieth	11110
32	XXXII	32nd thirty-second	100000
40	XL	40th	101000
50	L	50th	110010
60	LX	60th	111100
64	LXIV	64th	1000000
90	XC	90th	1011010
99	XCIX	99th	1100011
100	C	100th	1100100
128	CXXVIII	128th	10000000
200	CC	200th	11001000
256	CCLVI	256th	100000000
300	CCC	300th	100101100
400	CD	400th	110010000
500	D	500th	111110100

900	CM	900th	1110000100
1000	M	1000th thousandth	1111101000
1024	MXXIV	1024th	10000000000
1500	MD	1500th fifteen hundredth	10111011100
4000	M$\overline{\text{V}}$	4000th	111110100000
5000	$\overline{\text{V}}$	5000th	1001110001000
10,000	$\overline{\text{X}}$	10,000th	10011100010000
100,000	$\overline{\text{C}}$	100,000th	11000011010100000
1,000,000	$\overline{\text{M}}$	1,000,000th millionth	$10^{500,000}$

CONVERSIONS

Mile / kilometer

Miles – Kilometers		*Kilometers – Miles*	
Miles	*Kilometers*	*Kilometers*	*Miles*
1	1.6	1	0.6
2	3.2	2	1.2
3	4.8	3	1.8
4	6.4	4	2.4
5	8.0	5	3.1
6	9.6	6	3.7
7	11.2	7	4.3
8	12.8	8	4.9
9	14.4	9	5.5
10	16.0	10	6.2
20	32.1	20	12.4
30	48.2	30	18.6
40	64.3	40	24.8
50	80.4	50	31.0
60	96.5	60	37.2
70	112.6	70	43.4
80	128.7	80	49.7
90	144.8	90	55.9
100	160.9	100	62.1
1,000	1,609	1,000	621

For approximate conversions:

Miles – Kilometers: divide by 5, then multiply by 8

Kilometers – Miles: divide by 8, multiply by 5.

Metric Tyre Pressure Conversion Chart

Pounds per sq in	Kilograms per sq cm	KiloPascals (kPa)	(Atmospheres)
14	0.98	96.6	0.95
16	1.12	110.4	1.08
18	1.26	124.2	1.22
20	1.40	138.0	1.36
22	1.54	151.8	1.49
24	1.68	165.6	1.63
26	1.83	179.4	1.76
28	1.96	193.2	1.90
30	2.10	207.0	2.04
32	2.24	220.8	2.16
36	2.52	248.4	2.44
40	2.80	276.0	2.72
50	3.50	345.0	3.40
55	3.85	379.5	3.74
60	4.20	414.0	4.08
65	4.55	448.5	4.42

Clothing Sizes

Women

Dresses, Coats, Skirts/Junior Sizes Misses Sizes

American	7	9	11	13	15	8	10	12	14	16	18
British	9	11	13	15	17	10	12	14	16	18	20
Continental	34	36	38	40	42	38	40	42	44	46	48

Blouses, Sweaters

American	10	12	14	16	18	20
British	32	34	36	38	40	42
Continental	38	40	42	44	46	48

Shoes

American	4^1/$_2$	5	5^1/$_2$	6	6^1/$_2$	7	7^1/$_2$	8	8^1/$_2$	9	9^1/$_2$
British	3	3^1/$_2$	4	4^1/$_2$	5	5^1/$_2$	6	6^1/$_2$	7	7^1/$_2$	8
Continental	35^1/$_2$	36	36^1/$_2$	37	37^1/$_2$	38	38^1/$_2$	39	39^1/$_2$	40	40^1/$_2$

Children

American	3	4	5	6	6X
British	18	20	22	24	26
Continental	98	104	110	116	122

(For older children, sizes usually correspond with their ages.)

Shoes

American	8	9	10	11	12	13	1	2	3
British	7	8	9	10	11	12	13	1	2
Continental	24	25	27	28	29	30	32	33	34

Men

Suits

American	34	35	36	37	38	39	40	41	42
British	34	35	36	37	38	39	40	41	42
Continental	44	46	48	49^1/$_2$	51	52^1/$_2$	54	55^1/$_2$	57

Shirts

American	14^1/$_2$	15	15^1/$_2$	16	16^1/$_2$	17	17^1/$_2$	18
British	14^1/$_2$	15	15^1/$_2$	16	16 ^{1}/$_2$	17	17^1/$_2$	18
Continental	37	38	39	41	42	43	44	45

CHEMICAL ELEMENTS

An element is a substance not separable by ordinary chemical means into substances different from itself. Fewer than a hundred elements occur naturally, the others can only be made artificially.

Name	Symbol	Atomic number	Atomic weight	Valency
Actinium	Ac	89	(227)	
Aluminium	Al	13	26.98154	3
Americium	Am	95	(243)	3,4,5,6
Antimony	Sb	51	121.75	3,5
Argon	Ar	18	39.948	0
Arsenic	As	33	74.9216	3.5
Astatine	At	85	(210)	1,3,5,7
Barium	Ba	56	137.34	2
Berkelium	Bk	97	(247)	3,4
Beryllium	Be	4	9.01218	2
Bismuth	Bi	83	208.9804	3,5
Boron	B	5	10.81	3
Bromine	Br	35	79.904	1,3,5,7
Cadmium	Cd	48	112.40	2
Caesium	Cs	55	132.9054	1
Calcium	Ca	20	40.08	2
Californium	Cf	98	(251)	
Carbon	C	6	12.011	2.4
Cerium	Ce	58	140.12	3.4
Chlorine	Cl	17	35.453	1,3,5,7
Chromium	Cr	24	51.996	2,3,6
Cobalt	Co	27	58.9332	2,3
Copper	Cu	29	63.546	1,2
Curium	Cm	96	(247)	3
Dysprosium	Dy	66	162.50	3
Einsteinium	Es	99	(254)	
Erbium	Er	68	167.26	3
Europium	Eu	63	151.96	2,3
Fermium	Fm	100	(257)	
Fluorine	F	9	18.99840	1
Francium	Fr	87	(223)	1
Gadolinium	Gd	64	157.25	3
Gallium	Ga	31	69.72	2,3

Name	Symbol	Atomic number	Atomic weight	Valency
Germanium	Ge	32	72.59	4
Gold	Au	79	196.9665	1,3
Hafnium	Hf	72	178.49	4
Hahnium	Ha	105		
Helium	He	2	4.00260	0
Holmium	Ho	67	164.9304	3
Hydrogen	H	1	1.0079	1
Indium	In	49	114.82	3
Iodine	I	53	126.9045	1,3,5,7
Iridium	Ir	77	192.22	3,4
Iron	Fe	26	55.847	2,3
Krypton	Kr	36	83.80	0
Lanthanum	La	57	138.9055	3
Lawrencium	Lr	103	(260)	
Lead	Pb	82	207.2	2,4
Lithium	Li	3	6.941	1
Lutetium	Lu	71	174.97	3
Magnesium	Mg	12	24.305	2
Manganese	Mn	25	54.9380	2,3,4,6,7
Mendelevium	Md	101	(258)	
Mercury	Hg	80	200.59	1,2
Molybdenum	Mo	42	95.94	3,4,6
Neodymium	Nd	60	144.24	3
Neon	Ne	10	20.179	0
Neptunium	Np	93	237.0482	4,5,6
Nickel	Ni	28	58.70	2, 3
Niobium	Nb	41	92.9064	3,5
Nitrogen	N	7	14.0067	3,5
Nobelium	No	102	(255)	
Osmium	Os	76	190.2	2,3,4,8
Oxygen	O	8	15.9994	2
Palladium	Pd	46	106.4	2,4,6
Phosphorus	P	15	30.97376	3,5
Platinum	Pt	78	195.09	2,4
Plutonium	Pu	94	(244)	3,4,5,6
Polonium	Po	84	(209)	
Potassium	K	19	39.098	1
Praseodymium	Pr	59	140.9077	3

Name	Symbol	Atomic number	Atomic weight	Valency
Promethium	Pm	61	(145)	3
Protactinium	Pa	91	231.0359	
Radium	Ra	88	226.0254	2
Radon	Rn	86	(222)	0
Rhenium	Re	75	186.207	
Rhodium	Rh	45	102.9055	3
Rubidium	Rb	37	85.4678	1
Ruthenium	Ru	44	101.07	3,4,6,8
Rutherfordium	Ru	104		
Samarium	Sm	62	105.4	2,3
Scandium	Sc	21	44.9559	3
Selenium	Se	34	78.96	2,4,6
Silicon	Si	14	28.086	4
Silver	Ag	47	107.868	1
Sodium	Na	11	22.98977	1
Strontium	Sr	38	87.62	2
Sulphur	S	16	32.06	2,4,6
Tantalum	Ta	73	180.9479	5
Technetium	Tc	43	(97)	6,7
Tellurium	Te	52	127.60	2,4,6
Terbium	Tb	65	158.9254	3
Thallium	Tl	81	204.37	1,3
Thorium	Th	90	232.0381	4
Thulium	Tm	69	168.9342	3
Tin	Sn	50	118.69	2,4
Titanium	Ti	22	47.90	3,4
Tungsten(Wolfram)	W	74	183.85	6
Uranium	U	92	238.029	4,6
Vanadium	V	23	50.9414	3,5
Xenon	Xe	54	131.30	0
Ytterbium	Yb	70	173.04	2,3
Yttrium	Y	39	88.9059	3
Zinc	Zn	30	65.38	2
Zirconium	Zr	40	91.22	4

TIME
Periods of Time

annual	yearly	quadricentennial	every 400 years
biannual	twice a year	quincentennial	every 500 years
bicentennial	every 200 years	quindecennial	every 15 years
biennial	every two years	quinquennial	every five years
bimonthly	every two months; twice a month	semiannual	every six months
		semicentennial	every 50 years
biweekly	every two weeks; twice a week	semidiurnal	twice a day
		semiweekly	twice a week
centennial	every 100 years	septennial	every seven years
decennial	every 10 years	sesquicentennial	every 150 years
diurnal	daily	sexennial	every six years
duodecennial	every 12 years	thrice weekly	three times a week
millennial	every 1,000 years	tricennial	every 30 years
millenium	a thousand years	triennial	every three years
novennial	every nine years	trimonthly	every three months
octennial	every eight years	triweekly	every three weeks; three times a week
perennial	year after year		
quadrennial	every four years	undecennial	every 11 years
		vicennial	every 20 years

Birthstones

Month	Biblical	Present Day
January	Garnet	Garnet
February	Amethyst	Amethyst
March	Jasper	Aquamarine, Bloodstone
April	Sapphire	Diamond
May	Chalcedony, Carnelian, Agate	Emerald, chrysoprase
June	Emerald	Pearl, moonstone, alexandrite
July	Onyx	Ruby, carnelian
August	Carnelian	Peridot, sardonyx
September	Chrysolite	Saphire, lapis luzuli
October	Aquamarine, Beryl	Opal, tourmaline
November	Topaz	Topaz
December	Ruby	Turquoise, zircon

Traditional Anniversary Names

1st	Paper	10th	Tin, aluminium	35th	Coral
2nd	Cotton	11th	steel	40th	Ruby
3rd	Leather	12th	Silk, fine linen	45th	Sapphire
4th	Fruit, flowers	13th	Lace	50th	Golden
5th	Wood	14th	Ivory	55th	Emerald
6th	Iron, sugar	15th	Crystal	60th	Diamond
7th	Wool, copper	20th	China	75th	Diamond
8th	Bronze	25th	Silver		
9th	Pottery	30th	Pearl		

Days of the Week

Day	Derivation	Abbreviation
Sunday	The Sun	Sun. or S.
Monday	The Moon	Mon. or M.
Tuesday	Tiu, Norse God of War	Tues. or Tu.
Wednesday	Woden, Anglo-Saxon chief of Gods	Wed. or W.
Thursday	Thor, Norse God of Thunder	Thurs. or Th.
Friday	Frigg, Norse Goddess	Fri. or F.
Saturday	Saturn, Roman God of Harvests	Sat. or Sa.

Months of the Year

Month	Derivation	Abbreviation
January	Janus, Roman God of Doors and Gates	Jan.
February	Februa, Roman period of purification	Feb.
March	Mars, Roman God of War	Mar.
April	Aperire, Latin for 'to open'	Apr.
May	Maia, Roman Goddesss of Spring and Growth	My.
June	Juno, Roman Goddess of Marriage	Jun. or Je.
July	Julius Caesar	Jul. or Jy.
August	Augustus, First Emperor of Rome	Aug.
September	Septem, Latin for 'seven'	Sept. or Sep.
October	Octo, Latin for 'eight'	Oct.
November	Novem, Latin for 'nine'	Nov.
December	Decem, Latin for 'ten'	Dec.

Perpetual Calendar

To find the day on which a particular date falls in a specific year, look down the list of years and find the appropriate grid number.

Year	Grid	Year	Grid	Year	Grid	Year	Grid
1990	2	2005	7	2020	11	2035	2
1991	3	2006	1	2021	6	2036	10
1992	11	2007	2	2022	7	2037	5
1993	6	2008	10	2023	1	2038	6
1994	7	2009	5	2024	9	2039	7
1995	1	2010	6	2025	4	2040	8
1996	9	2011	7	2026	5	2041	3
1997	4	2012	8	2027	6	2042	4
1998	5	2013	3	2028	14	2043	5
1999	6	2014	4	2029	2	2044	13
2000	14	2015	5	2030	3	2045	1
2001	2	2016	13	2031	4	2046	2
2002	3	2017	1	2032	12	2047	3
2003	4	2018	2	2033	7	2048	11
2004	12	2019	3	2034	1	2049	6

1

```
JANUARY                 MAY                     SEPTEMBER
S  M  T  W  T  F  S      S  M  T  W  T  F  S      S  M  T  W  T  F  S
   1  2  3  4  5  6  7            1  2  3  4  5  6                     1  2
8  9 10 11 12 13 14      7  8  9 10 11 12 13      3  4  5  6  7  8  9
15 16 17 18 19 20 21     14 15 16 17 18 19 20     10 11 12 13 14 15 16
22 23 24 25 26 27 28     21 22 23 24 25 26 27     17 18 19 20 21 22 23
29 30 31                 28 29 30 31              24 25 26 27 28 29 30

FEBRUARY                JUNE                    OCTOBER
S  M  T  W  T  F  S      S  M  T  W  T  F  S      S  M  T  W  T  F  S
            1  2  3  4               1  2  3      1  2  3  4  5  6  7
5  6  7  8  9 10 11      4  5  6  7  8  9 10      8  9 10 11 12 13 14
12 13 14 15 16 17 18     11 12 13 14 15 16 17     15 16 17 18 19 20 21
19 20 21 22 23 24 25     18 19 20 21 22 23 24     22 23 24 25 26 27 28
26 27 28                 25 26 27 28 29 30        29 30 31

MARCH                   JULY                    NOVEMBER
S  M  T  W  T  F  S      S  M  T  W  T  F  S      S  M  T  W  T  F  S
            1  2  3  4   30 31             1                  1  2  3  4
5  6  7  8  9 10 11      2  3  4  5  6  7  8      5  6  7  8  9 10 11
12 13 14 15 16 17 18     9 10 11 12 13 14 15      12 13 14 15 16 17 18
19 20 21 22 23 24 25     16 17 18 19 20 21 22     19 20 21 22 23 24 25
26 27 28 29 30 31        23 24 25 26 27 28 29     26 27 28 29 30

APRIL                   AUGUST                  DECEMBER
S  M  T  W  T  F  S      S  M  T  W  T  F  S      S  M  T  W  T  F  S
30                1               1  2  3  4  5   31                1  2
2  3  4  5  6  7  8      6  7  8  9 10 11 12      3  4  5  6  7  8  9
9 10 11 12 13 14 15      13 14 15 16 17 18 19     10 11 12 13 14 15 16
16 17 18 19 20 21 22     20 21 22 23 24 25 26     17 18 19 20 21 22 23
23 24 25 26 27 28 29     27 28 29 30 31           24 25 26 27 28 29 30
```

2

```
JANUARY                 MAY                     SEPTEMBER
S  M  T  W  T  F  S      S  M  T  W  T  F  S      S  M  T  W  T  F  S
   1  2  3  4  5  6               1  2  3  4  5   30                   1
7  8  9 10 11 12 13      6  7  8  9 10 11 12      2  3  4  5  6  7  8
14 15 16 17 18 19 20     13 14 15 16 17 18 19     9 10 11 12 13 14 15
21 22 23 24 25 26 27     20 21 22 23 24 25 26     16 17 18 19 20 21 22
28 29 30 31              27 28 29 30 31           23 24 25 26 27 28 29

FEBRUARY                JUNE                    OCTOBER
S  M  T  W  T  F  S      S  M  T  W  T  F  S      S  M  T  W  T  F  S
         1  2  3                     1  2         1  2  3  4  5  6
4  5  6  7  8  9 10      3  4  5  6  7  8  9      7  8  9 10 11 12 13
11 12 13 14 15 16 17     10 11 12 13 14 15 16     14 15 16 17 18 19 20
18 19 20 21 22 23 24     17 18 19 20 21 22 23     21 22 23 24 25 26 27
25 26 27 28              24 25 26 27 28 29 30     28 29 30 31

MARCH                   JULY                    NOVEMBER
S  M  T  W  T  F  S      S  M  T  W  T  F  S      S  M  T  W  T  F  S
         1  2  3         1  2  3  4  5  6  7                  1  2  3
4  5  6  7  8  9 10      8  9 10 11 12 13 14      4  5  6  7  8  9 10
11 12 13 14 15 16 17     15 16 17 18 19 20 21     11 12 13 14 15 16 17
18 19 20 21 22 23 24     22 23 24 25 26 27 28     18 19 20 21 22 23 24
25 26 27 28 29 30 31     29 30 31                 25 26 27 28 29 30

APRIL                   AUGUST                  DECEMBER
S  M  T  W  T  F  S      S  M  T  W  T  F  S      S  M  T  W  T  F  S
   1  2  3  4  5  6               1  2  3  4      30 31
7  8  9 10 11 12 13      5  6  7  8  9 10 11      2  3  4  5  6  7  8
14 15 16 17 18 19 20     12 13 14 15 16 17 18     9 10 11 12 13 14 15
21 22 23 24 25 26 27     19 20 21 22 23 24 25     16 17 18 19 20 21 22
28 29 30                 26 27 28 29 30 31        23 24 25 26 27 28 29
```

3

JANUARY
S	M	T	W	T	F	S
		1	2	3	4	5
6	7	8	9	10	11	12
13	14	15	16	17	18	19
20	21	22	23	24	25	26
27	28	29	30	31		

FEBRUARY
S	M	T	W	T	F	S
					1	2
3	4	5	6	7	8	9
10	11	12	13	14	15	16
17	18	19	20	21	22	23
24	25	26	27	28		

MARCH
S	M	T	W	T	F	S
31					1	2
3	4	5	6	7	8	9
10	11	12	13	14	15	16
17	18	19	20	21	22	23
24	25	26	27	28	29	30

APRIL
S	M	T	W	T	F	S
1	2	3	4	5	6	
7	8	9	10	11	12	13
14	15	16	17	18	19	20
21	22	23	24	25	26	27
28	29	30				

MAY
S	M	T	W	T	F	S
			1	2	3	4
5	6	7	8	9	10	11
12	13	14	15	16	17	18
19	20	21	22	23	24	25
26	27	28	29	30	31	

JUNE
S	M	T	W	T	F	S
30						1
2	3	4	5	6	7	8
9	10	11	12	13	14	15
16	17	18	19	20	21	22
23	24	25	26	27	28	29

JULY
S	M	T	W	T	F	S
1	2	3	4	5	6	
7	8	9	10	11	12	13
14	15	16	17	18	19	20
21	22	23	24	25	26	27
28	29	30	31			

AUGUST
S	M	T	W	T	F	S
				1	2	3
4	5	6	7	8	9	10
11	12	13	14	15	16	17
18	19	20	21	22	23	24
25	26	27	28	29	30	31

SEPTEMBER
S	M	T	W	T	F	S
1	2	3	4	5	6	7
8	9	10	11	12	13	14
15	16	17	18	19	20	21
22	23	24	25	26	27	28
29	30					

OCTOBER
S	M	T	W	T	F	S
		1	2	3	4	5
6	7	8	9	10	11	12
13	14	15	16	17	18	19
20	21	22	23	24	25	26
27	28	29	30	31		

NOVEMBER
S	M	T	W	T	F	S
					1	2
3	4	5	6	7	8	9
10	11	12	13	14	15	16
17	18	19	20	21	22	23
24	25	26	27	28	29	30

DECEMBER
S	M	T	W	T	F	S
1	2	3	4	5	6	7
8	9	10	11	12	13	14
15	16	17	18	19	20	21
22	23	24	25	26	27	28
29	30	31				

4

JANUARY
S	M	T	W	T	F	S
			1	2	3	4
5	6	7	8	9	10	11
12	13	14	15	16	17	18
19	20	21	22	23	24	25
26	27	28	29	30	31	

FEBRUARY
S	M	T	W	T	F	S
						1
2	3	4	5	6	7	8
9	10	11	12	13	14	15
16	17	18	19	20	21	22
23	24	25	26	27	28	

MARCH
S	M	T	W	T	F	S
30	31					1
2	3	4	5	6	7	8
9	10	11	12	13	14	15
16	17	18	19	20	21	22
23	24	25	26	27	28	29

APRIL
S	M	T	W	T	F	S
		1	2	3	4	5
6	7	8	9	10	11	12
13	14	15	16	17	18	19
20	21	22	23	24	25	26
27	28	29	30			

MAY
S	M	T	W	T	F	S
				1	2	3
4	5	6	7	8	9	10
11	12	13	14	15	16	17
18	19	20	21	22	23	24
25	26	27	28	29	30	31

JUNE
S	M	T	W	T	F	S
1	2	3	4	5	6	7
8	9	10	11	12	13	14
15	16	17	18	19	20	21
22	23	24	25	26	27	28
29	30					

JULY
S	M	T	W	T	F	S
		1	2	3	4	5
6	7	8	9	10	11	12
13	14	15	16	17	18	19
20	21	22	23	24	25	26
27	28	29	30	31		

AUGUST
S	M	T	W	T	F	S
31					1	2
3	4	5	6	7	8	9
10	11	12	13	14	15	16
17	18	19	20	21	22	23
24	25	26	27	28	29	30

SEPTEMBER
S	M	T	W	T	F	S
1	2	3	4	5	6	
7	8	9	10	11	12	13
14	15	16	17	18	19	20
21	22	23	24	25	26	27
28	29	30				

OCTOBER
S	M	T	W	T	F	S
			1	2	3	4
5	6	7	8	9	10	11
12	13	14	15	16	17	18
19	20	21	22	23	24	25
26	27	28	29	30	31	

NOVEMBER
S	M	T	W	T	F	S
30						1
2	3	4	5	6	7	8
9	10	11	12	13	14	15
16	17	18	19	20	21	22
23	24	25	26	27	28	29

DECEMBER
S	M	T	W	T	F	S
1	2	3	4	5	6	
7	8	9	10	11	12	13
14	15	16	17	18	19	20
21	22	23	24	25	26	27
28	29	30	31			

5

JANUARY
S	M	T	W	T	F	S
				1	2	3
4	5	6	7	8	9	10
11	12	13	14	15	16	17
18	19	20	21	22	23	24
25	26	27	28	29	30	31

FEBRUARY
S	M	T	W	T	F	S
1	2	3	4	5	6	7
8	9	10	11	12	13	14
15	16	17	18	19	20	21
22	23	24	25	26	27	28

MARCH
S	M	T	W	T	F	S
1	2	3	4	5	6	7
8	9	10	11	12	13	14
15	16	17	18	19	20	21
22	23	24	25	26	27	28
29	30	31				

APRIL
S	M	T	W	T	F	S
			1	2	3	4
5	6	7	8	9	10	11
12	13	14	15	16	17	18
19	20	21	22	23	24	25
26	27	28	29	30		

MAY
S	M	T	W	T	F	S
31					1	2
3	4	5	6	7	8	9
10	11	12	13	14	15	16
17	18	19	20	21	22	23
24	25	26	27	28	29	30

JUNE
S	M	T	W	T	F	S
1	2	3	4	5	6	
7	8	9	10	11	12	13
14	15	16	17	18	19	20
21	22	23	24	25	26	27
28	29	30				

JULY
S	M	T	W	T	F	S
			1	2	3	4
5	6	7	8	9	10	11
12	13	14	15	16	17	18
19	20	21	22	23	24	25
26	27	28	29	30	31	

AUGUST
S	M	T	W	T	F	S
30	31					1
2	3	4	5	6	7	8
9	10	11	12	13	14	15
16	17	18	19	20	21	22
23	24	25	26	27	28	29

SEPTEMBER
S	M	T	W	T	F	S
		1	2	3	4	5
6	7	8	9	10	11	12
13	14	15	16	17	18	19
20	21	22	23	24	25	26
27	28	29	30			

OCTOBER
S	M	T	W	T	F	S
				1	2	3
4	5	6	7	8	9	10
11	12	13	14	15	16	17
18	19	20	21	22	23	24
25	26	27	28	29	30	31

NOVEMBER
S	M	T	W	T	F	S
1	2	3	4	5	6	7
8	9	10	11	12	13	14
15	16	17	18	19	20	21
22	23	24	25	26	27	28
29	30					

DECEMBER
S	M	T	W	T	F	S
		1	2	3	4	5
6	7	8	9	10	11	12
13	14	15	16	17	18	19
20	21	22	23	24	25	26
27	28	29	30	31		

6

JANUARY
S	M	T	W	T	F	S
31					1	2
3	4	5	6	7	8	9
10	11	12	13	14	15	16
17	18	19	20	21	22	23
24	25	26	27	28	29	30

FEBRUARY
S	M	T	W	T	F	S
1	2	3	4	5	6	
7	8	9	10	11	12	13
14	15	16	17	18	19	20
21	22	23	24	25	26	27
28						

MARCH
S	M	T	W	T	F	S
1	2	3	4	5	6	
7	8	9	10	11	12	13
14	15	16	17	18	19	20
21	22	23	24	25	26	27
28	29	30	31			

APRIL
S	M	T	W	T	F	S
				1	2	3
4	5	6	7	8	9	10
11	12	13	14	15	16	17
18	19	20	21	22	23	24
25	26	27	28	29	30	

MAY
S	M	T	W	T	F	S
30	31					1
2	3	4	5	6	7	8
9	10	11	12	13	14	15
16	17	18	19	20	21	22
23	24	25	26	27	28	29

JUNE
S	M	T	W	T	F	S
		1	2	3	4	5
6	7	8	9	10	11	12
13	14	15	16	17	18	19
20	21	22	23	24	25	26
27	28	29	30			

JULY
S	M	T	W	T	F	S
				1	2	3
4	5	6	7	8	9	10
11	12	13	14	15	16	17
18	19	20	21	22	23	24
25	26	27	28	29	30	31

AUGUST
S	M	T	W	T	F	S
1	2	3	4	5	6	7
8	9	10	11	12	13	14
15	16	17	18	19	20	21
22	23	24	25	26	27	28
29	30	31				

SEPTEMBER
S	M	T	W	T	F	S
			1	2	3	4
5	6	7	8	9	10	11
12	13	14	15	16	17	18
19	20	21	22	23	24	25
26	27	28	29	30		

OCTOBER
S	M	T	W	T	F	S
					1	2
3	4	5	6	7	8	9
10	11	12	13	14	15	16
17	18	19	20	21	22	23
24	25	26	27	28	29	30
31						

NOVEMBER
S	M	T	W	T	F	S
1	2	3	4	5	6	
7	8	9	10	11	12	13
14	15	16	17	18	19	20
21	22	23	24	25	26	27
28	29	30				

DECEMBER
S	M	T	W	T	F	S
			1	2	3	4
5	6	7	8	9	10	11
12	13	14	15	16	17	18
19	20	21	22	23	24	25
26	27	28	29	30	31	

7

JANUARY
S	M	T	W	T	F	S
30	31					1
2	3	4	5	6	7	8
9	10	11	12	13	14	15
16	17	18	19	20	21	22
23	24	25	26	27	28	29

MAY
S	M	T	W	T	F	S
1	2	3	4	5	6	7
8	9	10	11	12	13	14
15	16	17	18	19	20	21
22	23	24	25	26	27	28
29	30	31				

SEPTEMBER
S	M	T	W	T	F	S
				1	2	3
4	5	6	7	8	9	10
11	12	13	14	15	16	17
18	19	20	21	22	23	24
25	26	27	28	29	30	

FEBRUARY
S	M	T	W	T	F	S
		1	2	3	4	5
6	7	8	9	10	11	12
13	14	15	16	17	18	19
20	21	22	23	24	25	26
27	28					

JUNE
S	M	T	W	T	F	S
			1	2	3	4
5	6	7	8	9	10	11
12	13	14	15	16	17	18
19	20	21	22	23	24	25
26	27	28	29	30		

OCTOBER
S	M	T	W	T	F	S
30	31					1
2	3	4	5	6	7	8
9	10	11	12	13	14	15
16	17	18	19	20	21	22
23	24	25	26	27	28	29

MARCH
S	M	T	W	T	F	S
		1	2	3	4	5
6	7	8	9	10	11	12
13	14	15	16	17	18	19
20	21	22	23	24	25	26
27	28	29	30	31		

JULY
S	M	T	W	T	F	S
31					1	2
3	4	5	6	7	8	9
10	11	12	13	14	15	16
17	18	19	20	21	22	23
24	25	26	27	28	29	30

NOVEMBER
S	M	T	W	T	F	S
		1	2	3	4	5
6	7	8	9	10	11	12
13	14	15	16	17	18	19
20	21	22	23	24	25	26
27	28	29	30			

APRIL
S	M	T	W	T	F	S
					1	2
3	4	5	6	7	8	9
10	11	12	13	14	15	16
17	18	19	20	21	22	23
24	25	26	27	28	29	30

AUGUST
S	M	T	W	T	F	S
	1	2	3	4	5	6
7	8	9	10	11	12	13
14	15	16	17	18	19	20
21	22	23	24	25	26	27
28	29	30	31			

DECEMBER
S	M	T	W	T	F	S
				1	2	3
4	5	6	7	8	9	10
11	12	13	14	15	16	17
18	19	20	21	22	23	24
25	26	27	28	29	30	31

8

JANUARY
S	M	T	W	T	F	S
1	2	3	4	5	6	7
8	9	10	11	12	13	14
15	16	17	18	19	20	21
22	23	24	25	26	27	28
29	30	31				

MAY
S	M	T	W	T	F	S
		1	2	3	4	5
6	7	8	9	10	11	12
13	14	15	16	17	18	19
20	21	22	23	24	25	26
27	28	29	30	31		

SEPTEMBER
S	M	T	W	T	F	S
30						1
2	3	4	5	6	7	8
9	10	11	12	13	14	15
16	17	18	19	20	21	22
23	24	25	26	27	28	29

FEBRUARY
S	M	T	W	T	F	S
			1	2	3	4
5	6	7	8	9	10	11
12	13	14	15	16	17	18
19	20	21	22	23	24	25
26	27	28	29			

JUNE
S	M	T	W	T	F	S
					1	2
3	4	5	6	7	8	9
10	11	12	13	14	15	16
17	18	19	20	21	22	23
24	25	26	27	28	29	30

OCTOBER
S	M	T	W	T	F	S
	1	2	3	4	5	6
7	8	9	10	11	12	13
14	15	16	17	18	19	20
21	22	23	24	25	26	27
28	29	30	31			

MARCH
S	M	T	W	T	F	S
				1	2	3
4	5	6	7	8	9	10
11	12	13	14	15	16	17
18	19	20	21	22	23	24
25	26	27	28	29	30	31

JULY
S	M	T	W	T	F	S
1	2	3	4	5	6	7
8	9	10	11	12	13	14
15	16	17	18	19	20	21
22	23	24	25	26	27	28
29	30	31				

NOVEMBER
S	M	T	W	T	F	S
				1	2	3
4	5	6	7	8	9	10
11	12	13	14	15	16	17
18	19	20	21	22	23	24
25	26	27	28	29	30	

APRIL
S	M	T	W	T	F	S
1	2	3	4	5	6	7
8	9	10	11	12	13	14
15	16	17	18	19	20	21
22	23	24	25	26	27	28
29	30					

AUGUST
S	M	T	W	T	F	S
			1	2	3	4
5	6	7	8	9	10	11
12	13	14	15	16	17	18
19	20	21	22	23	24	25
26	27	28	29	30	31	

DECEMBER
S	M	T	W	T	F	S
30	31					1
2	3	4	5	6	7	8
9	10	11	12	13	14	15
16	17	18	19	20	21	22
23	24	25	26	27	28	29

9

JANUARY
S	M	T	W	T	F	S
	1	2	3	4	5	6
7	8	9	10	11	12	13
14	15	16	17	18	19	20
21	22	23	24	25	26	27
28	29	30	31			

MAY
S	M	T	W	T	F	S
			1	2	3	4
5	6	7	8	9	10	11
12	13	14	15	16	17	18
19	20	21	22	23	24	25
26	27	28	29	30	31	

SEPTEMBER
S	M	T	W	T	F	S
1	2	3	4	5	6	7
8	9	10	11	12	13	14
15	16	17	18	19	20	21
22	23	24	25	26	27	28
29	30					

FEBRUARY
S	M	T	W	T	F	S
				1	2	3
4	5	6	7	8	9	10
11	12	13	14	15	16	17
18	19	20	21	22	23	24
25	26	27	28	29		

JUNE
S	M	T	W	T	F	S
30						1
2	3	4	5	6	7	8
9	10	11	12	13	14	15
16	17	18	19	20	21	22
23	24	25	26	27	28	29

OCTOBER
S	M	T	W	T	F	S
		1	2	3	4	5
6	7	8	9	10	11	12
13	14	15	16	17	18	19
20	21	22	23	24	25	26
27	28	29	30	31		

MARCH
S	M	T	W	T	F	S
31					1	2
3	4	5	6	7	8	9
10	11	12	13	14	15	16
17	18	19	20	21	22	23
24	25	26	27	28	29	30

JULY
S	M	T	W	T	F	S
	1	2	3	4	5	6
7	8	9	10	11	12	13
14	15	16	17	18	19	20
21	22	23	24	25	26	27
28	29	30	31			

NOVEMBER
S	M	T	W	T	F	S
					1	2
3	4	5	6	7	8	9
10	11	12	13	14	15	16
17	18	19	20	21	22	23
24	25	26	27	28	29	30

APRIL
S	M	T	W	T	F	S
	1	2	3	4	5	6
7	8	9	10	11	12	13
14	15	16	17	18	19	20
21	22	23	24	25	26	27
28	29	30				

AUGUST
S	M	T	W	T	F	S
				1	2	3
4	5	6	7	8	9	10
11	12	13	14	15	16	17
18	19	20	21	22	23	24
25	26	27	28	29	30	31

DECEMBER
S	M	T	W	T	F	S
1	2	3	4	5	6	7
8	9	10	11	12	13	14
15	16	17	18	19	20	21
22	23	24	25	26	27	28
29	30	31				

10

JANUARY
S	M	T	W	T	F	S
		1	2	3	4	5
6	7	8	9	10	11	12
13	14	15	16	17	18	19
20	21	22	23	24	25	26
27	28	29	30	31		

MAY
S	M	T	W	T	F	S
				1	2	3
4	5	6	7	8	9	10
11	12	13	14	15	16	17
18	19	20	21	22	23	24
25	26	27	28	29	30	31

SEPTEMBER
S	M	T	W	T	F	S
	1	2	3	4	5	6
7	8	9	10	11	12	13
14	15	16	17	18	19	20
21	22	23	24	25	26	27
28	29	30				

FEBRUARY
S	M	T	W	T	F	S
					1	2
3	4	5	6	7	8	9
10	11	12	13	14	15	16
17	18	19	20	21	22	23
24	25	26	27	28	29	

JUNE
S	M	T	W	T	F	S
1	2	3	4	5	6	7
8	9	10	11	12	13	14
15	16	17	18	19	20	21
22	23	24	25	26	27	28
29	30					

OCTOBER
S	M	T	W	T	F	S
			1	2	3	4
5	6	7	8	9	10	11
12	13	14	15	16	17	18
19	20	21	22	23	24	25
26	27	28	29	30	31	

MARCH
S	M	T	W	T	F	S
30	31					1
2	3	4	5	6	7	8
9	10	11	12	13	14	15
16	17	18	19	20	21	22
23	24	25	26	27	28	29

JULY
S	M	T	W	T	F	S
		1	2	3	4	5
6	7	8	9	10	11	12
13	14	15	16	17	18	19
20	21	22	23	24	25	26
27	28	29	30	31		

NOVEMBER
S	M	T	W	T	F	S
30						1
2	3	4	5	6	7	8
9	10	11	12	13	14	15
16	17	18	19	20	21	22
23	24	25	26	27	28	29

APRIL
S	M	T	W	T	F	S
		1	2	3	4	5
6	7	8	9	10	11	12
13	14	15	16	17	18	19
20	21	22	23	24	25	26
27	28	29	30			

AUGUST
S	M	T	W	T	F	S
31					1	2
3	4	5	6	7	8	9
10	11	12	13	14	15	16
17	18	19	20	21	22	23
24	25	26	27	28	29	30

DECEMBER
S	M	T	W	T	F	S
	1	2	3	4	5	6
7	8	9	10	11	12	13
14	15	16	17	18	19	20
21	22	23	24	25	26	27
28	29	30	31			

11

JANUARY
S	M	T	W	T	F	S
				1	2	3	4
5	6	7	8	9	10	11
12	13	14	15	16	17	18
19	20	21	22	23	24	25
26	27	28	29	30	31	

FEBRUARY
S	M	T	W	T	F	S
						1
2	3	4	5	6	7	8
9	10	11	12	13	14	15
16	17	18	19	20	21	22
23	24	25	26	27	28	29

MARCH
S	M	T	W	T	F	S
1	2	3	4	5	6	7
8	9	10	11	12	13	14
15	16	17	18	19	20	21
22	23	24	25	26	27	28
29	30	31				

APRIL
S	M	T	W	T	F	S
			1	2	3	4
5	6	7	8	9	10	11
12	13	14	15	16	17	18
19	20	21	22	23	24	25
26	27	28	29	30		

MAY
S	M	T	W	T	F	S
31					1	2
3	4	5	6	7	8	9
10	11	12	13	14	15	16
17	18	19	20	21	22	23
24	25	26	27	28	29	30

JUNE
S	M	T	W	T	F	S
	1	2	3	4	5	6
7	8	9	10	11	12	13
14	15	16	17	18	19	20
21	22	23	24	25	26	27
28	29	30				

JULY
S	M	T	W	T	F	S
			1	2	3	4
5	6	7	8	9	10	11
12	13	14	15	16	17	18
19	20	21	22	23	24	25
26	27	28	29	30	31	

AUGUST
S	M	T	W	T	F	S
30	31					1
2	3	4	5	6	7	8
9	10	11	12	13	14	15
16	17	18	19	20	21	22
23	24	25	26	27	28	29

SEPTEMBER
S	M	T	W	T	F	S
		1	2	3	4	5
6	7	8	9	10	11	12
13	14	15	16	17	18	19
20	21	22	23	24	25	26
27	28	29	30			

OCTOBER
S	M	T	W	T	F	S
				1	2	3
4	5	6	7	8	9	10
11	12	13	14	15	16	17
18	19	20	21	22	23	24
25	26	27	28	29	30	31

NOVEMBER
S	M	T	W	T	F	S
1	2	3	4	5	6	7
8	9	10	11	12	13	14
15	16	17	18	19	20	21
22	23	24	25	26	27	28
29	30					

DECEMBER
S	M	T	W	T	F	S
		1	2	3	4	5
6	7	8	9	10	11	12
13	14	15	16	17	18	19
20	21	22	23	24	25	26
27	28	29	30	31		

12

JANUARY
S	M	T	W	T	F	S
					1	2	3
4	5	6	7	8	9	10
11	12	13	14	15	16	17
18	19	20	21	22	23	24
25	26	27	28	29	30	31

FEBRUARY
S	M	T	W	T	F	S
1	2	3	4	5	6	7
8	9	10	11	12	13	14
15	16	17	18	19	20	21
22	23	24	25	26	27	28
29						

MARCH
S	M	T	W	T	F	S
	1	2	3	4	5	6
7	8	9	10	11	12	13
14	15	16	17	18	19	20
21	22	23	24	25	26	27
28	29	30	31			

APRIL
S	M	T	W	T	F	S
					1	2	3
4	5	6	7	8	9	10
11	12	13	14	15	16	17
18	19	20	21	22	23	24
25	26	27	28	29	30	

MAY
S	M	T	W	T	F	S
30	31					1
2	3	4	5	6	7	8
9	10	11	12	13	14	15
16	17	18	19	20	21	22
23	24	25	26	27	28	29

JUNE
S	M	T	W	T	F	S
		1	2	3	4	5
6	7	8	9	10	11	12
13	14	15	16	17	18	19
20	21	22	23	24	25	26
27	28	29	30			

JULY
S	M	T	W	T	F	S
					1	2	3
4	5	6	7	8	9	10
11	12	13	14	15	16	17
18	19	20	21	22	23	24
25	26	27	28	29	30	31

AUGUST
S	M	T	W	T	F	S
1	2	3	4	5	6	7
8	9	10	11	12	13	14
15	16	17	18	19	20	21
22	23	24	25	26	27	28
29	30	31				

SEPTEMBER
S	M	T	W	T	F	S
		1	2	3	4	
5	6	7	8	9	10	11
12	13	14	15	16	17	18
19	20	21	22	23	24	25
26	27	28	29	30		

OCTOBER
S	M	T	W	T	F	S
31					1	2
3	4	5	6	7	8	9
10	11	12	13	14	15	16
17	18	19	20	21	22	23
24	25	26	27	28	29	30

NOVEMBER
S	M	T	W	T	F	S
1	2	3	4	5	6	
7	8	9	10	11	12	13
14	15	16	17	18	19	20
21	22	23	24	25	26	27
28	29	30				

DECEMBER
S	M	T	W	T	F	S
			1	2	3	4
5	6	7	8	9	10	11
12	13	14	15	16	17	18
19	20	21	22	23	24	25
26	27	28	29	30	31	

13

JANUARY
S	M	T	W	T	F	S
31					1	2
3	4	5	6	7	8	9
10	11	12	13	14	15	16
17	18	19	20	21	22	23
24	25	26	27	28	29	30

FEBRUARY
S	M	T	W	T	F	S
1	2	3	4	5	6	
7	8	9	10	11	12	13
14	15	16	17	18	19	20
21	22	23	24	25	26	27
28	29					

MARCH
S	M	T	W	T	F	S
		1	2	3	4	5
6	7	8	9	10	11	12
13	14	15	16	17	18	19
20	21	22	23	24	25	26
27	28	29	30	31		

APRIL
S	M	T	W	T	F	S
						1	2
3	4	5	6	7	8	9
10	11	12	13	14	15	16
17	18	19	20	21	22	23
24	25	26	27	28	29	30

MAY
S	M	T	W	T	F	S
1	2	3	4	5	6	7
8	9	10	11	12	13	14
15	16	17	18	19	20	21
22	23	24	25	26	27	28
29	30	31				

JUNE
S	M	T	W	T	F	S
			1	2	3	4
5	6	7	8	9	10	11
12	13	14	15	16	17	18
19	20	21	22	23	24	25
26	27	28	29	30		

JULY
S	M	T	W	T	F	S
31					1	2
3	4	5	6	7	8	9
10	11	12	13	14	15	16
17	18	19	20	21	22	23
24	25	26	27	28	29	30

AUGUST
S	M	T	W	T	F	S
1	2	3	4	5	6	
7	8	9	10	11	12	13
14	15	16	17	18	19	20
21	22	23	24	25	26	27
28	29	30	31			

SEPTEMBER
S	M	T	W	T	F	S
				1	2	3
4	5	6	7	8	9	10
11	12	13	14	15	16	17
18	19	20	21	22	23	24
25	26	27	28	29	30	

OCTOBER
S	M	T	W	T	F	S
30	31					1
2	3	4	5	6	7	8
9	10	11	12	13	14	15
16	17	18	19	20	21	22
23	24	25	26	27	28	29

NOVEMBER
S	M	T	W	T	F	S
		1	2	3	4	5
6	7	8	9	10	11	12
13	14	15	16	17	18	19
20	21	22	23	24	25	26
27	28	29	30			

DECEMBER
S	M	T	W	T	F	S
				1	2	3
4	5	6	7	8	9	10
11	12	13	14	15	16	17
18	19	20	21	22	23	24
25	26	27	28	29	30	31

14

JANUARY
S	M	T	W	T	F	S
30	31					1
2	3	4	5	6	7	8
9	10	11	12	13	14	15
16	17	18	19	20	21	22
23	24	25	26	27	28	29

FEBRUARY
S	M	T	W	T	F	S
		1	2	3	4	5
6	7	8	9	10	11	12
13	14	15	16	17	18	19
20	21	22	23	24	25	26
27	28					

MARCH
S	M	T	W	T	F	S
			1	2	3	4
5	6	7	8	9	10	11
12	13	14	15	16	17	18
19	20	21	22	23	24	25
26	27	28	29	30	31	

APRIL
S	M	T	W	T	F	S
30						1
2	3	4	5	6	7	8
9	10	11	12	13	14	15
16	17	18	19	20	21	22
23	24	25	26	27	28	29

MAY
S	M	T	W	T	F	S
	1	2	3	4	5	6
7	8	9	10	11	12	13
14	15	16	17	18	19	20
21	22	23	24	25	26	27
28	29	30	31			

JUNE
S	M	T	W	T	F	S
				1	2	3
4	5	6	7	8	9	10
11	12	13	14	15	16	17
18	19	20	21	22	23	24
25	26	27	28	29	30	

JULY
S	M	T	W	T	F	S
30	31					1
2	3	4	5	6	7	8
9	10	11	12	13	14	15
16	17	18	19	20	21	22
23	24	25	26	27	28	29

AUGUST
S	M	T	W	T	F	S
		1	2	3	4	5
6	7	8	9	10	11	12
13	14	15	16	17	18	19
20	21	22	23	24	25	26
27	28	29	30	31		

SEPTEMBER
S	M	T	W	T	F	S
					1	2
3	4	5	6	7	8	9
10	11	12	13	14	15	16
17	18	19	20	21	22	23
24	25	26	27	28	29	30

OCTOBER
S	M	T	W	T	F	S
1	2	3	4	5	6	7
8	9	10	11	12	13	14
15	16	17	18	19	20	21
22	23	24	25	26	27	28
29	30	31				

NOVEMBER
S	M	T	W	T	F	S
			1	2	3	4
5	6	7	8	9	10	11
12	13	14	15	16	17	18
19	20	21	22	23	24	25
26	27	28	29	30		

DECEMBER
S	M	T	W	T	F	S
31					1	2
3	4	5	6	7	8	9
10	11	12	13	14	15	16
17	18	19	20	21	22	23
24	25	26	27	28	29	30

UNITED STATES MAP

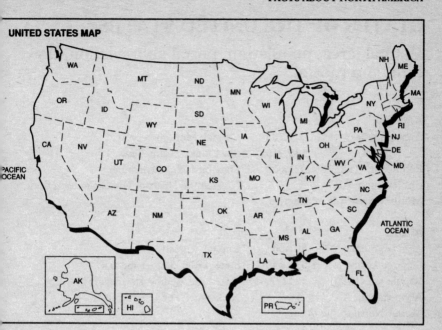

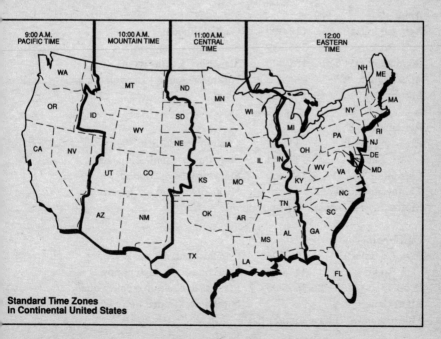

Standard Time Zones in Continental United States

STATES OF THE UNITED STATES

Capital, area, population, postal abbreviation, flower, bird, and motto

Alabama

Area (sq miles):   51,705   Capital: Montgomery
    (sq km):   133,915   State flower: Camellia
Population (1985): 4,021,000   State bird: Yellowhammer
Abbreviation: AL   Nicknames: Heart of Dixie; Camellia State
Motto: Crossroads of America

Alaska

Area (sq miles):   591,004   Capital: Juneau
    (sq km):   1,530,693   State flower: Forget-me-not
Population (1985):   521,000   State bird: Willow ptarmigan
Abbreviation: AK   Nickname: The Last Frontier
Motto: North to the future

Arizona

Area (sq miles):   114,000   Captial: Phoenix
    (sq km):   295,259   State flower: Saguaro
Population (1985): 3,187,000   State bird: Cactus wren
Abbreviation: AZ   Nickname: Grand Canyon State
Motto: *Diat Deus* ('God enriches')

Arkansas

Area (sq miles):   53,187   Capital: Little Rock
    (sq km):   137,754   State flower: Apple blossom
Population: (1985) 2,359,000   State bird: Mockingbird
Abbreviation: AR   Nickname: Land of Opportunity
Motto: *Regnat Populus* ('The people rule')

California

Area (sq miles):   158,706   Capital: Sacramento
    (sq km):   411,047   State flower: Golden poppy
Population (1985): 26,365,000   State bird: California valley quail
Abbreviation: CA   Nickname: Golden State
Motto: *Eureka* ('I have found it')

Colorado

Area (sq miles): 104,091 Capital: Denver
(sq km): 269,594 State Flower: Blue Colombine
Population (1985): 3,231,000 State Bird: Lark Bunting
Abbreviation: CO Nickname: Centennial State
Motto: *Nil sine numine* ('Nothing without providence')

Connecticut

Area (sq miles): 5,018 Capital: Hartford
(sq km): 12,997 State flower: Mountain laurel
Population (1985): 3,174,000 State Bird: American robin
Abbreviation: CT Nicknames: Constitution State; Nutmeg State
Motto: *Qui transtulit sustinet* ('He who transplanted still sustains')

Delaware

Area (sq miles): 2,044 Capital: Dover
(sq km): 5,294 State flower: Peach blossom
Population (1985): 622,000 State bird: Blue hen chicken
Abbreviation: DE Nicknames: First State; Diamond State
Motto: Liberty and independence

District of Columbia

Area (sq miles): 000 Capital: Washington
(sq km): 164 State flower: American beauty
Population (1985): 638,000 State bird: Wood thrush
Abbreviation: DC Nickname: Capital city
Motto: *Justitia omnibus* ('Justice for all')

Florida

Area (sq miles): 58,664 Capital: Tallahassee
(sq km): 151, 939 State flower: Orange blossom
Population (1985): 11,366,000 State bird: Mockingbird
Abbreviation: FL Nickname: Sunshine State
Motto: in God we trust

Georgia

Area: (sq miles): 58,910 Capital: Atlanta
(sq km): 152,576 State flower: Cherokee rose
Population (1985): 5,976,000 State bird: Brown thrasher
Abbreviation: GA Nicknames: Peace State; Empire State of
the South.
Motto: Wisdom, justice and moderation.

187

Hawaii

Area (sq miles):	6,471	Capital: Honolulu
(sq km):	16,760	State flower: Hibiscus
Population (1985):	1,054,000	State bird: Nene Goose
Abbreviation: HI		Nickname: Aloha State

Motto: The life of the land is perpetuated in righteousness.

Idaho

Area (sq miles):	83,564	Capital: Boise
(sq km):	216,430	State flower: Syringa
Population (1985):	1,005,000	State bird: Mountain bluebird
Abbreviation ID		Nickname: Gem State

Motto: *Esto perpetua* ('It is perpetual')

Illinois

Area (sq miles):	57,8ß71	Capital: Springfield
(sq km):	149,885	State flower: Native violet
Population (1985):	11,535,000	State bird: Cardinal
Abbreviation: IL		Nickname: Prairie State

Motto: State sovereignty - national union

Indiana

Area (sq miles):	36,413	Capital: Indianapolis
(sq km):	94,309	State flower: Peony
Population (1985):	5,499,000	State bird: Cardinal
Abbreviation: IN		Nickname: Hoosier State

Motto: Crossroads of America.

Iowa

Area (sq miles):	56,275	Capital: Des Moines
(sq km):	145,752	State flower: Wild rose
Population (1985):	2,884,000	State bird: Goldfinch
Abbreviation: IA		Nickname: Hawkeye State

Motto: Our liberties we prize and our rights we will maintain.

Kansas

Area (sq miles):	82,277	Capital: Topeka
(sq km) :	213,096	State flower: Sunflower
Population (1985):	2,450,000	State bird: Western meadowlark
Abbreviation: KS		Nickname: Sunflower State

Motto: *Ad astra per aspera* ('To the stars through difficulties')

Kentucky

Area (sq miles):	40,409	Capital: Frankfort
(sq km):	104,659	State flower: Goldenrod
Population (1985):	3,726,000	State bird: Kentucky cardinal
Abbreviation: KY		Nickname: Bluegrass State

Motto: United we stand, divided we fall.

Louisiana

Area (sq miles):	47,752	Capital: Baton Rouge
(sq km):	123,677	State flower: Magnolia
Population (1985):	4,481,000	State bird: Eastern brown pelican
Abbreviation: LA		Nickname: Pelican State

Motto: Union, justice, and confidence.

Maine

Area (sq miles):	33,265	Capital: Augusta
(sq km):	86,156	State flower: Pine cone and tassel
Population (1985):	1,164,000	State bird: Chickadee
Abbreviation: ME		Nickname: Pine Tree State

Motto: *Dirigo* ('I direct')

Maryland

Area (sq miles):	10,460	Capital: Annapolis
(sq km):	27,091	State flower: Black-eyed Susan
Population (1985):	4,392,000	State bird: Baltimore oriole
Abbreviation: MD		Nicknames: Old line state; Free State

Motto: *Fatti maschii, parole femine* ('Manly deeds, womanly words')

Massachusetts

Area (sq miles):	8,284	Capital: Boston
(sq km):	21,455	State flower: Mayflower
Population (1985):	5,822,000	State bird: Chickadee
Abbreviation: MA		Nicknames: Bay State; Colony State.

Motto: *Ense petit placidam sub libertate* ('By the sword we seek peace, but peace only under liberty')

Michigan

Area (sq miles):	97,102	Capital: Lansing
(sq km):	251,493	State flower: Apple
Population (1985):	9,088,000	State bird: Robin
Abbreviation: MI		Nicknames: Great lake State; Wolverine State

Motto: *Si quaeris peninsulam amoenam* ('If you seek a pleasant peninsula, look about you')

Minnesota

Area (sq miles):	86,614	Capital: St Paul
(sq km):	224,329	State flower: Showy lady slipper
Population (1985):	4,193,000	State bird: Common loon
Abbreviation: MN		Nicknames: North Star State; Gopher State.

Motto: *L'Etoile du nord* ('Star of the North')

Mississippi

Area (sq miles):	47,689	Capital: Jackson
(sq km):	123,514	State flower: Magnolia
Population (1985):	2,613,000	State bird: Mockingbird
Abbreviation: MS		Nickname: Magnolia State

Motto: *Virtute et armis* ('By valor and arms')

Missouri

Area (sq miles):	69,697	Capital: Jefferson City
(sq km):	180,415	State flower: Hawthorn
Population (1985):	5,029,000	State bird: Bluebird
Abbreviation: MO		Nickname: Show-Me-State

Motto: *Salus populi suprema lex esto* ('The welfare of the people shall be the supreme law')

Montana

Area (sq miles):	147,046	Capital: Helena
(sq km):	380,847	State flower: Bitterroot
Population (1985):	826,000	State bird: Western meadowlark
Abbreviation: MT		Nickname: Treasure State

Motto: *Oro y plata* ('Gold and silver')

Nebraska

Area (sq miles):	77,355	Capital: Lincoln
(sq km):	200,349	State flower: Goldenrod
Population (1985):	1,606,000	State bird: Meadowlark
Abbreviation: NE		Nickname: Cornhusker State

Motto: Equality before the law

Nevada

Area (sq miles):	110,561	Capital: Carson City
(sq km):	286,352	State flower: Sagebrush
Population (1985):	936,000	State bird: Mountain Bluebird
Abbreviation: NV		Nicknames: Sagebrush State; Battle-Born State

Motto: All for our country.

New Hampshire

Area (sq miles): 9,279
(sq km): 24,032
Population (1985): 998,000
Abbreviation: NH
Motto: Live free or die

Capital: Concord
State flower: Purple lilac
State bird: Purple finch
Nickname: Granite State

New Jersey

Area (sq miles): 7,787
(sq km): 20,168
Population (1985): 7,562,000
Abbreviation: NJ
Motto: Liberty and prosperity.

Capital: Trenton
State flower: Purple violet
State bird: Eastern goldfinch
Nickname: Garden State

New Mexico

Area (sq miles): 121,593
(sq km): 314,924
Population (1985): 1,450,000
Abbreviation: NM
Motto: *Crescit eundo* ('It grows as it goes').

Capital: Santa Fe
State flower: Yucca
State bird: Roadrunner
Nickname: Land of Enchantment

New York

Area (sq miles): 52,735
(sq km): 136,583
Population (1985): 17,783,000
Abbreviation: NY
Motto: *Excelsior* ('ever upward')

Capital: Albany
State flower: Rose (any color)
State bird: Bluebird
Nickname: Empire State

North Carolina

Area (sq miles): 52,669
(sq km): 136,412
Population (1985): 6,255,000
Abbreviation: NC
Motto: *Esse quam videri* ('To be rather than to seem')

Capital: Raleigh
State flower: Dogwood
State bird: Cardinal
Nicknames: Tar Heel State; Old North State

North Dakota

Area (sq miles): 70,702
(sq km): 183,117
Population (1985): 685,000
Abbreviation: ND
Motto: Liberty and union, now and forever, one and inseparable.

Capital: Bismarck
State flower: Wild prairie rose
State bird: Western Meadowlark
Nickname: Peace Garden State

FACTS ABOUT NORTH AMERICA

Ohio

Area (sq miles):	44,787	Capital: Columbus
(sq km):	115,998	State flower: Scarlet carnation
Population (1985):	10,744,000	State bird: Cardinal
Abbreviation: OH		Nickname: Buckeye State

Motto: With God all things are possible.

Oklahoma

Area (sq miles):	69,956	Capital: Oklahoma City
(sq km):	181,185	State flower: Mistletoe
Population (1985):	3,301,000	State bird: Scissor-tailed flycatcher
Abbreviation: OK		Nickname: Sooner State

Motto: *Labor omnia vincit* ('Labor conquers all things')

Oregon

Area (sq miles):	97,073	Capital: Salem
(sq km):	251,418	State flower: Oregon grape
Population (1985):	2,687,000	State bird: Western meadowlark
Abbreviation: OR		Nickname: Beaver State

Motto: The union.

Pennsylvania

Area (sq miles):	46,063	Capital: Harrisburg
(sq km):	119,251	State flower: Mountain laurel
Population (1985):	11,853,000	State bird: Ruffed grouse
Abbreviation: PA		Nickname: Keystone State

Motto: Virtue, liberty and independence.

Rhode Island

Area (sq miles):	1,212	Capital: Providence
(sq km):	3,139	State flower: Violet
Population (1985):	968,000	State bird: Rhode Island hen
Abbreviation: RI		Nicknames: Little Rhody; Ocean State

Motto: Hope

South Carolina

Area (sq miles):	31,113	Capital: Columbia
(sq km):	80,852	State flower: Carolina jessamine
Population (1985):	3,347,000	State bird: Carolina wren
Abbreviation: SC		Nickname: Palmetto State

Motto: *Dum spiro spero* ('While I breathe, I hope')

South Dakota

Area (sq miles):	77,116	Capital: Pierre
(sq km):	199,730	State flower: Pasque flower
Population (1985):	708,000	State bird: Pheasant
Abbreviation: SD		Nicknames: Coyote State; Sunshine State

Motto: Under God, the people rule.

Tennessee

Area (sq miles):	42,144	Capital: Nashville
(sq km):	109,152	State flower: Iris
Population (1985):	4,762,000	State bird: Mockingbird
Abbreviation: TN		Nickname: Volunteer State

Motto: Agriculture and commerce.

Texas

Area (sq miles):	266,807	Capital: Austin
(sq km):	691.027	State flower: Bluebonnet
Population (1985):	16,370,000	State bird: Mockingbird
Abbreviation: TX		Nickname: Lone Star State

Motto: Friendship

Utah

Area (sq miles):	84,899	Capital: Salt Lake City
(sq km):	219,887	State flower: Sego lily
Population (1985):	1,645,000	State bird: Seagull
Abbreviation: UT		Nickname: Beehive State

Motto: Industry

Vermont

Area (sq miles):	9,614	Capital: Montpelier
(sq km):	24,900	State flower: Red clover
Population (1985):	535,000	State bird: Thrush
Abbreviation: VT		Nickname: Green Mountain State

Motto: Freedom and unity

Virginia

Area (sq miles):	40,767	Capital: Richmond
(sq km):	105,586	State flower: Flowering dogwood
Population (1985):	5,706,000	State bird: Cardinal
Abbreviation: VA		Nickname: Old Dominion

Motto: *Sic semper tyannis* ('Thus always to tyrants')

Washington

Area (sq miles):	68,139	Capital: Olympia
(sq km):	176,479	State flower: Rhododendron
Populations (1985):	4,409,000	State bird: Willow Goldfinch
Abbreviations: WA		Nickname: Evergreen State

Motto: *Alki* ('By and by')

West Virginia

Area (sq miles):	24,231	Capital: Charlestown
(sq km):	62,758	State flower: Rhododendron
Population (1985):	1,936, 000	State bird: Cardinal
Abbreviation: WV		Nickname: Mountain State

Motto: *Montani semper liberi* ('Mountaineers are always free')

Wisconsin

Area (sq miles):	66,215	Capital: Madison
(sq km):	171,496	State flower: Wood violet
Population (1985):	4,775,000	State bird: Robin
Abbreviation: WI		Nickname: Badger State

Motto: Forward

Wyoming

Area (sq miles):	97,809	Capital: Cheyenne
(sq km):	253,324	State flower: Indian paintbrush
Population (1985):	509,000	State bird: Meadowlark
Abbreviation: WY		Nickname: Equality State

Motto: Equal rights.

Commonwealth

Puerto Rico

Area (sq miles):	3,349	Capital: San Juan
(sq km):	8,647	Flower: Maga
Population:	3,196,520	Bird: Reinita
Abbreviation: PR		Nickname: Equality State

Motto: *Joannes est nomen eius* ('John is his name')

PRESIDENTS OF THE UNITED STATES

No.	Name	Life Dates	Place of Birth	Politics	Dates of Term
1	George Washington	1732-1799	Virginia	Federalist	1789-1797
2	John Adams	1735-1826	Massachusetts	Federalist	1797-1801
3	Thomas Jefferson	1743-1826	Virginia	Dem.-Rep.	1801-1809
4	James Madison	1751-1836	Virginia	Dem.-Rep.	1809-1817
5	James Monroe	1758-1831	Virginia	Dem.-Rep.	1817-1825
6.	John Quincy Adams	1767-1848	Massachusetts	Dem.-Rep.	1825-1829
7	Andrew Jackson	1767-1845	South Carolina	Democrat	1829-1837
8	Martin Van Buren	1782-1862	New York	Democrat	1837-1841
9	William Henry Harrison	1773-1841	Virginia	Whig	1841
10	John Tyler	1790-1862	Virginia	Democrat	1841-1845
11	James Knox Polk	1795-1849	North Carolina	Democrat	1845-1849
12	Zachary Taylor	1784-1850	Virginia	Whig	1849-1850
13	Millard Fillmore	1800-1874	New York	Whig	1850-1853
14	Franklin Pierce	1804-1869	New Hampshire	Democrat	1853-1857
15	James Buchanan	1791-1868	Pennsylvania	Democrat	1857-1861
16	Abraham Lincoln	1809-1865	Kentucky	Republican	1861-1865
17	Andrew Johnson	1808-1875	North Carolina	Republican	1865-1869
18	Ulysses Simpson Grant	1822-1885	Ohio	Republican	1869-1877
19	Rutherford Birchard Hayes	1822-1893	Ohio	Republican	1877-1881
20	James Abram Garfield	1831-1881	Ohio	Republican	1881
21	Chester Alan Arthur	1830-1886	Vermont	Republican	1881-1885
22	Grover Cleveland	1837-1908	New Jersey	Democrat	1885-1889
23	Benjamin Harrison	1833-1901	Ohio	Republican	1889-1893
24	Grover Cleveland	1837-1908	New Jersey	Democrat	1893-1897
25	William McKinley	1843-1901	Ohio	Republican	1897-1901
26	Theodore Roosevelt	1858-1919	New York	Republican	1901-1909
27	William Howard Taft	1857-1930	Ohio	Republican	1909-1913
28	Woodrow Wilson	1856-1924	Virginia	Democrat	1913-1921
29	Warren Gamaliel Harding	1865-1923	Ohio	Republican	1921-1923
30	Calvin Coolidge	1872-1933	Vermont	Republican	1923-1929
31	Herbert Clark Hoover	1874-1964	Iowa	Republican	1929-1933
32	Franklin Delano Roosevelt	1882-1945	New York	Democrat	1933-1945

No.	Name	Life Dates	Place of Birth	Politics	Dates of Term
33	Harry S. Truman	1884-1972	Missouri	Democrat	1945-1953
34	Dwight David Eisenhower	1890-1969	Texas	Republican	1953-1961
35	John Fitzgerald Kennedy	1917-1963	Massachusetts	Democrat	1961-1963
36	Lyndon Baines Johnson	1908-1973	Texas	Democrat	1963-1969
37	Richard Milhous Nixon	1913-	California	Republican	1969-1974
38	Gerald Rudolph Ford	1913-	Nebraska	Republican	1974-1977
39	James Earl Carter Jr.	1924-	Georgia	Democrat	1977-1981
40	Ronald Wilson Reagan	1911-	Illinois	Republican	1981-1989
41	George Herbert Walker Bush	1924-	Massachusetts	Republican	1989-

VICE PRESIDENTS OF THE UNITED STATES

No.	Name	Life Dates	President	Politics
1	John Adams	1735-1826	George Washington	Federalist
2	Thomas Jefferson	1743-1826	John Adams	Federalist
3	Aaron Burr	1756-1836	Thomas Jefferson	Dem.-Rep.
4	George Clinton	1739-1812	Thomas Jefferson James Madison	Dem.-Rep.
5	Elbridge Gerry	1744-1814	James Madison	Dem.-Rep.
6	Daniel D. Tonpkins	1774-1825	James Madison	Dem.-Rep.
7	John C. Calhoun	1782-1850	John Quincy Adams Andrew Jackson	Dem.-Rep.
8	Martin Van Buren	1782-1862	Andrew Jackson	Dem.-Rep.
9	Richard M. Johnson	1780-1850	Martin Van Buren	Democrat
10	John Tyler	1790-1862	William Henry Harrison	Whig
11	George M. Dallas	1792-1864	James K. Polk	Democrat
12	Millard Fillmore	1800-1874	Zachary Taylor	Whig
13	William R. King	1786-1853	Franklin Pierce	Democrat

No.	Name	Life Dates	President	Politics
14	John C. Breckinridge	1821-1875	James Buchanan	Democrat
15	Hannibal Hamlin	1809-1891	Abraham Lincoln	Republican
16	Andrew Johnson	1808-1875	Abraham Lincoln	Republican
17	Schuyler Colfax	1823-1885	Ulysses S. Grant	Republican
18	Henry Wilson	1812-1875	Ulysses S. Grant	Republican
19	William A. Wheeler	1819-1887	Rutherford B. Hayes	Republican
20	Chester A. Arthur	1829-1886	James Garfield	Republican
21	Thomas A. Hendricks	1819-1885	Grover Cleveland	Democrat
22	Levi P. Morton	1824-1920	Benjamin Harrison	Republican
23	Adlai E. Steveson	1835-1914	Grover Cleveland	Democrat
24	Garret A. Hobart	1844-1899	William McKinley	Republican
25	Theodore Roosevelt	1858-1919	William McKinley	Republican
26	Charles W. Fairbanks	1852-1918	Theodore Roosevelt	Republican
27	James S. Sherman	1855-1912	William H. Taft	Republican
28	Thomas R. Marshall	1854-1925	Woodrow Wilson	Democrat
29	Calvin Coolidge	1872-1933	Warren G. Harding	Republican
30	Charles G. Dawes	1865-1951	Calvin Coolidge	Republican
31	Charles Curtis	1860-1936	Herbert C. Hoover	Republican
32	John N. Garner	1868-1967	Franklin D. Roosevelt	Democrat
33	Henry A. Wallace	1888-1965	Franklin D. Roosevelt	Democrat
34	Harry S. Truman	1884-1972	Franklin D. Roosevelt	Democrat
35	Alben W. Barkley	1877-1956	Harry S. Truman	Democrat
36	Richard M. Nixon	1913-	Dwight D. Eisenhower	Republican
37	Lyndon B. Johnson	1908-1973	John F. Kennedy	Democrat
38	Hubert H. Humphrey	1911-1978	Lyndon B. Johnson	Democrat
39	Spiro T. Agnew	1918-	Richard M. Nixon	Republican
40	Gerald R. Ford	1913-	Richard M. Nixon	Republican
41	Nelson A. Rockefeller	1908-1979	Gerald R. Ford	Republican
42	Walter F. Mondale	1928-	James (Jimmy) Carter	Democrat
43	George Bush	1924-	Ronald Reagan	Republican
44	J. Danforth Quayle	1947	George Bush	Republican

NATIONAL PARKS OF THE UNITED STATES

Park Name	Designation Date	Area (hectares)	Location
Arcadia	1916	15,770	Maine
Arches	1929	29,695	Utah
Badlands	1929	98,461	South Dakota
Big Bend	1935	286,565	Texas
Biscayne	1968	72,900	Florida
Bryce Canyon	1923	14,502	Utah
Canyonland	1964	136,610	Utah
Capitol Reef	1937	97,895	Utah
Carsbad Caverns	1923	18,921	New Mexico
Channel Islands	1938	100,910	South California
Crater Lake	1902	64,869	Oregon
Denaldi	1917	1,645,248	South Alaska
Everglades	1934	566,075	Florida
Gates of the Arctic	1978	2,845,000	Alaska
Glacier	1910	410,188	Montana
Glacier Bay	1925	1,569,481	Alaska
Grand Canyon	1908	493,059	Arizona
Grand Teton	1929	125,661	Wyoming
Great Smoky Mountains	1926	210,550	Tennessee
Guadalupe Mountains	1966	30,875	Texas
Haleakala	1916	11,596	Hawaii
Hawaii Volcanoes	1916	92,745	Hawaii
Hot Springs	1832	2,358	Arkansas
Isle Royale	1931	231,398	Michigan
Katmai	1918	1,792,810	Alaska
Kenai Fjord	1978	229,457	Alaska
Kings Canyon	1940	186,211	California
Kobuk Valley	1978	692,000	Alaska
Lake Clark	1978	987,000	Alaska
Lassen Volcanic	1907	43,047	California
Mammoth Cave	1926	21,230	Kentucky
Mesa Verde	1906	21,078	Colorado
Mount Rainier	1899	95,265	Washington
North Cascades	1968	204,227	Washington
Olympic	1909	370,250	Washington
Petrified Forest	1906	37,835	Arizona
Redwood	1968	44,280	California
Rocky Mountian	1915	106,762	Colorado
Sequoia	1890	162,885	California
Shenandoah	1926	78,.845	Virginia
Theodore Roosevelt	1947	78,845	Virginia
Virgin Islands	1956	5,947	Virgin Islands
Voyageurs	1971	88.678	Minnesota
Wind Cave	1903	11,449	South Dakota
Wrangell-St Elias	1978	3,297,000	Alaska
Yellowstone	1872	898,350	Montana / Wyoming
Yosemite	1890	307,932	California
Zion	1909	59,308	Utah

PROVINCES OF CANADA

Name	(Abb)	Area sq km	sq miles	Population (1986 est)	Capital
Alberta	AB	661,188	255,285	2,365,825	Edmonton
British Columbia	BC	930,532	359, 279	2,883,367	Victoria
Manitoba	MB	650,090	251,000	1,063,016	Winnipeg
New Bruntswick	NB	72,092	27,835'	709,442	Fredericton
Newfoundland	NF	404,519	156,185	568,349	St John's
Northwest Territories	NT	3,246,404	1,253,438	51,384	Yellowknife
Nova Scotia	NS	52,841	20,402	873,199	Halifax
Ontario	ON	891,198	344,092	9,100,000	Toronto
Prince Edward Island	PE	5656	2184	126,646	Charlottetown
Quebec	PQ	1,540,680	594,860	6,572,300	Quebec
Saskatchewan	SK	651,900	251,700	1,009,613	Regina
Yukon Territory	YT	536,327	207,076	26,166	Whitehorse

NATIONAL PARKS OF CANADA

Name	Location	Area sq miles	(km)
Banff	Alberta	2,585	(6,695)
Cape Breton Highlands	Cape Breton Island	390	(1,010)
Elk Island	Alberta	51	(132)
Fundy	New Brunswick	79	(205)
Georgian Bay Islands	Georgian Bay	5.4	(14)
Glacier	British Columbia	521	(1,350)
Jasper	Alberta	4,200	(10,880)
Kootenay	British Columbia	587	(1,520)
Mount Revelstoke	British Columbia	100	(259)
Point Pelee	Ontario	6	(16)
Prince Albert	Saskatchewan	1,869	(4,840)
Prince Edward Island	Prince Edward Island	7	(18)
Riding Mountain	Manitoba	1,148	(2,970)
St Lawrence Islands	Thousand Islands	0.3	(0.8)
Terra Nova	Newfoundland	153	(396)
Waterton Lakes	Alberta	220	(570)
Wood Buffalo	Alberta	17,300	(44,800)
Yoho	British Columbia	507	(1,310)

BASEBALL TEAMS

	Team	Stadium
National League	Atlanta Braves	Atlanta-Fulton County Stadium, GA
	Chicago Cubs	Wrigley Field, IL
	Cincinnati Reds	Riverfront Stadium, OH
	Houston Astros	Astrodome, TX
	Los Angeles Dodgers	Dodgers Stadium, CA
	Montreal Expos	Olympic Stadium, Quebec
	New York Mets	Shea Stadium, PA
	Philadelphia Phillies	Veterans Stadium,PA
	Pittsburgh Pirates	Three Rivers Stadium, PA
	St Louis Cardinals	Busch Stadium, MO
	San Diego Padres	Jack Murphy Stadium, CA\
	San Francisco Saints	Candlestick Park, CA

	Team	Stadium
American League	Baltimore Orioles	Memorial Stadium, MD
	Boston Red Sox	Fenway Park, MA
	California Angels	Anaheim Stadium, CA
	Chicago White Sox	Comiskey Park, IL
	Cleveland Indians	Cleveland Stadium, OH
	Detroit Tigers	Tiger Stadium, MI
	Kansas City Royals	Royal Stadium, MO
	Milwaukee Brewers	Milwaukee County Stadium, WI
	Minnesota Twins	Hubert H Humphrey Metrodome, MN
	New York Yankees	Yankees Stadium, NY
	Oakland A's	Oakland Coliseum, CA
	Seattle Mariners	Kingdome, WA
	Texas Rangers	Arlington Stadium, TX
	Toronto Blue Jays	Exhibition Stadium, Ontario

FOOTBALL TEAMS

	Team	City, State
National Conference	Atlanta Falcons	Suwanee, GA
	Chicago Bears	Lake Forest, IL
	Dallas Cowboys	Irving, TX
	Detroit Lions	Pontiac, MI
	Green Bay Packers	Green Bay, WI
	Los Angeles Rams	Anaheim, CA
	Minnesota Vikings	Eden Prairie, MN
	New Orleans Saints	New Orleans, LA
	New York Giants	East Rutherford, NJ
	Philadelphia Eagles	Philadelphia, PA
	Phoenix Cardinals	Phoenix, AZ
	San Francisco 49ers	Redwood City, CA

| | Tampa Bay Buccaneers | Tampa, FL |
| | Washington Redskins | Washington, DC |

	Team	*City, State*
American	Buffalo Bills	Orchard Park, NY
Conference	Cincinnati Bengals	Cincinnati, OH
	Cleveland Browns	Cleveland, OH
	Denver Broncos	Denver, CO
	Houston Oilers	Houston, TX
	Indianapolis Colts	Indianapolis, IN
	Kansas City Chiefs	Kansas City, MO
	Los Angeles Raiders	El Segundo, CA
	Miami Dolphins	Miami, FL
	New England Patriots	Foxboro, MA
	New York Jets	New York, NY
	Pittsburgh Steelers	Pittsburgh, PA
	San Diego Chargers	San Diego, CA
	Seattle Seahawks	Kirkland, WA

BASKETBALL TEAMS

	Team	*City, State*
Eastern	Atlanta Hawks	Atlanta, GA
Conference	Boston Celtics	Boston, MA
	Chicago Bulls	Chicago, IL
	Charlotte Hornets	Charlotte, NC
	Cleveland Cavaliers	Richfield, OH
	Detroit Pistons	Pontiac, MI
	Indiana Pacers	Indianapolis, IN
	Milwaukee Bucks	Milwaukee, WI
	New Jersey Nets	East Rutherford, NJ
	New York Knickerbockers	New York, NY
	Philadelphia 76ers	Philadelphia, PA
	Washington Bullets	Landover, MD

	Team	*City, State*
Western	Dallas Mavericks	Dallas, TX
Conference	Denver Nuggets	Denver, CO
	Golden State Warriors	Oakland, CA
	Houston Rockets	Houston, TX
	Los Angeles Clippers	Los Angeles, CA
	Los Angeles Lakers	Inglewood, CA
	Miami Heat	Miami, FL
	Phoenix Suns	Phoenix, AZ
	Portland Trails Blazers	Portland, OR
	Sacramento Kings	Sacramento, CA
	San Antonio Spurs	San Antonio, TX
	Seattle Super Sonics	Seattle, WA
	Utah Jazz	Salt Lake City, UT

TELEPHONE AREA CODES

Code	Area	Code	Area
201	New Jersey (Newark)	303	Colorado
202	Washington D C	304	West Virginia
203	Connecticut	305	Florida (Miami)
204	Manitoba	306	Saskatchewan
205	Alabama	307	Wyoming
206	Washington (Seattle)	308	Nebraska (North Platte)
207	Maine	309	Illinois (Peoria)
208	Idaho	312	Illinois (Chicago)
209	California (Fresno)	313	Michigan (Detroit)
212	New York City (Manhattan, Bronx)	314	Missouri (St Louis)
		315	New York (Syracuse)
213	Texas (Dallas)	316	Kansas (Wichita)
214	California (Los Angeles)	317	Indiana (Indianapolis)
215	Pennsylvania (Philadelphia)	318	Louisiana (Shreveport)
216	Ohio (Cleveland)	319	Iowa (Dubuque)
217	Illinois (Springfield)	401	Rhode Island
218	Minnesota (Duluth)	402	Nebraska (Omaha)
219	Indiana (South Bend)	403	Alberta Yukon North West Territories
418	Quebec (Quebec City)		
419	Ohio (Toledo)	404	Georgia (Atlanta)
501	Arkansas	405	Oklahoma (Oklahoma C)
502	Kentucky (Louisville)	406	Montana
503	Oregon	408	California (San Jose)
504	Louisiana (New Orleans)	409	Texas (Galveston)
505	New Mexico	412	Pennsylvania (Pittsburgh)
506	New Brunswick	413	Massachusetts (Springfield)
507	Minnesota (Rochester)	414	Wisconsin (Milwaukee)
509	Washington (Spokane)	415	California (San Francisco)
512	Texas (San Antonio)	416	Ontario (Toronto)
513	Ohio (Cincinnati)	417	Missouri (Spingfield)
514	Quebec (Montreal)	601	Mississippi
515	Iowa (Des Moines)	602	Arizona
516	NewYork (Hempstead)	603	New Hampshire
517	Michigan (Lansing)	604	British Columbia
518	New York (Albany)	605	South Dakota
519	Ontario (London)	606	Kentucky (Newport)
301	Maryland	607	New York (Binghamton)
302	Delaware	608	Wisconsin (Madison)

Code	Area	Code	Area
609	New Jersey (Trenton)	806	Texas (Amarillo)
612	Minnesota (Minneapolis)	807	Ontario (Thunder Bay)
613	Ontario (Ottawa)	808	Hawaii
614	Ohio (Columbus)	809	Bermuda, Puerto Rico, Virgin
615	Tennessee (Nashville)		Islands and other Caribbean
616	Michigan (Grand Rapids)		Islands
617	Massachusetts (Boston)	812	Indiana (Evansville)
618	Illinois (Centralia)	813	Florida (Fort Myers)
619	California (San Diego)	814	Pennsylvania (Altoona)
701	North Dakota	815	Illinois (Rockford)
702	Nevada	816	Missouri (Kansas City)
703	Virginia (Roanoke)	817	Texas (Fort Worth)
704	North Carolina (Charlotte)	818	California (Burbank)
705	Ontario (North Bay)	819	Quebec (Sherbrooke) North
707	California (Santa Rosa)		West Territories
709	Newfoundland	901	Tennessee(Memphis)
712	Iowa (Council Bluffs)	902	Nova Scotia
713	Texas (Houston)	903	Northwest Mexico
714	California (Orange)	904	Florida (Jacksonville)
715	Wisconsin (Eau Claire)	905	Mexico City
716	New York (Buffalo)	906	Michigan (Escanaba)
717	Pennsylvania (Harrisburg)	907	Alaska
718	New York City (Brooklyn,	912	Georgia (Savannah)
	Queens, Staten Island)	913	Kansas (Topeka)
801	Utah	914	New York (White Plain)
802	Vermont	915	Texas (Sweetwater)
803	South Carolina	916	California (Sacramento)
804	Virginia (Richmond)	918	Oklahoma (Tulsa)
805	California (Bakersfield)	919	North Carolina (Raleigh)

ZIP CODES

Aberdeen	SD	57401	Azusa	CA	91702
Abilene	TX	79604	Bakersfield	CA	93302
Addison	IL	60101	Baldwin Park	CA	91706
Akron	OH	44309	Baltimore	MD	21233
Alameda	CA	94501	Bangor	ME	04401
Albany	GA	31706	Barberton	OH	44203
Albuquerque	NM	87101	Bartleville	OK	74003
Alexandria	LA	71301	Baton Rouge	LA	70821
Alexandria	VA	22313	Battle Creek	MI	49016
Alhambra	CA	91802	Bay City	MI	48706
Allen Park	MI	48101	Bayonne	NJ	07002
Allentown	PA	18101	Baytown	TX	77520
Alton	IL	62002	Beaumont	TX	77704
Alttona	PA	16603	Beavercreek	OH	45401
Amarillo	TX	79120	Beaverton	OR	90201
Ames	LA	50010	Bell	CA	90201
Anaheim	CA	92803	Belleville	IL	62220
Anchorage	UK	99502	Belleville	NJ	07109
Anderson	IN	46018	Bellevue	WA	98009
Anderson	SC	29621	Bellflower	CA	90706
Annapolis	MD	21401	Bell Gardens	CA	90201
Ann Abor	MI	48106	Bellingham	WA	98225
Anniston	AL	36201	Beloit	WI	53511
Antioch	CA	94509	Bergenfield	NJ	07621
Appleton	WI	54911	Berkeley	CA	94704
Arcadia	CA	91006	Berwyn	IL	60402
Arlington	TX	76010	Bessemer	AL	35020
Arlington Heights	IL	60004	Bethel Park	PAS	15102
Arvada	CO	80001	Bethlehem	PA	18016
Asheville	NC	28810	Bettendorf	IA	52722
Ashland	KY	41101	Beverly	MA	01915
Athens	GA	30601	Beverley Hills	CA	90213
Atlanta	GA	30304	Billings	MT	59101
Atlantic City	NJ	08401	Biloxi	MS	39530
Attleboro	MA	02703	Binghamton	NY	13902
Auburn	AL	36830	Birmingham	AL	35203
Auburn	NY	13021	Bismarck	ND	58501
Auburn	WA	98002	Blacksburg	VA	24060
Augusta	GA	30901	Blaine	MN	55433
Aurora	CO	80010	Bloomfield	NJ	07003
Aurora	IL	60507	Blooningtton	IL	61701
Austin	TX	78710	Bloomington	IN	47401

Bloomington	MN	55420	Cape Girardeau	MO	63701
Blue Springs	MO	64015	Carbondale	IL	62901
Boca Raton	FL	33432	Carlsbad	CA	92008
Bolingbrook	IL	60439	Carlsbad	NM	88220
Bossier City	LA	71111	Carrolton	TX	75006
Boston	MA	02205	Carson	CA	90749
Boulder	CO	80302	Carson City	NV	89701
Bountiful	UT	84010	Casper	WY	82601
Bowie	MD	20715	Cedar Falls	IA	50613
Bowling Green	KY	42101	Cedar Rapids	IA	52401
Bowling Green	OH	43402	Cerritos	CA	90701
Boynton Beach	FL	33435	Champaing	IL	61820
Bradenton	FL	33506	Chandler	AZ	85224
Brea	CA	92621	Chapel Hill	NC	27514
Bremerton	WA	98310	Charleston	SC	29423
Bridgeport	CT	06602	Charleston	WV	25301
Bristol	CT	06010	Charlottesville	VA	22906
Brockton	MA	02403	Chattanooga	TN	37401
Broken Arrow	OK	74012	Chelsea	MA	02150
Brookfield	WI	53005	Chesapeake	VA	23320
Brooklyn Center	MN	55429	Chester	PA	10913
Brooklyn Park	MN	55007	Cheyenne	WY	82001
Brook Park	OH	44142	Chicago	IL	60607
Brownsville	TX	78520	Chicago Heights	IL	60411
Brunswick	OH	44212	Chico	CA	95926
Bryan	TX	77801	Chicopee	MA	01021
Buena Park	CA	90622	Chula Vista	CA	92010
Buffalo	NY	14240	Cicero	IL	60650
Burbank	CA	91505	Cincinnati	OH	45234
Burbank	IL	60459	Claremont	CA	91711
Burlingame	CA	94010	Clarksville	TN	37040
Burlington	IA	52601	Clearwater	FL	33575
Burlington	NC	27215	Cleveland	OH	44101
Burlington	VT	05401	Cleveland	TN	37311
Burnville	MN	55337	Cleveland Heights	OH	44118
Burton	MI	48502	Clifton	NJ	07015
Butte	MT	59701	Clinton	IA	52732
Calumet City	IL	60409	Clovis	CA	93612
Camarillo	Ca	93010	Clovis	NM	88010
Cambridge	MA	02140	College Station	TX	77840
Camden	NJ	08101	Colorado Springs	CO	80901
Campbell	CA	95008	Columbia	MO	65201
Canton	OH	44711	Columbia	SC	29201
Cape Coral	FL	33910	Columbia	TN	38401

Columbus	GA	31908	Des Moines	IA	50318
Columbus	IN	47201	Des Plaines	IL	60018
Columbus	MS	39701	Detroit	MI	48233
Columbus	OH	43216	Dothan	AL	36303
Compton	CA	90220	Downers Grove	IL	60515
Concord	CA	94520	Downey	CA	90241
Concord	NH	03301	Dubuque	IA	52001
Coon Rapids	MN	55433	Duluth	MN	55806
Coral Gables	FL	33114	Duncanville	TX	75138
Coral Springs	FL	33065	Dunedin	FL	33528
Corona	CA	91720	Durham	NC	27701
Corpus Christi	TX	78408	East Chicago	IN	46312
Corvallis	OR	97333	East Cleveland	OH	44112
Costa Mesa	CA	92626	East Detroit	MI	48021
Council Bluffs	IA	51501	East Lansing	MI	48823
Covina	CA	91722	Easton	PA	18042
Covington	KY	41011	East Orange	NJ	07019
Cranston	RI	02910	East Point	GA	30364
Crystal	MN	55428	East Providence	RI	02914
Culver City	CA	90230	East St Louis	IL	62201
Cumberland	MD	21502	Eau Claire	WI	54701
Cupertino	CA	95014	Edina	MD	55424
Cuyaboga Falls	OH	44222	Edmond	OK	73034
Cypress	CA	90630	Edmonds	WA	98020
Dallas	TX	75260	El Cajon	CA	92020
Daly City	CA	94015	El Dorado	AR	71730
Danbury	CT	06810	Elgin	IL	60120
Danville	IL	61832	Elizabeth	NJ	07207
Danville	VA	24541	Elk Grove	IL	60007
Davenport	IA	52802	Elkhart	IN	46515
Davis	CA	95616	Elmhurst	IL	60126
Dayton	OH	45401	Emira	NY	14901
Daytona Beach	FL	32015	El Monte	CA	91734
Dearhorn	MI	48120	El Paso	TX	79910
Dearhorn Heights	MI	48127	Elyria	OH	44035
Decatur	AL	35602	Emporia	KS	66801
Decatur	IL	62521	Englewood	CO	80110
Deerfield Beach	FL	33441	Enid	OK	73701
De Kalb	IL	60115	Erie	PA	16515
Del City	OK	73115	Escondido	CA	92025
Delray Beach	FL	33444	Euclid	OH	44117
Del Rio	TX	78840	Eugene	OR	97401
Denton	TX	76201	Evanston	IN	47708
Denver	CO	80202	Evansville	In	02149

Everett	MA	98201	Garden City	MI	48135
Fairborn	OH	45324	Garden Grove	CA	92640
Fairfield	CA	94533	Garfield	NJ	07026
Fairfield	OH	45014	Garfield Heights	OH	44125
Fair Lawn	NJ	07410	Garland	TX	75040
Fall River	MA	02722	Gary	IN	46401
Fargo	ND	58102	Gastonia	NC	28052
Farmington	NM	87401	Glendale	AZ	85301
Farmingotn Hills	MI	48024	Glendale	CA	91209
Fayetteville	AR	72701	Glendora	CA	91740
Fayetteville	NC	28302	Glenview	IL	60025
Ferndale	MI	45840	Gloucester	MA	01930
Findlay	OH	45840	Goldsboro	NC	27530
Fitchburg	MA	01420	Grand Forks	ND	58201
Flagstuff	AZ	86001	Grand Island	NE	68801
Flint	MI	48502	Grand Junction	CO	81501
Florence	AL	35631	Grand Prairie	TX	75051
Florence	SC	29501	Grand Rapids	MI	49501
Florisant	MO	63033	Granite City	IL	62040
Fond Du Lac	WI	54935	Great Falls	MT	59403
Fontana	Ca	92335	Greeley	CO	80631
Fort Collins	CO	80521	Green Bay	WI	53401
Fort Dodge	IA	50501	Greenfield	WI	53220
Fort Lauderdale	FL	33450	Greensboro	NC	27420
Fort Lee	NJ	07024	Greenville	MS	38701
Fort Myers	FL	33450	Greenville	NC	27834
Fort Smith	AR	72901	Greenville	SC	29600
Fort Wayne	IN	46802	Gresham	OR	97030
Fort Worth	TX	76101	Gulfport	MS	39503
Fountain Valley	CA	92778	Hackensack	NJ	07602
Frankfort	KY	40601	Hagerstown	MD	21740
Frederick	MD	61032	Hallandale	FL	33009
Freeport	IL	61032	Haltom City	TX	76117
Freeport	NY	11520	Hamilton	OH	45012
Fremont	CA	94538	Hammond	IN	46320
Fresno	CA	93706	Hampton	VA	23670
Fridley	MN	55432	Hanover Prk	IL	60103
Fullerton	CA	92631	Harlingen	TX	78551
Gadsen	AL	35901	Harrisburg	PA	17105
Gainseville	FL	32602	Hartford	CT	06101
Gaithersburg	MD	20877	Harvey	IL	60426
Galesburg	IL	61401	Hattiesburg	MS	39401
Galveston	TX	77553	Haverhill	MA	01830
Gardena	CA	90247	Hawthorne	CA	90250

Hayward	CA	94544	Jamesville	WI	53545
Hazelton	PA	18201	Jefferson City	MO	65101
Hempstead	NY	11551	Jersey City	NJ	07303
Haileah	FL	33010	Johnson City	TN	37601
Highland	IN	46322	Johnstown	PA	15901
Highland Park	IL	60035	Joliet	IL	60436
Highland Park	MI	48203	Jonesboro	AR	72401
High Point	NC	27260	Joplin	MO	64801
Hillsboro	OR	97123	Kalamazoo	MI	49001
Hilo	HI	96720	Kankalee	IL	60901
Hobbs	NM	88240	Kansas City	KS	66110
Hoboken	NJ	07030	Kansas City	MO	64108
Hoffman Estates	IL	60195	Kearny	NJ	07032
Holland	MI	49423	Kenner	LA	70062
Hollywood	FL	33022	Kennewick	WA	99336
Holyroke	MA	01040	Kenosha	WI	53141
Honolulu	HI	96820	Kent	OH	45429
Hopkinsville	KY	42240	Kentwood	MI	49508
Hot Springs	AR	71901	Kettering	OH	45429
Houma	LA	70360	Killeen	TX	76541
Houston	TX	77201	Kingsport	TN	37662
Huber Heights	OH	45424	Kingston	NC	28501
Huntington	WV	25704	Kingsville	TX	78363
Huntingdon Beach	CA	92647	Kirkwood	MO	63122
Huntington Park	CA	90255	Knoxville	TN	37901
Huntsville	AL	35813	Kokomono	IN	46902
Hurst	TX	76053	La Crosse	WI	54601
Hutchinson	KS	67501	Lafayette	IN	47901
Idaho Falls	ID	83401	Lafayette	LA	70501
Independence	MO	64501	La Habra	CA	90631
Indianopolis	IN	46202	Lake Charles	LA	70601
Inglewood	CA	90311	Lakeland	FL	33802
Inkster	MI	48141	Lakewood	CA	90714
Iowa City	IA	52240	Lakewood	CO	80215
Irvine	CA	92713	lakewood	OH	44107
Irving	TX	75061	Lake Worth	FL	33416
Irvington	NJ	07111	La Mesa	CA	92041
Itheca	NY	14850	La Mirada	CA	90638
Jackson	MI	49201	Lancaster	CA	93534
Jackson	MS	39205	Lancaster	OH	43130
Jackson	TN	38301	Lancaster	PA	17604
Jacksonville	AR	72076	Lansing	IL	60438
Jacksonville	FL	32203	Lansing	MI	48924
Jamestown	NY	14701	La Puenta	CA	91747

Laredo	TX	78041	Lufkin	TX	75901
Largo	FL	33540	Lynchburg	VA	24506
Las Cruces	NM	88001	Lynn	MA	01901
Las Vegas	NV	89114	Lynwood	CA	90262
Lauderdale Lakes	FL	33313	Macon	GA	31213
Lauderhill	FL	33313	Madison	WI	53707
Lawrence	IL	46226	Madison Heights	Mi	48071
Lawrence	KS	66044	Malden	MA	02148
Lawrence	MA	01842	Manchester	NH	03103
Lawton	OK	73501	Manhattan	KS	66502
Leavenworth	KS	66048	Manhattan Beach	CA	90266
Lebanon	PA	17042	Manitowoc	WI	54220
Lee's Summit	MO	64063	Mankato	MN	56001
Leominister	MA	01453	Mansfield	OH	44901
Lewiston	ID	83501	Maple Heights	OH	44137
Lewiston	ME	04240	Maplewood	MN	55109
Lexington	KY	40511	Margate	FL	33063
Lima	OH	45802	Marietta	GA	30060
Lincoln	NE	68501	Marion	IN	46952
Lincoln Park	MI	48146	Marion	OH	43302
Linden	NJ	07036	Marlborough	MA	01752
Lindenhurst	NY	11757	Marshalltown	IA	50158
Little Rock	AR	72231	Mason City	IA	50401
Littleton	CO	80120	Massilon	OH	44646
Livermore	CA	94550	Maywood	IL	60153
Livonia	MI	48150	McAllen	TX	78501
Lodi	CA	95240	McKeesport	PA	15134
Logan	UT	84321	Medford	MA	02155
Lombard	IL	60148	Medford	OR	97501
Lompoc	CA	93436	Melbourne	FL	32901
Long Beach	CA	90809	Melrose	MA	02176
Long Beach	NY	11561	Memphis	TN	38101
Long Branch	NJ	07740	Menlo Park	CA	94025
Longmont	CO	80501	Menomonee Falls	Wi	53051
Longview	TX	75602	Mentor	OH	44060
Longview	WA	98632	Merced	CA	95340
Lorain	OH	44052	Meriden	CT	06450
Los Altos	CA	94022	Meridian	MS	39301
Los Angeles	CA	90052	Merrillville	IN	46410
Los Gatos	CA	95030	Mesa	AZ	85201
Louisville	KY	40231	Mesquite	TX	75149
Loveland	CO	80537	MiamI	FL	33152
Lowell	MA	01853	Miami Beach	FL	33139
Lubbock	TX	79408	Michigan City	IN	46360

Middletown	CT	06457	New Albany	IN	47150
Middletown	OH	45042	Newark	CA	94560
Midland	MI	48640	Newark	DE	19711
Midland	TX	79702	Newark	NI	07102
Midwest City	OK	73140	Newark	OH	43055
Milford	CT	06460	New Bedford	MA	02741
Milpitas	CA	95035	New Berlin	WI	53151
Milwaukee	WI	53201	New Britain	CT	06050
Minneapolis	MN	55401	New Bruntswick	NJ	08901
Minnetonka	MN	55343	New Castle	PA	16101
Minot	ND	58701	New Haven	CT	06511
Miramar	FL	33023	New Iberia	LA	70560
Mishawaka	IN	46544	New London	CT	06320
Missoula	MT	59806	New Orleans	LA	70113
Mobile	AL	36601	Newport	RI	02840
Modesto	CA	95350	Newport Beach	CA	92660
Moline	IL	61265	Newport News	VA	23607
Monroe	LA	71203	New Rochelle	NY	10802
Monroeville	PA	15146	Newton	MA	02158
Monrovia	CA	91016	New York	NY	10001
Montclair	NJ	07042	Niagara Falls	NY	14302
Montebello	CA	90640	Niles	IL	60648
Monferey	CA	93940	Norfolk	VA	23501
Monterey Park	CA	91754	Normal	IL	64761
Montgomery	AL	36119	Norman	OK	73070
Moore	OK	73153	Norristown	PA	19401
Moorhead	MN	56560	Northampton	MA	01060
Morgantown	WV	26505	Northbrook	IL	60062
Mountain View	CA	94042	North Charleston	SC	29406
Mount Prospect	IL	60056	North Chicago	IL	60064
Mount Vernon	NY	10551	Northglen	CO	30233
Muncie	IN	47032	North Las Vegas	NV	89030
Murfreesboro	TN	37130	North Little Rock	AR	72114
Murray	UT	84107	North Miami	FL	33161
Muskegon	MI	49440	North Miami Beach	FL	33160
Muskogee	OK	74401	North Olmsted	OH	44070
Nacogdoches	TX	75961	North Richland Hills	TX	76118
Nampa	ID	83651	North Tonawanda	NY	14120
Napa	CA	94558	Norwalk	CA	50650
Naperville	IL	60556	Norwalk	CT	06856
Nashua	NH	03061	Norwich	CT	06360
Nashville	TN	37202	Norwood	OH	45212
National City	CA	92050	Novato	CA	94947
Naugatuck	CT	06110	Nutley	NJ	07110

Oak Forest	IL	60452	Pembroke Pines	FL	33024
Oakland	CA	94615	Pensacola	FL	32501
Oak Lawn	IL	60454	Peoria	IL	61601
Oak Park	IL	60301	Perth Amboy	NJ	08861
Oak Park	MI	48237	Petalum	CA	94952
Oak Ridge	TN	37830	Petersburg	VA	23804
Ocala	FL	32678	Phenix City	AL	36867
Oceanside	CA	92054	Philadelphia	PA	15219
Odessa	TX	79760	Pheonix	AZ	85026
Ogden	UT	84401	Pico Rivera	CA	90660
Oklahoma City	OK	73125	Pine Bluff	AR	71601
Okathe	KS	66061	Pinellas Park	FL	33565
Olympia	WA	98501	Pittsburg	CA	94565
Omaha	NE	68108	Pittsburgh	PA	15219
Ontario	CA	91751	Pittsfield	MA	01201
Orange	CA	92667	Placentia	CA	92670
Orange	NJ	07051	Plainfield	NJ	07061
Orem	UT	84057	Plano	TX	75074
Orlando	FL	32802	Plantation	FL	33318
Oshkosh	WI	54901	Pleasant Hill	CA	94523
Ottumwa	IA	52501	Pleasanton	CA	94566
Overland Park	KS	66204	Plum	PA	15239
Owensboro	KY	43201	Plymouth	MN	55447
Oxnard	CA	93030	Pocatello	ID	83201
Pacifica	CA	94044	Pomona	CA	91766
Paducah	KY	42001	Pompano Beach	FL	33060
Palatine	IL	60067	Ponca City	OK	74601
Palm Springs	CA	92263	Pontiac	MI	48056
Palto Alto	CA	94303	Portage	IN	46368
Panama City	FL	32401	Portage	MN	49081
Paramount	CA	90723	Port Arthur	TX	77640
Paramus	NJ	07652	Port Huron	MI	48060
Paris	TX	75460	Portland	ME	04101
Parkersburg	WV	26101	Portland	OR	97208
Park Forest	IL	60466	Portsmouth	NH	03801
Park Ridge	IL	60068	Portsmouth	OH	45662
Parma	PH	44129	Portsmouth	VA	23705
Pasadena	CA	91109	Poughkeepsie	NY	12601
Pasedena	TX	77501	Prichard	AL	36610
Pascagoula	MS	39567	Providence	RI	02940
Passaic	NJ	07055	Provo	UT	84603
Paterson	NJ	07510	Pueblo	CO	81003
Pawtucket	RI	02860	Quincy	IL	62301
Peabody	MA	01960	Quincy	MA	02269

Racine	WI	53401	St Clair Shores	MI	48080
Rahway	NJ	07065	St Cloud	MN	56301
Raleigh	NC	27611	St Joseph	MO	64501
Rancho Cucamonga	CA	91730	St Louis	MO	63155
Rancho Palos Verdes	CA	90274	St Louis Park	MN	55426
Rapid City	SD	57701	St Paul	MN	55101
Raytown	MO	64133	St Petersburg	FL	33730
Reading	PA	19603	Salem	MA	01970
Redding	CA	96001	Salem	OR	97301
Redlands	CA	92373	Salina	KS	67401
Redondo Beach	CA	90277	Salinas	CA	93907
Redwood City	CA	94064	Salt Lake City	UT	84119
Reno	NV	89510	San Angelo	TX	76902
Renton	WA	98057	San Antonio	TX	78284
Revere	MA	02151	San Bernardino	CA	92403
Rialto	CA	92376	San Bruno	CA	94066
Richardson	TX	75080	San Buenavetura		
Richfield	WA	55423	(Ventura)	CA	93002
Richland	WA	99352	San Clemente	CA	92672
Richmond	CA	94802	San Diego	CA	92199
Richmond	IN	47374	Sandusky	OH	44870
Richmond	VA	23232	Sandy City	UT	84070
Ridgewood	NJ	07451	San Francisco	CA	94188
Riverside	CA	92507	San Gabriel	CA	91776
Riviera Beach	FL	33404	San Jose	CA	95101
Roanoke	VA	24022	San Leandro	CA	94577
Rochester	MN	55901	San Luis Obispo	CA	93401
Rochester	NY	14692	San Mateo	CA	94402
Rockford	IL	61125	San Rafael	CA	94901
Rock Hill	SC	29730	Santa Ana	CA	94901
Rock Island	IL	61201	Santa Barbara	CA	93102
Rockville	MD	20850	Santa Clara	CA	95050
Rockville Center	NY	11570	Santa Cruz	CA	95060
Rocky Mount	NC	27801	Santa Fe	NM	87501
Rome	GA	30161	Santa Maria	CA	93456
Rome	NY	13440	Santa Monica	CA	90406
Rosemead	CA	91770	Santa Rosa	CA	95402
Roseville	MI	48066	Sarasota	FL	33578
Roseville	MN	55113	Saratoga	CA	95070
Rosewell	NM	88201	Savannah	GA	31401
Royal Oak	MI	48068	Sayreville	NJ	09972
Sacramento	CA	95813	Schaumburg	IL	60194
Saginaw	MI	48065	Schenectady	NY	12301
St Charles	MO	63301	Scottsdale	AZ	85251

Scranton	PA	18505	Superior	WI	54880
Seal Beach	CA	90740	Syracuse	NY	13220
Seaside	CA	93955	Tacoma	WA	98413
Seattle	WA	98109	Tallahassee	FL	32301
Selma	AL	36701	Tamarac	FL	33320
Shaker Heights	OH	44120	Tampa	FL	33630
Shawnee	KS	66202	Taunton	MA	02780
Shawnee	OK	74801	Taylor	MI	48180
Sheboygan	WI	53081	Tempe	AZ	85282
Shelton	CT	06484	Temple	AZ	76501
Sherman	TX	75090	Terre Haute	IN	47808
Shreveport	LA	71102	Texarkana	TX	75501
Simi Valley	CA	93065	Texas City	TX	75501
Sioux City	IA	51101	Thornton	CO	80229
Souix Falls	SD	57101	Thousand Oaks	CA	91360
Skokie	IL	60076	Tinley Park	IL	60477
Slidell	LA	70458	Titusville	FL	32780
Somerville	MA	02143	Toledo	OH	43601
Somerville	NJ	08876	Topeka	KS	66603
South Bend	IN	46624	Torrance	CA	90510
South Euclid	OH	44121	Torrington	CT	06790
Southfield	MI	48037	Trenton	NJ	08650
South Gate	CA	90280	Troy	MI	48099
Southgate	MI	48195	Troy	NY	12180
South San Francisco	CA	94080	Tucson	AZ	85726
Sparks	NV	89431	Tulsa	OK	74101
Spartanburg	SC	29301	Turlock	CA	95380
Spokane	WA	99210	Tuscaloosa	AL:	35403
Springfield	IL	62703	Tustin	CA	92680
Springfield	MA	01101	Twin Falls	ID	83301
Springfield	MO	65801	Tyler	TX	75712
Springfield	OH	45501	Union City	CA	94587
Springfield	OR	97477	Union City	NJ	07087
Stamford	CT	06904	University City	MO	68130
State College	PA	16801	Upland	CA	91786
Sterling Heights	MI	48077	Upper Arlington	OH	43221
Steubenville	OH	43952	Urbana	IL	61801
Stillwater	OK	74074	Utica	NY	13504
Stockton	CA	95208	Vacaville	CA	95688
Stow	OH	44224	Valdosta	GA	31601
Strongsville	OH	44136	Vallejo	CA	94590
Suffolk	VA	23434	Valley Stream	NY	11580
Sunnyvale	CA	94086	Vancouver	WA	98661
Sunrise	FL	33338	Vicksburg	MS	39180

Victoria	TX	77901	Westminster	CO	80030
Vineland	NJ	08360	West New York	NJ	07093
Virginia Beach	VA	23450	West Orange	NJ	07052
Visalia	CA	93277	West Palm Beach	FL	33401
Vista	CA	92083	Wheaton	IL	60187
Waco	TX	76701	Wheat Ridge	CO	80033
Walla Walla	WA	99362	Wheeling	WV	26003
Walnut Creek	CA	94596	White Plains	NY	10602
Waltham	MA	02154	Whittier	CA	90605
Warner Robins	GA	31093	Wichita	KS	67276
Warren	MI	48089	Wichita Falls	TX	76307
Warren	OH	44481	Wilkes-Barre	PA	18701
Warwick	RI	02887	Williamsport	PA	17701
Washington	DC	20013	Wilmette	IL	60091
Waterbury	CT	06701	Wilmington	DE	19850
Waterloo	IA	50701	Wilmington	NC	28402
Watertown	NY	13601	Wilson	NC	27893
Waukegan	IL	60085	Winona	MN	55987
Waukesha	WI	53186	Winston-Salem	NC	27102
Wausau	WI	54401	Woburn	MA	01801
Wauwatosa	WI	53213	Woodland	CA	95695
Weirton	WV	26062	Woonsocket	RI	02895
West Allis	WI	53213	Worcester	MA	01613
West Covina	CA	91793	Wyandotte	MI	48192
Westfield	MA	01085	Wyoming	MI	49509
Westfield	NJ	07090	Yakima	WA	98903
West Haven	CT	06516	Yonkers	NY	10701
West Jordan	UT	84084	Yorba Linda	CA	92686
Westland	MI	48185	York	PA	17405
West Memphis	AR	72301	Youngstown	OH	44501
West Miffin	PA	15122	Yuma	AZ	85364
Westminster	CA	92683	Zanesville	OH	43701

COUNTRIES OF THE WORLD

Country	Capital	Official Language(s)	Currency
Afghanistan	Kabul	Pushtu, Dari	Afghani (Af) =100 puls
Albania	Tirana/Tiranë	Albanian	Lek (L) =100 quintars
Algeria	El Djazair/Algiers	Arabic	Dinar (AD) =100 centimes
Andorra	Andorra la Vella	Catalan	French Franc and Spanish Peseta
Angola	Luanda	Portuguese	Kwanza (Kz) =100 lweis
Antigua and Barbuda	St John's	English	East Caribbean Dollar (EC$) =100 cents
Argentina	Buenos Aires	Spanish	Austral (Arg$) =100 centavos
Australia	Canberra	English	Dollar (A$) =100 cents
Austria	Vienna	German	Schilling (Sch) =100 groschen
Bahamas	Nassau	English	dollar (BA$) =100 cents
Hahrain	Manama	Araic	Dinar (BD) =1000 fils
Bangladesh	Khaka	Bangla (Bengali)	Taka (Tk) =100 poisha
Barbados	Bridgetown	English	Dollar (Bds$) =100 cents
Belgium	Brussels	Flemish, French	Franc (BFr) =100 cents
Belize	Belmopan	English	Dollar (Bz$) =100 cents
Benin	Porto Novo	French, English	CFA Franc (CFAFr) =100 centimes
Bhutan	Thimphu	Dzongkha (Tibetan/Burmese)	Ngultrum (N) =100 chetrums

Country	Capital	Official Language(s)	Currency
Bolivia	La Paz	Spanish	Peso (B£) =100 centavos
Botswana	Gaborone	English	Pula (Pu) =100 thebe
Brazil	Brasilia	Portuguese	Cruzado/Cruziero(Cr) =100 centavos
Brunei	Bandar Seri Begawan	Malay	Dollar (Br$) =100 cents
Bulgaria	Sofia	Bulgarian	Lev (Lv) =100 stotinki
Burkina Faso	Ouagadougou	French	CFA Franc (CFAFr) =100centimes
Burma	Rangoon	Burmese	Kyat (K) =100 pyas
Burundi	Bujumbura	Kirundi, French	Franc (BuFr) =100 centimes
Cameroon	Yaoundé	French, English	CFA Franc (CFAFr) =100 centimes
Canada	Ottawa	English, French	Dollar (C$) =100 cents
Cape Verde Islands	Praia	Creole Portuguese	Excudo (CVEsc) =100 centavos
Central African Republic	Bangui	French	CFA Franc (CFAFr) =100 centimes
Chad	N'Djamena	French	CFA Franc (CFAFr) =100 centimes
Chile	Santiago	Spanish	Peso (Ch$) =100 centesimos
China	Beijing (Peking)	Puronghua (Mandarin Chinese)	Renminbi Yan (RMBY or $) =100 fen
Colombia	Bogotá	Spanich	Peso (Col$) =100 centavos
The Comoros	Moroni	French, Arabic	CFA Franc (CFAFr) =100 centimes
Congo	Brazzaville	French	CFA Franc (CFAFr) =100 centimes

Country	Capital	Official Language(s)	Currency
Cook Islands	Avarua	English, Polynesian dialects	New Zealand Dollar (NZ$) =100 cents
Costa Rica	San José	Spanish	Colon (CRC) =100 centimos
Cuba	Havana	Spanish	Peso (Cub$) =100 centavos
Cyprus	Nicosia	Greek, Turkish	Pound (C£) =1000 mills
Czechoslovakia	Prague	Czech, Slovak	Koruna (Kcs) =100 heller
Denmark	Copenhagen	Danish	Krone (DKr) =100 øre
Djibouti	Djibouti-Ville	French, Arabic	Franc (DjFr) =100 cetimes
Dominica	Roseau	English	East Caribbean (EC$) Dollar =100 cents
Dominican Republic	Santo Domingo	Spanish	Peso (DR$) =100 centavos
Ecuador	Quito	Spanish	Sucre (Su) =100 Centavos
Egypt	Cairo	Arabic	Pound (E£) =100 piastres
El Salvador	San Salvador	Spanish	Colón (ESC) =100 centavos
Equatorial Guinea	Malabo	Spanish	Ekuele (E) =100 centimes
Ethiopa	Addis Ababa	Amharic	Birr (Br) =100 cents
Fiji	Suva	English, Fijian Hindi	Dollar (F$) =100 cents
Finland	Helsinki	Finnish	Markka (FMk) =100 penniä
France	Paris	French	Franc (Fr) =100 centimes
Gabon	Libreville	French	CFP Franc (CFPFr) =100 centimes

Country	Capital	Official Language(s)	Currency
The Gambia	Banjul	English	Dalasi (Di) =100 butut
German Democratic Republic (E Germany)	East Berlin	German	GDR Mark /Ostmark(M) =100 pfennig
Germany, Federal Republic of (West Germany)	Bonn	German	Deutsche Mark (DM) =100 pfennig
Ghana	Accra	English	Cedi (C) =100 pesawas
Greece	Athens	Greek	Drachma (Dr) =100 lepta
Grenada	St George's	English	East Caribbean dollar (EC$) =100 cents
Guatemala	Guatemala City	Spanish	Quetzal (Q) =100 centavos
Guinea	Conakry	French	Syli (Sy) =100 cauris
Guyana	Georgetown	English	Dollar (G$) =100 cents
Haiti	Port-au-Prince	French	Gourde (Gde) =100 centimes
Honduras	Tegucigalpa	Spanish	Limpira (La) =100 centavos
Hong Kong	Victoria	English, Chinese	Dollar (HK$) =100 cents
Hungary	Budapest	Hungarian	Forint (Ft) =100 fillér
Iceland	Reykjavik	Icelandic	Króna (IKr) =100 aurar
India	New Delhi	Hindi	Rupee (Re) =100 paisa
Indonesia	Jakarta	Bahasa Indonesian	Rupiah (Rp) =100 sen
Iran	Tehran	Farsi	Rial (RI) =100 dinar
Iraq	Baghdad	Arabic	Dinar ID) =1000 fils

Country	Capital	Official Language(s)	Currency
Ireland Republic of	Dublin	Irish, English	Pound/punt(IR)£ =100 pence/pighne
Israel	Jerusalem	Hebrew	Shekel (IS) =100 agorot
Italy	Rome	Italian	Lira (L) =100 centesimi
Ivory Coast	Abidjan (commercial) Yamoussoukro (political and administrative	French	CFA Franc (CFAFr) =100 centimes
Jamaica	Kingston	English	Dollar (J$) =100 cents
Japan	Tokyo	Japanese	Yen (Y) =100 sen
Jordan	Amman	Arabic	Dinar (JD) =1000 fils
Kampuchea	Phnom Penh	Khmer	Riel (CRl) =100 sen
Kenya	Nairobi	Kiswahili	Shilling (KSh) =100 cents
Kiribati	Tarawa	I-Kiribati English	Australian Dollar (A$) =100 cents
Korea, Democratic People's Republic of (N Korea)	Pyongyang	Korean	Won (NKW)
Korea, Republic of (S Korea)	Seoul	Korean	Won (W) =100 chun
Kuwait	Kuwait City	Arabic	Dinar (KD) =1000 fils
Laos	Vientiane	Lao	Kip (Kp) =100 at
Lebanon	Beirut	Arabic	Livre/Pound (L£) =100 piastres
Lesotho	Maseru	Sesotho, English	Malote (LSM) =100 lecente
Liberia	Monrovia	English	Dollar (L£) =100 cents
Libya	Tripoli	Arabic	Dinar (LD) =100 dirhams

Country	Capital	Official Language(s)	Currency
Liechtenstein	Vaduz	German	Swiss Franc (SFr) =100 centimes
Luxembourg	Luxembourg-Ville	German	Franc (LFr) =100 centimes
Macao	Macao City	Portuguese	Pataca (Pat) =100 avos
Madagascar	Antannanarivo	French, Malagasy	Franc (MgFr0 =100 centimes
Malawi	lilongwe	Chichewa, English	Kwacha (Mk) =100 tambala
Malaysia	Kuala Lumpur	Bahasa Malaysia (Malay)	Dollar (M$) =100 cents
Maldives	Malé	Dhivehi	Rufiyaa (MRf) =100 laris
Mali	Bamako	French	CFA Franc (CFAFr) =100 centimes
Malta	Valletta	English, Maltese	Pound (M£) =100 cents
Mauritania	Nouakchott	French, Arabic	Ouguiya (U) =5 khoums
Mauritius	Port Louis	English, French	Rupee (MR) =100 cents
Mexico	Mexico City	Spanish	Peso (Mex$) =100 centavos
Monaco	Monaco	French	Franc (MnFr) =100 centimes
Mongolia	Ulan Bator	Mongolian	Tugrik (Tug) =100 möngö
Morocco	Rabat	Arabic	Dirham (DH) =100 centimes
Mozambique	Maputo	Portuguese	Metical (MZM) =100 centavos
Namibia	Windhoek	Afrikaans, English	Rand (R) =100 cents
Nauru	Yaren District	English, Nauruan	Australian Dollar (A$) =100 cents
Nepal	Kathmandu	Nepali	Rupee (NRp) =100 pice

Country	Capital	Official Language(s)	Currency
Netherlands	Amsterdam (The Hague-seat of government)	Dutch	Guilder (Gld) Florin =100 cents
New Zealand	Wellington	English	Dollar (NZ$) =100 cents
Nicaragua	Managua	Spanish	Córdoba (C) =100 centavos
Niger	Niamey	French	CFA Franc (CFAFr) =100 centimes
Nigeria	Lagos	English	Naira (N) =100 kobo
Norway	Oslo	Norwegian	Drone (NKr) =100 ore
Oman	Muscat	Arabic	Rial Omani (RO) =1000 baizas
Pakistan	Islamabad	Urdu	Rupee (Rp) =100 paisa
Panama	Panama City	Spanish	Balboa (Ba) =100 centesimos
Papua New New Guinea	Port Moresby	English, Hiri Motu Melanisian Pidgin	Kina (K) =100 toca
Paraguay	Asunción	Spanish	Guarani (G) =100 centimos
Peru	Lima	Spanish	Sol (S) or Inti =100 centavos
Philippines	Manila	Tagalog, Cebuano	Peso (PP) =100 centavos
Poland	Warsaw	Polish	Zloty (ZI) =100 groszy
Portugal	Lisbon	Portuguese	Escudo (ESc) =100 centavos
Puerto Rico	San Juan	Spanich	Dollar ($) =100 cents
Qatar	Doha	Arabic	Riyal (QR) =100 dirhams
Romania	Bucharest	Romanian	Leu (pl. Lei) =100 bani
Rwanda	Kigali	French, Kinyarwanda	Franc (RWFr) =100 centimes

Country	Capital	Official Language(s)	Currency
St Kitts-Nevis	Basseterre	English	East Caribbean Dollar (EC$) =100 cents
St Lucia	Castries	English	East Caribbean Dollar (EC$) =100 cents
St Vincent	Kingstown	English	East Caribbena Dollar (EC$) =100 cents
San Marino	San Marino	Italian	Lira (SML) =100 centesimi
São Tomé and Principe	São Tomé	Portuguese	Dobra or Escudo (ESP) =100 centavos
Saudi	Riyadh	Arabic	Riyal (SAR) =100 halalas
Senegal	Dakar	French	CFA Franc (CFAFr) =100 centimes
Seychelles	Victoria	English, Creole	Rupee (SR) =100 cents
Sierra Leone	Freetown	English	Leone (Le) =100 cents
Singapore	Singapore City	Chinese, English Malay, Tamil	Ringgit or Dollar S$) =100 cents
Solomon Islands	Honiara	English	Dollar SI$) =100 cents
Somalia	Mogadishu	Somali, Arabic	Shilling (SoSh) =100 centesimi
South Arrica	Pretoria Kinyarwanda Cape Town (legislative)	Afrikaans English	Rand (R) =100 cents
Spain	Madrid	Spanish	Peseta (Pa) =100 centimos
Sri Lanka	Colombo	Sinhala, Tamil	Rupee (SLR) =100 cents
Sudan	Khartoum	Arabic	Pound (S£) =100 piastres

Country	Capital	Official Language(s)	Currency
Surinam	Paramaribo	Dutch	Guilder (SGld) or Florin =100 cents
Swaziland	Mbabane	English, SiSwati	Lilangeni (Li) =100 cents
Sweden	Stockholm	Swedish	Krona (SKr) =100 øre
Switzerland	Berne	German, French Italian, Romansch	Swiss Franc (SFr) =100 centimes
Syria	Damascus	Arabic	Pound (Syr£) =100 piastres
Taiwan	Taipei	Mandarin Chinese	New Dollar (NT$) =100 cents
Tanzania	Dar es Salaam	Swahili, English	Shilling (TSh0 =100 cents
Thailand	Bangkok	Thai	Baht (Bt) =100 satang
Togo	Lomé	French, Kabiye, Ewe	CFA Franc (CFAFr) =100 centimes
Tonga	Nuku'alofa	Tongan	Pa'anga or Tongan Dollar (T$) =100 seniti
Trinidad and Tobago	Port of Spain	English	Dollar (TT$) =100 cents
Tunisia	Tunis	Arabic	Dinar (TD) =1000 millemes
Turkey	Ankara	Turkish	Lira (TL) =100 kuros
Tuvalu	Funafuti	Tuvaluan (Samoan)	Australian Dollar (A$) =100 cents
Uganda	Kampala	English	Shilling (USh) =100 cents
Union of Soviet Socialist Republics	Moscow	Russian	Rouble (Rub) =100 kopeks
United Arab Emirates	Abu Dhabi	Arabic	Dirham (DH) =100 fils

Country	Capital	Official Language(s)	Currency
United Kingdom	London	English	Pound sterling (£) =100 pence
United States of America	Washinton DC	English	Dollar ($) =100 cents
Uruguay	Montevideo	Spanish	New Peso (UrugN$) =100 centesimos
Vanuatu	Port Vila	Bislama, English French	Vatu (V) =100 centimes
Venezuela	Caracas	Spanish	Bolivar (B) =100 centimos
Vietnam	Hanoi	Vietnamese	Dông (D) =100 hào
Western Samoa	Apia	English, Samoan	Tala or Western Samoan Dollar (WS$) =100 sene
Yemen Arab Republic (N Yemen)	Sana'a	Arabic	Riyal (YR) =100 fils
Yemen People's Democratic Republic (S Yemen)	Aden	Arabic	Dinar (YD) =1000 fils
Yugoslavia	Belgrade	Serbo-Croat, Slovene Macedonian	Dinar (D) =100 paras
Zaire	Kinshasa	French	Zaire (Z) =100 makuta
Zambia	Lusaka	English	Kwacha (K) =100 ngwee
Zimbabwe	Harare	English	Dollar (Z$) =100 cents

UNITED NATIONS MEMBER COUNTRIES

The United Nations Organization was set up in 1945. Originally, 50 nations signed its charter. Today there are 159 member countries.

Country	Year Joined	Country	Year Joined
Afghanistan	1946	Congo	1960
Albania	1955	Costa Rica	1945
Algeria	1962	Cuba	1945
Angola	1976	Cyprus	1960
Antigua and Barbuda	1981	Czechoslovakia	1945
Argentina	1945	Denmark	1945
Australia	1945	Djibouti	1977
Austria	1955	Dominica	1978
Bahamas	1973	Dominican Republic	1945
Bahrain	1971	Ecuador	1945
Bangladesh	1974	Egypt	1945
Barbados	1966	El Salvador	1945
Belgium	1945	Equatorial Guinea	1968
Belize	1981	Ethiopia	1945
Benin	1960	Fiji	1970
Bhutan	1971	Finland	1955
Bolivia	1945	France	1945
Botswana	1966	Gabon	1960
Brazil	1945	Gambia	1965
Brunei	1984	Germany, East	1973
Bulgaria	1955	Germany, West	1973
Burkina Faso (Upper Volta)	1960	Ghana	1957
Burma	1948	Greece	1945
Burundi	1962	Grenada	1974
Byelorussian SSR	1945	Guatemala	1945
Cameroon	1960	Guinea	1958
Canada	1945	Guinea-Bissau	1974
Cape Verde	1975	Guyana	1966
Central African Republic	1960	Haiti	1945
Chad	1960	Honduras	1945
Chile	1945	Hungary	1955
China	1945	Iceland	1946
Colombia	1945	India	1945
Comoros	1975	Indonesia	1950

Country	Year Joined	Country	Year Joined
Iran	1945	Pakistan	1947
Iraq	1945	Panama	1945
Ireland, Rep of	1955	Papua New Guinea	1975
Israel	1949	Paraguay	1945
Italy	1955	Peru	1945
Ivory Coast	1960	Philippines	1945
Jamaica	1962	Poland	1945
Japan	1956	Portugal	1955
Jordan	1955	Qatar	1971
Kampuchea (Cambodia)	1955	Romania	1955
Kenya	1963	Rwanda	1962
Kuwait	1963	St Lucia	1979
Laos	1955	St Vincent & the Grenadines	1980
Lebanon	1945	Samoa	1976
Lesotho	1966	São Tomé & Principe	1975
Liberia	1945	Saudi Arabia	1945
Libya	1955	Senegal	1960
Luxembourg	1945	Seychelles	1976
Madagascar	1960	Sierra Leone	1961
Malawi	1964	Singapore	1965
Malaysia	1957	Solomon Islands	1978
Maldive Islands	1965	Somali Republic	1960
Mali	1960	South Africa	1945
Malta	1964	Spain	1955
Mauritania	1961	Sri Lanka	1955
Mauritius	1968	St Christopher-Nevis	1983
Mexico	1945	Sudan	1956
Mongolia	1961	Surinam	1975
Morocco	1956	Swaziland	1968
Mozambique	1975	Sweden	1946
Nepal	1955	Syria	1945
Netherlands	1945	Tanzania	1961
New Zealand	1945	Thailand	1946
Nicaragua	1945	Togo	1960
Niger	1960	Trinidad & Tobago	1962
Nigeria	1960	Tunisia	1956
Norway	1945	Turkey	1945
Oman	1971	Uganda	1962

Country	Year Joined	Country	Year Joined
Ukrainian SSR	1945	Vietnam	1976
USSR	1945	Yemen Arab Republic	1947
United Arab Emirates	1971	Yemen PDR	1967
United Kingdom	1945	Yugoslavia	1945
United States	1945	Zaire	1960
Uruguay	1945	Zambia	1964
Vanuatu	1981	Zimbabwe	1980
Venezuela	1945		

UNITED NATIONS: AGENCIES

FAO   Food and Agriculture Organization
GATT   General Agreement on Tariffs and Trade
IAEA   International Atomic Energy Authority
IBRD   International Bank for Reconstruction and Development
            (World Bank)
ICAO   International Civil Aviation Organization
ICF   International Court of Justice
IDA   International Development Association
IFC   International Finance Corporation
ILO   International Labour Organization
IMCO   Inter-Governmental Maritime Consultative Organization
IMF   International Monetary Fund
ITU   International Telecommunications Union
UNCLOS United Nations Conference on the Law of the Sea
UNCTAD United Nations Conference on Trade and Development
UNEF   United Nations Emergency Fund
UNESCO United Nations Educational, Scientific and Cultural Organization
UNICEF United Nations Children's Emergency Fund
UNIDO   United Nations Industrial Development Organization
UNRWA   United Nations Relief and Works Agency
UPU   Universal Postal Union
WHO   World Health Organization
WMO   World Meteorological Organization

AIRPORT AND CITY CODES

Airport/City	Code
A	
Aberdeen, SD, USA	ABR
Abidjan, Ivory Coast	ABJ
Abu Dhabi, Utd. Arab Emirates	AUH
Acapulco, Mexico	ACA
Addis Ababa, Ethiopia	ADD
Aden, Dem. Rep. Yemen	ADE
Agadir, Morocco	AGA
Algiers, Algeria	ALG
Alexandria, Egypt	ALY
Amsterdam, Netherlands	AMS
Anchorage, AK, USA	ANC
Anguilla, Leeward Is.	AXA
Ankara, Turkey	ESB
Antigua, Leeward Is.	ANU
Aruba, Neth. Antilles	AUA
Asunción, Paraguay	ASU
Athens, Greece	ATH
Atlanctic City, NJ, USA	AIY
Atlantac, GA, USA	ATL
Auckland, New Zealand	AKL
B	
Baghdad-Saddam Intl., Iraq	BGW
Bahrain, Bahrain	BAH
Bangkok, Thailand	BKK
Banjul, Gambia	BJL
Barbados, Barbados	BGI
Barbuda, Leeward Is.	BBQ
Barcelona, Spain	BCN
Basel, Switzerland	BSL
Baton Rouge, LA, USA	BTR
Beirut, Lebanon	BEY
Belfast, N. Ireland	BFS
Belgrade, Yugoslavia	BEG
Benghazi, Libya	BWN
Berlin, West-Tegel Apt, Germany Fed. Rep	TXL
Berlin West, Germany Fed. Rep.	BER
Bermuda, Atlantic Ocean	BDA
Bird Island, Seychelles	BDI
Bogotá, Colombia	BOG
Boise, ID, USA	BOI
Bombay, India	BOM
Boston, MA, USA	BOS
Brasilia, Brazil	BSB
Brisbane, QL, Australia	BNE
Brussels, Belgium	BRU
Bucharest, Romania	BUH
Budapest, Hungary	BUD
Buenos Aires, Argentina Airport	EZE
Buffalo, NY, USA	BUF
C	
Cairo, Egypt	CAI
Calcutta, India	CCU
Calgary, Alberta, Canada	YYC
Cap Haitien, Haiti	CAP
Caracas, Venezuela	CCS
Chicago, IL, USA	ORD
Chihuahua, Mexico	CUU
Cincinnati, OH, USA	CVG
Clevelnad, OH, USA– Lakefront Airport	BKL
Cleveland, OH, USA,– Hopkins Airport	CLE
Cologne/Bonn APT, Germany Fed. Rep.	CGN
Colombo, Sri Landa	CMB
Columbus, OH, USA	CMH
Copenhagen, Denmark	CPH
Curaçao, Neth. Antilles	CUR
D	
Dakar, Senegal	DKR
Dallas/Ft. Worth, TX, USA	DFW

Airport/City	Code	Airport/City	Code
Damascus, Syria	DAM	**H**	
Dar es Salaam, Tanzania	DAR	Halifax, NS, Canada	YHZ
Delhi, India	DEL	Hamburg, Germany Fed. Rep.	HAM
Denver, CO, USA	DEN	Hamilton, Ontario, Canada	YHM
Des Moines, IA, USA	DSM	Hanover, Germany Fed. Rep.	HAJ
Detroit City Airport, MI, USA	DET	Harare, Zimbabwe	HRE
Detroit, MI, USA	DTT	Harrisburg, PA, USA	MDT
Detroit–Metropol APT,		Hartford Bradley Int., MA, USA	BDL
MI, USA	DTW	Havana, Cuba	HAV
Djakarta, Indonesia	HLP	Helsinki, Finland	HEL
Cubai, Utd. Arab Emirates	DXB	Hermosillo, Mexico	HMO
Düsseldorf, Germany Fed. Rep.	DUS	Hilo, Hawaii, HI, USA	ITO
		Honolulu, Int., HI, USA	HNL
E		Houston, Hoby Airport,	
Edinburgh, UK	EDI	TX, USA	HOU
Edmonton, Alberta, Canada	YEG	Houston–Intercont. APT,	
El Paso, TX, USA	ELP	TX, USA	IAH
Entebbe, Uganda	EBB	**I**	
		Indianapolis, IN, USA	IND
F		Innsbruck, Austria	INN
Fairbanks, AK, USA	FAI	Islamabad, Pakistan	ISB
Ft. de France, Martinique	FDF	Istanbul, Turkey	IST
Frankfurt, Germany Fed. Rep.	FRA		
Ft. Lauderdale, FL, USA	FLL	**J**	
		Jeddah, Saudi Arabia	JED
G		Jerusalem	JRS
Gander, Nfld., Canada	YQX	Johannesburg, South Africa	JNB
Geneva, Switzerland	GVA	Juneau, AK, USA	JNU
Gibraltar	GIB		
Glasgow, Scotland	GLA	**K**	
Prestwick Airport	PIK	Kabul, Afghanistan	KBL
Georgetown, Guvana	GEO	Kansas City, MO, USA	MCI
Grand Turk, Turks & Caicos Is.	GET	Karachi, Pakistan	KHI
Great Harbour Cay, Bahamas	GHC	Khartoum, Sudan	KRT
Grenada, Windward Is	GND	Kingston, Jamaica	KIN
Guadalajara, Mexico	GDC	Kinshasa, Zaïre	FIH
Guam Island, Guam	GUM	Kodiak, AK, USA,	
Guatanamo, Cuba	GAO	Kodiak Airport	ADQ
Guatemala City, Guatemala	GUA	Kuala Lumpur, Malaysia	KUL
		Kuwait, Kuwait	KWI

Airport/City	Code	Airport/City	Code
L		**N**	
Lagos, Nigeria	LOS	Nadi, Fiji	NAN
La Paz, Bolivia	LPB	Nairobi, Kenya	NBO
Las Vegas, NV, USA	LAS	Naples, Italy	NAP
Leningrad, USSR	LED	Nashville, TN, USA	BNA
Lima, Peru	LIM	Nassau, Bahamas	NAS
Lisbon, Portugul	LIS	New York–Newark	
London, UK–Gatwick Airport	LGW	Airport, NY, USA	EWR
London, UK–Heathrow Airport	LHR	New Orleans, LA USA	MSY
London, Ontario, Canada	YXU	Newport, RI, USA	NPT
Los Angeles, CA, USA	LAX	New York, NY, USA–	
Lusaka, Zambia	LUN	JF Kennedy Airport	JFK
		New York, NY, USA–	
M		La Guardia Airport	LGA
Madras, India	MAA	New York, NY, USA	NYC
Madrid, Spain	MAD	Nice, France	NCE
Malaga, Spain	AGP	Nome, AK, USA	OME
Malta, Malta	MLA	Nuremberg, Germany	NUE
Manaus, Brazil	MAO		
Manchester, UK	MAN	**O**	
Mandalay, Burma	MDL	Okinawa–Naha Airport, Japan	OKA
Maracaibo, Venezuela	MAR	Oklahoma City, OK, USA	OKC
Marseille, France	MRS	Osaka, Japan	OSA
Medicine Hat, Alberta, Canada	YXH	Oslo, Norway	OSL
Melbourne, Australia	MEL	Ottawa, Ontario, Canada	YOW
Memphis, TN, USA	MEM		
Mexico City, Mexico	MEX	**P**	
Miami, FL, USA	MIA	Pago Pago, American Samoa	PPG
Michigan city, IN, USA	MGC	Panama City, Panama	PTY
Milan, Iraly–Malpenso Airport	MXP	Papeete, Tahiti	PPT
Milwaukee, WI, USA	MKE	Paris, France–Charles	
Minneapolis/St. Paul, MN, USA	MSP	de Gaulle Airport	CDG
Monrovia, Liberia	ROB	Paris, France–Orly Airport	ORY
Montego bay, Jamaica	MBJ	Perth, WA, Australia	PER
Montevideo, Uruguay	MUD	Philadelphia, PA, USA	PHL
Montreal, Quebec, Canada	YIL	Phoenix, AS, USA	PHX
Montserrat, Leeward Is.	MNI	Pisa, Italy	PSA
Moscow, USSR–		Pittsburgh, PA, USA	PIT
Sheremetyevo Airport	SVO	Pointe-à-Pitre, Guadeloupe	PTP
Munich, Germany Red. Rep.	MUC	Port-au-Prince, Haiti	PAP

Airport/City	Code	Airport/City	Code
Portland, OR, USA	PDX	Seoul, Korean Republic	SEL
Port of Spain, Trinidad	POS	Shanghai, P R China	SHA
Prague, Czechoslovakia	PRG	Shannon, Ireland Rep.	SNN
Prince Albert, SA, Canada	YPA	Singapore, Singapore	SIN
Prince George, BC, Canada	YXS	Sofia, Bulgaria	SOF
Prince Rupert, BC, Canada	YPR	Stockholm, Sweden–	
		Arlanda Airport	ARN
Q		Stuttgart, West Germany	STR
Quebec City, QU, Canada	YQB	Sydney, NSW, Australia	SYD
Quito, Ecuador	UIO		
		T	
R		Taipei, Taiwan	TPE
Rabat, Morocco	RBA	Tampa, FL, USA	TPA
Rangoon, Burma	RGN	Tehran, Iran	THR
Reykjavik, Iceland	REK	Tel Aviv, Israel	TLV
Rio de Janeiro, Brazil	GIG	Tenerife, Canary Is	TCI
Rome, Italy–		Tobago, Trinidad & Tobago	TAB
Leonardo da Vinci Airport	FCO	Tokyo, Japan–Hanedo Airport	HND
		Tokyo, Japan–Narita Airport	NRT
S		Toronto, Ontario, Canada	YYZ
St. Johns, Ffld., Canada	YYT	Tripoli, Libya	TIP
St. Kitts, Leeward Is.	SKB	Tunis, Tunisia	TUN
Salt Lake City, UT, USA	SLC	Turin, Italy	TRN
San Francisco, CA, USA	SFO		
San José, Costa Rica	SJO	**V**	
San Juan, Puerto Rico–Isla Grande		Vancouver, BC, Canada	YV
Airport	SIG	Victoria, BC, Canada	YYJ
San Juan, Puerto Rico–Isla Verde		Vienna, Austria	VIE
Airport	SJU		
San Salvador, El Salvador	SAL	**W**	
Santiago, Chile	SCL	Warsaw, Poland	WAW
Santo Domingo, Dominican Rep	SDQ	Washington, DC, USA–	
São Paulo, Brazil–		National Airport	DCA
Congonhas Airport	CHG	Washington, DC, USA–	
São Paulo, Brazil–		Dulles Airport	IAD
Viracopos Airport	CGH	Winnipeg, MN, Canada	YWG
Saskatoon, SA, Canada	YXE		
Seattle, WA, USA–HM		**Z**	
		Zagreb, Yugolslavia	ZAG
Jackson Airport	SEA	Zurich, Switzerland	ZRH

AIRLINE CODES

Airline	Code	Airline	Code
American Airlines, Inc	AA	Air Sénégal	DS
Air Canada	AC	TAAG-Angola Airlines	ST
Air France	AF	DLT Deutsche Regionale	
Air Algérie	AH	Luftverkehrsgesellschaft	
Air India	AI	German Domestic Airlines	DW
US Air/Allegheny		Danair	DX
Commuter Airlines	AL	Douglas Airways	DZ
Aeromexico	AM	Eastern Air Lines	EA
Ansett Airlines of Australia	AN	Aer Lingus (Irish)	EI
Aviaco	AO	Ethiopian Airlines	ET
Aspen Airways, Inc	AP	Empresa Ecuatiriana de Aviación	EU
Aerolineas Argentinas	AR	East-West Airlines	EW
Alaska Airlines	AS	Ariana Afghan Airlines	FG
Royal Air Maroc	AT	Flugfelag-Icelandair	FI
Avianca	AV	Air Pacific	FJ
Finnair	AY	Frontier Airlines	FL
Alitalia	AZ	Garuda Indonesian Airways	GA
British Airways	BA	Airborne Express	GB
British Midland Airways	BD	Gulf Air	GF
Air BVI Ltd	BL	Ghana Airways	GH
Aero Trasporti Italiane	BM	Ansett Airlines of South Australia	GJ
Air Botswana Pty Ltd	BP	Greenlandair	GL
Airlines of Northern Australia	BT	Air Gabon	GN
Braathens SAFE Airtransport	BU	Gibraltar Airways	GT
BWIA International	BW	Aviateca	GU
Trans-Provincial Airlines Ltd	CD	Talair	GV
Faucett	CF	Guyana Airways Corporation	GY
China Airlines	CI	Hawaiian Airlines	HA
Continental Airlines, Inc.	CO	Air Melanesie	HB
CP Air	CP	NLM–Dutch Airlines	HN
Cubana Airlines	CU	Iraqi Airways	IA
Cathay Pacific Airways	CX	Iberia	IB
Cyprus Airways	CY	Indian Airlines	IC
Dan-Air Services	DA	Solomon Islands Airways	IE
Air Djibouti	DJ	Interflug	IF
Delta Air Lines	DL	Alisarda	IG
Dominicana De Aviación	DO	Imperial Airways	II

Airline	Code	Airline	Code
Touraine Air Transport	IJ	Air Mauritius	MK
Airlines of Tasmania	IP	Commercial Airways	MN
Caribbean Airways	IQ	Air Mauritaine	MR
Iranair	IR	Egyptair	MS
Eagle Air	IS	Mexicana de Aviación	MX
Air Inter	IT	Air Mali	MY
Yemen Airways	IY	Newair	NC
Arkia-Israeli Airlines	IZ	Nordair	ND
Japan Air Lines	JL	Executive Airlink	NE
Air Jamaica	JM	Air Vanuatu	NF
Yugoslav Airlines –JAT	JU	All Nippon Airways	NH
Korean Airlines	KE	American International Airways	NI
KLM–Royal Dutch Airlines	KL	Air Liberia	NL
Air Malta	KM	Mt Cook Airlines	NM
Kodiak Western Alaska Airlines	KO	Southwest Airlines	NU
Kenya Airways	KQ	Northwest Orient Airlines	NW
Karair	KR	New York Air	NY
Kuwait Airways	KU	Air New Zealand–Domestic	NZ
Cayman Airways	KX	Olympic Airways	OA
Lan Chile	LA	Emerald Airlines, Inc	OD
Lloyd Aero Boliviano	LB	Air Guadeloupe	OG
Luxair–Luxembourg Airlines	LG	Comair	OH
Lufthansa German Airlines	LH	CSA-Czechoslovak Airlines	OK
Liat	LI	Air Mongol–MIAT	OM
Sierra Leone Airways	LJ	Air Nauru	ON
Bell Air	LL	Air Panama Internacional	OP
ALM–Antillean Airlines	LM	Austrian Airlines	OS
Libyan Airlines	LN	Ozark Air Lines, Inc	OZ
LOT–Polish Airlines	LO	Pan American World Airways	PA
LACSA	LR	Air Burundi	PB
LAV–Linea Aeropostal Venezolana	LV	Fiji Air	PC
Crossair	LX	Pem Air Ltd	PD
El Al Israel Airlines	LY	Polynesian Airlines	PH
Bulgarian Airlines–Balkan	LZ	Piedmont Aviation	PI
Malev–Hungarian Airlines	MA	Pakistan International Airlines	PK
Air Madagascar	MD	Aeroperu	PL
Middle East Airlines/Airliban	ME	Philippine Airlines	PR
Malaysian Airline System	MH	Eastern Provincial Airways	PV

Airline	Code	Airline	Code
Pacific Western Airlines	PW	Trans-Australia Airlines	TN
Suriname Airways	PY	TAP Air Portugal	TP
LAP–Lineas Aereas Paraguayas	PZ	Transports Aeriens du Benin TAB	TS
Quebecair, Inc	QB	Tunis Air	TU
Qantas Airways	QF	TWA-Trans World Airlines, Inc	TW
Lesotho Airways	QL	TAN Airlines	TX
Air Malawi	QM	Air Calédonie	TY
Uganda Airlines	QU	Sansa	TZ
Zambia Airways	QZ	United Airlines	UA
Royal Nepal Airlines	RA	Burma Airways Corporation	UB
Syrian Arab Airlines	RB	Ladeco	UC
Varig, SA	RG	United Air Services	UE
Air Zimbabwe	RH	Flugfelag Nordurlands	UE
Eastern Airlines of Australia	RI	Air UK	UK
ALIA–Royal Jordanian Airlines	RJ	Air Lanka	UL
Air Afrique	RK	East Coast Airways	UN
Royal Air Inter	RN	Bahamasair	UP
Rarom–Romanian Air Transport	RO	UTA	UT
Reeve Aleutian Airways	RV	Cameroon Airlines	UY
South African Airways	SA	Air Resorts Airlines	UZ
Cruziero Do Sul SA	SC	VIASA	VA
Sudan Airways	SD	Air Volta	VH
SAHSA–Servicio Aereo		VASP	VP
De Honduras SA	SH	Air Polynésie	VT
SAS–Scandinavian		Air Ivoire	VU
Airlines System	SK	Western Airlines	WA
Sabena–Belgian World Airlines	SN	Wien Air Alaska, Inc	WC
SATA	SP	Windward Island Airways	
Singapore Airlines	SQ	International	W
Swissair	SR	Nigeria Airways	WT
Aeroflot Soviet Airlines	SU	Oman Aviation Services	WY
Saudi Arabian Airlines	SV	Munz Northern Airlines, Inc	XY
Taca International Airlines	TA	Air Tasmania	XZ
Air Tanzania Corporation	TC	Cyprus/Turkish Airlines	YK
Air New Zealand–International	TE	Air Midwest	ZV
THY–Turkish Airlines	TK	Virgin Air	ZP
Deta–LAM, Linhas Aereas			
De Mozambique	TM		

INTERNATIONAL DIALING CODES

Country	Code	Country	Code
Algeria	213	Egypt	20
American Samoa	684	Alexandria 3	
Andorra	33	Port Said 66	
all points 628		El Salvador	503
Argentina	54	Ethiopia	251
Buenos Aires 1		Addis Ababa 1	
Australia	61	Fiji	679
Melbourne 3		Finland	358
Sydney 2		Helsinki 0	
Austria	43	France	33
Vienna 222		Marseille 91	
Bahrain	973	Nice 93	
Belgium	32	Paris 13, 14 or 16	
Brussels 2		French Antilles	596
Ghent 91		French Polynesia	689
Belize	501	Gabon	241
Bolivia	591	German Democratic Republic	37
Santa Cruz 33		East Berlin 2	
Brazil	55	German Federal Republic	49
Brasilia 61		Frankfurt 69	
Rio de Janeiro 21		Munich 89	
Cameroon	237	West Berlin 30	
Chile	56	Greece	30
Santiago 2		Athens 1	
Columbia	57	Rhodes 241	
Bogata 1		Guam	671
Costa Rica	506	Guantanamo Bay U. S. Naval base	53
Cyprus	357	all points 99	
Czechoslovakia	42	Guyana	592
Prague 2		Georgetown 2	
Denmark	45	Haiti	509
Aalborg 8		Port-au-Prince 1	
Copenhagen 1 or 2		Honduras	504
Ecuador	593	Hong Kong	852
Cuneca 7		Hong Kong 5	
Quito 2		Kowloon 3	

Country	Code	Country	Code
Hungary	36	Liechenstein	41
Budapest 1		all points 75	
Iceland	354	Luxembourg	352
Akureyri 6		Malawi	265
Hahnarfjorour 1		Domasi 531	
India	91	Malaysia	60
Bombay 22		Kuala Lumpur 3	
New Delhi 11		Mexico	52
Indonesia	62	Mexico City 5	
Jakarta 21		Tijuana 66	
Iran	98	Monaco	33
Teheran 21		all points 93	
Iraq	964	Morocco	212
Baghdad 1		Agadir 8	
Ireland	353	Namibia	264
Dublin 1		Olympia 61	
Galway 2		Netherlands	31
Israel	972	Amsterdam 20	
Haifa 4		The Hague 70	
Jerusalem 2		Netherlands Antilles	599
Tel Aviv 3		Aruba 2978	
Italy	39	New Caledonia	687
Florence 55		New Zealand	64
Rome 6		Aukland 9	
Venice 41		Wellington 4	
Ivory Coast	225	Nicaragua	505
Japan	81	Managua 2	
Tokyo 3		Nigeria	234
Yokahama 45		Lagos 1	
Jordan	962	Norway	47
Amman 6		Bergen 5	
Kenya	254	Oslo 2	
Korea, South	82	Oman	968
Pusan 51		Pakistan	92
Seoul 2		Islamabad 51	
Kuwait	965	Panama	507
Liberia	231	Papua New Guinea	675
Libya	218	Paraguay	595
Tripoli 21		Asuncion 21	

Country	Code	Country	Code
Peru	51	Taiwan	886
Arequipa 54		Tainan 6	
Lima 14		Taipei 3	
Phillipines	63	Thailand	66
Manila 2		Bangkok 2	
Poland	48	Tunisia	216
Warsaw 22		Tunis 1	
Portugal	351	Turkey	90
Lisbon 1		Istanbul 1	
Qatar	974	Izmir 51	
Rumania	40	United Arab Emirates	971
Bucharest 0		Abu Dhabi 2	
Saipan	670	Al Ain 3	
San Merino	39	Dubai 4	
allpoints 541		Ras Al Khainah 77	
Saudia Arabia	966	Sharjah 6	
Riyadh 1		Umm Al Quwain 6	
Senegal	221	United Kingdom	44
Singapore	65	Belfast 232	
SouthAfrica	27	Cardiff 222	
Cape Town 21		Edinburgh 31	
Pretoria 12		Glasgow 41	
Spain	34	London Inner 71	
Barcelona 3		London Outer 81	
Las Palmas, Canary Islands 28		Uruguay	598
Madrid 1		Mercedes 532	
Seville 54		Montevideo 2	
Sri Lanka	94	Vatican City	39
Kandy 8		all points 6	
Suriname	597	Venezuela	58
Sweden	46	Caracas 2	
Göteborg 31		Maracaibo 61	
Stockholm 8		Yemen Arab Republic	967
Switzerland	41	Amran 2	
Geneva 22		Yugoslavia	38
Lucerne 41		Belgrade 11	
Zurich 1			

INTERNATIONAL VEHICLE LICENSE PLATES

Code	Country	Code	Country
A	Austria	EC	Ecuador
ADN	South Yemen	EIR	Ireland
AL	Albania	ET	Egypt
AND	Andorra	F	France
AUS	Australia	FJI	Fiji
B	Belgium	FL	Liechtenstein
BDS	Barbados	G	Gabon
BG	Bulgaria	GB	United Kingdom
BH	Belize	GBA	Alderney
BR	Brazil	GBG	Guernsey
BRN	Bahrain	GBJ	Jersey
BRU	Brunei	GBM	Isle of Man
BS	Bahamas	GBZ	Gibraltar
BUR	Bura	GH	Ghana
C	Cuba	GLA	Guatemala
CDN	Canada	GR	Greece
CH	Switzerland	GUY	Guyana
CI	Ivory Coast	H	Hungary
CL	Sri Lanka	HK	Hong Kong
CO	Colombia	HKJ	Jordan
CR	Costa Rica	I	Italy
CS	Czechoslovakia	IL	Israel
CY	Cyprus	IND	India
D	German Federal Republic	IR	Iran
DDR	German Democrtatic Republic	IRQ	Iraq
		IS	Iceland
DK	Denmark	J	Japan
DOM	Dominican Republic	JA	Jamaica
DY	Benin	K	Kampuchea
DZ	Algeria	L	Luxembourg
E	Spain	LAO	Lao People's Dem Republic
EAK	Kenya	LAR	Libya
EAT	Tanzania	LB	Liberia
EAU	Uganda	LS	Lesotho
EAZ	Zanzibar	M	Malta

Code	Country	Code	Country
MA	Morocco	RSR	Zimbabwe
MAL	Malaysia	RU	Burundi
MC	Monaco	RWA	Rwanda
MEX	Mexico	S	Sweden
MS	Mauritius	SD	Swaziland
MW	Malawi	SDV	Vatican City
N	Norway	SF	Finland
NA	Netherlands Antilles	SGP	Singapore
NIC	Nicaragua	SME	Suriname
NIG	Niger	SN	Sénégal
NL	Netherlands	SU	USSR
NZ	New Zealand	SWA	South West Africa (Namibia)
P	Portugal		
PA	Panama	SY	Seychelles
PAK	Pakistan	SYR	Syria
PE	Peru	T	Thailand
PI	Philippines	TG	Togo
PL	Poland	TN	Tunisia
PY	Paraguay	TR	Turkey
R	Romania	TT	Trinidad and Tobago
RA	Argentina	U	Uruguay
RB	Botswan	USA	USA
RC	Taiwan	VN	Vietnam
RCA	Central African Republic	WAG	Gambia
		WAL	Sierra Leone
RCB	Congo	WAN	Nigeria
RCH	Chile	WD	Dominica
RH	Haiti	WG	Grenada
RI	Indonesia	WL	St. Lucia
RIM	Mauritania	WS	Western Samoa
RL	Lebanon	WV	St. Vincent
RM	Madagascar	YU	Yugoslavia
RMM	Mali	YV	Venezuela
RNR	Zambia	Z	Zambia
ROK	Korea	ZA	South Africa
RSM	San Marino	ZR	Zaïre

INTERNATIONAL VOLTAGE GUIDE

Aden	220V	Egypt	110/220V
Afghanistan	220V	El Salvador	110V
Algeria	110/220V	Ethiopia	110/220V
Angola	220V	Fiji	220V
Anguilla	220V	Finland	220V
Antigua	110/220V	France	110/220V
†Argentina	220V	French Guiana	110/220V
Aruba	110V	Gabon	220V
†Australia	220V	Gambia	220V
Austria	220V	†Germany	110/220V
Azores	110/220V	Ghana	220V
Bahamas	110/220V	Gibraltar	220V
Bahrain	220V	†Greece	110/220V
Bangladesh	220V	Greenland	220V
Barbados	110/220V	Grenada	220V
Belgium	110/220V	Grenadines	220V
Belize	110/220V	Guadeloupe	110/220V
Benin	220V	Guatemala	110/220V
Bermuda	110/220V	Guinea	220V
Bhutan	220V	Guyana	110/220V
Bolivia	110/220V	Haiti	110/220V
Botswana	220V	Honduras	110/220V
†Brazil	110/220V	*Hong Kong	220V
British Virgin Islands	110/220V	Hungary	220V
Bulgaria	110/220V	Iceland	220V
Burma	220V	†India	220V
Burundi	220V	Indonesia	110/220V
Cameroon	110/220V	Iran	220V
Canada	110/220V	Iraq	220V
Canary Islands	110/220V	Ireland	220V
Cayman Islands	110V	Isle of Man (UK)	220V
Central African Republic	220V	Israel	220V
Chad	220V	Italy	110/220V
*Channel Islands (UK)	220V	Ivory Coast	220V
†Chile	220V	Jamaica	110/220V
China	220V	Japan	110V
Colombia	110V	Jordan	220V
Costa Rica	110/220V	Kampuchea	110/220V
Cuba	110V	Kenya	220V
Curacao	110V	Korea, South	220V
*Cyprus	220V	Kuwait	220V
Czechoslovakia	110/220V	Lao Peoples Democratic	
Denmark	220V	Republic (Laos)	110/220V
Dominica	220V	Lebanon	110/220V
Dominican Republic	110/220V	Lesotho	220V
Ecuador	110/220V	Liberia	110/220V

Libya	110/220V	Saudi Arabia	110/220V
Liechtenstein	220V	Sénégal	110V
Luxembourg	110/220V	Seychelles	220V
Macao	110/220V	Sierra Leone	220V
Madagascar	220V	*Singapore	110/220V
Madeira	220V	Somalia	110/220V
Majorca	110V	South Africa	220V
Malawi	220V	Spain	110/220V
Malaysia	110/220V	Sri Lanka	220V
Mali	110/220V	Sudan	220V
Malta	220V	Suriname	110/220V
Martinique	110/220V	Swaziland	220V
Mauritiana	220V	†Sweden	110/220V
Mexico	110/220V	Switzerland	110/220V
Monaco	110/220V	Syria	110/220V
Montserrat	220V	Tahiti	110/220V
Morocco	110/220V	Taiwan	110/220V
Mozambique	220V	Tanzania	220V
Nepal	220V	Togo	110/220V
Netherlands	110/220V	Tonga	220V
Netherland Antilles	110/220V	Trinidad and Tobago	110/220V
Nevis	220V	Tunisia	110/220V
New Caledonia	220V	Turkey	110/220V
New Zealand	220V	Turks and Caicos Islands	110V
Nicaragua	110/220V	Uganda	220V
Niger	220V	Upper Volta (Burkina Faso)	220V
*Nigeria	220V	Uruguay	220V
Norway	220V	United Arab Emirates	220V
Oman	220V	*United Kingdom	220V
Pakistan	220V	USA	110V
Panama	110V	USSR	110/220V
Papua New Guinea	220V	US Virgin Islands	110V
†Paraguay	220V	Vanuatu	200V
Peru	220V	Venezuela	110/220V
Philippines	110/220V	Vietnam	110/220V
Poland	110/220V	Yemen	220V
Portugal	110/220V	Yugoslavia	220V
Puerto Rico	110V	Zaire	220V
Qatar	220V	Zambia	220V
Romania	110/220V	*Zimbabwe	220V
Rwanda	220V		
St Barthélemy	220V		
St Eustatius	110/220V		
St Kitts	220V		
St Lucia	220V		
St Maarten	110/220V		
St Vincent	220V		

*Countries where plugs with 3 square pins are mainly used.

†Countries where DC is used in some areas.

WORLDWIDE WEATHER GUIDE

			J	F	M	A	M	J	J	A	S	O	N	D
Accra														
Temperature	F	Max	87	88	88	88	87	84	81	80	81	85	87	88
		Min	73	75	76	76	75	74	73	71	73	74	75	75
Temperature	C	Max	31	31	31	31	31	29	38	38	38	29	31	31
		Min	23	24	24	24	24	23	23	22	23	23	24	24
Humidity %		am	95	96	95	95	96	96	97	97	96	97	97	97
		pm	61	61	63	65	68	64	76	77	72	71	66	64
Amsterdam														
Temperature	F	Max	40	42	49	56	64	70	72	71	67	57	48	42
		Min	31	31	34	40	46	51	55	55	50	44	38	33
Temperature	C	Max	4	5	10	13	18	21	22	22	19	14	9	5
		Min	-1	-1	1	4	8	11	13	13	10	7	3	1
Humidity %		am	90	90	86	79	75	75	79	82	86	90	92	91
		pm	82	76	65	61	59	59	64	65	67	72	81	85
Athens														
Temperature	F	Max	55	57	60	68	77	86	92	92	84	85	66	58
		Min	44	44	46	52	61	68	73	73	67	60	53	47
Temperature	C	Max	13	14	16	20	25	30	33	33	29	24	19	15
		Min	6	7	8	11	16	20	23	23	19	15	12	8
Humidity %		am	77	74	71	65	60	50	47	48	58	70	78	78
		pm	62	57	54	48	47	39	34	34	42	52	61	63
Auckland														
Temperature	F	Max	73	73	71	67	62	58	56	58	60	63	66	70
		Min	60	60	59	56	51	48	46	46	49	52	54	57
Temperature	C	Max	23	23	22	19	17	14	13	14	16	17	19	21
		Min	16	16	15	13	11	9	8	8	9	11	12	14
Humidity %		am	71	72	74	78	80	83	84	80	76	74	71	70
		pm	62	61	65	69	70	73	74	70	68	66	64	64
Bahrain														
Temperature	F	Max	68	70	75	84	92	96	99	100	96	90	82	71
		Min	57	59	63	70	78	82	85	85	81	75	69	60
Temperature	C	Max	20	21	24	29	33	36	37	38	36	32	28	22
		Min	14	15	17	21	26	28	29	29	27	24	21	16
Humidity %		am	85	83	80	75	71	69	69	74	75	80	80	85
		pm	71	70	70	66	63	64	67	65	64	66	70	77
Bangkok														
Temperature	F	Max	89	91	93	95	93	91	90	90	89	88	87	87
		Min	68	72	75	77	77	76	76	76	76	75	72	68
Temperature	C	Max	32	33	34	35	34	33	32	32	32	31	31	31
		Min	20	22	24	25	25	24	24	24	24	25	22	20
Humidity %		am	91	92	92	90	91	90	91	92	94	93	92	91
		pm	53	55	56	58	64	67	66	66	70	70	65	56

			J	F	M	A	M	J	J	A	S	O	N	D
Beirut														
Temperature	F	Max	62	63	66	72	78	83	87	89	86	81	73	65
		Min	51	51	54	58	64	69	73	74	73	69	61	55
Temperature	C	Max	17	17	19	22	26	28	31	32	30	27	23	18
		Min	11	11	12	14	18	21	23	23	23	21	16	12
Humidity %		am	72	72	72	72	69	67	66	65	64	65	67	70
		pm	70	70	69	67	64	61	58	57	57	62	61	69
Berlin														
Temperature	F	Max	35	37	46	56	66	72	75	74	68	56	45	38
		Min	26	26	31	39	47	53	57	56	50	42	36	29
Temperature	C	Max	2	3	8	13	19	22	24	23	20	13	7	3
		Min	-3	-3	0	4	8	12	14	13	10	6	2	-1
Humidity %		am	89	89	88	84	80	80	84	88	92	93	92	91
		pm	82	78	67	60	57	58	61	61	65	73	83	86
Bombay														
Temperature	F	Max	83	83	86	89	91	89	85	85	85	89	89	97
		Min	67	67	72	76	80	79	77	76	76	76	73	79
Temperature	C	Max	28	28	30	32	33	32	29	29	29	32	32	31
		Min	12	12	17	20	23	21	22	22	22	21	18	13
Humidity %		am	70	71	73	75	74	79	83	83	85	81	73	70
		pm	61	62	65	67	68	77	83	81	78	71	64	62
Brussels														
Temperature	F	Max	40	44	51	58	65	72	73	72	69	60	48	42
		Min	30	32	36	41	46	52	54	54	51	45	38	32
Temperature	C	Max	4	7	10	14	18	22	23	22	21	15	9	6
		Min	-1	0	2	5	8	11	12	12	11	7	3	0
Humidity %		am	92	92	91	91	90	87	91	93	94	93	93	92
		pm	86	81	74	71	65	65	68	69	69	77	85	86
Buenos Aires														
Temperature	F	Max	85	83	79	72	64	57	57	60	64	69	76	82
		Min	63	63	60	53	47	41	42	43	46	50	56	61
Temperature	C	Max	29	28	26	22	18	14	14	16	18	21	24	28
		Min	17	17	16	12	8	5	6	6	8	10	13	16
Humidity %		am	81	83	87	88	90	91	92	90	86	83	79	79
		pm	61	63	69	71	74	78	79	74	68	65	60	62
Cairo														
Temperature	F	Max	65	69	75	83	91	95	96	95	90	86	78	68
		Min	47	48	52	57	63	68	70	71	68	65	58	50
Temperature	C	Max	18	21	24	28	33	35	36	35	32	30	26	20
		Min	8	9	11	14	17	20	20	22	20	18	14	10
Humidity %		am	69	64	63	55	50	55	65	69	68	67	68	70
		pm	40	33	27	21	18	20	24	28	31	31	38	41
Calcutta														
Temperature	F	Max	80	84	93	97	96	92	89	89	90	89	84	79
		Min	55	59	69	75	77	79	79	78	78	74	64	55
Temperature	C	Max	27	29	34	36	36	33	32	32	32	32	29	26
		Min	13	15	21	24	25	26	26	26	26	24	18	13
Humidity %		am	85	82	79	76	77	82	86	88	86	85	79	80
		pm	52	45	46	56	62	75	80	82	81	72	63	55

			J	F	M	A	M	J	J	A	S	O	N	D
Christchurch														
Temperature	F	Max	70	69	66	62	56	51	50	52	57	62	66	69
		Min	53	53	50	45	40	36	35	36	40	44	47	51
Temperature	C	Max	21	21	19	17	13	11	10	11	14	17	19	21
		Min	12	12	10	7	4	2	2	2	4	7	8	11
Humidity %		am	65	71	75	82	85	97	97	81	72	63	64	67
		pm	59	60	69	71	69	72	76	66	69	60	64	60
Colombo														
Temperature	F	Max	86	87	88	88	87	85	85	85	85	85	85	85
		Min	72	72	74	76	78	77	77	77	77	75	73	72
Temperature	C	Min	30	31	31	31	31	29	29	29	29	29	29	29
		Min	22	22	23	24	25	26	25	25	25	24	23	22
Humidity %		am	73	71	71	74	78	80	79	78	76	77	77	74
		pm	67	66	66	70	76	78	77	76	75	76	75	69
Copenhagen														
Temperature	F	Max	36	36	41	51	61	67	71	70	64	54	45	40
		Min	28	28	31	38	46	52	57	56	51	44	38	34
Temperature	C	Max	2	2	5	10	16	19	22	21	18	12	7	4
		Min	-2	-3	-1	3	8	11	14	14	11	7	3	1
Humidity %		am	88	86	85	79	70	70	74	78	83	86	88	89
		pm	85	83	78	68	59	60	62	64	69	76	83	87
Delhi														
Temperature	F	Max	70	75	87	97	105	102	96	93	93	93	84	73
		Min	44	49	58	68	79	83	81	79	75	65	52	46
Temperature	C	Max	21	24	31	36	41	39	36	34	34	34	29	23
		Min	7	9	14	20	26	28	27	26	24	18	11	8
Humidity %		am	72	67	49	35	35	53	75	80	72	56	51	69
		pm	41	35	23	19	20	36	59	64	51	32	31	42
Djakarta														
Temperature	F	Max	84	84	86	87	87	87	87	87	88	87	86	85
		Min	74	74	74	75	75	74	73	73	74	74	74	74
Temperature	C	Max	29	29	30	31	31	31	31	31	31	31	30	29
		Min	23	23	23	24	24	23	23	23	23	23	23	23
Humidity %		am	95	95	94	94	94	93	92	90	90	90	92	92
		pm	75	75	73	71	69	67	64	61	62	64	68	71
Frankfurt														
Temperature	F	Max	38	41	51	60	69	74	77	76	69	58	47	39
		Min	29	30	35	42	49	55	58	57	52	44	38	32
Temperature	C	Max	3	5	11	16	20	23	25	24	21	14	8	4
		Min	-1	-2	2	6	9	13	15	14	11	7	3	0
Humidity %		am	86	86	84	79	78	78	81	85	89	91	89	88
		pm	77	70	57	51	50	52	53	54	60	68	77	81
Haifa														
Temperature	F	Max	65	67	71	77	83	85	88	90	88	85	78	68
		Min	49	50	53	58	65	71	75	76	74	68	60	53
Temperature	C	Max	18	19	22	25	28	29	31	32	31	29	26	20
		Min	9	10	12	14	18	22	24	24	23	20	16	12
Humidity %		am	66	65	62	60	62	67	70	70	67	66	61	66
		pm	56	56	56	57	59	66	68	69	66	66	56	56

			J	F	M	A	M	J	J	A	S	O	N	D
Hamilton, Bda.														
Temperature	F	Max	68	68	68	71	76	81	85	86	84	79	74	70
		Min	58	57	57	59	64	69	73	74	72	69	63	60
Temperature	C	Max	20	20	20	22	24	27	29	30	29	26	23	21
		Min	14	14	14	15	18	21	23	23	22	21	17	16
Humidity %		am	78	76	77	78	81	82	81	79	81	79	76	77
		pm	70	69	69	70	75	74	73	69	73	72	70	70
Harare														
Temperature	F	Max	78	78	78	78	74	70	70	74	79	83	81	79
		Min	60	60	58	55	49	44	44	47	53	58	60	60
Temperature	C	Max	26	26	26	26	23	21	21	23	26	28	27	26
		Min	16	16	14	13	9	7	7	8	12	14	16	16
Humidity %		am	74	77	75	68	60	58	56	50	43	43	56	67
		pm	57	53	52	44	37	36	33	28	26	26	43	57
Hong Kong														
Temperature	F	Max	64	63	67	75	82	85	87	87	85	81	74	68
		Min	56	55	60	67	74	78	78	78	77	73	65	59
Temperature	C	Max	18	17	19	24	28	29	31	31	29	27	23	20
		Min	13	13	16	19	23	26	26	26	25	23	18	15
Humidity %		am	77	82	84	87	87	86	87	87	83	75	73	74
		pm	66	73	74	77	78	77	77	77	72	63	60	63
Instanbul														
Temperature	F	Max	46	47	51	60	69	77	82	82	76	68	59	51
		Min	37	36	38	45	53	60	65	66	61	55	48	41
Temperature	C	Max	8	9	11	16	21	25	28	28	24	20	15	11
		Min	3	2	3	7	12	16	18	19	16	13	9	5
Humidity %		am	82	82	81	81	82	79	79	79	81	83	82	82
		pm	75	72	67	62	61	58	56	55	59	64	71	74
Jeddah														
Temperature	F	Max	84	84	85	91	95	97	99	99	96	95	91	88
		Min	66	65	67	70	74	75	79	80	87	83	81	67
Temperature	C	Max	29	29	29	33	35	36	37	37	36	35	33	30
		Min	19	18	19	21	23	24	26	27	25	23	22	19
Humidity %		am	58	52	52	52	51	56	55	59	65	60	55	55
		pm	54	52	52	56	55	55	50	51	61	61	59	54
Johannesburg														
Temperature	F	Max	78	77	75	72	66	62	63	68	73	77	77	78
		Min	58	58	55	50	43	39	39	43	48	53	55	57
Temperature	C	Max	26	25	24	22	19	17	17	20	23	25	25	26
		Min	14	14	13	10	6	4	4	6	9	12	13	14
Humidity %		am	75	78	79	74	70	70	69	64	59	64	67	70
		pm	50	53	50	44	36	33	32	29	30	37	45	47
Kathmandu														
Temperature	F	Max	65	67	77	83	86	85	84	83	83	80	74	67
		Min	35	39	45	53	61	67	68	68	66	56	45	37
Temperature	C	Max	18	19	25	28	30	29	29	28	28	27	23	19
		Min	2	4	7	12	16	19	20	20	19	13	7	3
Humidity %		am	89	90	73	68	72	79	86	87	86	88	90	89
		pm	70	68	53	54	61	72	82	84	83	81	78	73

		J	F	M	A	M	J	J	A	S	O	N	D
Kuala Lumpur													
Temperature F	Max	90	92	92	91	91	91	90	90	90	89	89	89
	Min	72	72	73	74	73	72	73	73	73	73	73	72
Temperature C	Max	32	33	33	33	33	33	32	32	32	32	32	32
	Min	22	22	23	23	23	22	23	23	23	23	23	22
Humidity %	am	97	97	97	97	97	96	95	96	96	96	97	97
	pm	60	60	58	63	66	63	63	62	64	65	66	61
Lagos													
Temperature F	Max	88	89	89	89	87	85	83	82	83	85	88	88
	Min	74	77	78	77	76	74	74	73	74	74	75	75
Temperature C	Max	31	32	32	32	31	29	28	28	28	29	31	31
	Min	23	25	26	25	24	23	23	23	23	23	24	24
Humidity %	am	84	83	82	81	83	87	87	85	86	86	85	86
	pm	65	69	72	72	76	80	80	76	77	76	72	68
Lima													
Temperature F	Max	82	83	83	80	74	68	67	66	68	71	74	78
	Min	66	67	66	63	60	58	57	56	57	58	60	62
Temperature C	Max	28	28	28	27	23	20	19	19	20	22	23	26
	Min	19	19	19	17	16	14	14	13	14	14	16	17
Humidity %	am	93	92	92	93	95	95	94	95	94	94	93	93
	pm	69	66	64	66	76	80	77	78	76	72	71	70
Lisbon													
Temperature F	Max	57	59	63	67	71	77	81	82	79	72	63	58
	Min	46	47	50	53	55	60	63	63	62	58	52	47
Temperature C	Max	14	15	17	20	21	25	27	28	26	22	17	15
	Min	8	8	10	12	13	15	17	17	17	14	11	9
Humidity %	am	85	80	78	69	68	65	62	64	70	75	81	84
	pm	71	64	64	56	57	54	48	49	54	59	68	72
London (UK)													
Temperature F	Max	43	44	50	56	62	69	71	71	65	58	50	45
	Min	36	36	38	42	47	53	56	56	52	46	42	38
Temperature C	Max	6	7	10	13	17	20	22	21	19	14	10	7
	Min	2	2	3	6	8	12	14	13	11	8	5	4
Humidity %	am	86	85	81	71	70	70	71	76	80	85	85	87
	pm	77	72	64	56	57	58	59	62	65	70	78	81
Madrid													
Temperature F	Max	47	52	59	65	70	80	87	85	77	65	55	48
	Min	35	36	41	45	50	58	63	63	57	48	42	36
Temperature C	Max	9	11	15	18	21	27	31	30	25	19	13	9
	Min	2	2	5	7	10	15	17	17	14	10	5	2
Humidity %	am	86	83	80	74	72	66	58	62	72	81	84	86
	pm	71	62	56	49	49	41	33	35	46	58	65	70
Manila													
Temperature F	Max	86	88	91	93	93	91	88	87	88	88	87	86
	Min	69	69	71	73	75	75	75	75	75	74	72	70
Temperature C	Max	30	31	33	34	34	33	31	31	31	31	31	30
	Min	21	21	22	23	24	24	24	24	24	23	22	21
Humidity %	am	89	88	85	85	88	91	91	92	93	92	91	90
	pm	63	59	55	55	61	68	74	73	73	71	69	67

			J	F	M	A	M	J	J	A	S	O	N	D
Melbourne														
Temperature	F	Max	78	78	75	68	62	57	56	59	63	67	71	75
		Min	57	57	55	51	47	44	42	43	46	48	51	54
Temperature	C	Max	26	26	24	20	17	14	13	15	17	19	22	24
		Min	14	14	13	11	8	7	6	6	8	9	11	12
Humidity %		am	58	62	64	72	79	83	82	76	68	61	60	59
		pm	48	50	51	56	62	67	65	60	55	52	52	51
Mexico City														
Temperature	F	Max	66	69	75	77	78	76	73	73	74	70	68	66
		Min	42	43	47	51	54	55	53	54	53	50	46	43
Temperature	C	Max	19	21	24	25	26	24	23	23	23	21	20	19
		Min	6	6	8	11	12	13	12	12	12	10	8	6
Humidity %		am	79	72	68	66	69	82	84	85	86	83	82	81
		pm	34	28	26	29	29	48	50	50	54	47	41	37
Miami														
Temperature	F	Max	74	75	78	80	84	86	88	88	87	83	78	76
		Min	61	61	64	67	71	74	76	76	75	72	66	62
Temperature	C	Max	23	24	26	27	29	30	31	31	31	28	26	24
		Min	16	16	18	19	22	22	24	24	24	22	19	17
Humidity %		am	81	82	77	73	75	75	75	76	79	80	77	82
		pm	66	63	62	64	67	69	68	68	70	69	64	65
Moscow														
Temperature	F	Max	15	22	32	50	66	70	73	72	61	48	35	24
		Min	3	8	18	34	46	51	55	53	45	37	26	15
Temperature	C	Max	-9	-6	0	10	19	21	23	22	16	9	2	-5
		Min	-16	-14	-8	1	8	11	13	12	7	3	-3	-10
Humidity %		am	82	82	82	73	58	62	68	74	78	81	87	85
		pm	77	66	64	54	43	47	54	55	59	67	79	83
Nairobi														
Temperature	F	Max	77	79	77	75	72	70	69	70	75	76	74	74
		Min	54	55	57	58	56	53	51	52	52	55	56	55
Temperature	C	Max	25	26	25	24	22	21	21	21	24	24	23	23
		Min	12	13	14	14	13	12	11	11	11	13	13	13
Humidity %		am	74	74	81	88	88	89	86	86	82	82	86	81
		pm	44	40	45	56	62	60	58	56	45	43	532	53
Nassau														
Temperature	F	Max	77	77	79	81	84	87	88	89	88	85	81	79
		Min	65	64	66	69	71	74	75	76	75	73	70	67
Temperature	C	Max	25	25	26	27	29	31	31	32	31	29	27	26
		Min	18	18	19	21	22	23	24	24	24	23	21	19
Humidity %		am	84	82	81	79	79	81	80	82	84	83	83	84
		pm	64	62	64	65	65	68	69	70	73	71	68	66
New York														
Temperature	F	Max	37	38	45	57	68	77	82	80	79	69	51	41
		Min	24	24	30	42	53	60	66	66	60	49	37	29
Temperature	C	Max	3	3	7	14	20	25	28	27	26	21	11	5
		Min	-4	-4	-1	6	12	16	19	19	16	9	3	-2
Humidity %		am	72	70	70	68	70	74	77	79	79	76	75	73
		pm	60	58	55	53	54	58	58	60	61	57	60	61

			J	F	M	A	M	J	J	A	S	O	N	D
Oslo														
Temperature	F	Max	28	30	39	50	61	68	72	70	60	48	38	32
		Min	19	19	25	34	43	50	55	53	46	38	31	25
Temperature	C	Max	-2	-1	4	10	16	20	22	21	16	9	3	0
		Min	-7	-7	-4	1	6	10	13	12	8	3	-1	-4
Humidity %		am	86	84	80	75	68	69	74	79	85	88	88	87
		pm	82	74	64	57	52	55	59	61	66	72	83	85
Ottawa														
Temperature	F	Max	21	22	33	51	66	76	81	77	68	54	39	24
		Min	3	3	16	21	44	54	58	55	48	37	26	9
Temperature	C	Max	-6	-6	1	11	19	24	27	25	20	12	4	-4
		Min	-16	-16	-9	-1	7	12	14	13	9	3	-3	-13
Humidity %		am	83	88	84	76	77	80	80	84	90	86	84	83
		pm	76	73	66	58	55	56	53	54	59	63	68	75
Papeete														
Temperature	F	Max	89	89	89	89	87	86	86	86	86	87	88	88
		Min	72	72	72	72	70	69	68	68	69	70	71	72
Temperature	C	Max	32	32	32	32	31	30	30	30	30	31	31	31
		Min	22	22	22	22	21	21	20	20	21	21	22	22
Humidity %		am	82	82	84	85	84	85	83	83	81	69	80	81
		pm	77	77	78	78	78	79	77	78	76	76	77	78
Paris														
Temperature	F	Max	42	45	55	61	69	75	80	79	73	61	50	43
		Min	30	31	37	42	49	55	59	58	53	45	38	33
Temperature	C	Max	5	7	13	16	20	24	27	26	23	16	10	6
		Min	-1	0	3	6	9	13	15	14	12	7	4	0
Humidity %		am	89	87	87	84	83	82	79	85	89	92	91	90
		pm	80	72	60	56	56	55	50	54	60	69	78	80
Port-of-Spain														
Temperature	F	Max	87	88	89	90	90	89	88	88	89	89	89	88
		Min	69	68	68	69	71	71	71	71	71	71	71	69
Temperature	C	Max	31	31	32	32	32	32	31	31	32	32	32	31
		Min	21	20	20	21	22	22	22	22	22	22	22	21
Humidity %		am	89	87	85	83	84	87	88	87	87	87	89	89
		pm	68	65	63	61	63	69	71	73	73	74	76	71
Prague														
Temperature	F	Max	49	53	64	73	82	88	91	89	84	71	57	50
		Min	7	10	18	29	36	44	49	47	38	29	24	14
Temperature	C	Max	10	11	18	23	28	31	33	32	29	22	14	10
		Min	-13	-12	-8	-2	2	7	9	8	4	-2	-5	-10
Humidity %		am	84	83	82	77	75	74	77	81	84	87	87	87
		pm	73	67	55	47	45	46	49	48	51	60	73	78
Rangoon														
Temperature	F	Max	89	92	96	97	92	86	85	86	86	88	88	88
		Min	65	67	71	76	77	76	76	76	76	76	73	67
Temperature	C	Max	32	33	36	36	33	30	29	29	30	31	31	31
		Min	18	19	22	24	25	24	24	24	24	24	23	19
Humidity %		am	71	72	74	71	80	87	89	89	87	83	79	75
		pm	52	52	54	64	76	75	88	88	86	77	72	61

			J	F	M	A	M	J	J	A	S	O	N	D
Rio de Janeiro														
Temperature	F	Max	84	85	83	80	77	76	75	76	75	77	79	82
		Min	73	73	72	69	66	64	63	64	65	66	68	71
Temperature	C	Max	29	29	28	27	25	24	24	24	24	25	26	28
		Min	23	23	22	21	19	18	17	18	18	19	20	22
Humidity %		am	82	84	87	87	87	87	86	84	84	83	82	82
		pm	70	71	74	73	70	69	68	66	72	72	72	72
Rome														
Temperature	F	Max	52	55	59	66	74	82	87	86	79	71	62	55
		Min	40	42	45	50	56	63	67	67	62	55	49	44
Temperature	C	Max	11	13	15	19	23	28	30	30	26	22	16	13
		Min	5	5	7	10	13	17	20	20	17	13	9	6
Humidity %		am	85	86	83	83	77	74	70	73	83	86	87	85
		pm	68	64	56	54	54	48	42	43	50	59	66	70
San Francisco														
Temperature	F	Max	55	59	61	62	63	66	65	65	69	68	63	57
		Min	45	47	48	49	51	52	53	53	55	54	51	47
Temperature	C	Max	13	15	16	17	17	18	19	18	21	20	17	14
		Min	7	8	9	9	11	11	12	12	13	12	11	8
Humidity %		am	85	84	83	83	85	88	91	92	88	85	83	83
		pm	69	66	61	61	62	64	69	70	60	58	60	68
Singapore														
Temperature	F	Max	86	88	88	88	89	88	88	87	87	87	87	87
		Min	73	73	75	75	75	75	75	75	75	74	74	74
Temperature	C	Max	30	31	31	31	34	31	31	31	31	31	31	31
		Min	23	23	24	24	24	24	24	24	24	23	23	23
Humidity %		am	82	77	76	77	79	79	79	78	79	78	79	82
		pm	78	71	70	74	73	73	72	72	72	72	75	78
Stockholm														
Temperature	F	Max	30	30	37	47	58	67	71	68	60	49	40	35
		Min	23	22	26	34	43	51	57	56	49	41	34	29
Temperature	C	Max	-1	-1	3	8	14	19	22	20	15	9	5	2
		Min	15	15	14	1	6	11	14	13	9	5	1	-2
Humidity %		am	85	83	82	76	66	68	74	81	87	88	89	88
		pm	83	77	68	60	53	55	59	64	69	76	85	86
Sydney														
Temperature	F	Max	78	78	76	71	66	61	60	63	67	71	74	77
		Min	65	65	63	58	52	48	46	48	51	56	60	63
Temperature	C	Max	26	26	24	22	19	16	16	17	19	22	23	25
		Min	18	18	17	14	11	9	8	9	11	13	16	17
Humidity %		am	68	71	73	76	77	77	76	72	67	65	65	66
		pm	64	65	65	64	63	62	60	56	55	57	60	62
Tehran														
Temperature	F	Max	45	50	59	71	82	93	99	97	90	76	63	51
		Min	27	32	39	49	58	66	72	71	64	53	43	33
Temperature	C	Max	7	10	15	22	28	34	37	36	32	24	17	11
		Min	-3	0	4	9	14	19	22	22	18	12	6	1
Humidity %		am	77	73	61	54	55	50	51	47	49	53	63	76
		pm	75	59	39	40	47	49	41	46	49	54	66	75

		J	F	M	A	M	J	J	A	S	O	N	D
Tokyo													
Temperature	F	Max 47	48	54	63	71	76	83	86	79	69	60	52
		Min 29	31	36	46	54	63	70	72	66	55	43	33
Temperature	C	Max 8	9	12	17	22	24	28	30	26	21	16	11
		Min -2	-1	2	8	12	17	21	22	19	13	6	1
Humidity %		am 73	71	75	81	85	89	91	92	91	88	83	77
		pm 48	48	53	59	62	68	69	66	68	64	58	51
Vancouver													
Temperature	F	Max 41	44	50	58	64	69	74	73	65	57	48	43
		Min 32	34	37	40	46	52	54	54	49	54	39	35
Temperature	C	Max 5	7	10	14	18	21	23	23	18	14	9	6
		Min 0	1	3	4	8	11	12	12	9	7	4	2
Humidity %		am 93	91	91	89	88	87	89	90	92	92	91	91
		pm 85	78	70	67	63	65	62	62	72	80	84	88
Vienna													
Temperature	F	Max 34	38	47	58	67	73	76	75	68	56	45	37
		Min 25	28	30	42	50	56	60	59	53	44	37	30
Temperature	C	Max 1	3	8	15	19	23	25	24	20	14	7	3
		Min -4	-3	-1	6	10	14	15	15	11	7	3	-1
Humidity %		am 81	80	78	72	74	74	74	78	83	86	84	84
		pm 72	66	57	49	52	55	54	54	56	64	74	76
Warsaw													
Temperature	F	Max 32	32	42	53	67	73	75	73	66	55	42	35
		Min 22	21	28	37	48	54	58	56	49	41	33	28
Temperature	C	Max 0	1	6	13	19	23	24	23	19	14	6	3
		Min -7	-6	-2	3	8	12	14	13	9	5	1	-2
Humidity %		am 83	82	83	83	79	82	84	88	90	89	90	86
		pm 74	71	64	59	55	60	63	63	63	67	78	78
Zurich													
Temperature	F	Max 36	41	51	59	67	73	76	75	69	57	45	37
		Min 26	28	34	40	47	53	56	56	51	43	35	29
Temperature	C	Max 2	5	10	15	19	23	25	24	20	14	7	3
		Min -3	-2	1	4	8	12	14	13	11	6	2	-2
Humidity %		am 88	88	86	81	80	80	81	85	90	92	90	89
		pm 74	65	55	51	52	52	52	53	57	64	73	76

OLYMPIC GAMES

Summer

Year	Location
1896	Athens Greece.
1900	Paris, France.
1904	St. Louis, United States.
1908	London, England.
1912	Stockholm, Sweden.
1920	Antwerp, Belgium.
1924	Paris, France.
1928	Amsterdam, Netherlands.
1932	Los Angeles, United States.
1936	Berlin, Germany.
1948	London, England.
1952	Helsinki, Finland.
1956	Melbourne, Australia.
1960	Rome, Italy.
1964	Tokyo, Japan.
1968	Mexico City, Mexico.
1972	Munich, West Germany.
1976	Montreal, Canada.
1980	Moscow, USSR.
1984	Los Angeles, United States.
1988	Seoul, South Korea.
1992	Barcelona, Spain.

Winter

Year	Location
1924	Chamonix, France.
1928	St. Moritz, Switzerland.
1932	Lake Placid, United States.
1936	Garmisch, Germany.
1948	St. Moritz, Switzerland.
1952	Oslo, Norway.
1956	Cortina, Italy.
1960	Squaw Valley, United States.
1964	Innsbruck, Austria.
1968	Grenoble, France.
1972	Sapporo, Japan.
1976	Innsbruck, Austria.
1980	Lake Placid, United States.
1984	Sarajevo, Yugoslavia.
1988	Calgary, Canada.
1992	Albertville, France.

Olympic Games Events

ATHLETICS

Men
100-meter Run
200-meter Run
400-meter Run
800-meter Run
1,500-meter Run
3,000-meter Steeplechase
5,000-meter Run
10,000-meter Run
Marathon
20-kilometer Walk
50-kilometer Walk
110-meter Hurdles
400-meter Hurdles
High Jump
Long Jump
4 x 100-meter Relay
4 x 400-meter Relay
Pole Vault
Hammer Throw
Discus Throw
Triple Jump
Shot Put
Javelin
Decathlon

Women
100-meter Run
200-meter Run
400-meter Run
800-meter Run
1,500-meter Run
3,000-meter Run
10,000-meter Run
100-meter Hurdles
400-meter Hurdles
High Jump
Long Jump
4 x 100-meter Relay
4 x 400-meter Relay
Discus Throw
Shot Put
Javelin Throw
Heptathlon
Marathon

MODERN PENTATHLON: Individual and Team
BASKETBALL: Men and Women
FIELD HOCKEY: Men and Women
HANDBALL: Men and Women
SOCCER
VOLLEYBALL: Men and Women
WATER POLO
SYNCHRONIZED SWIMMING: Individual and Duet

CYCLING

Men	30-kilometer Points Race
Individual Pursuit	100-kilometer Road Team Time Trials
Individual Road Race	*Women*
1,000-meter	Sprint
Team Pursuit	Individual Road Race
Sprint	

GYMNASTICS

Men	Horse	Floor Exercise
All-round - Individual	Rings	Beam
All-round - Team	Vault	Asymetric Bars
Floor Exercise	*Women*	Vault
Horizontal Bar	All-round - Individual	Apparatus
Parallel Bars	All-round - Team	Rythmic

EQUESTRIAN

Three-day Event - Individual	Grand Prix Jumping - Team
Three-day Event - Team	Dressage - Individual
Grand Prix Jumping - Individual	Dressage - Team

FENCING

Men	Epee - Individual	*Women*
Foil - Individual	Epee - Team	Foil - Individual
Foil - Team	Sabre - Individual	Foil - Team
	Sabre - Team	

SWIMMING: Men

Men	Women
50-meter Freestyle	50-meter Freestyle
100-meter Freestyle	100-meter Freestyle
200-meter Freestyle	200-meter Freestyle
400-meter Freestyle	400-meter Freestyle
1,500-meter Freestyle	800-meter Freestyle
4 x 100-meter Medley Relay	4 x 100-meter Medley Relay
4 x 100-meter Freestyle Relay	4 x 100-meter Freestyle Relay
800-meter Freestyle Relay	100-meter Backstroke
100-meter Backstroke	200-meter Backstroke
200-meter Backstroke	100-meter Breaststroke
100-meter Breaststroke	200-meter Breaststroke
200-meter Breaststroke	100-meter Butterfly
100-meter Butterfly	200-meter Butterfly
200-meter Butterfly	200-meter Individual Medley
200-meter Individual Medley	400-meter Individual Medley
400-meter Individual Medley	

DIVING: Men

Men	Women
Springboard Diving	Springboard Diving
High Diving	High Diving

ARCHERY

Men	Women
Individual and Team	Individual and Team

TENNIS

Men	Women
Singles and Doubles	Singles and Doubles

TABLE TENNIS

Men	Women
Singles and Doubles	Singles and Doubles

CANOEING

Men
500-meter 1-man Canadian
500-meter 2-man Canadian
500-meter 1-man Kayak
500-meter 2-man Kayak
1,000-meter 1-man Kayak
1,000-meter 2-man Kayak
1,000-meter 4-man Kayak

1,000-meter 1-man Canadian
1,000-meter 1-man Canadian
Women
500-meter 1-woman Kayak
500-meter 2-woman Kayak
500-meter 4-woman Kayak

ROWING

Men
Single Sculls
Double Sculls
Coxed Pairs
Coxless Pairs
Coxless Fours

Quadruple Sculls (Coxed)
Quadruple Sculls
(Coxless)
Coxed Eights
Women
Single Sculls

Double Sculls
Coxless Pairs
Coxed Fours
Quadruple Sculls (Coxless)
Coxed Eights

YACHTING

Men
Soling Class
Flying Dutchman Class
Star Class

Finn Class
Tornado Class
470 Class

Windsurfing
Women
470 Class

WRESTLING

All-In Wrestling
48 kilograms (106 pounds)
52 kilograms (115 pounds)
57 kilograms (126 pounds)
62 kilograms (137 pounds)
68 kilograms (150 pounds)
74 kilograms (163 pounds)
82 kilograms (181 pounds)
90 kilograms (198 pounds)
100 kilograms (220 pounds)
Over 100 kilograms (220 pounds)

Greco-Roman
48 kilograms (106 pounds)
52 kilograms (115 pounds)
57 kilograms (126 pounds)
62 kilograms (137 pounds)
68 kilograms (150 pounds)
74 kilograms (163 pounds)
82 kilograms (181 pounds)
90 kilograms (198 pounds)
100 kilograms (220 pounds)
Over 100 kilograms (220 pounds)

BOXING

48 Kilograms (106 pounds)	67 kilograms (147.75 pounds)
51 kilograms (112.5 pounds)	71 kilograms (156.5 pounds)
54 kilograms (119 pounds)	75 kilograms (165.33 pounds)
57 kilograms (126 pounds)	81 kilograms (178.5 pounds)
60 kilograms (132.25 pounds)	95 kilograms (209.5 pounds)
63.5 kilograms (140 pounds)	More than 95 kilograms (209.5 pounds)

JUDO

60 kilograms (132.25 pounds)	86 kilograms (189.5 pounds)
65 kilograms (143.25 pounds)	95 kilograms (209.5 pounds)
71 kilograms (156.5 pounds)	More than 95 kilograms (209.5 pounds)
78 kilograms (172 pounds)	

SHOOTING

Men		*Women*
Airgun	Rapid-fire Pistol	Airgun
Airgun 10 meters	Moving Target	Airgun 10 meters
Trap shooting	Small-bore Rifle, 3	small-bore Rifle,
Small-bore Rifle, Prone	Positions	· 3 Positions
Free Pistol	Clay Target Skeet	Sport Pistol

WEIGHT LIFTING

52 kilograms (115 pounds)	82.5 kilograms (181.75 pounds)
56 kilgrams (123.5 pounds)	100 kilograms (220 pounds)
60 kilograms (132.25 pounds)	110 kilograms (242.5 pounds)
67.5 kilograms (148.75 pounds)	More than 110 kilograms (242.5 pounds)
75 kilograms (165.33 pounds)	

Winter Olympics

BIATHLON	ALPINE SKIING	90-meter Ski Jump
10 kilometers	*Men*	70-meter Ski Jump
20 kilometers	Downhill	*Women*
40-kilometer Relay	Giant Slalom	5 kilometer (3.1-mile)
BOBSLEDDING	Slalom	10 kilometer
4-man Bob	*Women*	20 kilometer
2-man Bob	Downhill	20-kilometer Cross-
FIGURE SKATING	Giant Slalom	country Relay
Men's Singles	Slalom	SPEED SKATING
Woman's Singles	NORDIC SKIING	*Men*
Pairs	*Men*	500 meters
Ice Dancing	15-kilometer (9.3-mile)	1,000 meters
ICE HOCKEY	Cross-country	1,500 meters
LUGE	30-kilometer (18.6-mile)	5,000 meters
Men	Cross-country	10,000 meters
Singles	50-kilometer (31.2-mile)	*Women*
Doubles	Cross-country	500 meters
Women	40-kilometer Cross-	1,000 meters
Singles	country Relay	1,500 meters
	Combined Cross-	3,000 meters
	country and Jumping	